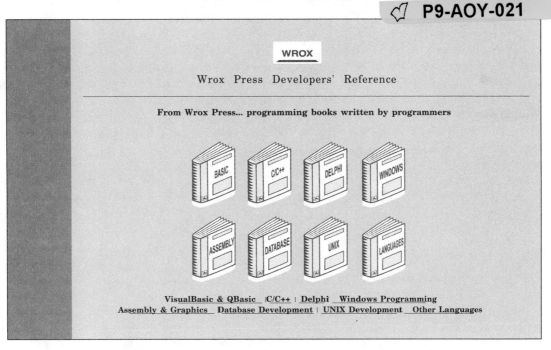

Professional
Microsoft SQL Server 6.5
Admin

Sharon Dooley
Kevin Kline
Robert Smith
Ed Carter
Dwayne Seiber
Christian Gross
Thomas Walsh

Wrox Press Ltd.®

Professional Microsoft SQL Server 6.5 Admin

© 1996 Wrox Press

Published by Wrox Press Ltd. 30 Lincoln Road, Olton, Birmingham, B27 6PA
Printed in Canada
Library of Congress Catalog no. 96-60557

ISBN 1-874416-49-4

Trademark Acknowledgements

Wrox has endeavored to provide trademark information about all the companies and products mentioned in this book by the appropriate use of capitals. However, Wrox cannot guarantee the accuracy of this information.

Credits

Authors
Sharon Dooley
Kevin Kline
Robert Smith
Ed Carter
Dwayne Seiber
Christian Gross
Thomas Walsh

Development Editor
John Franklin

Technical Editors
Chris Ullman

Technical Reviewers
Mike Yocca
Anne Zorner
Lars Lindstedt
Marcel Wingate
Tej Dhawan
Sameer Padhye
Jim Polizi
Kalen Delaney

Production Manager
Neil Gallagher

Design/Layout
Neil Gallagher
Andrew Guillaume
Hetendra Parekh

Proof Readers
Pam Brand
Melanie Orgee
Simon Gilks
Robin Morris

Indexers
Robin Morris
Simon Gilks

Cover Design
Third Wave

For more information on Third Wave, contact Ross Alderson on 44-121 236 6616
Cover photo supplied by The Telegraph Colour Library

About the Authors

Sharon Dooley

Sharon Dooley has been working with databases since before some of the potential readers of this book were born. She runs a small database consultancy, specializing in database design and tuning, out of the third floor of her Philadelphia row-house with the able assistance of Zebra, a small tabby cat, and Tank, a large Maine Coon cat. She also teaches for Learning Tree International where she is the author of their Hands On Introduction to Sybase and Hands On Microsoft SQL Server Admin courses.

Kevin Kline

Kevin Kline is the SQL Server Database Administrator and CASE-tools Administrator for Deloitte & Touche LLP's PracticeServerCenter, where he designs, develops and administers large-scale client/server OLTP, DSS and VLDB systems. Kevin's expertise in query analysis and troubleshooting, database tuning and optimization, application design and implementation also extends to Oracle, having published a book on that DBMS in 1994. *I dedicate this work to Kelly - my one true love. And to Dylan and Emily - the joys of my life - your bright eyes and happy laughter always make the burden light.*

Robert Smith

Robert Smith is a graduate of Oxford University who is now director of Amethyst Ltd. About half his time is spent developing with Access and SQL Server and the remainder is spent on consultancy in client-server design and development issues.

Ed Carter

Ed Carter is currently based in Tampa, where he is a consultant to several Fortune 400 companies in the Florida area. He is a specialist in Client-Server application development with extensive experience in Oracle and MSSQLServer systems which has led to being an ODBC API connoisseur. Though, at the end of the day, daughter Allison, wife Julie and DiscGolfing remain the driving passions.

Dwayne Seiber

Dwayne has been a Database Administrator for over 8 years, progressing from mainframe-based DBMS's to Microsoft SQL Server. He is currently employed by Deloitte & Touche, LLP in Hermitage, Tennessee. His favorite activity is spending time with his 15-month old son, Matt.

Christian Gross

Christian Gross is an Internet expert who has the ability to share his technical visions with management and IT professionals. He regularly speaks at professional developers' conferences such as the "Borland Developers' Conference" and "Client Server 95" conference. He also writes articles for technical magazines. As an IT consultant, Christian has advised companies such as National Westminster Bank of England, NCR, Standard Life and Union Bank of Switzerland.

Thomas Walsh

Tom Walsh is an Information Technology management consultant and lecturer in the New York/New Jersey metropolitan area, specializing in modern development methods and in the use of tools such as Microsoft SQL Server and Visual Basic. He has worked for such companies as Lucent Technologies, AT&T and Squibb Corporation. Tom also provides training to transition developers from legacy to client/server and intranet-based systems. He has trained Microsoft Solution Providers and has developed several courses for colleges and training companies such as The Chubb Institute. Tom can be reached at twalsh@msn.com.

6.5

Table of Contents

6.5

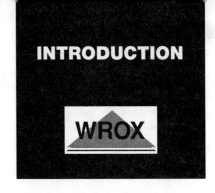
Who Is This Book For?

This book isn't an introductory text. It is designed to cover the main concerns of database administrators (DBAs) when they adopt Microsoft's new SQL Server 6.5 platform. Therefore, we have omitted some of the features common to any SQL Server and the DBA basics. It has been written by experienced DBAs and client-server developers to provide useful insights, methods and shortcuts–from people doing the same job as you.

It's possible to successfully administer a heavily used SQL Server database without really learning or using much SQL. However, true competence for the DBA comes from not only knowing how to use the SQL Enterprise Manager, but also the SQL and Transact-SQL commands that are frequently issued behind the scenes by Enterprise Manager. Consequently, you'll be presented with database management techniques through both Transact-SQL and SQL Enterprise Manager and, where relevant, in VBA.

If you haven't worked with the Microsoft Transact-SQL (a dialect of standard SQL), you'll find a concise tutorial in Appendix A. The book also assumes a familiarity with Windows NT, whilst showing you all that you need to know in order to fit SQL Server into that environment.

Professional Microsoft SQL Server 6.5™ Admin is written for:

- ▲ Database professionals who are new to Microsoft SQL Server 6.5
- ▲ DBAs of earlier releases of Microsoft's SQL Server
- ▲ Back-Office designers or developers who need to know how SQL Server 6.5 works and how to make it perform effectively
- ▲ People preparing for Microsoft's Certified Professional examinations

What's Covered In This Book?

In this guide, you will be taken from the nuts and bolts of installing SQL Server through to the things you will need to know in order to help SQL Server communicate with the rest of the world.

This book is designed to help an experienced database professional establish and maintain a SQL Server 6.5 environment for use in business-critical applications. The book is written with client/server application development in mind and presents the material in the context of SQL Server. You'll find a lot of emphasis on pro-active management of SQL Server to prevent problems from happening.

What's Not In This Book?

This book does not attempt to cover every feature of SQL Server 6.5. The product GUI, basic normalization, user details and reporting details are best taken from the free documentation that comes with the product.

It is assumed that DBAs already know the fundamentals of relational databases and basic SQL.

SQL Server Environment

Major Changes to 6.5

While SQL Server 6.0 was undoubtedly a massive leap forwards from its predecessor 4.2, both in terms of presentation and functionality, there was still room for improvement.

Microsoft have already taken criticism for the way SQL Server handled data changes on multiple servers. In 6.0, there is a process called a two phased commit which guaranteed that changes to multiple servers were either all committed or all rolled back, and this required programmers to code the phases manually. Microsoft SQL Server 6.5 introduces the Distributed Transaction Coordinator (DTC) to ensure that users can now simply execute Transact-SQL routines that update multiple servers within a transaction. The DTC works behind the scenes to track and coordinate changes.

Replication is already handled well by the point and click interface of the Enterprise Manager in 6.0. In 6.5, the current capabilities are expanded by a feature allowing replication to other databases besides SQL Server. This feature is known as heterogeneous replication.

Internet support is notably lacking from 6.0, but this is rectified in 6.5 by the introduction of the Web Assistant. This is a tool for producing web pages that incorporate database contents. The Web Assistant has a wizard that lets Web page designers enter selection criteria and formatting information.

Also, the concept of allowing SQL Server to call external procedures via DLLs has been expanded by a set of predefined stored procedures which facilitate OLE automation. These can be called in Transact-SQL routines and allow access to OLE servers and their automation methods.

Insert Row-level locking. This is the first stage in the performance improvements at table level for Microsoft SQL Server. This essentially addresses the last page 'bottleneck' for clustered and non-clustered indexing. This page can become overheated - commonly called a 'hot page', where all index inserts start to congregate.

OLAP extensions - the new cube & rollup extensions address all combinations of aggregations

These improvements have put Microsoft SQL Server 6.5 at the forefront of client/server technology and ensure that the DBA will be conducting the same practices for some time to come.

The Client/Server World of the Nineties

Although client/server computing seems to have emerged with the advent of the Sybase® SQL Server in the late 1980s, client/server computing first began in the early '80s as part of the UNIX operating system. The true definition of client/server is:

▲ Two mutually cooperating processes, one of which (the client) requests a service from the other (the server) which provides it.

The client and server may reside on the same platform or on different platforms. The service provided may or may not be data. The figure shows a 'pure' architecture of a typical business in which no business function happens on either the client or the database server.

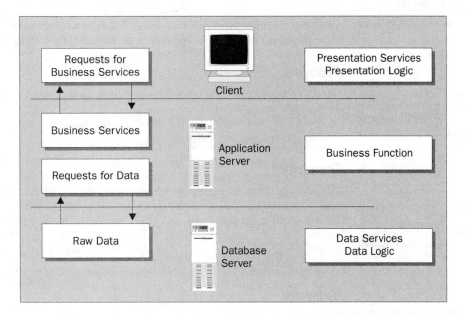

In practice, of course, this often gets muddy. We should note that, while the illustration shows the different types of processing happening on different physical pieces of hardware, it is possible to build both two and three tier architectures entirely in software. It is not necessary to have multiple computers in order to have a layered architecture.

The DBA's job is affected by the physical design of the system and that, in turn, is affected by the physical network model upon which the architecture resides.

The Network OSI Model

The OSI network model was developed by the International Standards Organization as a standard, with the expectation that it would replace the proprietary network protocols (such as IBM's SNA and DEC's DECNet) then in use. At this point, although network vendors are becoming more in compliance with this model, none implement it completely. The model specifies seven layers and requires that each layer be cleanly separated from the others by a well-defined interface.

Application

This is the layer the 'outside' world interacts with. It includes the operating system itself as well as any programs running on it. When something in this layer wants to access a network resource, it passes a message of some sort (we won't concern ourselves with the physical details here) to the next, or presentation, layer. From there messages go down all the way to the physical layer.

Presentation

This layer is responsible for masking differences in computers sharing the network. When the message comes from the application layer, the presentation layer translates it to a common format for use by the subordinate layers. The presentation layer is also responsible for any encryption required for security purposes. When a message needs to go to the application layer, the presentation layer does the same thing in reverse.

Session

This layer initiates and monitors the communications between computers on the network. It knows which messages are destined for whom and monitors the routing of those messages. It makes sure the communications continue until the parties end the conversation.

Transport

The transport layer is responsible for preparing the bits of data that get sent across the network. This layer breaks messages up into chunks, called *packets*, that are of the appropriate size and shape for the underlying network hardware. After it formats a packet, it hands it off to the network layer for actual routing. The transport layer is also the one that makes sure that messages sent are received.

Network

The network layer studies the map of the network and figures out how to get each packet from Point A to Point B. It is responsible for addressing and delivering the packets prepared by the transport layer.

Data Link

This is the most complicated of the layers. It is responsible for generating the electronic patterns that are fed into the network cables, and for translating those that come back out of the cables. It is the only layer that is intimately connected with the particular network hardware that comprises the network.

Physical

This layer represents the 'wires'—the network adapter cards in the computers and the cables connecting them.

What Happens Next?

Any number of rumors abound for the future of SQL Servers within client-server architecture. What's obvious is that the Back Office suite will become more & more integrated in order to produce a regular interface for the user and developer. SQL Server is already declaring its major elements as 'objects', so it's a natural progression for it to offer true object families for use within Back Office.

The 6.5 product supports 100GB databases today, but Microsoft claim Terrabyte capabilities within a couple of years. This will go hand-in-hand with scaling to 8 processor systems.

Most of the 6.5 features operate on the Power PC (except Web Assistant & MSQuery) as enhancements for Pentium Pro & Alpha continue apace.

Conventions

Finally, we've used a number of different font and layout styles to indicate different types of information in the book. Here are examples of them and what they mean.

> **Comments in boxes like these are bits of interesting information that you should take a look at.**

Whereas this style indicates a comment that, while interesting, is more of an aside. It's a bit of friendly chit-chat.

```
This is how TRANSACT SQL syntax is specified. It can't be typed in. It's a
template for creating commands.
```

```
This is the style for actual code that can be run on SQL Server
```

```
This is the output you will see from SQL Server
-----------------------------------------------------------------------------------
select * from pubs..authors

(1 row(s) affected)
```

When we're talking about **bits of code** in the main text, then they'll be in a **chunky font** as well.

Text that appears on your screen, for example on a menu or dialog box, also has its own font.

Tell Us What You Think

We've worked hard on this book to make it useful. We've tried to understand what you are willing to exchange your hard earned money for, and tried to make the book live up to your expectations.

Please let us know what you think about this book. Tell us what we did wrong and what we did right. This isn't just marketing flannel–we really do all huddle around the e-mail to find out what you think. If you don't believe it, then send us a note. We'll answer, and we'll take whatever you say on board for future editions. The easiest way is to use e-mail:

feedback@wrox.com
Compuserve 100063,2152

You can also find more details about Wrox Press on our web site. Here you'll find the code from our latest books, sneak previews of forthcoming titles and information about the authors and editors. You can order Wrox titles directly from the site or find out where your nearest local bookstore with Wrox titles is located. Look at the advert in the back of this book for more information. The address of our site is:

http://www.wrox.com

6.5

Installing and Configuring SQL Server

CHAPTER

1

One administration task that's often forgotten is the installing or upgrading of the software itself. Your very first administration task might be to get the software out of the box and install it. For this very reason, we'll begin this book with a detailed description of how to get SQL Server 6.5 up and running.

While being a relatively straightforward task, there are some decisions you'll have to make and we'll provide you with some guidelines for making them. We'll cover both how to install SQL Server 6.5 and how to upgrade an existing SQL Server installation to the new version. We'll also show you how to make the new version of SQL Server coexist with previous versions.

Pre-install Decisions

Even before you can install SQL Server, there are several decisions that you'll need to make about the server and network you install it on. You'll have to:

▲ Decide which computer in your network should be used for SQL Server (and perhaps even change the name of that computer).

▲ Choose the file system for that computer and identify the directories where you want to place the various components of SQL Server.

▲ Decide upon the character set, case sensitivity and sort order that SQL Server will use.

▲ Decide which network transport or transports you want to install.

Once you've made these decisions you'll need to create an SQL Executive account which you can use to log on to SQL Server.

The installation process itself is relatively simple. Like every other Microsoft Setup, it's simply a case of following the bouncing ball, so we'll only cover the actual installation process briefly. Once SQL Server has been installed, you then need to configure it so that it meets your needs.

Where Should I Put SQL Server?

Probably the first decision that you'll have to make is to select the NT Server where SQL Server will be installed. If your network includes several NT Servers, you must decide which one will be home to SQL Server 6.5. You'll usually want to avoid installing SQL Server on the machines that serve as Primary Domain Controllers (PDC) and Backup Domain Controllers (BDC). The PDC and BDC maintain and replicate the network accounts database and are always available for authenticating network logons. These tasks use a lot of resources. While it's possible to install SQL Server on either a PDC or BDC, you'll get better performance if you install it on a machine which does not need to devote resources to these functions. You also don't want to put an application SQL Server on the computer where you're running SMS.

The server you choose must have at least 16MB of memory (32 if you plan to use the replication feature). You'll need 81MB of free disk space, 56 for SQL Server itself and 25 MB for the master device. If you plan to install the on-line documentation, you need an additional 1 MB if you leave the files on the CD, 15 MB if you plan to put them on the disk.

NT File Systems and SQL Server

NT provides two major file systems: FAT (File Allocation Table) and NTFS (NT File System).

> **In addition, there's a version of HPFS (High Performance File System) for backwards compatibility with previous versions of OS/2. Since SQL Server doesn't work with HPFS, it won't be discussed any further.**

The FAT file system is identical to the file system that underlies MSDOS. It uses the 8.3 file naming convention of that operating system, and performs extremely well on small disk volumes. FAT lacks such sophisticated features as recoverability and security. In addition, many people feel that the short file names make it harder to use.

NTFS overcomes the limitations of FAT. It's designed to quickly perform standard file operations such as read, write and search. It also has built-in security at the file level and allows file names of up to 255 characters. NTFS files also have an 8.3 character name so that they can be accessed over a network from MSDOS and Windows 3.x. If one of these applications saves a file onto an NTFS volume, then both the short and long names are retained.

Microsoft states that the performance of SQL Server is about the same regardless of which file system is used, but there *is* a performance penalty if you install SQL Server on a compressed NTFS volume. In general, NTFS is faster for reads and FAT is faster for writes. You pay for NTFS's built-in fault tolerance at write time. You should choose your file system based on how you evaluate the following advantages and disadvantages in terms of your corporate needs rather than for any SQL-Server specific reasons.

File System	Advantages	Disadvantages
NTFS	Supports complete NT file level security. Keeps a log of activities so that a disk can be restored in the event of a power failure. Supports long file names and maintains MS DOS names. Allows MS DOS and Windows applications to access NTFS files across a network.	Recognized only by NT and Windows 95. If the computer is running another operating system such as MS DOS, Windows 3.x or OS/2, files must be on an NTFS partition on that computer.
FAT	Allows full access to files when the computer is running another operating system such as MS DOS. The most widely used file system for PCs. Enables you to share data on the partition with MS DOS. With NT Version 3.5, FAT supports long file names.	Files are not under the control of NT security. FAT does not support extremely large files. Less robust than NTFS.

Choosing the Server Name

This might sound like a relatively trivial task, but you should note that the SQL Server will have the same name as the name of the computer on which it's installed. You need to be sure that the name is a valid SQL Server identifier before you install SQL Server. A valid SQL Server name must start with an underscore (_) or a letter. Subsequent characters can be letters, numbers or the #, $ and _ characters. SQL Server names do not allow embedded spaces. If the name of the target computer does not conform to these rules then you'll need to change it. You can change the name of the computer from the Network Settings dialog. This can be accessed via the Network icon of the NT control panel.

If you rename a computer that's a member of an NT Server domain, make sure that the new computer name is added to the domain and the old one is removed. To do this, open the Server Manager application from the Administrative Tools program group, and select the target computer. You can then use the Computer menu to add or remove the selected computer from the domain.

Directories

By default, the setup program will place all of the SQL Server files in a directory **C:\MSSQL**. You can change this directory name if you want, but you can't use a long file name, not even if you're using NTFS; the root directory must conform to the FAT 8.3 format and can't contain spaces. The following directories will be created as part of the installation:

- **BACKUP** - Empty directory.
- **BIN** - MSDOS and Windows client executables and Windows Dynamic Link Library (DLL) files.
- **BINN** - NT executable files and on-line help files.
- **CHARSETS** - Character set and sort order files.
- **DATA** - Database devices.
- **DLL** - NT DLL files.
- **INSTALL** - Scripts for installing various options and log files from the install.
- **LOG** - Error Logs.
- **REPLDATA** - Working directory for replication.
- **SNMP** - Files to support SNMP.
- **SQLOLE** - Sample files.
- **SYMBOLS** - Debugging aids you can use in NT versions 3.51 and higher.

In most cases, you can use the defaults as long as you have disk space for the install. However, you may want to consider where to place the master device. The master device holds the *master, model* and *tempdb* databases, and the setup program places the **MSDBDATA** and **MSDBLOG** devices here as well. By default, this will be **C:\MSSQL\DATA**. You can choose where to place the master device when you install the system and, when making your choice, you'll want to consider drive speeds, any needs for removable media and any special device characteristics such as RAID devices. You may find it helpful to read the material in Chapter 3 concerning RAID devices before making that decision.

You also need to consider how big to make your master database. The default is 25 megabytes. If you have adequate disk space, you may want to make it larger at install time so that you avoid the headache of running out of space later. This will be important if you intend to create many different databases or add a lot of system stored procedures. If you don't know at install time what your future needs will be, don't worry. You can always use the **DISK RESIZE** command (see your Transact-SQL reference manual for details) to change the size of the master device.

Character Sets, Case Sensitivity and Sort Order

During the installation process, you'll be asked to select the character set, case sensitivity and sort order. In this section, we'll briefly outline the options available and tell you why you might choose one option over another.

> **The decisions you make here are critical. Once you make a choice, you can't change it without unloading your database to a character format. After the option is changed, you'll need to rebuild the database.**

Character Set

A character set is simply a list of up to 256 characters that SQL Server will recognize in your data. If your chosen character set has more than 128 characters, it's important to use the same ones on both the clients and the server. Microsoft continues to develop new character sets to support additional foreign languages but there are three primary ones.

ISO 8859-1(Latin 1 or ANSI) — This is the default character set and the one used by the Windows and NT operating systems. Use this set when you intend to have Windows and Windows NT clients exclusively, or if you need to maintain exact compatibility with a SQL Server environment for UNIX or DEC's VMS. This character set also provides compatibility with languages other than English.

Code page 850 (Multilingual) — This includes all the characters used by most of the languages of the European, North American and South American countries. You'll need this code page if you require strict compatibility with SQL Server 1.x case insensitive databases.

Code page 437 — This is the most commonly used character set in the United States. However, you should use it only when you have character-based applications that depend on the extended graphics characters in this code page (things like smiley faces and little hearts). You can tell if you need this code page by installing the ISO 8859-1 set. If your DOS applications look funny, you will need this code page.

Case-Sensitivity and Sort Order

Case-sensitivity and sort order go together. The case-sensitivity of your servers determines whether upper and lowercase letters are treated as the same (case-*insensitive*), or considered to be different (case-*sensitive*). Case-sensitivity is important in sorting and in comparisons of data with constants in an SQL **WHERE** clause.

If your server is case-sensitive, every SQL statement must have the names of tables and columns in the correct case. You need to make the decision based on the kinds of data you expect to deal with.

I worked with one Pharmaceutical company that required all servers to be case-sensitive because the names of chemicals follow that format. I also worked with a steel mill that builds steel out of common chemical elements-they wanted their servers to be case-insensitive because all of their historical mainframe data was in uppercase! So it's your choice.

There are several possible sort orders. The sort order specifies how SQL Server sorts the data it presents in response to queries. The choices are illustrated in the following table.

Sort Order	Example Comparisons	Order in which Values Are Returned
Dictionary order, case-insensitive	A=a, É =é, Ê ≠ E	E, e, È, É, é It's not possible to predict whether uppercase will precede lowercase. However, unaccented characters will precede accented ones.
Binary	Uses numeric (0-255) value for the character.	Ditto.
Dictionary order, case-sensitive	E ≠ e, Ë ≠ ë	E, e, È, è, É, é, ê, ë
Dictionary order, case-insensitive, uppercase preference	E = e, Ë = ë	E, e, È, è, É, é Uppercase is guaranteed to precede lowercase.
Dictionary order, case-insensitive, accent-insensitive	E = e = Ë = ë	E, e, È, è, É, é
Strict compatibility with Version 1.x case-insensitive databases (requires code page 850)	The first 128 characters are compared in the same way as case-insensitive dictionary order. The next 128 characters are compared in the same way as the binary sort order.	Ditto.
Custom	Comparisons depend on the sort order.	Ditto.

By default, the setup program will install the Server with Dictionary order and case-insensitive sorting.

There are some performance differences between the various sorts. Binary is the fastest but your data will not always be presented in dictionary order. For instance, ZYZZY will sort ahead of abcde, because uppercase Z precedes the lowercase a in the collating sequence. The case-sensitive, case-insensitive and case-sensitive with uppercase preference sort orders are about 20% slower than binary. The case-insensitive, accent-insensitive order is about 35% slower than binary.

> If your organization uses multiple SQL Servers then it's a good idea to have them all use the same sort and case rules. Otherwise you'll find it extremely difficult to move applications from one server to another.

Networks

SQL Server supports several different Network protocols. The basic protocol used is Named Pipes. This will be installed by default, and you should not remove it. When you install SQL Server, you can select additional network protocols to install. These include:

- ▲ Multi-protocol
- ▲ Novell Netware (IPX/SPX)
- ▲ TCP/IP
- ▲ Banyan Vines

The network protocols are supplied as a set of Dynamic Link Libraries (DLLs) called Net-Libraries. The Net-Libraries carry out all of the operations necessary to communicate across the network. SQL Server can handle multiple networks. It will simply 'listen' to all the protocols you install.

Multi-protocol

The Multi-protocol Net-Library uses NT's powerful Remote Procedure Call (RPC) capability. In SQL Server, the Multi-protocol Net-Library has been tested with TCP/IP Windows Sockets, Named Pipes and NWLink IPX/SPX.

The Multi-protocol library allows you to have integrated security over all the protocols supported by the RPC mechanism. This includes Windows-based Novell clients using SPX or IPXODI. This library offers performance comparable to that of the native interprocess communication Net-Libraries.

Multi-protocol Encryption

The Multi-protocol library also supports encryption for both user password identification and data. This is encrypted network traffic; the database itself isn't encrypted. When you choose the Multi-protocol netlib, the setup program will ask you if you want encryption. You can choose this option if it's appropriate for your installation.

NWLink IPX/SPX

This Net-Library allows SQL Server to communicate with Netware Clients using the IPX/SPX protocol. If you plan to use this Net-Library, you need to supply the Novell Bindery service name in which to register the SQL Server when you install it. The default is the name of the Novell Server computer.

TCP/IP (Windows Sockets)

This Net-Library allows you to communicate with the TCP/IP protocol. If you plan to use this library, you need to supply the TCP/IP port number on which the SQL Server will listen when you install it. The default value for this port is 1433, the official Internet Assigned Authority (IANA) socket number for Microsoft SQL Server.

Banyan Vines

SQL Server supports the Banyan Vines Sequenced Packet Protocol (SPP) on Intel platforms only. This protocol isn't supported on Alpha (AXP) or MIS platforms. When you install SQL Server using the Banyan Vines Net-Library, the setup program will prompt you for the StreetTalk PC-based service name. These names have the form *servicename@group@org,* where service name is the name of the service, group is the name of the group and org is the organization. You must create this name with the MSERVICE program included with the Vines software before you install SQL Server.

AppleTalk®

Server-side AppleTalk (ADSP) Net-Libraries are available to allow Alpha, Intel and MIPS computers to support Apple Macintosh-based clients. This Net-Library allows these clients to communicate with SQL Server via Native AppleTalk instead of TCP/IP. If you plan to use this Net-Library, you need to give the name of the AppleTalk service object name when you install SQL Server. This name is assigned by the AppleTalk System Administrator. It will be simplest if the AppleTalk service object name is the same as the SQL Server machine name. SQL server always registers the service in the local zone.

DECnet

SQL Server includes server-side Net-Libraries that provide connectivity with PATHWORKS networks. This allows VMS clients to connect to SQL Server using DECNet sockets. When you install this Net-Library, you need to provide the DECnet object ID that SQL Server will listen on. This ID is set by your VMS System Administrator and must be unique in the network. It can be an alphanumeric ID or a numeric ID, in which case you must preface it with a # sign when you install the Net-Library

Creating an Account for the SQL Executive Service

Before you install SQL Server, you need to create an account for the SQL Executive. If you don't do this, the install will use the computer's LocalSystem account and the SQL Executive will not be able to perform many connectivity related tasks. You can create multiple SQL Executive accounts, but it's usually easier to let one account manage several servers. If you are planning to use replication, it's particularly desirable to have the publishing server and all its subscribing servers share the same account. The account you create should be a domain user account and must have the following rights:

- ▲ Log on as a service
- ▲ Act as part of the operating system
- ▲ Replace a process level token
- ▲ Increase quotas

To create an account for the SQL Executive, use the NT's User Manager for Domains as found in the Administrative Tools program group. Choose New User from the User menu.

Create
SQL
Executive

```
┌─────────────────────────────────────────────────────────────────┐
│ ▬                        New User                                 │
├───────────────────────────────────────────────────────────────────┤
│                                                                   │
│  Username:     SQL Executive                          [ Add ]     │
│                                                                   │
│  Full Name:    SQL Executive Account                  [ Cancel ]  │
│                                                                   │
│  Description:  Needed to allow replication and scheduling         │
│                                                       [ Help ]    │
│  Password:     *******                                            │
│  Confirm                                                          │
│  Password:     *******                                            │
│                                                                   │
│  ☐ User Must Change Password at Next Logon                        │
│  ☒ User Cannot Change Password                                    │
│  ☒ Password Never Expires                                         │
│  ☐ Account Disabled                                               │
│                                                                   │
│  [Groups]  [Profile]  [Hours]  [Logon To]  [Account]              │
└───────────────────────────────────────────────────────────────────┘
```

You must fill in the UserName and Password fields. It's also important to check the User cannot change password and Password never expires boxes.

> It's important that the password isn't changed or allowed to expire. If the SQL Executive doesn't run after having been assigned a Windows NT user account, it's possible that the password has been changed. (It's also possible that there is no domain controller available to validate the password.) If the password or user ID must be changed, use the SQL Executive Configuration dialog to change it. (See Configuring the SQL Executive later in this chapter.)

The SQL Executive logon should belong to the local administrators group. To do this you should click the Groups button, and in the next dialog box add the Logon to the Administrators group. You will see the New User dialog again and should press the Add button. Then press Close to return to the User Manager screen. The next thing you need to do is to give the new account the rights it needs:

▲ Act as part of the operating system

▲ Increase quotas

▲ Log on as a service

▲ Replace a process level token

To do this, select User Rights from the Policies menu:

Create User right

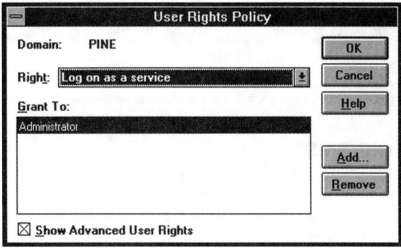

This isn't an intuitive dialog! When this screen is first presented, the Show Advanced User Rights box is unchecked. Check it and then pull down the list box. Once you find the right you want to grant, select it and then click on Add.... This will bring you to a second dialog. Make sure that the name of your domain shows in the drop-down list at the top. Then click the Show Users button so that your SQL Executive account will show. Scroll through the list in the top part of the screen until you find your account, and then select it. Now click the Add button and your account will magically appear at the bottom part of the screen. Click OK, and repeat this process for each of the rights. After that, you can close the User Manager down and get ready to install SQL Server.

SQL Server Installation

There are various ways to install SQL Server so we'll look at each of these briefly.

Installing from a SQL Server CD

You'll find that the CD contains 4 hardware specific subdirectories: **ALPHA**, **I386**, **MIPS** and **PPC**. You should run the setup program (**SETUP.EXE**) from the directory appropriate to your hardware platform.

When you start **SETUP.EXE**, go through the traditional welcome screen and setup will then prompt you for your name and organization, as well as the Product ID from the back of the CD jewel case.

After providing the required information, you'll see a screen that shows you several different options. At this point, you should choose Install SQL Server and Utilities.

Installing from the MSDN Enterprise Edition

This procedure is correct for the July 1996 edition of the MSDN and covers installation on NT 3.51 only. All the Back Office Test Platform products install from the first CD in the US set. The setup program on this CD installs the Back Office installer.

> When you try to run this installer, it will not work unless you have installed NT
> Service Pack 4. It obligingly proposes to install this service pack for you.

Once you have the Installer available, use it to install SQL Server. It will ask you to agree with a License, and offer you more information. Ultimately, it will present you with a screen from which you can choose to install SQL Server. It will then request CD 2. From there, the installation proceeds in the standard fashion.

Installing with SMS

This section assumes that you know how to deploy products with SMS. There are three files located in the root directory of the CD-ROM which will help you install SQL Server.

Filename	Description
`SMSSQL65.PDF`	Package Definition Format (PDF) file that automates creating a SQL Server package in SMS. The SQL Server package can then be distributed and installed on SMS computers. The PDF file also enables SMS to detect SQL Server on SMS computers and report that information in the SMS computer inventory.
`SMSSQL65.CMD`	Batch file that detects the platform of the computer and runs the appropriate version of setup.
`SMSSQL65.INI`	Installation script for unattended setup. This file can easily be edited to specify any drive, subdirectory, or installation option.

Unattended Setup

It's possible to install SQL Server by preparing a text file of parameters for the setup utility. Detailed instructions for doing this are in SQL Books On-Line.

Determining the Correct Licensing Mode

The next thing you need to do is to choose the Licensing Mode you want to use. Like the other BackOffice products, SQL Server requires both server and client licenses. There are two different types of client license available.

- ▲ **Per Seat** - a license is required for any computer or workstation that will access any Microsoft SQL Server in the world. It does not matter whether the client computer is using Microsoft client software or software provided by third parties. This is the most economical choice if your clients are likely to connect to multiple SQL Servers.

- ▲ **Per Server** - in this mode, you specify what the maximum number of client connections is and purchase a license for each of these connections.

You must choose the license mode when you install SQL Server. If you choose Per Seat, you can't subsequently change the licensing mode to Per Server. Per Server licenses can be converted to Per Seat licenses at no additional cost.

> If you don't know which licensing mode to choose, start off with per server. That way, you can change over if your choice proves to be incorrect or if your requirements change.

If you are installing a workstation version of SQL Server or the MSDN Back Office Test Platform, these decisions may have been made for you.

Many SQL Server applications obtain multiple SQL Server connections. Starting with SQL Server 6.0, Microsoft began supporting *Node-based Client Access*. This recognizes that multiple connections issued from the same workstation are not separate users. These connections are counted against a *single* client license. (This feature is available in both per seat and per server licensing modes.) Microsoft-supplied SQL Server client software for versions 6.0 and 6.5 (both ODBC and DBLibrary) support Node-based Client Access. Applications which use earlier versions of ODBC or DBLibrary will not have this support; each *connection* will require a *separate* license. Third party applications may or may not support node-based access.

If you choose per server, you must enter a number of concurrent **users**. This is the number of Client Access Licenses you have purchased. Once you choose per server licensing, you'll see a screen which tells you what the rules are.

Installation Options

Once licensing has been completed, the installation can begin in earnest. The following steps are all handled by self explanatory dialogs, and the decisions required should all have been resolved through your advance planning:

- Setting the Installation Path
- Placing and Sizing the Master Device
- Installing OnLine Documentation
- Selecting the Character Set
- Selecting the Sort Order
- Additional Network Support

> Remember, when you come to choose the Net-Libraries you want to install, you should leave the Named Pipes library in the list.

At the bottom of the dialog, where you are choosing character set, sort order and network support, are two check boxes. These say whether or not you want the SQL Server and SQL Executive started when you boot NT. In most cases, this is what you want, so you should check them.

The SQL Executive Log On Account

The SQL Executive Log On Account is where you finally get to use the User that you created when you set up NT for SQL Server. The install process assumes that you want the Administrator account. You should replace this with the name of the user you created for the SQL Executive.

SQL Executive Log On Account

◆ Install SQL Executive Service to log on to Windows NT as:

Account: | PINE\Administrator |

Password: | xxxxxxxx |

Confirm Pwd: | xxxxxxxx |

[Continue]
[Back]
[Exit]
[Help]

◇ Install to log on as Local System account.

Enter the name and password of that user on this screen and don't check the Install to log on as Local System account option. After you click the Continue button, you'll be asked whether or not you want to have encryption of the Multi-protocol network traffic. You can check the box if your organization requires this level of security. The default isn't to encrypt.

At this point in the install, the **SETUP** program copies what it needs from the CD to the hard disk. You can watch the progress bar while it does this, or go and refill your coffee cup. Eventually, the files will be copied and you'll see a screen informing you that Setup is now creating your master database device. Once you see this screen, you can choose to watch the sand flow up and down inside the Q (it's apparently a substitute for the hourglass) or you can take the advice provided on the screen and continue with another task. Once the installation is complete, you'll need to reboot.

Upgrading SQL Server 4.2 to SQL Server 6.0 or SQL Server 6.5

Of course, not everyone will be installing afresh. No doubt some of you will have an existing 4.2 SQL Server, as well as all its databases, and will need to upgrade to the new version. We'll run through the steps involved with an NT SQL Server. If you have an OS/2 SQL Server, you'll first have to upgrade the operating system because SQL Server 6.0 and above does not run on OS/2.

> Upgrading databases from 4.2 to 6.x isn't reversible. While the actual database format is unchanged, there are new system tables and new datatypes. You will not be able to convert the upgraded databases back to 4.2 databases, nor can you restore an SQL Server 6.x dump to a 4.2 server. Client applications that ran with 4.2 databases will still continue to work with Version 6 databases.

There are some things to think about before you start upgrading. You will probably want to do the upgrades in a test environment first. That way, you can identify problems and resolve them without having a negative impact on your production systems. The upgrade assumes that the sort order, file system and network protocols are the same as those you used for your 4.2 installation. If you want to change any of these, you should not upgrade your SQL Server, but instead do a complete install of SQL Server 6.5.

Checking that the Upgrade Will Be Successful

There are new keywords in SQL Server 6.0 and in SQL Server 6.5. You can't upgrade a database that uses these keywords as column names. The upgrade requires that the correct information exists in the **text** column of the **syscomments** table. Finally, you can't upgrade any databases that are in read-only mode. The Setup utility will check for these conditions, but you'll find it easier to work out ahead of time whether the upgrade will succeed. To do this, you must run a program called **CHKUPG65.EXE** if you are upgrading to 6.5 or **CHKUPG.EXE** if you are upgrading to 6.0. These programs are on the install CD.

You can run it in the command prompt box, or from the file manager by selecting File | Run. CHKUPG65 takes several input values, each of which is preceded by the appropriate switch.

Switch & Value	Meaning
/U *sa*	User; must be the system administrator.
/P *password*	System administrator password. If no value is provided, NULL is assumed.
/S *server*	The name of the server you are upgrading. If you don't provide a value, the **CHKUPG65** program will work with the local server.
/o *filename*	The full path name for the output file.

After the program has been completed, you can view the log with any text editor. It will contain messages about any trouble spots it finds.

```
===========================================================
=======  Database: master

        Status: 8
                (No problem)

        Missing objects in Syscomments
                None

        Keyword conflicts
                Column name: MSscheduled_backups.DAY [SQL-92
keyword]


===========================================================
=======  Database: pubs

        Status: 0
                (No problem)
```

```
        Missing objects in Syscomments
                None

        Keyword conflicts
                Column name: sales.DATE    [SQL-92 keyword]
```

This run of **CHKUPG65** did not find any errors but it does warn about column names that conflict with the SQL 92 standard. These reserved words are not used in SQL Server 6.5, but will be used in future versions. This gives you advance notice so that you can plan to change the conflicting words before subsequent releases of SQL Server.

> Even though Setup will run **CHKUPG**, it's a good idea for you to do it before you start the upgrade. That way, you can deal with any problems before they arise.

Upgrading from SQL Server 6.0 to SQL Server 6.5

You can upgrade from SQL Server 6.0 to SQL Server 6.5 by a similar process. Run **CHKUPG65** to make sure there won't be any problems.

> There are a lot more reserved words in SQL Server 6.5 so you may need to change some of your applications before you can upgrade.

Before You Begin the Upgrade

Upgrading your SQL Server isn't difficult. However, there are several things you must do before you start.

First, **back up all of your databases**. You may want to back them up twice and send one backup off to a remote location. There is no such thing as being too cautious in this business!

You can't upgrade any databases which are marked as read only. If you have any of these, use **sp_dboption** to set the read only option to false.

Determine whether or not you'll have any problems running 4.2 applications against a version 6.5 SQL Server. There are two particular areas to look at.

Keywords

CHKUPG65 looks only at database objects in determining whether or not there will be keyword conflicts. You need to make sure that there are no other places where keyword problems could appear. For example, **CHKUPG65** won't know about a table an application creates and then drops.

Changes to Support ANSI Standards

Microsoft has changed the rules for queries involving **GROUP BY**. Now these queries must conform to the ANSI standard. This means that the select list can **only** include aggregates and the columns named in the **GROUP BY** clause, and that **all columns** used in the **GROUP BY** clause **must** appear in the select list. If applications previously took advantage of the relaxation of these rules, they will now fail with a fatal error message.

> If you have applications that used the non-standard forms of the GROUP BY, it's possible to set trace flag T202 that will make Version 6 emulate the earlier versions characteristics. This is only appropriate as a short-term solution.

The following table shows how much disk space is required to upgrade to 6.5 from a previous version of SQL Server:

Upgrade From	Disk Space	Master Device Space	Books On-line
6.0	20 MB	2 MB	1 or 15MB
4.2	65 MB	9 MB	1 or 15 MB

If your 4.2 SQL Server is configured to have **tempdb** in RAM, which you can determine by looking at configuration options or by running isql and issuing the sp_configure command, the upgrade process will change the configuration so that **tempdb** is on the default device. You must make sure that the default disk device will be big enough to hold **tempdb** when the Version 6.5 SQL Server is started. If you are not familiar with the techniques for managing devices, see Chapter 3. You can also use the isql/w procedures outlined in that chapter with your 4.2 SQL Server.

Starting the Upgrade

When you're ready to run Setup to upgrade your SQL Server, you should shut down all other applications on that Server. In particular, you must shut down any applications that might use any of the SQL Server DLLs. These include any SQL Server client tools (isql/w, SQL Administrator and SQL Object Manager), SQL Monitor and SQL Transfer Manager. If you are upgrading from Version 6.0, stop replication and make sure that the log is empty. In addition, you should shut down any Word for Windows applications, the Microsoft Visual C++ Development environment and any applications which use the Visual C++ Runtime library.

Once you've dealt with all of these things, you're ready to do the upgrade! Once again the dialogs are all self-explanatory. Upgrading does not differ much from a full installation. Once the upgrade is complete, you'll find that in SQL Server 6.5, SQL Administrator and SQL Object Manager have been replaced by SQL Enterprise Manager. However, they are still usable. When you upgrade a 4.2 SQL Server, the upgrade process installs the necessary stored procedures to make these programs work with a Version 6.5 server.

Using SQL Server 6.5 and SQL Server 4.2 Concurrently

SQL Server 6.5 and SQL Server 4.2 coexist quite happily. You can even have 4.2 and 6.5 servers on the same machine, as long as the servers have different names. It isn't possible to run SQL Server 6.0 servers and SQL Server 6.5 servers on the same machine.

Version 4.2 clients can connect to Version 6.5 servers and Version 6.5 clients can connect to Version 4.2 servers. Both versions can be set up as remote servers and ODBC connections can be made to both 4.2 and 6.5 servers.

Replication is *not* available for Version 4.2 servers. Replication from 6.5 servers to 6.0 servers is done with ODBC so you must install the proper ODBC drivers.

If you use extended stored procedures, you should rebuild the appropriate DLLs with the new SQL Server Libraries.

Using SQL Administrator and Object Manager with SQL Server 6.5

SQL Administrator and SQL Object Manager have been replaced by SQL Enterprise Manager in Version 6.5. When you upgrade a server from version 4.2 to version 6.5, the upgrades that will allow you to continue to use the older programs are done automatically. If you want to use these programs with newly installed Version 6.5 servers, you need to run some upgrade scripts. Both of these scripts can be run from ISQL/W.

If you want to use SQL Administrator, run **C:\mssql\install\admin60.sql**. If you want to use SQL Object Manager, run **C:\mssql\install\object60.sql**.

> Note that the scripts are still called xxxx60 even in SQL Server Version 6.5. If you are using SQL Server version 6.0, the scripts will be in the c:\sql60\install subdirectory.

You will be able to use the new SQL Enterprise Manager to administer both Version 4.2 and Version 6.5 SQL Servers. Its capabilities far exceed those of SQL Administrator and SQL Object Manager combined. If you want to use a 6.5 SQL Enterprise Manager to administer a 4.2 server, you must run the **SQLOLE42.SQL** script found in your install directory. To use a SQL Server 6.5 Manager with a 6.0 server, you must run the **SQLOLE65.SQL** script which is also in your install directory.

Using Dump and Load with Both Versions of SQL Server

You can load a database dumped with the 4.2 Dump Database command into a Version 6.5 server, but this only applies to servers that are running on the same hardware platform. You can't restore, for example, a database dumped on an Intel machine to a server running on a MIPS machine regardless of version. It's a good idea to run the **CHKUPG65** utility before doing so as you may encounter the same problems you would have run into if you had upgraded the database directly.

You can't dump a Version 6.5 database and restore it to a 4.2 server. SQL Server 6.0 backups can be loaded into 6.5 and SQL Server 6.5 backups can be loaded into Version 6.0, by using Microsoft SQL Server 6.0 Service Pack 3, which is available separately from Microsoft.

Transferring Data between Versions

As long as you are not using any of the new SQL Server 6.5 datatypes or the identity property, you can move data between Version 4.2 and 6.5 servers with Bulk Copy in both character and native modes. You can also use the Database/Object transfer functions of SQL Enterprise Manager 6.5 or the SQL Transfer Manager program of earlier versions.

Sanity Testing Your Installation

Whether you have completed a new installation or have upgraded an existing 4.2 installation, you'll want to make sure that your new server works.

If you did not reboot your NT Server after you installed SQL Server 6.5, do so now. If you did not choose to have the server started when NT starts, you will have to do that now too. Find the SQL Service Manager in the SQL Server Program Group, and double click on it. Then double click on the Green light to start the server. Once the server is running, start isql/w. You will see a connect dialog.

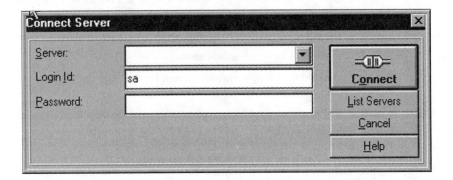

Type your server name and the sa password, then choose Connect. When you see the Query window, type the following query:

```
select @@servername, @@version
```

Execute it by pressing *Ctrl+E* or choosing Execute from the Query menu. You should see the name of the server you have just installed and the SQL Server version.

Client Configuration and Setup

When you install SQL Server, the appropriate client software is also installed on the server itself. However, your organization probably has many computers that need to use the Microsoft SQL Server client software to communicate with the server.

In this section, we will discuss first what the software is, and second, how to install it on the most common client hardware platforms. We will also discuss installing ODBC, since Microsoft Access, Microsoft Visual C++, Microsoft Visual Basic, replication to non-SQL servers and many third party tools require the ODBC software. At the end of the section, there is a brief discussion of the most common things that go wrong with client workstations and how to solve these problems.

When you install the client software, the Setup program automatically installs the libraries and DLLs needed by client applications. There are some additional utilities you can install if you choose to do so.

Utility Choice	Description
BCP	Installs the bulk copy utility (bcp) which is used to copy data between the database and operating system files.
ISQL/W	Installs both ISQL/W and isql, the interactive SQL processors. ISQL/W runs in a Windows environment, isql in the DOS environment.
SQL Enterprise Manager	Installs SQL Enterprise Manager which is used for server and database administration tasks (only available in a 32-bit environment).
SQL Security Manager	Installs the SQL Security manager, which is used to manage SQL Server accounts when security is integrated with the NT security.
Configuration Diagnostics	Installs the SQL Client Configuration Utility, which you use to determine whether the versions of various DLLs are installed on a client, and the makepipe and readpipe programs used to test the named pipes network connections.
SQL Server Books Online	The complete set of on-line SQL Server 6 documentation.
MS Query	Query tool for relational databases.
MS DTC	Monitoring and Administrations tool for the Distributed Transaction Coordinator.
SQL Server Web Assistant	Tool to assist in publishing query results on the Web.
SQL Trace	Graphical utility that monitors and records SQL Server 6.5 database activity.

Your application developers will need at least BCP, ISQL, SQL Trace and the SQL Server Books Online. Administrators will need SQL Enterprise Manager. Your system administrator should also have SQL Security Manager on his or her workstation, assuming it's running a 32-bit environment.

> **It's a good idea to put Configuration Diagnostics on every workstation where client software is installed since you never know when you will need it!**

Installing Client Software on 16-bit Computers

Client software can be installed from the SQL Server 6.5 CD on a local drive or on a network drive.

DOS

There is no setup program for the DOS client software. You need to create a directory on the client machine. This directory will usually be named `C:\MSSQL\BIN`, although there is no requirement that it has that name. Copy the desired programs from the `\CLIENTS\MSDOS` directory on the SQL Server CD to the directory you have created on the client. You must copy the appropriate network TSR:

Network Protocol	TSR
Named Pipes	DBNMIPE.EXE
Novell SPX	DBMSSPX.EXE
Banyan Vines	DBMSVINE.EXE

Add the directory where you installed the software to the path. If you want, you can add the command **DBNMPIPE** (or **DBMSSPX** or **DBMSVINE**) to the **AUTOEXEC.BAT**. This will install the appropriate TSR each time the computer is rebooted.

Windows or Windows For Workgroups

The setup program for Windows and Windows for Workgroups is in the **\CLIENTS\WIN16** subdirectory of the SQL Server CD. To install the client software, simply run **SETUP.EXE** from that directory. You will need to:

1   Provide the name of the drive and the directory where the software should be installed. This is usually **C:\MSSQL** but this isn't compulsory.

2   Choose the optional tools (ISQL/W and the SQL Client Configuration Utility) which you want to install.

3   Specify the appropriate network protocol. This can be Named Pipes, Novell SPX, Banyan Vines, TCP/IP or Multi-protocol.

4   Choose whether or not you want to install SQL Server Books on-line.

> If you are upgrading either a DOS or a Windows installation, be sure none of the client software is running when you begin the install.

Installing Client Software on 32-bit Computers

These clients are installed using the same setup program you used to install SQL Server. You will find it on the standard SQL Server CD in the **\ALPHA**, **\I386**, **\PPC**, or the **\MIPS** directory. You can install the software from a local or a network drive. If you are installing on NT, you can install client software on remote computers as well.

The 32-bit setups will (optionally) install SQL Books Online. You need to decide whether to install the entire documentation on the local hard drive or to leave it on the CD. The disk install is faster but takes more space. Of course, if the Client machine does not have access to a CDROM drive containing the SQL Books files, you'll have to install them to the local hard disk.

> It's possible to install the 16-bit client software in a 32-bit environment. If you wish to do so, please follow the instructions above. There is no particular reason to install the 16-bit software in these environments, and it's generally preferable to use the 32-bit versions.

NT

For NT the steps are as follows:

1 Start the Setup program and respond to the questions. You can choose whether to do a local or remote installation.

2 Select the directory into which you want the client software installed.

3 Select the Utilities you want to install.

4 Install SQL Books Online if desired

5 Reboot the computer.

The **AUTOEXEC.BAT** file will automatically be updated with the path of the SQL Server root directory. The previous **AUTOEXEC** will be saved as **AUTOEXEC.nnn**, where **nnn** is a number between 001 and 999. It will be the highest numbered one in the root directory when you finish the install.

Windows 95

For Windows 95 the steps are as follows:

1 Start the Setup program and respond to the questions.

2 When you see the Install or Remove Utilities screen, choose INSTALL.

3 Select the directory into which you want the client software installed.

4 Select the Utilities you want to install.

5 Install SQL Books Online if desired

> If you're upgrading a previous installation, make sure that there's no SQL Server software running.

ODBC Installation

The method with which you install ODBC varies depending on the platform you are installing client software on.

NT

When you install Client software on an NT platform, the ODBC driver is automatically installed by the Setup program.

Windows 95

To install the ODBC drivers for Windows 95, use the ODBCST32 program in the ODBC directory for your platform.

Windows/Windows for Workgroups   *for Windows 3.1*

Use the setup program in the **\CLIENTS\WIN16\ODBC** directory of the SQL Server 6.5 CD.

> If you are upgrading a previous installation, you may want to make a backup copy of the files **SQLSRVR.DLL** and **DRVSSRVR.HLP**, which are in your **\WINDOWS\SYSTEM** directory, before installing the new software.

Changing SQL Server Options

Once you've installed SQL Server, you'll find that you've already dealt with some of the available SQL Server options. Server options are general settings for SQL Server that specify:

▲ Directories

▲ Auto start options and parameters

▲ Logging and integration

In this section, we will look how to set the server options, and then describe the options in detail.

How to Set Server Options

You can set the options with SQL Setup. Many of them can also be specified with SQL Enterprise Manager, which you'll meet in the next chapter. To specify them with SQL Setup, start Setup and select Set Server Options and from the Options dialog. You will see the following Server Options Screen.

Setting Directory Options

When you installed SQL Server, you specified a root directory and the directory for the Master device. If you move the code or the master device, you can change the directories here. You can also specify a different location for the SQL Server Errorlog. The installation process creates **\MSSQL\LOG\ERRORLOG** with no file type. If you do not want an SQL Server error log, leave this field empty. You might choose not to have an SQL Server error log when you have integrated its messages with the NT Application log. If you don't maintain this log file, you will not be able to review the log in SQL Enterprise Manager.

> Note that putting a space in the errorlog field isn't the same as deleting all the characters. If you put a space in, SQL Enterprise manager looks for a file name of . and gets very confused!
>
> Also, don't use a file type for the errorlog. This similarly confuses SQL Enterprise Manager!

Assuming that there is a file name for the error log, a new log file is created each time SQL Server is started. Six prior versions are maintained, named **ERRORLOG.1**, **ERRORLOG.2** etc. **ERRORLOG.1** is the newest.

Autostart Options

You use the Auto Start options to specify which services should be started when the NT server is booted. In most cases, you want the SQL Server and the SQL Executive to start automatically. If you don't have these services started at boot time, you can use SQL Service Manager to start them whenever you want. You can also start these services from the command line. If you need to start SQL Server with special switches, particularly when you want to recover from a failed setting of configuration options, you would want to tell it not to start the SQL Server at boot time.

You can also specify whether a Mail Client session should be started automatically at the same time as SQL Executive service. You need to have SQL Mail if you are using any Mail Application Programming Interface (MAPI) features of SQL Server. These include Alerts and scheduled tasks that use e-mail to notify operators of their results, as well as any mail enabled applications your organization may have developed. When you check Auto Start Mail Client, you should click the Mail Login button and make sure the login information is correct. Note that Mail must already be installed on the NT Server before you can use SQL Mail.

> In SQL Server 6.0, the Enterprise Manager allows you to check a non-existent option called 'autostart license logging'. If you do so, you may experience problems. See the Microsoft Knowledgebase article Q143213 for detailed instructions on how to correct the problems.

Logging and Integration Options

It's possible, and customary, to integrate the SQL Server event log with the Windows NT application log. This means that SQL Server and SQL Executive events are logged in the same place as the events of other applications. If you want to use the Alerting capabilities of SQL Server, you must integrate the SQL Server event log with the NT log. You can only set or change this option with SQL Setup.

It's also possible, and customary, to integrate the SQL Server performance monitor with the NT performance monitor. Since SQL Server operates in conjunction with everything else that is happening on the NT Server, it makes sense to study its behavior at the same time as you are studying the behavior of its environment. You can only set or change this option with SQL Setup. Once you have chosen integration, you can use either SQL Setup or SQL Enterprise Manager to set or change the way it's integrated. You have two choices: Direct Response Mode and On Demand Mode.

With the default, Direct Response Mode, SQL Server statistics gathering is separate from its display. In this option, data is immediately available to the performance monitor and the performance monitor response time is optimized. However, data displayed with this option is one period behind; that is, the previous period's statistics are displayed while the current period's are being collected. When you choose On Demand Mode, the NT Performance Monitor requests and waits for SQL Server data during each refresh period.

This mode gives you the latest data but the Performance Monitor response time will be slower than it is in Direct Response mode. On Demand Mode is useful when you are comparing SQL Server statistics with other system statistics in the same view, and also when you are studying a statistic that is updated infrequently. When you are using On Demand Mode, you should make sure that the refresh interval is long enough so that the SQL Server isn't overloaded with requests from Performance Monitor.

xp_cmdshell Option

The extended procedure xp_cmdshell allows the execution of commands in the command shell of the SQL Server computer. Usually this procedure executes Windows NT commands in SQL Server's security context which, by default, is a user account with local administrator authority.

If you check this option, when someone who isn't sa executes xp_cmdshell, the requested command runs in the SQLExecutiveCmdExec user account, which is the same account used by SQL Executive for scheduled tasks entered by non-system administrators. When you grant execute permission for xp_cmdshell to users, the users can execute any operating-system command at the Windows NT command shell that the account running SQL Server (usually a local system account) has privilege to execute.

To restrict xp_cmdshell access to users who have administrator permission on the Windows NT-based computer where SQL Server is running, select the xp_cmdshell - Use SQLExecutiveCmdExecAccount for Non-SAs option.

Commands issued by clients logged on to SQL Server as sa are executed under SQL Server's security context regardless of the setting of this option. There is additional information about the SQL Executive CmdExec account and the SQL Server Login Account later in this chapter.

SNMP Support

If your NT machine has the SNMP (Simple Network Management Protocol) service installed when you install SQL Server, you will be given the option to enable SQL Server to interact with this service. The necessary files for this tool are installed when you install SQL Server.

Tape Support

When you click the Tape Support button, you get a dialog box that will allow you to specify how SQL Server should behave when it tries to read a tape that has not been inserted in the drive.

Startup Options

SQL Server can be started with various options. These options are specified either:

▲ On the command line used to start SQL Server

▲ By modifying the Startup Parameters line in Control Panel's Services application

▲ With the Parameters button in the Server Options dialog

▲ By defining Registry Keys

▲ Using Visual Basic For Applications (VBA).

Switch & Value	Meaning
-d *master_device_path*	Fully qualified path for the MASTER database device.
-e *error_log_path*	Fully qualified path for the error log file.
-n	Does not use the NT event log for errors.

> **If you use the -n switch, you should also use the -e switch so that there will be some logging of SQL Server events.**

Switch & Value	Meaning
-m	Starts SQL Server in single-user mode.
-s *registry_key*	Starts SQL Server using an alternate set of startup parameters stored in the Registry under the key *registry_key*.
-f	Starts SQL Server in minimal mode.

Use the -f switch to recover from a failed configuration. This switch causes SQL Server to start with minimum values for User Connections, open databases, locks, open objects, language information and asynchronous I/O. The procedure cache is set to 50%. The server starts in single user mode and the CHECKPOINT mechanism isn't started. Remote access and read-ahead are disabled, if tempdb is in RAM it's set to 2MB and autoexec procedures are not run.

Use the -f switch on the command line
```
        sqlserver -f
```
or use the Services application in Control Panel and place -f in the startup parameters box.

Switch & Value	Meaning
`-c`	Speeds startup by starting SQL Server independently of the Windows NT Service Control Manager.
`-x`	Turns off the collection of CPU and cache hit statistics to allow for maximum performance.
`-p` *precision_level*	Maximum level of precision for decimal and numeric datatypes. Default is 28 digits but can range from 1 to 38. If precision_level isn't supplied but the -p switch is, SQL Server will assume a maximum of 38.
`-r` *master_mirror_path*	Fully qualified path for the device used to mirror the MASTER database device.
`/T` *trace#*	Start with the specified trace flag (See Chapter 10 for details of trace flags).

Even though a /t (lowercase) will be accepted, you should not use this unless specifically directed to do so by Microsoft support services.

Changing Startup Options with SQL Setup

When you want to change startup options from the Server Options dialog, you click the Parameters button in the Server Options dialog.

To add a new switch, type it and any value in the top text box, and then click the <u>A</u>dd button. To remove a switch, select it in the existing parameters list and then click the remove button.

> It's also possible to change startup options with the SQL Enterprise Manager.

Adding Registry Keys for Alternate Startup Options

At install time, Setup records default parameters in the registry under

```
HKEY_LOCAL_MACHINE
    \SOFTWARE
        \Microsoft
            \MSSQLServer
                \MSSQLServer
                    \Parameters
```

SQL Server Startup options are **SQLArg0**, **SQLArg1**, and so on. When you want to create a new key with different start up options, you should follow this procedure:

- Use **REGEDT32**
- Copy an existing key
- Modify it appropriately for the new startup options

Be sure to backup the registry before you start making changes to it. Only experienced users should edit the Registry! For example, suppose you want to create a Registry Key that you can use when you want to start SQL Server in Single User mode.

You start by selecting the highest level **MSSQLServer** key, and choosing the Add Key option from the Edit menu. When you do this, you're prompted for the name of the key. You might name your key **SingleUser**. Next, you should select the lower level **MSSQLServer** key. Save its contents to a text file by choosing Save Key from the Registry menu. Now select the **SingleUser** key you added, and load the text file into it by choosing Restore from the Registry menu. Select **Parameters** under the **SingleUser** key and, using the Add Value function of the Edit menu, add the value **SQLArg2** with a string of **-m**.

When you want to start SQL Server in single user mode, issue the command

```
sqlservr -sSingleUser
```

in the command box.

Changing Startup Options with VBA

SQL Servers can be started with the **START** method. This method takes the path of the master device, the path of the errorlog, the path of the master mirror device, if any, and the Start Mode as parameters. Start Mode is one of

- NoServiceControl
- NTErrorLogging
- SingleUser
- StartAndConnect
- RealTime
- Defaults

Changing Network Support

Changing network support is similar to the process used when installing SQL Server for the first time. Simply check or uncheck the desired netlibs. If you're installing a netlib that isn't one of the standard supported ones, you'll need the manufacturer's software.

Changing the SQL Server Login Account

On Windows NT 3.51 or later-based systems, to take advantage of SQL Server features that require the SQL Server service to access the network (such as replicating data to an ODBC subscriber or generating web pages), you must set up the MSSQLServer service to log on under a user account.

During SQL Server installation, the setup program asks you to provide the domain, username, and password of a Windows NT user account, which it then assigns to SQL Executive. SQL Server setup installs the MSSQLServer service to run under the LocalSystem account, not under a user account.

After installation, you can modify SQL Server to run under a different user account. For example, to explicitly control SQL Server permissions to access resources on other computers, run SQL Server under a domain user account. You can change account assignments by using the Control Panel Services application.

To set up the MSSQLServer service to log on under a different user account. From Windows NT, open Control Panel, open the Services application and select the MSSQLServer service. Choose the Startup button. Under the Log On As option, select This Account, and then type in the account information.

> The account under which MSSQLServer service logs on must meet the same requirements as the account under which SQL Executive logs on. It makes sense to run the MSSQLServer service and the SQL Executive service under the same user account; that way, you only have one account to worry about.

SQL Executive CmdExec Account

When you install SQL Server, the process creates an NT domain user account named SQLExecutiveCmdExec. This account has a randomly generated password, so it's impossible to use it to log on. This account is used to run CmdExec tasks that are owned by users other than system administrators (sas). This means that all users can execute CmdExec tasks in the security context that's provided by the SQLExecutiveCmdExec account.

By controlling the rights, permissions, and group memberships of the SQLExecutiveCmdExec account, you can control the operating system privileges of tasks that are owned by users other than System Administrators. To configure the rights, permissions, and group memberships of the SQLExecutiveCmdExec account, use the User Manager application from the Administrative Tools program group under Program Manager.

CmdExec tasks that are owned by sas run in the security context of the user account that is assigned to SQL Executive. Generally, the SQL Executive account belongs to the local group of the Administrators on the server.

SQL Server Configuration

SQL Server has many different values you can configure. The options you're most likely to change affect memory, I/O and the maximums for various components such as locks. Configuration values can be changed with Transact-SQL commands, SQL Enterprise Manager and Visual Basic for Applications (VBA). We will show you the mechanics of changing configurations after introducing SQL Enterprise Manager in the next chapter, but we want to cover the overall concepts now.

Dynamic and Static

Configuration options are divided into Dynamic and Static options and Advanced and Standard options. Dynamic options take effect immediately after they are changed. Changes to static options do not take effect until you stop and restart the SQL Server. Advanced options are only displayed when you request them by setting the 'Show advanced options' to true. We will point out which options are dynamic and advanced as we discuss them. This section covers all of the commonly changed options and many of the ones that are less often used. There are some which are rarely changed which won't be covered. Many of these say 'change only when told to do so by Microsoft.' The manual does a decent job of explaining them.

> Be careful. The Administrator's Companion published with version 6.0 of the product has the *standard* options in plain type and the *advanced* options in bold type, despite a paragraph to the contrary.

Memory Configuration

One of the most important changes you will make to SQL Server's configuration is the amount of memory available to it. In this section, we'll discuss how SQL Server uses memory, how you should change it and we'll also cover the possibility of putting *tempdb* in RAM.

How SQL Server Uses Memory

You can allocate up to 2 gigabytes of memory to SQL Server. If the Server will be used as a distribution server, there must be at least 32 MB of memory on the machine and you must allocate at least 16 MB to SQL Server. It uses this memory for:

- ▲ SQL Server kernel and resource structures
- ▲ The procedure cache
- ▲ The data cache (buffers)

SQL Server will take its memory first. This memory is used for the code itself, locks, user connections, and so forth. The remainder is divided between the procedure and data caches. You specify the total available memory and the percent that should be given to the procedure cache. Both the procedure and data buffers are managed with a Least Recently Used (LRU) strategy, in which, when space is needed for a new item, it replaces the one that was least recently used.

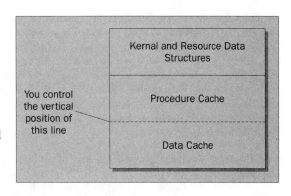

When you install SQL Server, it sets the memory option based on the amount of available memory in the machine.

Available in Machine	Allocated to SQL Server
< 32MB	8MB
>= 32 MB	16MB

Because SQL Server 'locks' memory for itself, you should be careful not to 'crowd' NT. The following table contains guidelines for dividing memory between NT and SQL Server. Keep in mind that these numbers assume that SQL Server has a machine to itself. If other applications are running on the same NT server, you'll have to balance their needs with the needs of SQL Server.

Available Memory	Give SQL Server
16 MB	4 MB
24 MB	8 MB
32 MB	16 MB
48 MB	28 MB
64 MB	40 MB
128 MB	100 MB
256 MB	216 MB
512 MB	464 MB

In general, you should avoid allocating memory in 'dribs and drabs'. In most cases (again depending on whether or not other applications are running on the server) there is no measurable difference between giving SQL Server 14MB, 16MB, and 18MB on a 32MB machine. The reason for this is that additional memory is generally given to the data cache. Most cache hit ratio studies indicate that there is a fairly flat performance increase curve beyond several megabytes. To determine whether or not additional memory will be useful, you should check the Cache Hit Ratio of the SQL Server while the system is under typical load. If it's 90% or higher, you will not benefit from additional memory.

In allocating memory to SQL Server, make sure there is enough disk space for the NT virtual memory support files (**pagefile.sys, ...**). These will need to accommodate the additional memory.

To determine whether you have given the right amount of memory to SQL Server, you'll want to watch the Page Faults/Sec counter of the NT Memory Object. If there are page faults, SQL Server has too much memory and you should give some back to the operating system.

Don't configure SQL Server for more virtual memory then there is physical memory; this can result in poor performance.

There are two configuration options that you'll work with to tune memory for your SQL Server: **memory** and **procedure cache**. These are discussed in the next section.

Memory Configuration Options

The memory configuration option specifies the amount of memory available to SQL Server in 2K units. This means that if you want to give SQL Server 16 MB of memory, you set the memory to 8192. Memory can range from 1000 to 1048576. The memory option is static and one of the standard options. When you change memory, you must stop and restart the server.

The procedure cache configuration option specifies the percentage of available memory that should be allocated for caching stored procedures. The default is 30%. The optimal value for the procedure cache varies from application to application. For example, if you run more stored procedures than ad hoc queries, you may benefit from increasing this percentage. This value may also need to be changed when you move from development into production. You want to find the right balance between space for procedures that are run concurrently and space for data buffers. You can study the behavior of the procedure cache with the DBCC MEMUSAGE and the SQLPERF LRUSTATS commands. The procedure cache configuration option is static and one of the standard options.

tempdb *in RAM*

It's possible to request that *tempdb* be placed in RAM. This reduces memory that is available for the data cache. It's important to understand that the memory used for *tempdb* isn't part of the amount specified in the memory setting. For example, if memory is currently configured at 16MB and you want use 10 of those 16MB for tempdb, you would change the memory configuration option, so that only 6MB are available to SQL Server.

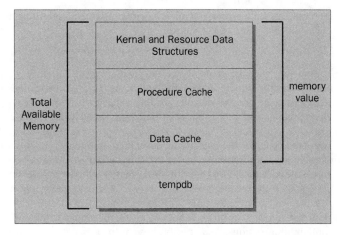

In most cases, it will be better to devote memory to data cache since *tempdb* pages will use the cache just like other database pages. However, if your applications make extensive use of *tempdb*, you may want to evaluate whether this will help you or not. You want to consider putting *tempdb* in RAM when you have plenty of available memory, the cache hit ratio is low, and applications have a lot of *tempdb* activity.

Use sp_lock or SQL Enterprise Manager to see how applications use tempdb.

To evaluate the performance of *tempdb* in RAM:

1 Select a small set of your *tempdb* intensive queries

2 Run these several times with *tempdb* on disk, noting the execution times

3 Reconfigure to put tempdb in RAM

4 Re-run queries

5 If little improvement, give the memory back to the data cache

If you put *tempdb* in RAM, you'll still be able to use the ALTER DATABASE command to increase it if necessary. When you do so, the memory allocations will not be contiguous. You must stop and restart the server to get contiguous allocations. If you alter *tempdb* 10 times, you must stop and restart the server.

Miscellaneous Configuration Options

Configuration options are used to change a lot of different elements of SQL Server. In this section we will look at a few that are particularly important. These options are all part of the standard configuration set.

You can configure the number of *open databases* for the server. When this maximum is reached, you'll receive an error message if someone tries to open another one. The default is 20, and this value can range from 5 to 32,767. This is a static option. You can also configure the maximum number of *open objects* (tables, views, etc.). The default is 500, and the value can range from 100 to 2,147,483,647. You should increase this only when you receive error messages indicating that you do not have enough open objects. Each allowed open object consumes 70 bytes of memory, so you may need to increase the amount of memory available to SQL Server if you increase this value. This is a static option.

You specify whether or not you want *nested triggers*. When triggers are nested and a trigger on TableA performs some update action on TableB, any trigger associated with that action on TableB is invoked. Nested triggers are the default. Set this value to 0 if you do not want nested triggers. Nested triggers tend to be smaller and more modular than non-nested triggers. This is a dynamic option.

You can configure the maximum number of simultaneous *user connections*. Each connection requires 37 KB of memory. The minimum value for this option is 5, the default is 20 and the maximum is 15 for the SQL Workstation, and 32, 767 for the SQL Server. If you do not have enough connections, users will be prevented from logging on to the server. This is a static option.

With the 6.5 release of SQL Server, all of the options that can be set with the SET statement are also configuration options. You specify these with *user_option* which takes a bitmap representing one or more of the following options:

Configuration Value	Description
1	DISABLE_DEF_CNST_CHK. When enabled, default constraint checking is disabled.
2	IMPLICIT_TRANSACTIONS. When enabled, starts a transaction automatically when an SQL statement is about to be processed.
4	CURSOR_CLOSE_ON_COMMIT. When enabled, closes any open cursors whenever the transaction count goes to 0.
8	ANSI_WARNINGS. When enabled, warns users of any non-standard ANSI behavior.
16	ANSI_PADDING. When enabled, prevents trimming of column values.
32	ANSI_NULLS. When enabled, enforces ANSI null behavior in equality comparisons.
64	ARITHABORT ON. When enabled, terminates a query when an overflow or divide-by-zero error occurs during query execution.
128	ARITHIGNORE. When enabled, returns NULL when an overflow or divide-by-zero error occurs during a query.
256	QUOTED_IDENTIFIER. When enabled, causes the new sessions to differentiate between single and double quotation marks when evaluating an expression.
512	NOCOUNT. When enabled, turns off the message returned at the end of each statement that states how many rows were affected by the statement.
1024	ANSI_DEFAULTS. When enabled, alters the session's behavior not to use ANSI compatibility for nullability. New columns defined without explicit nullability will be defined not to allow NULLS.
2048	ANSI_DEFAULTS. When enabled, alters the session's behavior to ANSI compatibility for nullability. New columns defined without explicit nullability will be defined to allow NULLs.

You should note that this establishes values for the *server as a whole* rather than affecting only an individual connection like the SET statement does. An individual user can override these settings for a session with the SET statement. This option is dynamic. However, changes will only be seen by new logins. They do not apply retroactively to users who have already connected to the server.

Options You *Almost* Never Change

There are two options which are 'dangerous'. The first one allows ad hoc updates to the system catalogue tables and the second one changes the default sort order id.

In most cases, you don't want to update the system tables directly. For instance, you want new rows to be added to the the *sysdatabases* table as a result of a CREATE DATABASE statement. After all, inserting a new row in this table doesn't actually cause a database to exist! In some cases, however, the only way to solve a problem will be to modify one or more of these tables. When you want to do this, you'll need to change the value of *allow updates* from its default (0) to a value of 1. Once you've done this, you can modify system tables. This is a dynamic option and part of the standard set of options.

> It's a good idea to put the SQL Server in single user mode before you change this option. Then you don't risk inadvertent changes.

You can change the *default sortorder id* configuration option but you shouldn't do so. Remember that the sort order affects indexes and comparisons of data. If you want to change the sort order, you'll need to use SQL Setup. If you already have data in databases on the server, you'll need to copy it out to character format and reload it. This is a static option and part of the advanced set.

SQL Executive Configuration

With the 6.5 release, you get the ability to configure some aspects of the SQL Executive. These features can only be configured using the SQL Enterprise Manager. Even though it's possible to change things like the start-up account with the Services tool in Control Panel, you should not do it that way. The table below lists the configurable aspects of the SQL Executive.

Parameter	Description
Auto-start SQL Mail when SQL Executive starts.	If true, SQL Executive will automatically start SQL Mail. SQL Server needs to be running when the SQL Executive starts SQL Mail.
Auto-restart server after unexpected server shut-down.	If true, when SQL Server stops unexpectedly (in response to something other than a shutdown or net stop command), the SQL Executive will restart the server and record a message in the NT event log
Server down polling interval.	Specifies how often the SQL Executive should check for an unexpected stopped server. The default is 5 minutes.

Table Continued on Following Page

Parameter	Description
Local Host Server	The name of the local SQL Server. This will be the default unless you have configured the SQL Server to listen on an alternate pipe. In that case, you should use the listen-on name from the Local Host Server list in the configuration dialog.
Error Log File	Specifies a path and file name for the SQL Executive error log file. If you use an error log file, it will add a substantial amount of processing overhead. However, if you are trouble-shooting the SQL Executive, it can be useful.
System Account	If true, the SQL Executive is assigned to run in the LocalSystem account. Remember that this will prevent the server from participating in replication and scheduled tasks involving other servers.
This Account	The name of the domain user account the SQL Executive is running under.
Password	The password for the SQL Executive Account.

Configuring NT for SQL Server

There are two NT options that you may want to change: Server Tasking and Throughput.

When you install SQL Server, Setup configures NT so that foreground and background tasks are equally responsive. This arrangement allows SQL Server to run as a background application at equal priority with any foreground applications and is the recommended configuration for SQL Server. However, if SQL Server must coexist with other applications on the same NT Server, you may want to restore NT's default, which is the opposite of the way Setup has left it. You can change this via the System dialog in the control panel. There is a Best Foreground Application Response Time option which can be set under the Tasking section of the dialog.

SQL Server setup has also configured NT to maximize throughput for network applications. This allows NT Server to accommodate more connections and is the recommended configuration for SQL Server. If you have different requirements, you may want to restore NT's default which gives priority to the local applications. You can change in the Network dialog on the control panel. On the Installed Network Software list under the Server option, if you select Configure you are then able to set Maximum Throughput for File Sharing. This option only applies if you are running SQL Server on NT Server. It does not apply if your underlying platform is NT Workstation.

Summary

In this chapter we looked at the main tasks that an administrator might have to perform when installing and setting up SQL Server.

Most of the decisions that the administrator will have to make during setup should be determined in advance of the physical process of installation. The configuration process is very flexible and allows backtracking at most points, in case mistakes are made. Although setting up a server might initially seem a very daunting task, the online documentation guides you through most of the basics quite painlessly.

6.5

Concepts and Facilities

Once you've installed SQL Server, you'll be greeted with a bewildering array of tools and objects. The purpose of this chapter is to give you a quick run through of all the tools that are available and what they're used for. Once you have a feeling for what everything does, then we'll look at the whole object model within SQL Server 6.5, and how the different tools and objects interact. Then we'll look at the Enterprise Manager and supply guidance on how to use this most essential tool to register servers and to define server groups. Finally, we'll look at how you can use the Enterprise Manager and SQL Executive to customize the way SQL Server operates via various configuration options.

SQL Server Tools and Utilities

There are three main services that are installed with SQL Server:

- The SQL Server engine
- The SQL Executive
- The Microsoft Distributed Transaction Coordinator

In addition to these, you will also find several different tools. The main items you'll encounter in the Program Group(on the server) are:

- SQL Service Manager
- SQL Transfer Manager
- SQL Security Manager
- SQL Enterprise Manager
- SQL Client Configuration Utility
- SQL Performance Monitor
- SQL Trace
- SQL Web Page Wizard
- ISQL/W
- A couple of help files
- A readme

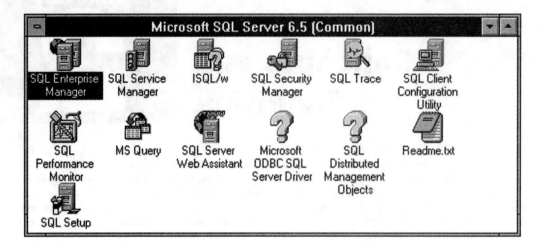

Under the covers are two more utilities that run in the NT command shell-**isql** and **bcp**. However, we'll get started by describing the different SQL Server services and their functions.

Services

The **SQL Server** service (MSSQLSERVER) *is* the RDBMS. It handles all of the query processing. This kernel parses SQL, manages the allocation of pages to data, and stores and updates data in the database. It manages buffers, monitors the network for requests and packages results in response to those requests. This service also has responsibility for user authentication.

The **SQL Executive** service is responsible for handling the alerting, task scheduling, and replication features of the Version 6.0 SQL Server. The alerting feature allows you to associated alerts with events. When a particular event happens, the alert can execute some kind of task and/or send e-mail or pager notification to a particular individual or set of individuals. The task scheduling feature allows you to schedule Transact-SQL commands or any programs that can run in the command shell to be run at a specified time or on a regular basis. Chapter 4 covers the alerting and scheduling features of SQL Server. Replication allows you to keep SQL Server or ODBC-compliant databases 'in sync' with each other. These databases can reside on different servers. Replication is covered in detail in Chapter 11.

The **Distributed Transaction Coordinator** service (MSDTC) coordinates transactions across a network of NT and Windows 95-based systems. It's designed to support operations other than database transactions but, in the current release, it only deals with SQL Server. With MSDTC, SQL Server can:

- ▲ Update data that resides on two or more SQL Server systems.
- ▲ Participate in transactions that are controlled by X/Open™ DTP XA-compliant transaction-processing monitors.

The DTC can handle all the complexities of the two-phase commit protocol which is needed when transactions are distributed across platforms. This makes it much easier to develop distributed applications than it has been in previous releases of SQL Server. This feature was introduced in the 6.5 release.

SQL Service Manager

This little goodie has a single screen containing a traffic light. It runs on the machine where the SQL Server is installed. You use it to start, pause or stop one or all of the services. Click on the red light to stop the service, the yellow to pause it, the green to make it go. That's all this does.

Administrative Tools

The administrative tools allow you to manage SQL Server. New with SQL Server 6.5 is the Enterprise Manager, which replaces the SQL Administrator tool of previous versions. The other administrative tool available to you is the SQL Security Manager. You might also consider the Distributed Transaction Coordinator to be an administrative tool, since it allows you to monitor and manage these transactions.

SQL Enterprise Manager

This is a tool that was introduced in 6.0, and will rapidly become your constant companion (if it hasn't already). With it you can do almost every DBA chore purely by pointing and clicking. We'll present it in detail later in the chapter, and from then on, we'll be using it to perform most of the administrative tasks. While the 6.5 release of the tool is much improved over the 6.0 version, there are still some 'warts' and these will be pointed out as we go along. You'll find that about 90% of the things you need to do can be done with SQL Enterprise Manager, but you'll be stuck with Transact-SQL commands for the rest!

SQL Security Manager

This is the tool you use to manage users when you are integrating SQL Server security with NT security. We'll talk about it in detail during Chapter 7. It's somewhat more primitive than most of Microsoft's tools but it does do a good job of making SQL Server users out of NT users.

Query Tools

There are three query tools that come with SQL Server. Two of them, ISQL/W and isql, are simple vehicles that allow you to issue Transact-SQL statements and view the results. The third, MSQUERY, is a slightly higher level tool that lets you form queries with a drag-and-drop approach similar to that of Microsoft Access. All three tools can run on the server or on a client.

ISQL/W

No matter how much point and click you have, you will still have to use Transact-SQL. ISQL/W is a Windows-hosted (both 16- and 32-bit) version of the command line isql that makes it easy to enter queries in Transact-SQL. It gives you a multiple document interface for queries and results. It can read and write ASCII files and has the common Windows editing functions (cut, paste, copy). This makes it a whole lot easier to use than isql. The same tool shows up inside SQL Enterprise Manager as the Query Tool. It's the ideal vehicle for doing all the things you can't do in Enterprise Manager and for exploring data. When you install clients, they get ISQL/W too.

isql

isql is a command line program that just feeds Transact-SQL to the server. It runs in every SQL Server environment. If you support both Microsoft and SYBASE SQL Servers, you'll find isql in the SYBASE environments as well. It doesn't have many editing capabilities, though it's wired to Notepad. But, because it reads ASCII files and can send its output (including error messages) to files then it's the perfect thing, in conjunction with NT **.BAT** or **.cmd** files, for batch type operations. For example, suppose you want to create a development database that matches your production one. You can prepare ASCII files which contain the create table statements. (There are several ways to do this in SQL Enterprise Manager.) Then you could create a file of commands that look like:

```
isql -Uuser -Ppwd -Sserver -iinputfile -ooutputfile
```

where each run of isql would create one of the tables. Error messages would be in the output file so that you could check your results. Building up command files in this way means that you can run jobs like this at night or as a background task, unlike the GUI tools which require your full and undivided attention. Isql is the only query tool available on a character mode client.

MS Query (SQL Server 6.5 only)

This is the point-and-click query tool that has shipped with Word, Excel and Powerpoint for a while. It has been ported to 32 bits and gives you a query engine similar to that provided by Microsoft Access. It provides a drag-and-drop window for forming queries as well as some point-and-click table definition facilities. It's available on both the server and on 32-bit clients. It uses ODBC to connect to the server from client machines, so you'll need to set up an ODBC data source name for each server the client will access. On the server, the ODBC connectivity is set up when you install SQL Server.

Internet

SQL Server's Internet connectivity is very important. SQL Server 6.5 includes an ODBC interface to Microsoft's Internet Information Server which is a part of NT 4.0 as well as the SQL Web Page Wizard. The SQL Web Page Wizard generates HTML (HyperText Markup Language) that helps you publish query results on the Web. You'll need to be running a Web Server to use this, of course. There are some system procedures you can use for Web publishing.

Data Conversion and Migration Tools

Many of us don't have the luxury of building only brand-new SQL Server applications. Instead, we find ourselves converting data from some prior version of an application on some other platform, from a previous version of SQL Server, or from an OS/2 or SYBASE SQL Server. There are a couple of things in SQL Server you can use to help you with this thankless task. The first is a program called Bulk Copy and the second is the database/object transfer facility of SQL Enterprise Manager.

Bcp

Bcp stands for Bulk Copy Program. This program is the workhorse for moving data between different environments. There is probably more replication being done today with bcp than is done with SQL Server's built-in replication capability. Its mission in life is to read a sequential file and populate a database table or to read a database table and create a sequential file. Because it can read and write ASCII text files in either a delimited or a fixed format, bcp is very useful for moving data between a SQL Server and a mainframe, for example.

Transfer Tool

Previous versions of SQL Server (including the 6.0 version) had a program called Transfer Manager, which could be used to transfer data between different versions of Microsoft SQL Server as well as between SYBASE servers and Microsoft SQL Server. In SQL Server 6.5, the transfer functions are part of SQL Enterprise Manager. The transfer functions provide the ability to move the definitions of object and/or their associated data. This function generates scripts and files that can be used by isql and bcp and allows you to automate much of what you would otherwise have to do manually.

Monitoring and Troubleshooting Tools

Some of the tools that come with SQL Server will assist you in the troubleshooting task that's part of the job of every SQL Server administrator. We'll be covering these in more detail in Chapter 9 so only a brief description of each is supplied here.

SQL Performance Monitor

As its name implies, this is the tool you'll use to study the behavior (or misbehavior) of your SQL Servers. It can be integrated with the NT performance monitor so that you can study the behavior of SQL Server and NT at the same time.

Client Configuration Utility

You'll find that there are always problems with the client workstations. This isn't unique to SQL Server. People often refer to these problems as the 'DLL Wars'. What will happen is that some piece of software you know nothing about will happily install its own version of one of the SQL Server or ODBC DLLs on top of the more recent one installed by you. This is where the SQL Client Configuration Utility comes in handy. This program lets you see the versions of DBLibrary and the Net Libraries that are actually being used by the client. You can also use this program to change default settings.

SQL Trace (SQL Server 6.5 only)

SQL Trace is a graphical utility you can use to monitor and record database activity. It can display all server activity in real time. You can also create filters that allow you to study specific users or specific applications. This is a pretty neat tool that lets you see the SQL statements and Remote Procedure Calls people have issued. All of its results can be saved to files for later review. Since you can add Login Name, the domain and user name, application name and host name to each record, you can use this facility to build in some SQL Server auditing.

Documentation

Microsoft ships a full documentation set on CD-ROM. You can install this to your hard drive if you won't always have access to a CD-ROM. Since the powerful Microsoft Search Engine (the same one that comes with the Microsoft Developer Network and TechNET) is included, the on-line documentation is actually more useful than the paper documentation (unless you want to read it on the bus!). When you install clients, you'll have the option of installing SQL Books, the on-line documentation set. The standard install doesn't put it on the server but you can change this at install time.

SQL Server Objects

SQL Server 6.5 is a relational DBMS, not an object database. The term database object is commonly used with regards to SQL Server just as a way of saying 'thing in the database'. We're not talking about objects in terms of inheritance, reusability, or polymorphism here. First, we'll talk about the databases that are created as part of the installation process. Then we'll talk about the catalog and control tables (the system tables) that are in those databases. After that, we'll briefly review the other database objects: user tables, datatypes, constraints, views, stored procedures, triggers and indexes. All of the database objects can be created with SQL Enterprise Manager.

System Databases

When you install SQL Server, five databases will be created for you:

- *master*
- *model*
- *msdb*
- *tempdb*
- *pubs*

The master *Database*

The *master* database contains tables that describe all other databases on the server. This database also has all the login and privilege information stored in it. All physical devices that have been created have their definitions stored here. *Master* contains information about executing processes, configuration options that have been set and other critical information.

> As you can imagine, the *master* database is extremely important. In general, you will not want to give people permission to create objects in it. You will want to be rigorous about backing it up after each and every change to it. Think of it as both the brains and the heart of SQL Server.

The model *Database*

The *model* database is a template that's used every time a new database is created. It defines the minimum size of any database on the server. It contains the catalogue tables that are used in every database.

> As a database administrator, you may find it appropriate to add objects to *model* so that they're available in every database you create.

The msdb *Database*

The *msdb* database exists to support the SQL Executive and Replication (see below). It contains scheduling information for SQL Executive. If this server is a distribution server, *msdb* has information about subscribers and articles. If this server is a subscribing server, *msdb* has status information about the last successfully processed replication.

The tempdb *Database*

tempdb is a scratch pad area that's available to all users and to SQL Server itself. Objects created in this database are transient; that is, they exist only while the user who created them is connected to the server.

> The *tempdb* that's created at Setup time is almost never big enough. We'll talk about that a bit more in Chapter 3.

The pubs *Database*

This database is the one used in all the examples in the SQL Server documentation. You will generally want to make it available to everyone so that they can practice using SQL Server. Microsoft supplies a script so that you can easily build a fresh copy after people have been experimenting. We've tried to illustrate many of our examples with the *pubs* database, where possible.

> If you don't need this training vehicle, you can choose not to install it. You can also drop *pubs* with no damage to the SQL Server.

System Tables

SQL Server, like most relational databases, maintains its catalog and administrative information in tables in the database. Some of these tables exist only in *master*; the rest exist in all databases. *The Microsoft SQL Server Transact-SQL Reference Manual* contains a detailed, column-by-column description of each of these tables so only a brief description is presented here.

Tables in master

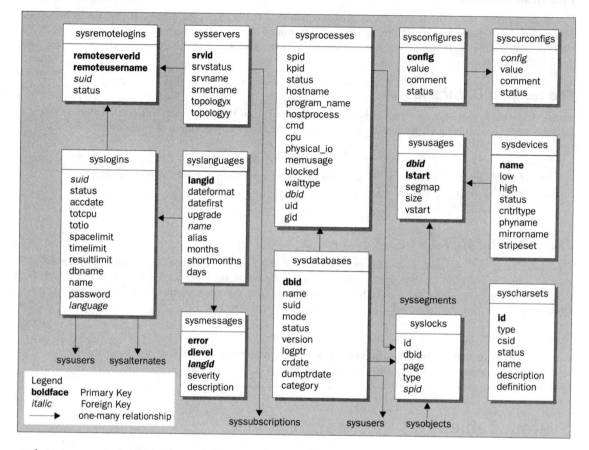

syscharsets	- Available character sets & current default character set
sysconfigures	- Configuration options & current settings
syscurconfigs	- Built from sysconfigures when referenced by **sp_configure**
sysdatabases	- Information about each database on the server
sysdevices	- Entry for each physical device
syslanguages	- One row for each available language
syslocks	- Built when referenced
syslogins	- An entry for each valid login
sysmessages	- An entry for each error or warning message
sysprocesses	- Built when referenced by **sp_who**
sysremotelogins	- Login ids which are allowed to execute procedures on this server from a remote server
sysservers	- A row for each remote SQL Server that's accessible to this server
sysusages	- Physical disk space used by databases

System Tables in All Databases

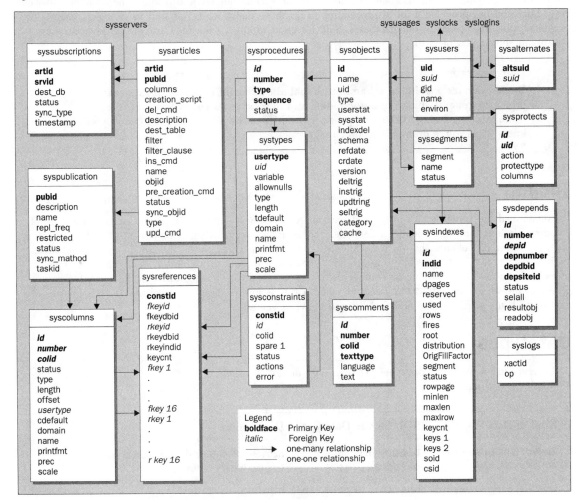

sysalternates	- Maps login names to names in the database
sysarticles	- Information about published articles
syscolumns	- Describes columns
syscomments	- SQL text used to create all objects except tables
sysconstraints	- The mapping of constraints to objects
sysdepends	- References to tables, views, or procedures
sysindexes	- Information about indexes
syslogs	- The transaction log
sysobjects	- The master catalog for the database
sysprocedures	- Query trees or plans
sysprotects	- Privileges that have been granted or revoked
syspublications	- A row for each publication
sysreferences	- Mappings for all the foreign key constraints
syssegments	- Disk storage used by the database
syssubscriptions	- Relates published articles to subscribing servers
systypes	- System-supplied and user-defined data types
sysusers	- Names of users and groups

In the 'old days', one had to write a lot of SQL to get information about even simple things like the names of all the tables in the database. Database Administrators quickly got to know these tables real well. Now Microsoft has provided a lot of procedures to do those things for us, as well as giving us neat graphical tools for looking at our databases. Still, it's good to know what they are so that you can work with them should you need to.

> By the way, it's possible to set an option that allows modification of the system tables. In general, that's not a good idea, and in most cases you will want to treat these tables as being Microsoft's property and leave them unchanged. Be sure you know what you're doing if you do change them.

Tables

We mentioned the system tables in the last section. An SQL Server table is a named object with a set of columns. Each column has a name, a datatype, and an indication of whether or not **NULL** values (missing data) are allowed. Columns that do not allow **NULL** values can generally be thought of as required data. With SQL Server 6.0, it's possible to attach an **IDENTITY** property to a column. A column with this property is an auto-incrementing or counter field, and is useful for creating surrogate keys. SQL Server generates the values for **IDENTITY** columns when a row is inserted into the database. It's possible to control both the starting value and the distance between values.

Datatypes

SQL Server has a wealth of datatypes. They're only described briefly as they're covered in detail in the *Transact-SQL Reference Manual*.

Kind of Data	SQL Server Datatype	Description
Binary (non-printable)	**binary(n),** **varbinary(n)**	n bytes of binary data, varbinary is variable length, binary is fixed length.
Character (printable)	**char(n)**, **varchar(n)**	n bytes of character data.
Date and time	**datetime,** **smalldatetime**	Special data type that combines both date and time into a single field. **Datetime** is 8 bytes long, **smalldatetime** is 4.
Exact numeric datatypes	**int, integer** **smallint** **tinyint** **decimal[(p [,s])]** **numeric[(p [,s])]**	4 byte integer. 2 byte integer. 1 byte, unsigned integer (values from 0 to 255). Precise decimal with p digits and s places to the right of the decimal point
Approximate numeric	**float(n)** **double precision** **real**	Single or double precision floating point. Single precision floating point.
Currency	**money, smallmoney**	4 decimal digits of precision. **Money** is 8 bytes long, **smallmoney** is 4.

Table Continued on Following Page

Kind of Data	SQL Server Datatype	Description
BLOB	**text, image**	Datatype managed by SQL Server as a linked list of pages. Suited for large images and text files.
Other	**bit**	Holds only 0 or 1.
	timestamp	Field is automatically updated each time the containing row is changed. Used for optimistic concurrency management schemes.

It's also possible to create what are called user-defined datatypes. These datatypes are based on the supplied system datatypes. The names of these datatypes must be unique in the database. Once a user-defined datatype has been created, it can be used in tables just as the system-supplied datatypes can. It's possible to associate rules and defaults (see below) with a user-defined datatype.

> **Organizations that use these datatypes (often referred to as 'shop types') will often add the definitions to model so that they're consistently used in all databases.**

Constraints, Defaults and Rules

Some of the SQL Server objects allow you to maintain:

- ▲ Primary key integrity
- ▲ Domain integrity
- ▲ Referential integrity

You'll do this using constraints, defaults, rules, and potentially, triggers, which we'll discuss a little later. The constraints are new to SQL Server 6.5. Previous versions had only rules, defaults and triggers.

Views

A view is simply a stored SQL **SELECT** statement that serves as a virtual table. It can be used anywhere a table can be used. Views are often used to simplify complex data (for example, joining tables so that an user sees a 'flat file') and to provide logical data independence. Views are also often used to provide row-level security. SQL Server allows more updates through views than many of the other RDBMS products do.

Stored Procedures

SYBASE® 'invented' stored procedures with its first SQL Server. They're written in Transact-SQL, which provides a rich SQL dialect and some procedural statements. They're named, reusable objects that reside in the database and execute on the server. Because they're pre-compiled, and because frequently used ones are kept in a memory cache, they provide some real performance enhancements. (In days gone by, Oracle have complained that SYBASE was 'unfairly' using its own technology in a bench mark. Now Oracle, and almost everybody else, has added stored procedures to their product.) Stored procedures are extremely useful because they can act as an interface to front-end applications. If the interface remains unchanged, the stored procedures can be modified as necessary to accommodate changes to the underlying database. Procedures are also a useful part of a security scheme, since a user can be given the privilege of executing a procedure without having the privilege to see or change the data that the procedure can.

Microsoft has added the concept of extended stored procedures. These extended procedures allow you to load and execute functions within a DLL (dynamic link library) as if they were stored procedures. These procedures are created using Open Data Services, which is discussed below.

Microsoft-supplied Procedures

There are hundreds of system procedures supplied by Microsoft. These procedures:

- Get information from the catalog tables
- Support replication
- Support the SQL Executive
- Manage logins and databases

The procedures supplied by Microsoft generally start with the letters **sp_**, although there are a few that start with **xp_**. The latter are used for integrated security, mail and a few miscellaneous functions.

Triggers

Triggers are a special kind of stored procedure that are executed automatically when rows are inserted, updated or deleted. It's possible to have three different triggers: one for insert, one for delete and one for update. They can also be combined. Before SQL Server 6.0, triggers were the only tool for enforcing referential integrity. Today, they're still useful for enforcing business rules, and they remain the only way of implementing cascaded update and delete. Triggers happen in the context of a user transaction and after the update has been made to the database. Triggers have access to two 'magic' tables. The word 'magic' is used, because they don't really exist. They are in fact views of the transaction log, but you can manipulate them just as if they were real tables. These tables are identical in structure to the table being operated on. The table named **inserted** contains the after image of the data; that is, the way the rows look after the update. The table named **deleted** contains the before image of the data; that is, the way the rows looked before the update. It's possible to do all sorts of interesting things with triggers. It's common to use triggers to timestamp or mark the id of the updating user in all the affected rows. Triggers also give you a place to build any audit trails or other change journals your application might require. The most important thing about triggers is that they're guaranteed to happen-there's no way to bypass a trigger. The only way to avoid it is to drop the trigger, and that's a privileged operation.

Indexes

Technically, indexes aren't database objects but an extension of the table object. In SQL Server, as in other relational database management systems, indexes have nothing to do with whether data can be retrieved. It's always possible to scan a table in order to answer a query. Indexes do, however, have everything to do with how quickly data can be retrieved. SQL Server has two different indexing strategies, providing both unique and non-unique indexes.

Programming Interfaces

There are four ways that application programs can interact with SQL Server:

- ▲ Through Transact-SQL
- ▲ Through DBLibrary
- ▲ Through ODBC
- ▲ Through OLE

Transact-SQL

Transact-SQL is Microsoft's dialect of the ANSI Standard SQL. It's compliant with the 89 standard and has many of the features of the 92 standard. In addition to the SQL statements, it has procedural statements such as **if...else, while, begin...end, execute** and **raiserror**. You can also use most of the system stored procedures in Transact-SQL programs.

DBLibrary

DBLibrary is the lowest level of interface; it's also the level at which SYBASE and Microsoft have agreed to maintain compatibility. If your application works with the 4.2 DBLibrary, it's supposed to continue to work with either the Microsoft or SYBASE product. It's a function call interface, and applications written in C and Visual Basic™ can call these functions directly. Applications written in MicroFocus COBOL use Embedded SQL. Embedded SQL simply consists of statements written in SQL that are prefaced by some recognizable words. A pre-processor translates these statements to the appropriate function calls. The MicroFocus pre-processor is pretty smart and recognizes points where it should generate a stored procedure. Windows applications must have access to the file **MSDBLIB3.DLL** if they are using DBLibrary. Programmers who are writing DOS applications will also need a character mode version of DBLibrary. This file, together with the necessary header files, is included in the SQL Server Programmer's Toolkit.

ODBC

ODBC stands for Open Data Base Connectivity. This is a specification published by Microsoft but with wide industry acceptance. It's vendor-neutral and is based on the SQL Access Group's function call interface for relational databases. One of the goals of ODBC is to make the back-end data source transparent to applications. Effectively, we have a picture that looks a lot like this.

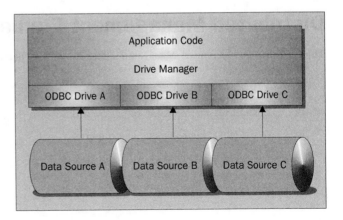

The ODBC drivers are generally supplied by the data-source vendors or by some other third party provider. The ODBC Driver Manager has typically been provided by Microsoft as a DLL. The ODBC drivers themselves are also DLLs. However, ODBC is now also appearing in the UNIX® environment, where some other format will be used.

Microsoft is very strongly committed to ODBC, and has stated that the performance of the SQL Server ODBC driver is better than the performance achieved using the native DBLibrary interface. It's possible to write both VB and C programs directly to the ODBC API.

OLE

OLE stands for object linking and embedding and was originally a technique for creating compound documents. OLE was used during the creation of this book. The illustrations within this chapter were originally created in Visio and linked into a Microsoft Word document. By clicking on the picture in Word it's possible to make immediate alterations to the diagram in Visio, when needed. OLE, in this sense, has made it possible to create compound documents which combine data from different application sources.

The definition of OLE has expanded somewhat to include what is called OLE Automation. If an object is suited to OLE automation, it exposes a set of properties that can be manipulated by an application.

OLE is Microsoft's standard interface mechanism, and is built on a Remote Procedure Call (RPC) architecture. OLE allows one application (called an Automation Controller) to programmatically access the capabilities of another application (called an Automation Server). Each automation server exposes a set of objects that have:

▲ Properties that describe their state

▲ Methods that can be used to query or modify properties

OLE provides the mechanism that allows Back Office components (Exchange, SMS, etc.) to communicate with each other. It's also becoming the primary method for client applications to communicate with server-side applications, although the performance of OLE in this area is still somewhat lacking.

Distributed Management Framework

The SQL Server Distributed Management Framework has been designed from the ground up to allow:

▲ A flexible and scaleable management framework

▲ Centralized management of distributed servers

▲ A proactive management environment

▲ Lights-out operations

Here's a diagram of the architecture of SQL Server.

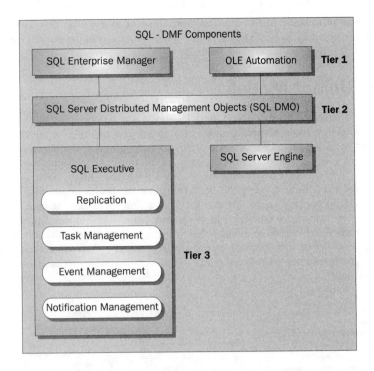

The Distributed Management Framework is a three-tiered distributed OLE architecture of interconnected objects, interfaces and services. The first tier is the 'outside world'-the client-side applications. This is where you'll find SQL Enterprise Manager, as well as applications developed with tools such as Excel, Visual Basic, Microsoft Project and Visual C++.

The second tier consists of the SQL Server Distributed Management Objects–SQL-DMO for short. Like all of the Microsoft products, SQL Server has an 'object model'. The SQL Enterprise Manager uses this object model extensively. You can manipulate the SQL Server objects with Visual Basic for Applications (VBA).

The third tier of the Distributed Management Framework contains the SQL Server engine–the core RDBMS, and the services provided by the SQL Executive.

SQL Server Distributed Management Objects

The middle tier of the Distributed Management Framework is the Distributed Management Objects layer. This is the SQL Server **object model**. You're going to be seeing a lot more of these! Each Microsoft Office™ and Back Office™ application exposes its functions through an object interface.

An object model is a picture of the objects that represent things a particular application can *do*. An *object* is something that can be controlled. Objects can be organized into hierarchical levels.

The objects which comprise an object model have **properties** and **methods**. Properties are characteristics of the object such as color, shape, location on the planet. Methods are things that the object can do; for example, walk, chew gum, walk and chew gum at the same time. Objects can be organized into **collections**.

Collections are made up of multiple instances of the same type of object. The objects which are visible through an object model are said to be **exposed**. This means that the outside world is able to change their properties and operate on them by using their methods.

An Example Object Model

For example, consider a sheep. It's an object. A flock of sheep is a collection of sheep. It's possible to talk about the flock as a whole or about a specific sheep or a sheep as a member of the flock. As one might expect, collections are in fact objects in their own right and have properties and methods also. For example, the number of sheep in the flock is a property of the flock. All collections have a count property like this. To push this sheep analogy to the limit, let's consider what we might have as a method for this collection. The shepherd may want to move the flock from one pasture to another. If each sheep has a 'move' method, it would be possible to do this one sheep at a time. But then, at least, if they were smart sheep, the first ones to be moved would have run away long before the last ones got to the new pasture. What the shepherd needs is a FlockMove method that will move the whole collection from one place to another. Microsoft has developed a method of graphically representing these object models. Let's take a look one of these diagrams and see what it looks like. The diagrams only represent objects and collections, not properties and methods.

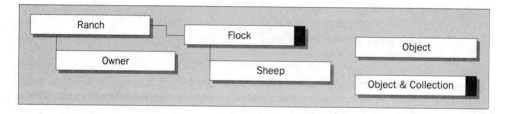

What this drawing says is: a ranch has an owner object and a collection of flocks. Each flock has sheep objects. It's important to understand that when we're talking about a sheep, we're talking about a sheep that belongs to a particular instance of a flock. That is, if we have a 'North Forty' flock, a 'South Forty' flock and a 'Back Forty' flock, and we're talking about a sheep named 'Lambkin', we're talking about the 'Lambkin' who belongs to the 'Back Forty' (or whichever) flock.

The SQL Server Object Model

SQL Server 6 exposed what Microsoft calls the Distributed Management Objects. These are 32-bit Component Object Model objects and are OLE Automation compatible. Any tool which supports OLE Automation, including Visual Basic (32-bit version) and Visual C++ (32-bit version), can be used to manipulate these objects. Now let's look at the SQL Server Object Model. First, we have the Application object and the things that it contains.

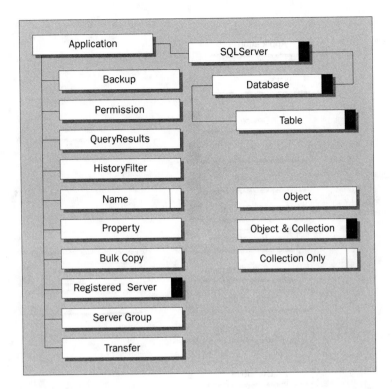

As you might expect, an application has a collection of SQL Servers, and these in turn have collections of databases, and databases have collections of tables. The Application object also contains several objects.

One of the objects contained by the application object is the *Backup* object. This object has properties which describe the backup devices, and other information that's used when you want to perform a backup or a restore operation. This object is discussed in greater detail in the chapter on Backup and Recovery. The *HistoryFilter* object is used for managing task histories. With SQL Server 6.5, both the *BulkCopy* process and the *Transfer* process are application objects, which allows them to be managed with the SQL Executive scheduler. ServerGroup and the RegisteredServer collection are used by SQL Enterprise Manager. The remaining objects: Permission, QueryResults, Names and Property are generic objects which may appear at multiple levels in the object hierarchy. For instance, database objects and users may have associated Permissions objects. QueryResults contains rows and columns that are returned by Transact-SQL statements. Many of the methods of the DMO will return QueryResults objects. The Property Object is meta-data about a particular property of a SQL DMO. It contains information such as whether the property is readable, setable and what its name is. Property objects belong to the Properties collection associated with most SQL DMOs. Finally, there's the mysterious 'Collection Only' Names collection. This is a collection of **strings** rather than a collection of objects. Microsoft could have made it a 'proper' collection by having it contain a single object–Name–with a single property–String, but they chose to leave out the unnecessary layer. Let's move on to the next layer of the SQL Server Object Model.

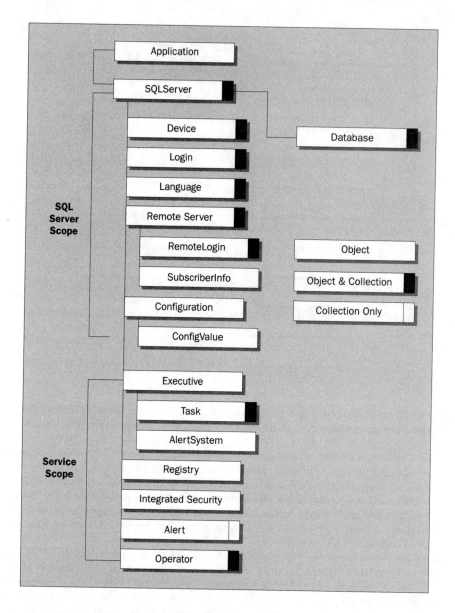

This is getting more interesting. Here are some SQL Server elements you've actually heard about. These objects are divided into two groups: those that belong to the SQL Server itself and those that belong to the SQL Server through the SQL Executive and other NT services. For example, physical devices belong to the SQL Server per se, while Integrated Security is part of the service scope. Now let's have a look at the database part of the SQL Server Object Model.

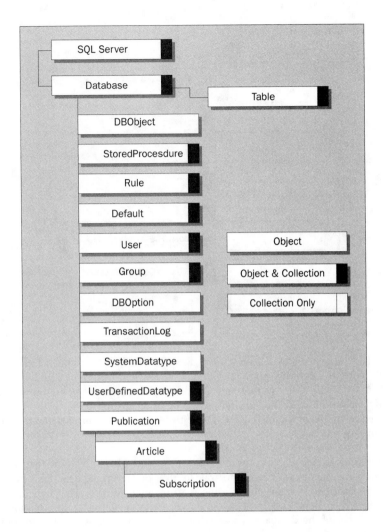

Now, if you've not worked with SQL Server at all, this may seem a bit confusing. Why is DBObject not a collection? And why doesn't DBObject include all these other things we've always called Database Objects–stored procedures, rules, defaults, and so on? The answer is that a DBObject is a generic object that has properties appropriate to all kinds of database objects. DBObjects can represent a Table, View, Rule, Default, Stored Procedure, Trigger or UserDefined Datatype Object. Now let's take a look at the final part of the SQL Server Object Model, the Tables collection.

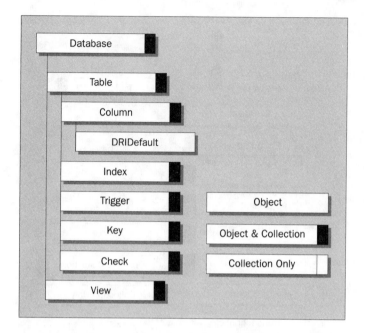

There are a couple of interesting things to notice here. First, the Tables collection includes a collection of Views. That's actually not too surprising, given that a view is a virtual table and functions in much the same way as a table does. Notice that the Key and Check constraint objects appear only at the table level. Although Transact-SQL allows them to be declared at the table or column level, in the Object Model they're only considered at the table level. The DRIDefault object, representing a Default constraint, is the only object that belongs to a column.

There's one important thing to notice about the SQL Server Object Model. That is, that it doesn't include the actual data stored in the data base. There's no way to 'drill down' through the table object to the actual rows. You can't use the Distributed Management Objects to manipulate data. That function is the province of application tools like Visual Basic and Visual C++ which are gradually acquiring the ability to encapsulate the data content of the database. That's what VB does with its Remote Data Objects.

Our focus is on the administration of SQL Server. In the next section, we'll look at SQL Enterprise Manager, the administrative tool built on SQL Server's Distributed Management Object Model.

Getting Started with SQL Enterprise Manager

Microsoft's SQL Enterprise Manager is a tool with a graphical user interface that's intended to let a system administrator manage all the servers in the enterprise from her desk top. Using this tool, you can configure and manage the server itself, SQL Executive, SQL Mail, and the Distributed Transaction Coordinator for all of the servers you're responsible for. This tool gives you a graphical interface to backup and restore operations. It provides the facilities for managing scheduled tasks and defining alerts that fire in response to various events. With the 6.5 release, you can use SQL Enterprise Manager to transfer data between servers. SQL Enterprise Manager also allows you to create and manage all of the SQL Server database objects.

If you plan to implement replication, you'll probably want to use SQL Enterprise Manager to set up your replication scheme. For those cases where you want to do something that isn't built in to SQL Enterprise manager, there's the Query Tool. This is a version of ISQL/W which lets you issue any Transact-SQL statement and see the results. You can even add your favorite tools (perhaps your word processor or spreadsheet) to it so that they're just a button click away. SQL Enterprise Manager is a rich product, and merits a lot of exploration.

SQL Enterprise Manager Server Manager Display

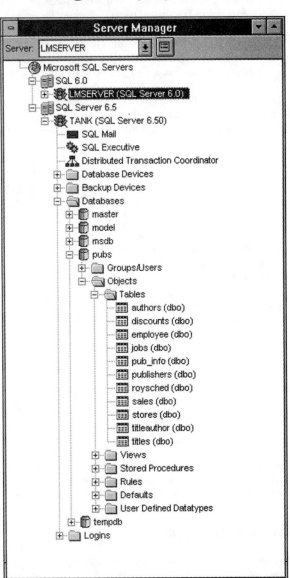

'Home Base' in SQL Enterprise Manager is its Server Manager window. This display shows everything there is to know about all the servers you've registered with SQL Enterprise Manager (details coming up) in a hierarchical display like the Windows Explorer. Click on a plus sign and the tree expands. Click on a minus and it contracts. Let's examine the contents of the illustration here.

First, there are two servers: LMSERVER, a 6.0 SQL Server, and TANK, a 6.5 SQL Server. Both servers are running; you can tell that from the green light in the traffic signal icon. You can also tell that you're connected to both of them since the traffic light has a red squiggly line through it.

> Note: SQL Enterprise Manager runs on both Windows NT (Server and Workstation) and Windows 95. If you run it in Windows 95, you will not be able to tell if a server is running. Also, the Windows 95 version does not allow you to start and stop servers nor does it allow you to configure the SQL Executive.

The display for the server TANK has been expanded. Immediately following the server name are three icons that display the status of SQL Mail, the SQL Executive and the Distributed Transaction Coordinator. If you're using the 6.0 version, you won't have icons for SQL Mail or the MS DTC. Below those are folders containing Database Devices, Backup Devices, Databases and Logins. If you look back at the SQL Server objects from the model, you'll notice that there's a folder corresponding to most of the collections that have SQL Server as a parent. Further down the tree, the pubs database has been expanded. Notice that the database contains folders for each of its collections as well. Once you get to a specific object such as a table, it's treated as a unit rather than a hierarchy.

You can work with the elements of the Server Manager display in several different ways. First, you can select an element and then choose appropriate actions from a menu (see the discussion of menus below). Second, you can double-click on an element and a default screen (usually the one for editing that object) will be displayed.

The Server Manager Display also has right-mouse button menus. If you select an object and click the right mouse button, a menu will drop down as illustrated here.

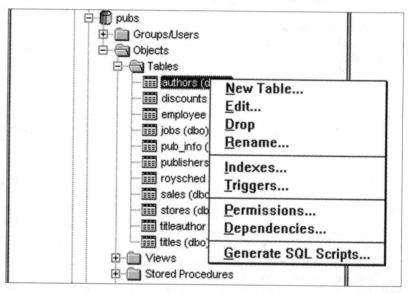

Now that we've covered the basic mechanics of using SQL Enterprise Manager, we'll look at some basic DBA task. The first is organization of Server Groups and the second is the process of registering a server with SQL Enterprise Manager. Finally, we'll show you how to change the sa password with this tool.

Server Groups

Server groups allow you to visually organize servers in the SQL Enterprise Manager window. These groups don't serve any other function. That is, putting two servers in the same group says nothing about, for instance, whether they're remote servers for each other or whether they're running on the same domain. You use groups to make your life easier when you're managing servers in your organization.

Server groups can contain subgroups, so that you can set up a hierarchy of groups and servers. For example, you might develop the following organization for the servers you manage.

> Development Servers
> > Project 1 Servers
> > Project 2 Servers
> Production Servers
> > Chicago Office Servers
> > > Marketing Servers
> > > Admin Servers
> > Boston Office Servers
> > > Marketing Servers

Or you might choose to organize your servers by SQL Server version, e.g. SQL Server 4.2, SQL Server 6.0, SQL Server 6.5.

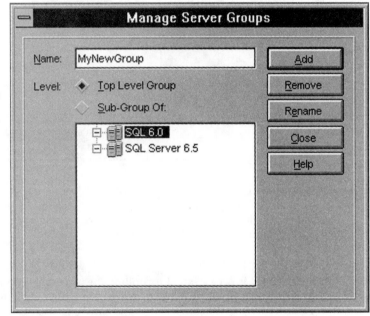

SQL Enterprise Manager will create a default group for you, but you need not use it. If you want to create your own group, do so before you register your server(s). To create, maintain or remove groups, choose Server Groups from the Server Menu and you'll see this screen.

You can create hierarchies of groups that meet your particular needs. The groups you create are part of the profile and will be stored according to the Application configuration settings you've chosen.

Registering an SQL Server

SQL Enterprise Manager needs to know what SQL Servers you want to administer. To tell it about a server, you **register** the server. You can't do anything with the server in SQL Enterprise Manager until you do this. All the tool buttons will be disabled and most of the menu choices will be grayed. To register the server, you must provide the server name, the login id and password you'll use to log on to it, and whether you'll connect to it with standard security or trusted connections. The information you provide here will be used each time you connect to the server, including when you use the SQL Query tool.

When you choose
Register Server from the
Server menu or when
you click on the Register
Server tool button, you'll
see the following screen.

The server will be placed in which ever group is highlighted in the Server Group box at the bottom of the screen. If you forgot to define a group, click the Groups button and you'll see the group definition screen. The Servers button will give you a list of servers if you're running under Windows NT but won't show you anything if you're running under Windows 95.

> **The server list isn't developed by polling the available servers on the network. It only shows servers you've connected to at some time in the past. It's possible to register a server that doesn't show up in the Active server list, and it's possible for a server that no longer exists to show up in the list as well.**

When you register a server, SQL Enterprise Manager will try to connect to it. It will tell you if it can't do so. You'll be able to register the server even if the connection fails. If you believe you should be able to connect to the server, there are several things to check. Do you have the login id and password correct? If so, is the target server running? Can you connect to it with other tools?

It's important to note that, when you register a server, the default is to store all the registration information locally. This means that *any* user who signs on to the workstation and starts SQL Enterprise Manager has access to this configuration. You can change this and develop profiles specific to an NT logon id. To do this, you must choose **Preferences/Configure** from the **Tools** menu. This will bring up the Application dialog. Clear the **Store User Independent** check box *before* you register servers, particularly if you're registering them with the **sa** login.

SQL Enterprise Manager in Version 6.0 didn't provide this capability. This created a fairly gaping security hole when a server was registered with the **sa** password. Fortunately, Microsoft has fixed this in the 6.5 release.

These profiles include the groups discussed in the next section. You can also store profiles remotely so that an administrator can have the same profile regardless of the workstation he or she signs on to. Remote profiles can also be shared between several administrators, giving them all the same picture of the servers in the organization.

Changing the *sa* Password

When you install SQL Server, there is *no* password on the **sa** login! Probably the most important thing you can do is to change it as soon as possible! You can change the password with SQL Enterprise Manager, Transact-SQL and VBA.

Using SQL Enterprise Manager to Change the **sa** Password

To change the **sa** password, open the Logins folder for a server. Select the **sa** login and double-click to see the Manage Logins screen.

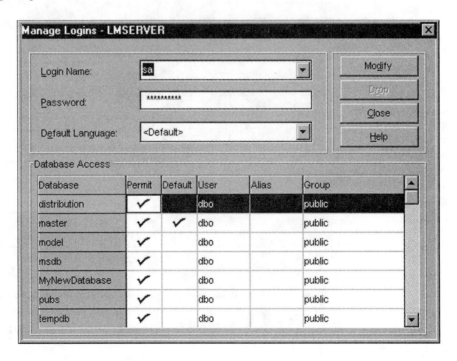

Type the new sa password and click modify. You'll need to confirm the new password.

Changing the sa Password with Transact-SQL

To change the sa password with Transact-SQL, you log in as sa and use the **sp_password** command.

```
sp_password old, new [, login_id]
```

For example, to set the sa password to 'secret', you would issue the following command:

```
sp_password null, secret
```

Changing the sa Password with VBA

To change the sa password with VBA, you use the SetPassword method to change the password property of the appropriate login object.

Configuring SQL Server

You can use either Enterprise Manager, Transact-SQL or VBA to set the configuration options.

Using SQL Enterprise Manager to Set Configuration Options

First, choose Configurations from the Server Menu, then click on the Configuration tab in the dialog box.

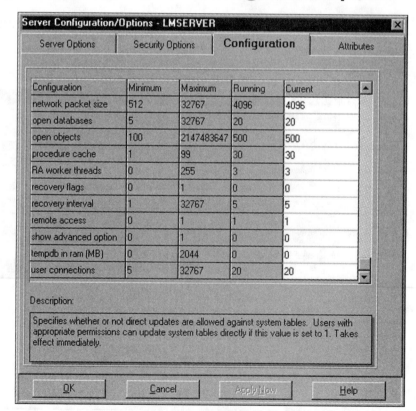

Configuration	Minimum	Maximum	Running	Current
network packet size	512	32767	4096	4096
open databases	5	32767	20	20
open objects	100	2147483647	500	500
procedure cache	1	99	30	30
RA worker threads	0	255	3	3
recovery flags	0	1	0	0
recovery interval	1	32767	5	5
remote access	0	1	1	1
show advanced option	0	1	0	0
tempdb in ram (MB)	0	2044	0	0
user connections	5	32767	20	20

Description:

Specifies whether or not direct updates are allowed against system tables. Users with appropriate permissions can update system tables directly if this value is set to 1. Takes effect immediately.

Change the values in the Current column as desired and press Apply Now to change a dynamic option without leaving the Configuration dialog. Press OK to close the dialog window and apply all of your changes to dynamic options. If you've changed any static options, stop the SQL Server and then restart it.

To see Advanced Options while working in SQL Enterprise Manager, scroll down through the list until you come to Show Advanced Options. Set the current value to 1 and press Apply now. Close and re-open the dialog so that SQL Enterprise Manager will refresh the display.

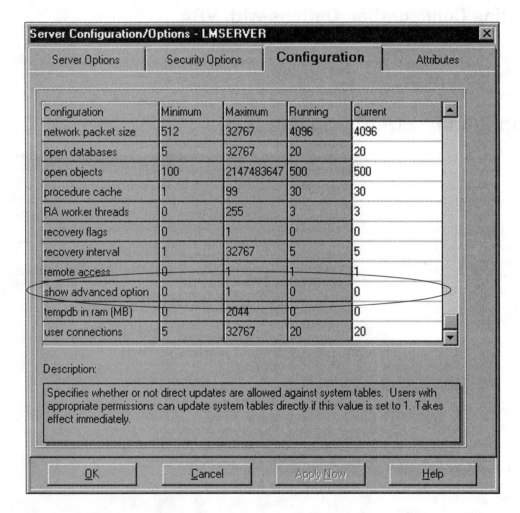

Setting Configuration Options with Transact SQL

With isql, ISQL/W, the query window in Enterprise Manager or any other tool that allows you to issue Transact-SQL, you can set configuration options with the system procedure **sp_configure** which displays the max, min and current values:

```
sp_configure
```

Or displays or sets the value for a configuration option

```
sp_configure config_name [, config_value]
```

After using **sp_configure** to change options, use the **RECONFIGURE** command to apply them. Stop the SQL Server and restart it to apply any static configuration options.

Setting Configuration Options with VBA

Each of the SQL Server Configuration options has a corresponding object in the ConfigValues collection of the Configuration object. You examine Configuration option details like minimum and maximum value, and change a Configuration option value, using the ConfigValue object for that Configuration option.

Configuring SQL Executive

To configure the SQL Executive, you can right-click on it in the Server Manager Display or select its configuration option from the Server menu. You will see the following dialog:

You can also use this dialog to change the account or password used for the CMD Exec account. You should change those here, not through the NT User Manager. You can't configure SQL Executive with Transact-SQL or VBA.

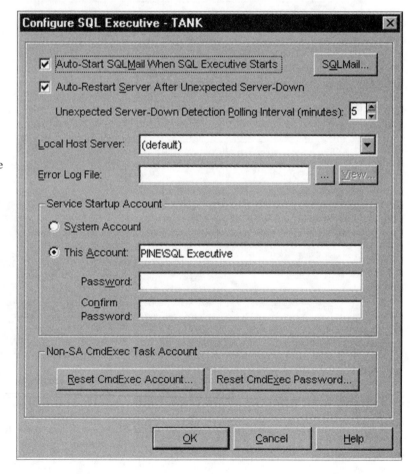

Summary

In this chapter, we've reviewed the tools that come with SQL Server as well as the various database objects that you'll find in a SQL Server database. We talked briefly about the system tables that SQL Server uses to keep track of objects and processes. Then we covered the Microsoft Distributed Management Framework and SQL Server's Distributed Management Object Model. You had an overview of the SQL Enterprise Manager Tool that will probably be your constant companion. We showed you how to get started with SQL Enterprise Manager by defining Server Groups and by registering servers. Finally, we demonstrated how you can use SQL Enterprise Manager, Transact-SQL and VBA to change the sa password and to configure the SQL Server. In the next chapter, we'll get into the nitty-gritty of managing the disk resources you'll be responsible for allocating to SQL Server.

6.5

CHAPTER

3

Physical Device Management

Physical device management is to SQL Server what rails are to the train system. Neither are celebrated or studied to the degree of the 'engine', but both are crucial to the success of the system overall. In this chapter, we'll start by looking at the basics of physical disk subsystems and at the default devices on which the databases and transaction logs are stored. We'll then examine how we can create, delete and alter devices within SQL Server from the Enterprise Manager using Transact SQL. We'll look at how to designate a default device on which we'll create new databases and the decisions that we need to make on where to place new devices. Finally, we'll touch upon topics of maintenance, performance and device recovery.

Physical Disk Subsystems

Devices are the physical disk files allocated by SQL Server to hold databases and transaction logs. If you want to create a new database on your newly installed SQL Server, you'll probably need to create new devices for it. You can create devices on a variety of physical mediums, including hard disks, floppy disks, WORM drives and CD-ROMS.

When you create a device, you are actually creating a file with a name that corresponds to that device. For instance, if you create a device called **TEST_DATA**, a corresponding file **TEST_DATA.DAT** is created. You can use this file to hold a database or transaction log. The two things to remember here are that, first, devices are physical files that are vulnerable to deletion or corruption when SQL Server isn't running, and second, the relationship between databases and logs to their devices is not direct. You can have several databases or logs on a single device. Conversely, a database or log can span many devices.

> There's another type of device used for backup and recovery: the dump device.
> We'll discuss this more fully in Chapter 6 *Database Backup and Recovery*.

SQL Server Supplied Devices

By default, SQL Server ships with three database devices in the **\MSSQL\DATA** directory: **MASTER.DAT**, **MSDBData.DAT** and **MSDBLog.DAT**. The **MASTER.DAT** device can be relocated using the SQL Server Setup utility. This illustration shows the setup of the default databases and devices:

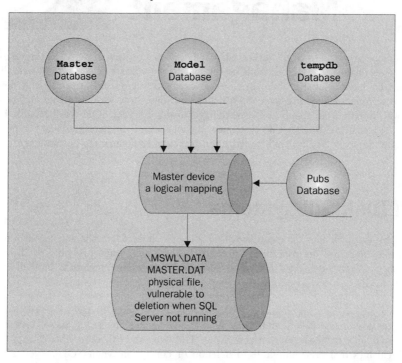

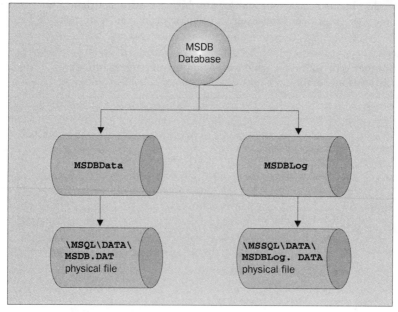

MASTER.DAT

MASTER.DAT is the most critical device that you'll encounter using SQL Server. It holds the *master, model, pubs* and *tempdb* databases which store all the information needed to run and administer SQL Server. Never use the **MASTER.DAT** device for any other database or log! Needless to say, you should pay special attention to this device to ensure that it's properly backed up. If this device is damaged, no other database on the server will be accessible until **MASTER.DAT** is restored.

tempdb

tempdb is another database on the **MASTER.DAT** device that could use some special attention. As we described in Chapter 2, *tempdb* is critical to the operation of just about every kind of database application because it's the workspace for temporary operations and tables. For example, any time a **SELECT** statement has an **ORDER BY** clause, the result set is temporarily stored in *tempdb* so that it can be sorted. However, *tempdb* is given only 2 megabytes on the **MASTER.DAT** device during SQL Server setup. That just isn't enough for any robust DBMS activity!

> After you've installed SQL Server, you should immediately create a new device for the *tempdb* database. The default 2MB size of *tempdb* isn't enough for any kind of heavy-duty processing. I usually create a new device called **TEMP_DATA.DAT** of 50 to 100MB in size (depending on available hard disk space and the needs of the application) and then allocate that device to the *tempdb* database.

MSDBData.DAT and MSDBLog.DAT

MSDBData.DAT and **MSDBLog.DAT** store the MSDB database and all scheduling information associated with the Enterprise Manager Task Scheduler. **MSDBData** stores the database, while **MSDBLog** stores the transaction log. These devices, like **MASTER.DAT**, are extremely important to SQL Server operations. Ensure that they are free from corruption and frequently backed up.

Managing Devices

Now that you've learned a little about the nature of devices, it's time to learn how to create, drop and alter them using the different methods at hand.

> Whenever you create or drop a device, you should backup the master database.

Creating Devices

The Enterprise Manager offers you two means of creating devices: the GUI and several TSQL commands.

A Device with Enterprise Manager

In the Enterprise Manager, select the server where you want information. Click the Manage Device button on the toolbar. Alternatively, you can select Database Devices option from the Manage Menu. Notice that the look of the dialog box has been changed using the properties and options pop-ups:

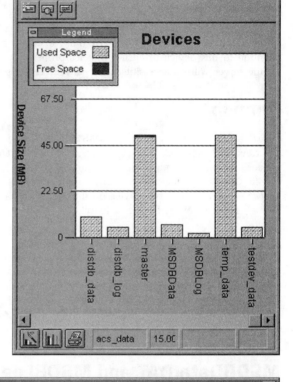

Click the New Device button on the Devices toolbar. The New Database Device dialog box will appear as shown:

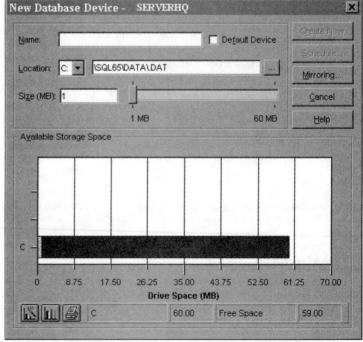

Alternatively, you can click the Database Devices folder, right-click any device in the folder or the folder itself and select New Device.

Providing Parameters for New Devices

When you're creating a new device, you need to provide values for the appropriate parameters:

- ▲ **Name:** the name of the new device up to 30 characters in length. Be sure to use a clear and consistent naming convention.

> I always append the suffix _DATA or _LOG to the device name to indicate if it is a database or transaction log device respectively.

- ▲ **Default Device:** a toggle that sets the device as a default used when a new database is created without specifying a device.

- ▲ **Location:** the logical drive location of the device. It must be on the local machine and cannot be a shared network drive.

- ▲ **Path**: the path on the local drive where the file is located. By default, the path to the **MASTER.DAT** file is used. Instead of entering a value here, you can click the Locate button.

- ▲ **Locate**: the Locate button provides you with a GUI to select the drive and path for your device file:

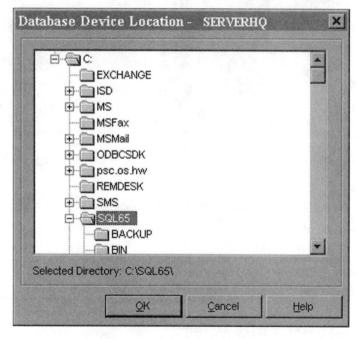

- ▲ **Size (MB)**: this parameter is the size of the device in megabytes. You can change the size by directly typing in a new value or by using the sliders.

- ▲ **Available Storage Space**: the number of megabytes of free space on the drives of the server.

▲ **Graph Controls**: the Graph Control buttons invoke the Graph Properties and Bar Graph Options dialog boxes (which we'll discuss shortly).

▲ **Create Now**: clicking this button causes SQL Server to create the device as described in the parameter fields of the New Device dialog box. This is generally an extremely fast operation.

▲ **Schedule**: clicking the Schedule button invokes the Schedule dialog box. You can then specify the time to execute the exact TSQL command needed to create the device that you've defined in the New Device dialog box:

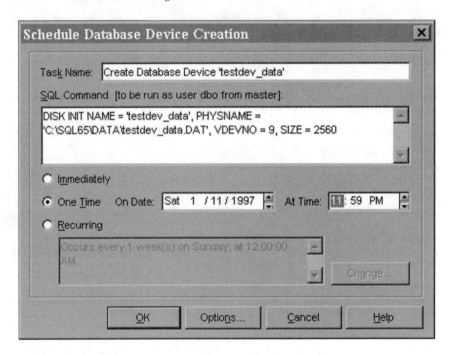

▲ **Mirroring**: clicking this button calls the Mirroring Device dialog box. Mirroring is discussed in further detail later this chapter.

Creating a Device with Transact-SQL

In the SQL Query Tool, we use the command **DISK INIT** to create a new device:

```
DISK INIT
    NAME = 'logical_name',
    PHYSNAME = 'physical_name',
    VDEVNO = virtual_device_number,
    SIZE = number_of_2K_blocks
[, VSTART = virtual_address]
```

DISK INIT is an extremely useful command for creating database and transaction log devices. In fact, any time you create a device with the Enterprise Manager, it's basically executing this command behind the scenes. Like many SQL Server stored procedures, **DISK INIT** makes the necessary entries into the underlying system tables, in this case *master.dbo.sysdevices*.

▲ **NAME** is the logical name of the device in 30 characters or less. It corresponds to the Name field use in the New Database Device dialog.

▲ **PHYSNAME** is the path and file name of the physical file for the database device.

▲ **VDEVNO** is a unique number from 1 to 255, retaining the number until the device is dropped.

▲ **SIZE** is the size of the device in 2K blocks (2048 bytes).

▲ **VSTART** is a seldom used parameter telling SQL Server the number of 2K blocks required to offset the physical device. Never use this parameter unless instructed to by your support provider.

Dropping a Device

It's not at all uncommon to want to drop a device. Dropping a device can be deceptive because you must remove both the logical definition of the device from the *master.dbo.sysdevices* table and the physical file from your file system.

> **Dropping a device from SQL Server also drops any databases or transaction logs stored on it, even if only a portion of the databases or logs reside there. SQL Server will prompt you with a warning and give you a chance to rollback the operation. The databases or logs will be dropped first, followed by the device. Beware! Once the device is gone, your only recourse is to recreate the device and restore from your backups.**

Once you drop the device in SQL Server, the row describing the device is removed from *sysdevices*, now rendering the device name and number available for reuse. However, you must be certain to then delete the physical file or else you'll be needlessly wasting disk space. Plus, you won't be able to create a new physical file with the same path and name while the old one remains. If you only have to remove one or two devices, the Enterprise Manager provides an easy and efficient way to do this. If you have to drop many devices or devices from many servers, TSQL provides a powerful set of commands to do this too.

Dropping a Device with the Enterprise Manager

In the Enterprise Manager, select the server on which you want information. Click the Manage Device button on the toolbar. Alternately, you can select Database Devices from the Manage menu. Click the Delete Device button on the Devices toolbar. SQL Server will verify that the device is unused by checking *master.dbo.sysusages*. If one or many databases or logs reside on the device, a warning dialog will appear:

Alternatively you can click the Database Devices folder, right-click the appropriate device and select D̲elete Device.

Dropping a Device with Transact-SQL

In the SQL Query Tool, use the system stored procedure **SP_DROPDEVICE** to drop a device.

```
sp_dropdevice logical_device_name [, delfile]
```

For example:

```
sp_dropdevice testdev_data, delfile
```

Only the SA can use this command to remove devices. By adding the **delfile**, you automatically ensure that the physical file is deleted, as well as the logical definition of the device that is stored in *sysdevices*. Note that you can't drop a device using this command if it contains databases and/or transaction logs.

Expanding a Device

You've seen how to find information about a device and how to create a new one from scratch. What if you want to take an existing device and alter it? With SQL Server, the only aspect of a device that you can easily change is the size of the device or its default/non-default status (discussed later). If you need to decrease the size of the device, rename it or relocate it, you're pretty much stuck with the task of backing up its contents, dropping the old device, creating a new device and restoring its contents. To increase the size of a database device, you have the two basic options: the Enterprise Manager or TSQL. In either case, the physical disk drive must have enough free disk space to support the expansion of the device.

Expanding a Device in Enterprise Manager

To increase the size of a device in the Enterprise Manager:

- ▲ Select the server on which you want information.
- ▲ Click the Manage Device button on the toolbar or use the equivalent option from the Manage menu.
- ▲ Click the Edit Device button on the Devices toolbar. As a shortcut, you can click the Database Devices folder, right-click the appropriate device and select Edit Device. The Edit dialog box will appear.
- ▲ Increase the value of the Size parameter and then click OK.

Expanding a Device in Transact-SQL

As SA, you can expand any device, including **MASTER.DAT**, using the command **DISK RESIZE**.

```
DISK RESIZE
    NAME = logical_device_name,
    SIZE = final_size in 2k blocks
```

For example, to increase the **MASTER.DAT** file from 25 megabytes to 32 megabytes in size:

```
DISK RESIZE
    NAME = 'MASTER',
    SIZE = 16384
```

DISK RESIZE cannot shrink a database; it can only expand one. Nor can it affect dump devices or *tempdb* when it is in RAM.

Getting Information about Devices

The Enterprise Manager offers you two ways to get information about the devices that already exist on the server: the GUI and through several TSQL commands.

> Throughout the chapter, we'll use the term *device* to describe devices containing both databases and transaction logs.

Obtaining Information about Devices with the Enterprise Manager

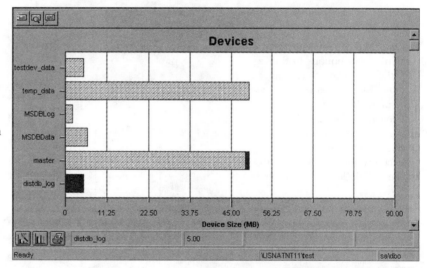

In the Enterprise Manager, select the server where you want information. Click the **Manage Device** button on the toolbar to get to the **Devices** dialog:

You can adjust the appearance of the Devices dialog box according to your taste by invoking the Graph Properties dialog box:

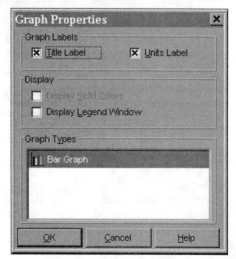

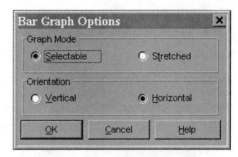

You can further adjust the Devices dialog box's appearance by making changes in the Bar Graph Options dialog box that you see here:

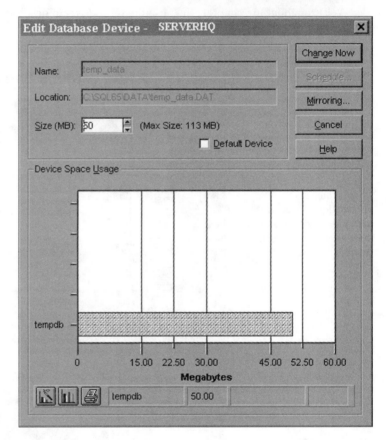

You can experiment with the graph properties and options to find a look that you like. Once you've identified the database device you want more information about, double-click either the device name or bar graph to get to the Edit Devices dialog box (more instructions about editing devices appear a little later in this chapter).

Obtaining Information about Devices with Transact-SQL

In the SQL Query Tool, we use the **sp_helpdevice** command, with or without a device name, to provide device information.

```
sp_helpdevice {device_name}
```

sp_helpdevice provides lots of good information about the devices currently residing on your server. If the **device_name** parameter is left null, **sp_helpdevice** provides information about all the devices and dump devices as contained in the *master.dbo.sysdevices* table.

> The sysdevices table contains information about every database device and dump device on the server. We can add database devices through the Enterprise Manager or by using the DISK INIT command. We add dump devices with the sp_addumpdevice system procedure.

Once you execute this stored procedure, you'll get a tidy report showing:

- ▲ The device name.

- ▲ The physical name and path.

- ▲ A brief description, including media type, database type, and size of device.

- ▲ Status, a number that corresponds to the database type shown in the description.

- ▲ **Cntrltype**, a numeric specification for the controller type of the server. 0 = database devices , 2 = a hard drive dump device, 3 or 4 = a diskette dump device, 5 = a tape device.

- ▲ The device number. Dump devices and **MASTER.DAT** always have a 0 device number. All other devices have a unique number from 1 to 255.

- ▲ Low and High, the virtual page number for high and low 2K data page of the device. If you like to do math, you can calculate the exact size of the device with this formula (high - low = number of 2048 byte data pages).

Designating a Default Device

When you go through the process of creating a new database, SQL Server gives you the option of immediately assigning the database (or transaction log) to a specific device. If you fail to tell SQL Server where you want to locate your new database or log, SQL Server will automatically assign the database to a **default device** (assuming there's enough space on the device, of course). When SQL Server is installed, only the **MASTER.DAT** device is designated as a default device.

> SQL Server has set MASTER.DAT as the initial default device. IMMEDIATELY set MASTER.DAT as a non-default device! You want to avoid unintentionally assigning a new database or log to the MASTER.DAT device.

Only the SA can assign the default/non-default status to a device. The rule of thumb to remember is to always specify the device where you would like your database or log to reside. In many situations, it's best to declare the master device as non-default and then *not* declare a default device. Why do this, you ask? The reason behind having no default devices on your server is that you can now no longer throw databases on the server without a little research beforehand. Without a default device, you must always declare the device where a database will reside. It's just a way to enforce good practices.

Setting a Default Device in Enterprise Manager

▲ When you're creating a new device or editing an existing device, toggle the Default Device box to checked, then click OK. This will set the device to default status.

▲ Set the device to non-default status by ensuring that the Default Device box is unchecked, then click OK.

Setting a Default Device in Transact-SQL

`sp_diskdefault` *logical_device_name* `[, defaulton | defaultoff]`

For example:

```
sp_diskdefault master, defaultoff
```

In this example, you would have set the **MASTER.DAT** device to non-default status. By setting the default status off through either the Enterprise Manager or the SQL Query Tool, you are basically altering the record of the device in the *master.dbo.sysdevices* table. Default devices have a status bit set to 1, while non-default devices have a status bit set to 0.

Guidelines for Device Placement

When you're creating and placing your devices, there are a number of choices you can make. Where should they go? How should they be partitioned to provide optimal performance? How can I reduce the risk of failure? How can I minimize damage in the event of failure? This section discusses the important techniques available to you through SQL Server and your server hardware to answer these questions.

> Although Version 6.5 features support for a 'fallback server', i.e. a secondary server ready to pick up database operations in the event of a catastrophic system failure, this section focuses on the means to deploy robust and fault tolerant subsytems within a single server. We'll give you more information about fallback servers in Chapter 6.

Despite the claims of many hardware vendors, equipment fails. Fault tolerance is the degree to which your system, both hardware and software, is protected from physical device failure and the level at which data integrity is ensured. A system that provides good protection from failure and recovery options in the event of a failure is said to be **fault tolerant**.

Three factors act as the primary influence on how you implement fault tolerance: cost, risk and performance. When deciding which factor will take precedence, you must analyze the business rules behind your application. Will down time cost the firm much money? Does the system need to operate 24 hours a day, 7 days per week? Is there a backup system (even a paper-based one) in the event of a failure during business hours? You can probably lay bets that it's a better choice to spend additional money up front to minimize your risk than to save a few dollars on a less reliable system.

Separate Physical Drives for Log and Database

Although SQL Server doesn't require it, there are a number of reasons to maintain logs and databases on separate devices. There are also some very good reasons to maintain these devices on entirely separate physical (not logical) disk drives. In this section, we'll go over the basics of each issue.

Separate Devices for Log and Database

It's adequate to put very small and unimportant databases entirely onto one device, but there are some important reasons to explain why you should create a separate transaction log device and database device for every new database you create.

- ▲ The **DUMP TRANSACTION** command, which is essential when the transaction log overflows, can't be used without separate devices.

- ▲ **TRUNCATE LOG ON CHECKPOINT** can't be used without separate devices.

- ▲ Replication can't be used.

Although each of these issues are discussed in other chapters, suffice it to say that each of these capabilities are very important in most production environments. Even if you don't plan on supporting all of these capabilities when you deploy, it's almost always considered good practice to place the logs and databases on separate devices.

Separate Physical Devices for Log and Database

There is one basic overriding reason to locate your log and database on separate devices: the I/O nature of the log and database devices are contradictory. Transaction logs write each transaction that occurs within a database serially. Because transaction logs writes one transaction after another as sequential I/O and at a much higher volume than database writes, you want to minimize head movement on the drive holding the transaction log. Databases, on the other hand, have to fetch data from all over the hard disk. Because databases are constantly seeking and writing, you should separate it from the transaction log drive.

> On our production systems, we place the databases, transaction logs and operating system each on their own physical disk.

On database devices, both index and databases are frequently the subject of random reads and writes. Consequently, you should separate them from the transaction log device. In fact, if you can afford it, it's best to place the database and log on separate I/O channels so that there's no I/O contention between the two at all. The Windows NT operating system files like the virtual memory file **PAGEFILE.SYS** is also typically accessed through sequential reads. Plus, the virtual memory file is frequently cached and seldom accessed. So, if you're strapped for space, you can combine the transaction log files and operating system files on a single physical drive. The following diagram shows the differing nature of transaction log device I/O and database device I/O.

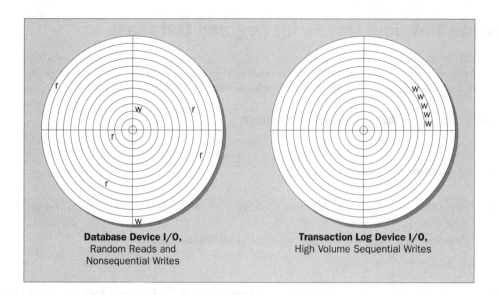

Database Device I/O,
Random Reads and
Nonsequential Writes

Transaction Log Device I/O,
High Volume Sequential Writes

Device Placement Options

With Windows NT and SQL Server 6.5, there are several ways to achieve fault tolerance and enhance performance. On the hardware side, you have RAID. On the operating system side, you have NT disk striping, mirroring and duplexing. On the SQL Server side, you have device mirroring and segments. Which options you choose to implement will be gauged by the priorities: cost, risk and performance. In general, though, you can count on better performance, improved reliability and less administrative overhead by sticking with the hardware-based options. We'll discuss each of these options in greater detail below. They are listed in order of the preference which you should give to them, which is based on performance provided, ease of implementation and enhanced data reliability.

RAID

One of the best ways to implement fault tolerance is to implement RAID, or Redundant Arrays of Inexpensive Disks, technology. The basic concept behind RAID is to substitute a single, fixed disk with multiple disks capable of simultaneous and parallel reads and writes. As you can guess, the multiple read-write heads of a RAID storage system are much faster than older disk technology. RAID also provides dramatic improvements in reliability, up-time and recoverability when compared to other disk technology.

Striping, Parity and Mirroring

To understand fault tolerance, you must comprehend the following concepts:

- ▲ **Striping** is the process of breaking large data blocks into small blocks and writing them across many disks. Instead of having one long I/O to a single disk drive, you have a burst of small I/Os across several disk drives, writing the data in a 'stripe'.

- ▲ **Parity** is the technique of storing parity information on one or many drives to rebuild a failed drive in the array. Parity slows performance but improves reliability.

- ▲ **Mirroring** is the technique of making a complete second copy of a drive. Under mirroring, every I/O is repeated on another drive. Consequently, reliability is greatly enhanced but performance is degraded.

There's a variation of mirroring known as duplexing. Under duplexing, not only are repeating hard drives used but they are supplemented with repeating hard disk controllers. Although duplexing can yield some significant performance improvements, especially for transaction logs, they are treated as synonymous for this discussion.

This diagram illustrates the basic behavior of data striping, parity and mirroring:

RAID uses varying combinations of striping, parity and mirroring in order to offer you different choices in performance, reliability and cost. There are six levels of RAID, levels 0 through 5.

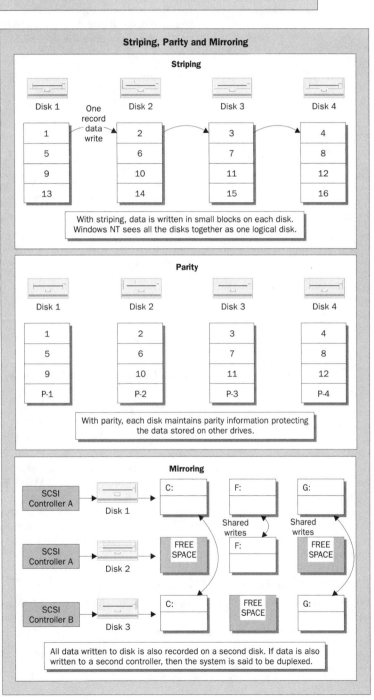

Striping, Parity and Mirroring

Striping

With striping, data is written in small blocks on each disk. Windows NT sees all the disks together as one logical disk.

Parity

With parity, each disk maintains parity information protecting the data stored on other drives.

Mirroring

All data written to disk is also recorded on a second disk. If data is also written to a second controller, then the system is said to be duplexed.

The Six Levels of RAID

Level	Quick Reference	Details	Recommendation
0	Data striping with no fault tolerance.	Extremely fast because data is broken into tiny blocks and spread across multiple disks. If one disk in the RAID fails, none of the disks are accessible.	Best read/write performance for the lowest cost, but low reliability. RAID 0 is ideal for constant read/write situations, like a tempdb device.
1	Hardware mirroring without striping.	All disks in the RAID have a backup disk. Uses lots of disk space and has no provision for data striping.	High reliability coupled with high performance on small block writes. Costly. A good choice for *mission-critical* OLTP applications.
2	Parallel access only.	All disks are accessed concurrently. Improved error detection and correction. If one disk in the RAID fails, none of the disks are accessible.	Not recommended.
3	Parallel access with parity and striping.	All disks are accessed concurrently, but allows hot swapping of failed drives. Single parity drive slows I/O and is a single point of failure.	Not recommended.
4	Parity without striping.	A single disk tracks parity information, which can be an I/O bottleneck and a single point of failure. RAID 4 is an independent array with fast, asynchronous access.	Not recommended.
5	Parity with striping.	Often regarded as the best form of RAID for production systems. Stripes data and parity across all disks. Allows hot swapping of any failed disk. Has slightly slower I/O due to overhead needed to calculate parity information.	Highly reliable with lower cost than RAID 1. Very quick reads, but slower at writes. Good for DSS or less critical OLTP applications.

Although there are situations where other RAID levels provide better choices for your application, I usually recommend choosing RAID 5 as your starting point. RAID 5 provides maximum fault tolerance without adding a huge burden of cost. It does have the poorest performance of the three recommended levels of RAID. However, RAID 5 allows a single disk to fail in the array without causing a system-wide failure. Depending upon your hardware, you can often just pull out a failed RAID 5 disk and replace it with new one without even shutting down the server. The RAID array will automatically rebuild the lost data onto your new disk.

Choosing which Level of RAID to Use

When you're determining which level of RAID to choose, use the following table as a shortcut, the key for which is:

TPS = Transactions per second
R   = A single read
W   = A single write
D   = Number of disks in array

RAID Level	Cost	Reliability	Performance	I/Os Generated	Storage Requirement
0	Best	Worst	Best	TPS * (R + W)	D
1	Worst	Moderate	Moderate	TPS * (R + 2W)	D * 2
5	Moderate	Best	Worst	TPS * (R + 4W)	D * 1.3

As you can see, performance is strongly linked to I/Os generated. In a RAID 5 array, for example, reads occur as quickly as at any of the other RAID levels. However, writes generate a significantly larger number of I/Os due to the large amount of parity information that must be recorded.

> For each write at RAID 5, the controller first reads the block where the data will be written to determine whether the block is occupied. It then reads the parity block and factors in the information found in the first block, if any. Finally, the new parity is calculated followed by the data being written and the parity being written. Wow! A total of 4 I/Os for one write request.

You can also see how cost and storage requirements are linked. Let's say you want 16 gigabytes of free storage space on your new system. At RAID 0, you could purchase 4 disks with 4 gigabytes of storage space. Hmmm, not too costly. At RAID 1, you would have to purchase 8 disks, because each disk is mirrored to a duplicate. Ouch, that will cost a lot. At RAID 5, you would need 5 disks; just one extra disk to help offset the space required to write parity data.

To be truly fault tolerant, your hardware should include protection features beyond those provided by RAID. You should ensure that your server is equipped with redundant cooling and power supply systems. It should also feature 'hot-swappable' disk drives as we mentioned earlier. If possible, you should also have redundant hard disk controllers. One controller should be used to maintain the RAID striping, while the other maintains I/O to the computer.

Windows NT File Systems

As an aside, you might be wondering what file system under NT works best for SQL Server devices? Testing shows that there' s only a minute difference between FAT and NTFS partitions, with FAT showing slightly faster writes and NTFS showing slightly faster reads.

However, the performance gain is so minimal that you shouldn't choose a file system as a means of improving SQL Server performance. As a general recommendation, you may want to place OS and **PAGEFILE.SYS** on an FAT boot partition and use NTFS partitions for your database and transactions logs.

Windows NT Disk Striping, Mirroring and Duplexing

Without a doubt, hardware-based RAID is less costly, less work, more reliable and gives far better performance that any of the other options for fault tolerance. However, hardware-based RAID is not always an option, particularly with older systems. Fortunately, in these cases you can use Windows NT disk management to provide gains in reliability and data integrity on those systems with multiple hard disks. In fact, you can use Windows NT to configure OS-controlled striping (with or without parity) and mirroring (with or without duplexing). Unfortunately, since this form of RAID-compliance is maintained by software, you should expect about a 10% hit on the CPU. Disk management basically allows NT to present a collection of drives as a single, logical drive and treat them as RAID0, RAID1, or RAID5. This can be extremely useful if you are refitting an older computer for use as your database server. Refer to your Windows NT Administration documentation for step-by-step instructions on implementing disk striping.

SQL Server Mirroring

If, for some reason you can't support hardware-based RAID and Windows NT-based RAID, you still have an alternative. SQL Server provides mirroring as an added measure against drive failure. When you tell SQL Server to mirror a drive, you tell it to make a complete duplicate of the device, keeping both in synch at all times. This means that your database operations will generate two I/Os, one on the original device and one on the duplicate. Mirroring constitutes a CPU hit (as much as 10% on some systems) and consumes extra disk space, but the added protection can be well worth it if you don't have other hardware or OS-based options in place.

Not only can you mirror across devices, you can also mirror across controllers if you have multiple controllers in place. By distributing several disks to each controller you have installed, and then mirroring your devices across disks on each controller, you eliminate the possibility of your controller acting as a single point of failure.

> Remember that databases and logs can span multiple devices. If you're aiming to mirror a database and/or its logs, you must mirror every device that contains the database(s) and log(s).

When you're setting up device mirrors, remember that device mirrors aren't actually devices. They don't get distinct **VDEVNOs**, nor do they contribute to the maximum total of 255 devices. Also note that the keyword **serial | noserial** shown in the example before is for older versions and non-Intel based versions of SQL Server. Non-Intel based versions of SQL Server can support non-serial (i.e. asynchronous) writes to device mirrors. Intel-based SQL Server uses serial writes, which write first to the primary device, then to its mirror. If an unrecoverable error occurs on the primary device, SQL Server automatically unmirrors the primary and operations immediately roll over the mirror. The mirror then becomes the primary without allowing you to encounter any down time.

Mirroring a Device in Enterprise Manager

Select the device to be mirrored, right-click the device, then select Mirror. The Mirror Database Device dialog will appear:

The Mirror Name defaults to the name and path of the original device, but with an extension of .mir. You can accept it or alter it if you prefer. Click the Mirror Now button. The device will be mirrored. All data in the primary device must be copied, so if the device already contains a large amount of data, mirroring could take a while.

Mirroring a Device in Transact-SQL

To mirror a device using SQL Query Tool use the **DISK MIRROR** command:

```
DISK MIRROR
     NAME = 'logical name of primary device',
     MIRROR = 'physical name of device mirror'
     [, WRITES = {SERIAL | NOSERIAL}]
```

NAME is the logical name of the device that will be mirrored.

MIRROR is the full path and filename of the device file. The quotation marks *are* required. This value is stored in the mirrorname column of the sysdevices table. So, in a sense, a device mirror is an attribute of a device.

WRITES enforces serial writes to the primary device and device mirror. This is an optional command included for compatibility with older and non-Intel versions of SQL Server.

> The **DISK MIRROR** command is slated for discontinuation in future versions of SQL Server. In fact, SQL Server-based mirroring is on the way out. Microsoft are currently recommending that you only use hardware-based mirroring (RAID) or Windows NT based mirroring (striping). You can still use it in Version 6.5, but now is the time to start weaning yourself off this technology.

Unmirroring a Device in Enterprise Manager

Select the device to be unmirrored, right-click the device, then select Mirror. The Unmirror Device dialog will appear as shown:

Toggle the appropriate radio button, then click Unmirror.

▲ Switch to Mirror Device - Retain Original Device makes the device mirror the primary device, while retaining the original device.

▲ Switch to Mirror Device - Replace Original Device makes the device mirror the primary device, while replacing the original device with the device mirror.

▲ Turn Off Mirror Device - Retain Original Device temporarily suspends mirroring to the device mirror, while retaining the device mirror for future use.

▲ Turn Off Mirror Device - Remove Original Device suspends mirroring to the device mirror and deletes the logical device. You must delete the physical device mirror using an OS command.

Unmirroring a Device in Transact-SQL

To unmirror a device in SQL use the **DISK UNMIRROR** command:

```
DISK UNMIRROR
     NAME = 'logical_device_name'
     [, SIDE = {PRIMARY | SECONDARY}]
     [, MODE = {RETAIN | REMOVE}]
```

NAME is the logical name of the database device to unmirror.

SIDE tells SQL Server whether you want to unmirror the primary device or the device mirror (secondary).

MODE causes the unmirroring to be temporary or permanent. **RETAIN**, the default, continues to store all of the device mirror information, such as the status column of *master.dbo.sysdevices*, so you can re-mirror the same device in the future. **REMOVE** clears all data about the device mirror, though you must remove the operating-system file that had been used as a mirror device.

To unmirror the device mirror and retain it for possible use in the future, you would issue a command like this:

```
DISK UNMIRROR name = 'testdev_data'
```

That's all you need! The defaults for the command would enable the rest of the functionality you might want. To unmirror the primary device and remove its definition for the *master.dbo.sysdevices* table and then delete the actual physical file of the mirror, you might issue a command like this:

```
disk unmirror
  name = 'testdev_data',
  side = primary,
  mode = remove
go

xp_cmdshell "del c:\sql65\data\testdev_data.mir"
go
```

Re-mirroring a Device

Not only can you unmirror a device using the **DISK UNMIRROR** command, you may also have to correct for **failover**. Failover is SQL Server's automatic process by which a corrupted device is replaced by the device mirror. The definition of the device mirror must still exist in the *master.dbo.sysdevices* table. When you re-mirror a device, SQL Server must completely resynch the device mirror, so re-mirroring could take a long time. To re-establish the mirror of an unmirrored or failed device, follow these steps:

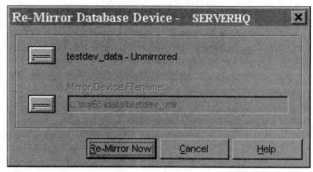

Select the device to be mirrored, right-click the device, then select Mirror. The Re-mirror Database Device dialog will appear as shown:

Click Re-Mirror Now button.

You can accomplish the same functionality by using the **DISK REMIRROR** command:

```
disk remirror name = 'logical_device_name'
```

SQL Server will then look at the information in the *master.dbo.sysdevices* based on the name of the device. No other information or parameters is necessary.

Using Segments in SQL Server

Let's start with the benefits of segments. Segments enable you to control, in very specific detail, exactly how tables, indexes and transaction logs are assigned to devices. Now, the drawback of segments. Segments incur an inordinate amount of administrative overhead and provide no added benefits in performance or reliability compared to RAID or disk striping. Segments also complicate database restoration and recovery.

> **Because they are controlled by software, segments can contribute to as much as a 10% CPU hit, depending on how they are implemented.**

Segments are an anachronism from the early days of SQL Server, when hardware technology was nowhere near as advanced as it is today. A segment is basically a predefined location on a specific hard disk where other database objects can be assigned. As you can guess, segments at one time actually provided a performance improvement because the DBA and system designers could identify I/O bottlenecks and build segments to counteract them. Nowadays, RAID and striping do a much better job than the typical implementation of segments. The only advantage that segments can contribute to a SQL Server 6.5 database is to limit the growth of a database object. That is, any object placed on a segment cannot outgrow the segment. So, you can place a variety of objects within their own segments and ensure that the segment prevents dramatic growth in the entire database.

> **Customized segments are seldom used beyond the command segregation of the transaction log to its own segment. As much as 5% of the SQL Server user community makes active use of segments.**

When you're working with segments, remember that they are database specific. You must be in the database where the segments were defined to act upon them. Also note that when you create or extend a segment, it will take up the entire device you designate. There are several stored procedures included with SQL Server that enable you to implement segments:

Syntax	Function
`sp_addsegment` *segment_name*[, *device_name*]	Create a segment.
`sp_dropsegment` *segment_name*[, *device_name*]	Drop or unmap a segment.
`sp_extendsegment` *segment_name*[, *device_name*]	Extend a segment to a new device and unmap existing segments.
`sp_helpsegment` [*segment_name*]	Get information about a segment or segments.
`create [table	index] ... on` *segment_name*	Place a specific object on a segment.
`sp_placeobject` *segment_name*, *object_name*	Spread an object across multiple segments.

As you can tell, this table only scratches the surface of the actual use and execution of the stored procedures used to create and maintain segments. If you're really convinced that segments are going to aid you with your application, review the section on segments in the SQL Server Administrator's Companion and the TSQL syntax for each of the stored procedures shown above in the TSQL Reference Guide.

Summary

You've seen the fundamentals of SQL Server devices: how to create, alter and drop the physical file structures used to hold SQL Server database objects and structures. You've also seen the most common methods of ensuring data integrity and availability through technologies like RAID, disk striping and mirroring. In the next chapter, we'll discuss how to manage databases and transaction logs in conjunction with the devices that you've seen in this chapter.

6.5

Database and Server Management

In SQL Server, databases are named objects. This model is different from that used by some other DBMSs in which tables belonging to all applications are placed in a single repository. It's important to fully understand databases, because they contain not only the tables in which your data is stored, but also views, triggers, stored procedures, data integrity rules, user data access rights and other objects that comprise your applications.

In this chapter, we'll touch on a number of topics that will show you the tools and techniques for managing an individual server and its databases. We'll begin by discussing the starting and stopping of the server, including the autostart features of SQL Server and the SQL Executive. We'll cover all of the intricacies of the database and its mate, the transaction log and, in particular, how you'd create them. We'll examine some of the tools you have available for monitoring the usage of database space. Finally, we'll discuss methods of automatically executing tasks and automated methods of reaction to alerts in order to ensure the good health and efficient operations of your server.

Server Operations

As a DBA, you'll be spending a lot of time controlling the uptime of your servers. You will encounter a number of situations that will necessitate shutting down and restarting SQL Server from time to time. Normally, you'll shut down SQL Server to remedy some errant operation on the server, but there are a few benefits outside of problem-correction to be gained from restarting SQL Server occasionally. In fact, some organizations routinely shutdown and restart all of their SQL Server machines on a weekly basis. In addition, you'll need to know how to control SQL Executive, SQL Server's scheduling service, which is detailed later in this chapter.

Automatic Startup

During server installation, you can assign SQL Server and SQL Executive to startup automatically whenever the server is booted. It's a good idea to enable this option on any machine that will serve as a SQL Server platform on a regular basis. Once you've installed SQL Server you can still easily control whether SQL Server and SQL Executive are automatically started when Windows NT boots up.

To enable automatic startup of SQL Server and SQL Executive after installation, invoke the Windows NT Services option of the Windows NT Control Panel. When the Services window appears select the desired service (MS SQL Server or SQL Executive) and click the Startup button to get to the Services Startup window.

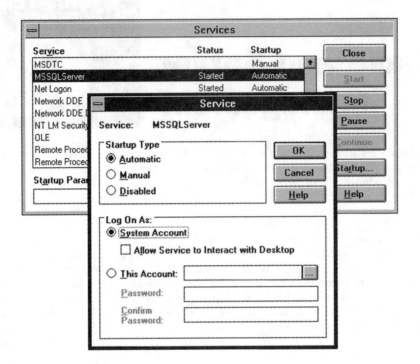

Then, simply click the button to set the service to either Automatic or Manual startup, and click OK.

Starting, Pausing, and Stopping Servers

When you install SQL Server you have the option to make SQL Server and SQL Executive autoboot options. You can further configure SQL Executive to automatically start SQL Mail when it's started. These options, which cause Windows NT to automatically start the SQL Server and SQL Executive services whenever the computer is rebooted, are usually a very good choice if you plan on using SQL Server consistently on a particular machine.

Starting

Starting SQL Server, SQL Executive, or SQL Mail initiates an instance of the service on the Windows NT server according to the startup options you've specified.

Occasionally, you may encounter a situation where SQL Server will not start. For example, if you have allocated more memory for SQL Server than actually exists on the server or have improperly allocated *tempdb* in RAM. In a circumstance like this, you should start SQL Server using the **-f** parameter. There are a whole set of SQL Server startup options available to you:

Startup Parameter	Description
-c	Shortens startup time by starting SQL Server without interaction with the Windows NT Service Control Manager.
-d *master_path*	Overrides the Registry setting for the fully qualified path of the Master device.
-e *errorlog_path*	Overrides the Registry setting for the fully qualified path of the errorlog.
-f	Starts SQL Server in minimal operating mode. Used to troubleshoot problems, especially those associated with startup. It's also a good idea not to run the SQL Executive service while in this mode.
-m	Start SQL Server in single-user mode and disables the *CHECKPOINT* mechanism. Used to troubleshoot problems, especially those associated with startup. Also a good idea not to run the SQL Executive service while in this mode.
-n	Disables Windows NT event logging for SQL Server events. Usually used in combination with the **-e** option.
-p *precision_level*	Defines the maximum precision of decimal and numeric datatypes from 1 to 38. The default is 28.
-r *mirror_path*	Defines the fully qualified path for the mirror device of the Master database device. Used to start SQL Server from the mirror device when Master is damaged.
-s *registry_key*	This command-line only option starts SQL Server with an alternate set of parameters stored in the Registry under the name **registry_key** and applies only to the SERVER subkey. This is useful for maintaining a emergency startup configuration.
/T *trace_flag_nbr*	Starts SQL Server with the specified trace flag enabled. (Refer to the **DBCC TRACEON** command for more information about trace flags). Use this trace flag exactly as shown. Substituting a **-t** for /**T** is *not* acceptable.
-x	Starts SQL Server without keeping maintenance information on CPU time and cache-hit ratio statistics. Sometimes provides a performance improvement.

Pausing

Pausing SQL Server merely prevents users and processes from establishing any new connections to the server. Processes currently connected to the server continue normally, but if the process disconnects then a new connection can't be established. Pausing the server is usually considered a courtesy of the DBA prior to an actual shutdown. You can't pause the SQL Executive or SQL Mail services.

Stopping

When you stop SQL Server, you end the Windows NT service MSSQLServer. You'll encounter serious application or database errors where stopping and restarting SQL Server (also known as **recycling** the server) will solve your problem. When you stop SQL Server, users can't access SQL Server and all operations, both user-initiated and automatic, are suspended. Stopping SQL Server has a few other effects too that can't be achieved through any other means. For example, when you shut down SQL Server, you also increment the errorlog. Every time SQL Server is shutdown and restarted, the current listing of service events and errors are written to a file. When SQL Server is restarted, it drops the oldest errorlog (usually **ERRORLOG.6** in the **\MSSQL\LOG** directory), increments the **ERRORLOG.1** through **ERRORLOG.5** by 1 and creates a new current errorlog stored in the file **ERRORLOG**.

You may also stop SQL Executive and SQL Mail. In either of these cases, shutting down this service terminates their current set of operations. No new operations can be performed until the service is restarted. You might wish to shutdown SQL Executive to prevent *any* tasks from firing on a given server, rather than going into the Task Scheduler (discussed later in this chapter) and manually disabling all your tasks.

Controlling Startup, Pause and Shutdown

You have several different methods available to manually start, pause, or stop SQL Server and its related services:

- Windows NT commands
- Transact-SQL commands
- SQL Server Manager
- SQL Enterprise Manager

Windows NT

You can control SQL Server and SQL Executive in Windows NT opening the Windows NT Services dialog box found in the Windows NT Control Panel.

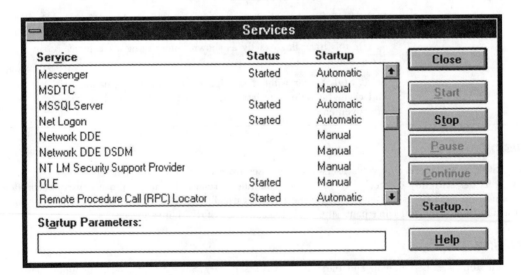

From there, choose the service MSSQLServer for SQL Server or SQLExecutive for SQL Executive and click Start, Pause or Stop as needed.

> You should note that SQL Executive can't be paused.

If needed, you can add startup parameters for SQL Server in the parameters box. Since SQL Mail isn't an NT service, you can't start it in this way. Alternatively, you can start SQL Server and SQL Executive, respectively, from a Windows NT DOS-prompt by issuing either of these commands:

```
net [ start / pause / stop ] sqlservr parameter_list
net [ start / stop ] sqlsexec
```

Or you can start the services from the command line in the **\MSSQL\BINN** directory by using these commands:

```
sqlervr  parameter_list
sqlexec
```

TSQL

You have limited options to control SQL Server or SQL Executive from within a TSQL command. However, you can stop SQL Server by issuing the command **SHUTDOWN**.

SQL Service Manager

The SQL Service Manager is one of the most convenient tools for starting, pausing and shutting down SQL Server and SQL Executive. The SQL Service Manager window provides the added benefit of informing you about the status of the server.

SQL Enterprise Manager

SQL Enterprise Manager also enables you to start and stop SQL Server, SQL Mail, and SQL Executive from within the Service Manager window. When running SQL Enterprise Manager from Windows NT, the stoplight beside each registered server shines green when running as with the SQL Service Manager. To control a given service, such as SQL Executive or SQL Mail, right-click on the icon, then select the Start or Stop option. To control SQL Server through the Enterprise Manager, right-click the server icon, then select the Start, Pause or Stop button.

> Note that the Enterprise Manager doesn't provide the server status or control options when run on a Windows 95 platform. You can manage SQL Executive and SQL Mail as normal.

Autostart Stored Procedures

You may find yourself in a position where you'd be much better off if only you could get SQL Server to kick off a certain program or process as soon as it started. For example, you could write a stored procedure to have SQL Server e-mail a notification to an operator as soon as it became available. You have that option through **autostart stored procedures**. There are three stored procedures that enable you to implement autostart stored procedures:

Syntax	Description
sp_makestartup *procedure_name*	Enables a procedure to run upon startup.
sp_unmakestartup *procedure_name*	Disables a procedure from running at startup.
sp_helpstart	Displays a list of all autostart procedures.

Autostart procedures can only be created by the sa and only in the *master* database. If you designated numerous autostart procedures, they will all execute in parallel. If you want to avoid this functionality, make one procedure the autostart procedure and code that procedure to call all other procedures. Each autostart procedure consumes one connection, though there's no limitation to the number of autostart connections.

The autostart procedures begin to execute after the last database has been recovered at startup. They will not execute at all if you start SQL Server with the **-f** (minimal configuration) parameter.

> **You can skip the autostart procedures by specifying the trace flag 4022 as a startup parameter.**

Databases and Transaction Logs

When you think of database management systems, you think of databases. So what's SQL Server's transaction log about and why is it so important? Transaction logs are the record of all activity within a database, so every action that alters data, changes security permissions, or alters the database environment is stored in the transaction log. This log isn't a journal that you can refer to or any kind of audit trail and is only used by SQL Server to allow it to recover from a system crash or media failure. Each database has its own transaction log and this can be embedded in the database or kept separate from the data itself.

SQL Server uses a methodology known as **write-ahead logging** to buffer writes to the database. In effect, SQL Server writes all changes to the transaction log first and, once written, they're re-recorded in the database. Most of the time, transactions are written to the log, then processed en masse into the database only after a SQL Server **CHECKPOINT**. One of the consequences of this approach is that there are far more writes to the transaction log than there are to the database itself.

Another important behavior of the transaction log is the way in which it fills up. Transactions are written in the log as they are processed. Many transactions result in more than one write to the log. For example, SQL Server frequently processes updates not as a single change or set of changes, but as a single **DELETE** statement (or set of **DELETE**s) followed by a single **INSERT** statement or set of **INSERT**s. Thus, the transaction log might write two I/Os (a delete, then and insert) where the database has only one (an update). As you can see, a large set of transactions could potentially fill up the whole transaction log.

Your transaction log should be separate from the database. The only exception to this rule is when you have a toy database like Pubs.

> The *master* database can't have a separate transaction log. It and its log are an indivisible unit and must always be backed up together.

There are three reasons for this: performance, recovery and backup. The behavior described above influences performance. You will get a significant performance boost by moving the database and log to separate physical devices located on separate drives. You can gain an additional boost if you're able to move the transaction log to a separate disk controller from the database. You should consider placing your transaction log on your fastest device since there's more activity in it than in the database itself. Separating the log from the data also reduces table fragmentation and consequently increases scan efficiency, and this is important, since a full scan of a table is often the only way to retrieve data. (Table scan and other SQL Server search techniques are covered in Chapter 9–*Managing Performance.*)

There's another, perhaps more important, reason to keep the database and the transaction log separate. A separate transaction log increases your ability to recover from disasters. If the data and the log are on separate physical devices, you're not going to lose both of them in a single disk crash. If you lose the database device, you can recover all the data from the transaction log up to the point of failure. Putting the transaction log on a device with a separate controller also increases fault tolerance.

Finally, a separate transaction log allows you to develop a backup strategy that combines full database backups with transaction log backups. You can't do this if the transaction log is embedded in the database. Backups are limited to full database backups, unless you separate the database and log. However, when they're separated, you can perform full backups of the database and perform incremental backups of the transaction log. We'll cover this concept in detail in Chapter 6.

> The transaction log is stored in a system table called *syslogs.* This table contains the columns **XACTID**, a binary column, and **OP**, a tinyint column. Some third-party tools allow you to look directly at the *syslogs* table, but never attempt to do this yourself. And since it contains only binary, it's virtually unintelligible to all but Mr. Spock himself.
>
> NEVER write ANYTHING directly to the *syslogs* table. This results in an infinitely looping transaction to the log that will continue until the log is completely filled and the database crashes.
>
> Sometimes the *syslogs* information gets out of date. This doesn't cause system problems but is reported as an error by the database consistency check command (DBCC). You can fix this problem with the command `DBCC CHECKTABLE(SYSLOGS)`. DBCC is covered in more detail in Chapter 6 on backup and recovery and Chapter 10 on troubleshooting.

Databases and Devices

In Chapter 3, we looked at devices, the physical storage allocated to SQL Server. These devices are used for all your databases and their associated transaction logs. There are many ways of placing databases on devices. The following picture illustrates some of them.

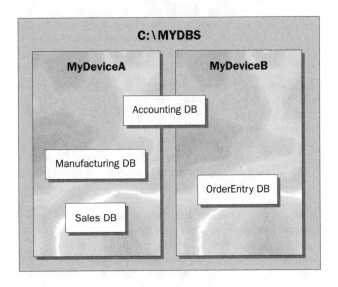

In this example, devices hold more than one database and the accounting database spans multiple devices. It's generally a good idea to give each database and log its own devices—this will make recovery from a disk crash much easier. It's fine to spread a database over several devices; it may be necessary to do this as a database grows. Just don't put more than one database or log on the same device.

Creating Databases and Transaction Logs

Your ultimate goal, when creating a database, is to implement a system that properly stores your data, consumes minimal space, provides adequate performance, good reliability, and quick recovery from a system failure. Creating a database is one step in a logical and systematic process. There are several things you need to do when you're creating a database:

- ▲ Create the database using SQL Enterprise Manager, Transact-SQL or VBA.

- ▲ Back up the *master* database (Remember, all databases are defined in the Sysdatabases table of that database).

- ▲ If you created the database with SQL Enterprise Manager or VBA, use the **sp_helprevdatabase** stored procedure to generate the Transact-SQL statements you will need if you've recreate the database after a disk crash. This procedure is described in Chapter 6.

However, the very first step in creating your database is to estimate its size.

Estimating the Database Size

If you're building on an existing system, like a DOS-based program or mainframe legacy system, start with double the size of the current system. This gives you some room to grow, as well as some space to add new data structures to improve performance. If you're building a system from scratch, estimate the volume of data based on the recommendations in Appendix B of the *SQL Server Administrator's Companion*. These formulae are tedious in the extreme, and there's a neat stored procedure that almost all administrators use instead of their calculators. It's named **sp_estspace**, and was originally developed by a couple of folks at Sybase: Hal Spitz and Malcolm Colton. There's a Microsoft SQL Server specific version available on Compuserve (**estspace.sql**).

Estimating the Transaction Log Size

You can estimate a reasonable starting size for the transaction log based on your size estimate for the database. In a typical decision support system (DSS), the transaction log might need to be 5% to 10% of the database size. Transaction logs for heavy transaction processing systems (OLTP) systems usually run from 20 to 30% of the database size. Batch systems usually need large transaction logs. Anywhere from 50% to 200% of the database size is common for batch systems.

> **Estimates for transaction log size are just that—rule-of-thumb estimates. Also keep in mind that you can always increase the size of a transaction log, but you CAN'T decrease it without a lot of extra work. On the other hand, if the log fills up, all work on that database stops dead until the full log is taken care of! This is one of those dreadful trade-offs administrators are faced with.**

Once you've got your estimates down for the database and transaction log, you will usually want to create the physical device(s) for the new database and log, following the procedures outlined in the last chapter.

> **Never place any database on the *master* device. It should only contain the databases that were placed on it during the setup process.**

Creating Databases Using SQL Enterprise Manager

The process starts within the Server Manager dialog box. Select and open the server and right-click the Databases icon, then choose New Database. Alternatively, you can click the Manage Databases button on the toolbar or select Databases from the Manage menu. When the Manage Databases dialog box appears, click the New Database icon to get to the New Databases dialog box:

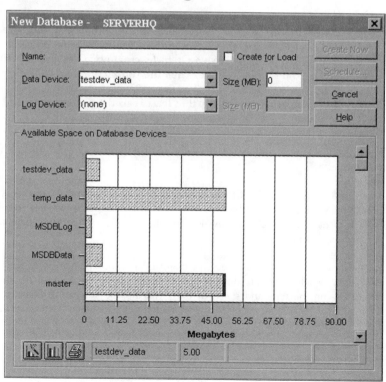

Enter a Name for the database that is 30 characters or less. Don't forget that, if you have a case-sensitive server, database names will be case-sensitive. You'll be typing it frequently in Transact-SQL statements. Make it short *and* understandable to others.

Select the database device where the database will be stored by typing in the name or selecting it from the drop-down listbox of the Data Device field. Note that the default device name will appear in the Data Device field. You can also select the option (new) from the drop-down list if you realize that you need a new device after you've started the create database process.

> **The database device that's presented in the data device field is the first device in the pool of default devices. If the Master device appears in this field, that device is marked as a default device. You should edit the Master device and set it to non-default status.**

Enter the database size in megabytes. This value will default to the total available space on the device. A database can't be smaller than 1 megabyte. Remember, it's easy to change the size of a database if you've estimated it incorrectly.

Select the log device where the transaction will reside by typing in the name or by selecting it from the drop-down list of the Log Device field. You can leave this field null if you like (that is, leave the value (none)), but it's generally not a good idea, since that will put the transaction log on the same device as the data. You can also select option (new) if you realize you need a new log device after you've started the create database process.

> **If you choose the same device for both the database and the transaction log, define two devices even if they point to the same underlying physical device. For example, if you only have a C: drive, create two devices–MyDB.Dat and MyLog.Dat on the C: drive. Then the transaction log will be separated from the data. This won't give you all of the recovery benefit of having the log on a different disk from the data, but you'll at least reap the performance and backup benefits.**

Enter the log size in megabytes. As with databases, this value will default to the total available space on the device.

You should only check the Create for Load option when you're creating a database that will be immediately loaded from a backup. This option tells SQL Server not to initialize the data pages as it would for a new database. You will only do this when you're recovering a database or moving a database from one server to another.

Click OK to create the database. This could take a while, since SQL Server must initialize each page in the allocation. Benchmarks rate this process as lasting 20 to 60 minutes per gigabyte of database space depending on the type and speed of the physical disk subsystem. Once you're done creating your new database with SQL Enterprise Manager, remember to backup the *master* database and to run `sp_helprevdatabase.`

Creating Databases using Transact-SQL

To create a database with Transact-SQL, you use the **CREATE DATABASE** command.

```
CREATE DATABASE  database_name
[ON {DEFAULT  |  database_device} [= size in megabytes]
     [,  database_device [= size in megabytes]]...]
[LOG ON log_device [= size in megabytes]
     [,  log_device [= size in megabytes]]...]
[FOR LOAD]
```

The **database_name** value is a name up to 30 characters in length. **ON** specifies the database device(s) where database will be located. **LOG ON** specifies the database device(s) where the transaction log will be located. Note that by using the **CREATE DATABASE** command, you're able to specify that the database and log are located on more than one device at initialization. SQL Enterprise Manager only gives you the capability to initialize one database device and one transaction log device at the time of database creation. Don't leave the **size** value blank unless you want the size to default to the value specified in the Server Configurations or the Model database, whichever is larger. The **FOR LOAD** option provides the same functionality as the Create for Load option in SQL Enterprise Manager.

You might have noticed that the **CREATE DATABASE** command specifies size in megabytes, while the **DISK INIT** command used to create new physical devices specifies space in 2K pages. This is just one of the little inconsistencies in SQL Server that you'll encounter. You'll find that it's better to look up the syntax than to try to issue a command from memory.

To create a new 40 megabyte database named MyDatabase with 10MB transaction log on devices named MyDataDev and MyLogDev, you would issue the following command:

```
CREATE DATABASE MyDatabase
   ON MyDataDev=40
   LOG ON MyLogDev=10
```

> When you use the CREATE DATABASE command, SQL Server will not give you an error if the amount of space you specify is unavailable. It will actually get as close to the size value you specify in half-megabyte increments. SQL Server will then report back the actual size of the database that it created.

Don't forget to back up *master* after you create the database. If you didn't save your Transact-SQL command, you should also run **sp_help_revdatabas**e.

Creating a Database with VBA

To create a database with VBA, you must declare a new **Database** object and set its properties appropriately. Then you add the object to the **Databases** collection of the appropriate SQL Server.

Don't forget to back up *master* and create the necessary Transact-SQL commands with **sp_help_revdatabase**.

Behind the Scenes

SQL Server performs many processes behind the scenes when it creates a new database. First, SQL Server begins by allocating the database space. It then inserts a row into master.dbo.sysdatabases and an additional row in master.dbo.sysusages for each device used. Then, SQL Server initializes the database space in extent blocks (eight 2k data page). This step of the process takes the lion's share of time in the procedure and is the portion of the process that's skipped when you use the **FOR LOAD** or **CREATE FOR LOAD** options. SQL Server concludes the process by recreating everything in the Model database in your new database.

> If you have tables, views, triggers, or stored procedures you want to appear in all of your new database, then place them in *model*. If, for some reason, there isn't enough space in your new database to recreate the *model* database, the CREATE DATABASE process will fail.

Removing a Database

Dropping a database, which can only be done by the sa or dbo, results in the removal of the database from the devices where it's housed. All objects, data and permissions stored by the database are gone. Dropping a database doesn't make the disk space it had been using available to other applications. The space used for its devices still belongs to SQL Server. You can, though, use this space to create a new database.

You must drop the devices and delete the underlying physical files to return the disk space to the application. To drop a database with SQL Enterprise Manager, simply open the Database folder within the Server Manager and select the database to be dropped. Click the right-mouse button and select Delete. SQL Enterprise Manager will ask you to confirm the deletion.

To drop a database with Transact-SQL, use the following commands:

```
drop database database_name [, database_name ...]
```

or

```
sp_dbremove database_name[, dropdev]
```

sp_dbremove is preferable for two reasons. First, **sp_dbremove** will drop suspect, loading or recovering databases. **Drop Database** will only drop a database in 'normal' operating conditions. Second, **sp_dbremove** allows you to drop the database devices at the same time that you drop the database. Note that you can only drop the devices if they're used exclusively by the database you're dropping.

To drop a database with VBA, use the **Remove** method of the appropriate database. Remember that you should back up the *master* database when you drop a database.

Removable Media

With the advent of SQL Server 6.0, support for databases deployed on removable media such as CD-ROM, WORM drives, optical drives, and even floppies are now possible options. SQL Server allows you, as sa, to install a copy of a regular database to a removable media. You must manage removable media databases with Transact-SQL. Neither SQL Enterprise Manager nor VBA currently has support for these databases.

Creating a Removable Database

To create a removable database, you use the system stored procedure **sp_create_removable**. This command creates three (or more) devices on the removable media and installs a copy of the database on the devices. Each device serves a different purpose. One device stores all necessary system catalog tables, one stores the transaction log, and one or more devices store the data. You must have at least three devices for a removable media database. Here's the syntax of the stored procedure:

```
sp_create_removable  database_name,
     system_logical_name, 'system_physical', system_size,
     log_logical_name, 'log_physical', log_size,
     data_logical_name1, 'data_physical1', data_size1
     [... , data_logical16]
```

For example:

```
sp_create_removable TEST,
    test_sys01, 'c:\sql65\test_sys01.dat', 5,
    test_log01, 'c:\sql65\test_log01.dat', 5,
    test_data01, 'c:\sql65\test_data01.dat', 5
```

In the example, a removable database called TEST would be created on the C: drive of the server. The TEST database should be used only for development. Once you complete the development of the TEST database, you can then use the system stored procedure **sp_certify_removable** to ready the database for deployment. A few rules about **sp_create_removable**. Retain the sa as the dbo of the database and don't add any users to the database, though you may add groups. Don't add any new database or log devices. And commonsense dictates that you shouldn't make any reference to objects outside of the database.

Certifying a Removable Database

The next step in deploying a removable database is to certify it using the system stored procedure **sp_certify_removable**. This stored procedure verifies that the database doesn't violate any rules associated with a removable database, such as nonusers. If the database checks out, it's set off line, the transaction log is merged into the system device and dropped, and other information is reported to the DBA. The syntax for **sp_certify_removable** is shown below:

```
sp_certify_removable  database_name [, auto]
```

For example:

```
sp_certify_removable TEST, auto
```

This example would completely certify the TEST database for deployment on a removable media. If the procedure is run without the **AUTO** setting, it will only issue a report on the readiness of the database. You can then alter the database until it complies with certification. If you use the **AUTO** setting, SQL Server will complete the certification process by dropping any non-sa users and completing the transfer of data and objects.

> **Retain the report generated by sp_certify_removable. You will need it to properly install the database.**

Installing a Removable Database

Once you've certified and deployed the removable media, you can install it on another server using the **sp_dbinstall** system stored procedure. This procedures installs the database and its devices, one command being issued per device of the database. When run, **sp_dbinstall** moves the system device and transaction log to your new server's hard disk, but allows you the option of leaving the read-only data on the distribution media or moving it to the server. **Sp_dbinstall** uses this command syntax:

```
sp_dbinstall database_name, logical_device_name, 'physical_device_name', size,
'device_type' [, 'location']
```

where:

- ▲ *Database_name* is the logical database name.
- ▲ *Logical_device_name* is the logical name of the device being install.
- ▲ *Physical_device_name* is the fully qualified path and file name of the device.
- ▲ *Size* is the size of the device in megabytes.
- ▲ *Device_type* indicates the device is either SYSTEM (system tables and log) or DATA.
- ▲ *Location* is the location on the destination server's hard disk—a fully qualified path and filename. A location is only required for a system device.

You can now activate the device by issuing the command:

```
sp_dboption database_name, offline, FALSE
go
```

This activates a newly installed database where the *database_name* is a value you provide. If you think you may have to restart SQL Server during the deployment of a removable database, you may want to ensure that the offline database isn't initialized by SQL Server during startup. You can control this functionality by using the system stored procedure **sp_devoption**, as shown below:

```
sp_devoption [device_name [, deferred | 'read only' {, true | false} [,
override]]]
```

For example:

```
sp_devoption TEST_SYS01, deferred, true
```

This command tells SQL Server not to automatically open the device TEST_SYS01 when the server is started.

> You can use the system stored procedure **sp_dbremove** to drop a removable database.

Keeping Tabs on your Database

You will frequently be checking up on your databases–for a multitude of reasons. SQL Server provides a number of methods to gain information about the status of a database.

In the Enterprise Manager, you can invoke the Edit Database window by simply double-clicking the database:

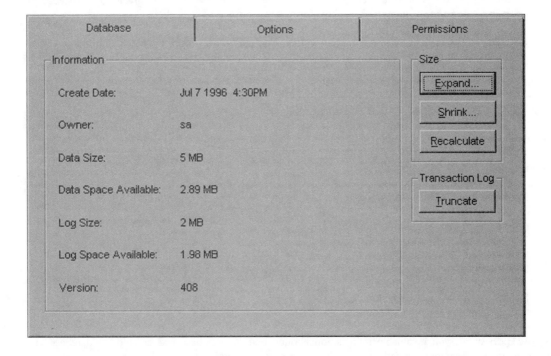

The Edit Database window provides a great deal of information about the general condition of the database. The create date, owner and version of SQL Server code are shown as well as a quick report on the contents of the database. The data size and data space available are shown in megabytes, as are the log size and log space available. If the log isn't on a separate device from the database, the log size and log space available will show a value of 'Shared with Data'. The buttons on the Edit Database window are all discussed below, except the final two options, Expand and Shrink, which are discussed later.

> In older versions of SQL Server, it was not uncommon for the transaction log information to be out of sync with the actual status of the log, sometimes even reporting negative values for **log size** and **log space available**. This problem could be rectified by issuing the command DBCC Checktable(Syslogs) in the database where you're encountering the error.

The Recalculate button recalculates the latest space usages of the database. Always recalculate the current size of the database before shrinking it. Note that completing this command could take several minutes.

The Truncate button is a nifty little one-click access to the TSQL equivalent of **DUMP TRAN (current database) WITH NO_LOG**. Thus, you can use this command to truncate all of the inactive transactions from the transaction log. You lose the opportunity to backup the transaction log once this command is issued, and even the transaction that clears the log isn't written to the transaction log.

SQL Enterprise Manager gives you only a small amount of the rich information you can pull out using system stored procedures in Transact-SQL. The first and most fundamental Transact-SQL procedure is **sp_helpdb 'database_name'**. A slightly formatted example of it is shown below:

```
sp_helpdb 'test'
go
```

```
name   db_size   owner   dbid   created   status
------   -----------   --------   -------   -----------   ---------
test   12.00 MB   sa   8   Jul 7 1996   no options set
```

```
device_fragments       size       usage
--------------------------   ------------   ---------
testdev_data     5.00 MB    data only
testdev_log     2.00 MB    log only
testdev_data1     5.00 MB    data only
```

```
    device              segment
    ----------           ------------
    testdev_data          default
    testdev_data          system
    testdev_data1         default
    testdev_data1         system
    testdev_log          logsegment
```

Sp_helpdb shows you invaluable information about when the database was created, its database id number, device fragments, and device usage. It's important to keep track of the type and number of devices because this can have an impact on database recovery, should you ever have to load from a backup.

You could also use the **sp_spaceused** command to get a snapshot of the space usage of the database, though **sp_spaceused** is known to be slightly inaccurate. You execute **sp_spaceused** in the database where you're gauging the space allocation, as shown on the following page:

```
use test
go

sp_spaceused
go
```

database_name	database_size	unallocated space
test	12.00 MB	11.38 MB

reserved	data	index_size	unused
640 KB	70 KB	40 KB	530 KB

Using this procedure, you can get a pretty good ball-park figure for the total amount of database space, the used portion, and unused portion. The unallocated space in the report is available for use by any table or index. The unused space has been assigned to specific tables but hasn't been filled by data or index nodes for those tables. You should monitor the database usage regularly. If unallocated space is low and the database is subject to growth, you will want to expand the database before you get an 'out of space' message. If the database is stable but has a large amount of unallocated space, you may want to shrink it so that you can use the space other databases.

Expanding the Database and Log

Expanding a database or transaction log is quick and easy work, but there are a couple of points to remember. First, there must be space on one or more devices for you to expand the database or log. Second, only the sa can expand or shrink the database or log. Third, you can only alter the size of the database or log 32 times. So try not to make changes in the database or log size impulsively. Finally, you should always make a backup of the *master* database and run **sp_help_revdatabase** once your change is complete but *before* you do anything else.

Expanding a Database with SQL Enterprise Manager

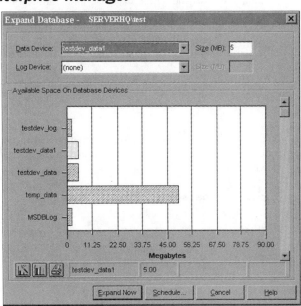

You expand a database or transaction log using SQL Enterprise Manager by first invoking the Edit Database window and then clicking the Expand button. The Expand Database dialog box will appear:

To expand a database or transaction log, select the device where it will be expanded from the drop-down list box. If you need to create a new device, simply select the (new) option from the list box to be taken directly to the New Database Device window. When you select a device to extend your database or log, the total space available in that device will appear as the default value in the Size field. If this value is incorrect, simply type in the new value or use the sliders. It may take a few moments to allocate the space, particularly if you're adding a lot of it.

Expanding a Database with Transact-SQL

You can also expand a database or transaction log using the Transact-SQL command **ALTER DATABASE**. The syntax is shown below:

```
ALTER DATABASE database_name
[ON {DEFAULT | device_name} [= size], ...]
LOG ON device_name [= size]
[FOR LOAD]
```

This command, in most ways, resembles the **CREATE DATABASE** statement. However, when you specify size, you're indicating the amount of space you want to *add* to the database or transaction log, not the final size. As an example, look at the **CREATE DATABASE** and **ALTER DATABASE** statements shown below:

```
CREATE DATABASE TEST
      on TESTDEV_DATA = 5, TESTDEV_DATA1 = 5
   log on TESTDEV_LOG = 2
GO
ALTER DATABASE TEST
   on TESTDEV_DATA1 = 5
GO
ALTER DATABASE TEST
   log on TESTDEV_LOG = 8
GO
```

This example creates the TEST database and transaction log as 10 and 2 megabytes respectively. Later, an additional 5 megabytes are added to the database and 8 megabytes are added to the log, for a total of 15 and 10 megabytes respectively. The **ALTER DATABASE** functionality for the **LOG ON** clause will only work if you had created the database using **LOG ON**.

> **ALTER DATABASE can be performed while users are working in the database.**

If you'd created the database without a separate transaction log, but later discovered that you want to separate them, you can separate the transaction log by using the Transact-SQL command **sp_logdevice**, as shown below:

```
sp_logdevice database_name, device_name
```

For example:

```
sp_logdevice TEST, TESTDEV_LOG1
```

This example would create a separate transaction log for the TEST database on a device called **TESTDEV_LOG1**. Of course, the device must already exist. All available space in the device is given to the new transaction log.

> Once you've altered the database or log, make a backup of the *master* database and run **sp_help_revdatabase**.

Expanding a Database with VBA

To expand a database with VBA, you use the **ExtendOnDevices** method of the appropriate database.

Shrinking a Database

You can expand both a database and a transaction log. You can shrink only databases. The database must be in single-user mode when you shrink it. It's a good idea to **Recalculate** the size of the database before you shrink it.

Shrinking a Database Using Enterprise Manager

To shrink a database with SQL Enterprise Manager, select the specific database you will shrink from the Database folder. Double-click the database to invoke the Edit Database window.

If you haven't already done so, click the Recalculate button. Recalculation of the database's space allocation may take some time. Click the Shrink button. If the database isn't in single-user mode, SQL Server will ask you if you'd like to continue. If you say Yes, SQL Server will set the database to single-user mode for you. The Shrink Database window will appear:

The window will show you the smallest possible size the database can be reduced to in the Minimum Size (MB) field. This is the aggregate size of the objects and data stored in the database. Enter the desired size for the database in the Database Size (MB) field, or use the sliders. Click OK to resize the database. The process might take a few minutes.

> Remember that even though you're shrinking the database, you're *not* freeing up any disk space. You're only freeing up allocated space on one or more of your database devices. If you need to free up disk space, you must also drop or alter your database devices.

Shrinking a Database Using Transact-SQL

To shrink a database using Transact-SQL, you must use the command **DBCC SHRINKDB**. You must put the database in single-user mode before you can shrink it The syntax is shown below:

```
dbcc shrinkdb (database_name [, new_size in 2K pages [, 'MASTEROVERRIDE']])
```

When specified with only the **database_name** clause, **ShrinkDB** returns information about the minimum possible size of the database. Unlike the SQL Enterprise Manager interface, **ShrinkDB** may shrink both the log and database. If this occurs to your dissatisfaction, you'll have to shrink the whole database then enlarge the database or transaction log using an **ALTER DATABASE** statement.

> Fortunately, **dbcc shrinkdb** is fully logged and fully recoverable.

You can also use the **dbcc shrinkdb** command to shrink the *master* or *tempdb* databases, though you must start the server in single-user mode (execute the **sqlservr** command-line executable with the **-m** parameter). You must use the **MasterOverride** clause to effect a reduction in the *master* database. Do not undertake this lightly!

Shrinking a Database with VBA

To recalculate the size of the database, you use the **Recalculate** method of the appropriate database. To put the database in single-user mode, you set the **SingleUser** property of the **DBOption** object to TRUE. You shrink a database with the **Shrink** method of the appropriate database.

Renaming a Database

The sa can rename a database any time subsequent to its creation using the system stored procedure **sp_renamedb**. Note that changing the name of a database in no way ensures that stored procedures and triggers will continue to work if they use explicit references to the database. You may only rename a database that has been placed in single-user mode. The syntax for **sp_renamedb** is shown below:

```
sp_renamedb  old_database_name,  new_database_name
```

Database Options

When setting up a new database, there are a collection of features and behaviors, known as **database options**, that you can enable or disable according to the needs of your application. The database options affect a number of different factors such as transaction log behavior, ANSI SQL-92 compatibility, checkpointing and user access. First, we look at the options, then we'll look at how to set them with the SQL Enterprise Manager, Transact-SQL and VBA.

Upon installation of SQL Server, all options are set to false, except for the select into/bulkcopy option in *tempdb* which is set to true. If you want to set a given option for all databases on your server, then simply set the option in Model. All databases created after the option is set in Model will be enabled in subsequently created databases. Options, when set, take effect immediately. The following section describes each of the database options.

Select Into/Bulk Copy

Setting this option **=** **TRUE** enables you to perform these operations:

    ▲   **SELECT INTO** a destination table: This variation of the **SELECT** statement enables you to rapidly create tables and populate them with data from an existing table.

▲ Fast bcp: bcp can run very quickly with this option set **= True** because it isn't logged. Fast bcp is disabled when it acts upon a table with triggers or indexes.

▲ **Writetext** operations on Text and Image fields are not logged.

If you attempt to perform a **SELECT INTO** command with the option set to false, you'll receive an error message. bcp and Writetext will both perform logged operations when **SELECT INTO = FALSE**. Usually production environments run with this option set to **FALSE**, while development environments run with this option set to **TRUE**.

Columns Null By Default

It's always best to specify NULL or NOT NULL when issuing a CREATE TABLE statement. Setting this option tells SQL Server how to assign NULL or NOT NULL status when you neglect to do it explicitly. Setting this value = FALSE defines the default column status of NOT NULL. Setting this value = TRUE sets the column status to NULL. This feature was added to support ANSI standards which dictate that default is nulls are allowed.

No Checkpoint on Recovery

The option, when set = TRUE, prevents SQL Server from issuing a checkpoint record to the log after the recovery (a.k.a. startup) process is complete.

Truncate Log on Checkpoint

This option, when set = TRUE, causes SQL Server to truncate the transaction log after every system-generated checkpoint. The log isn't truncated after user-issued checkpoints. Any attempt to explicitly dump the transaction log will result in an error. This option is commonly set in development databases, where there's less requirement to have a secure backup and a stronger requirement to keep the transaction log clear.

Single User

Only one user at a time including sa may use a database with this option set = TRUE.

DBO Use Only

Only the dbo or sa can access a database with this option set = TRUE. If the dbo and sa are separate users, then they may both be in the database at the same time.

Read Only

In a database where READ ONLY = TRUE, tables may be read but not written to. Read only databases can be very fast because they incur no locking overhead.

Offline

In a removable media database where OFFLINE = TRUE, the database is no longer available because it's unmounted.

Published

When PUBLISHED = TRUE, the database is the source for a SQL Server replication publication.

Subscribed

When SUBSCRIBED = TRUE, the database is the destination of a SQL Server replication publication.

To set options for the database using SQL Enterprise Manager, invoke the Edit Database window then choose the Options tab.

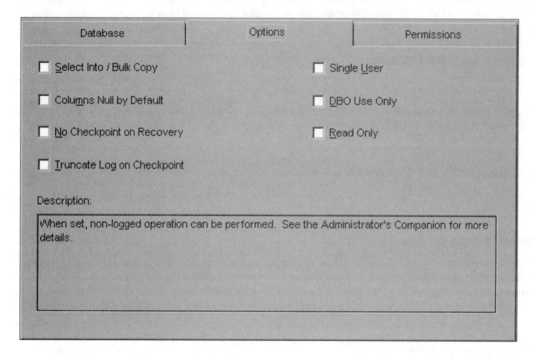

To set options using Transact-SQL, use the system stored procedure **sp_dboption** as shown below:

```
sp_dboption database_name, 'unique_string_option', {true | false}
```

Sp_dboption must be executed from the *master* database by the dbo or sa. Running **sp_dboption** by itself tells you all the available options. The 'unique_string_option' means that SQL Server will accept a unique abbreviation of the option you want to change. For example, you could use the value 'select' instead of 'select into/bulkcopy'.

Each SQL Server database has a DBOption object. Each option is a property of that object, and you use VBA to set the appropriate property to TRUE or FALSE.

SQL Executive, Automated Tasks and Scheduling

You may have noticed earlier in the chapter that we discussed the SQL Executive service. SQL Executive is the tool SQL Server uses to automate tasks, schedule processes, and raise alerts. Common uses of the SQL Executive include scheduling replication tasks, scheduling backup tasks, controlling processes that monitor the servers, and raising alerts when the monitor detects a problem.

Scheduling Tasks

One of the big improvements in SQL Server 6.0 was the addition of a strong task manager. The task manager very effectively schedules processes to run at the time and frequency of your bidding. The task manager utilizes the *msdb* database to store task information and the SQL Executive as an agent to control the timing and execution of those tasks.

Tasks are grouped into five basic types. Two of the five task groups are usable by DBAs: TSQL statements (like **DUMP TRAN**, a local stored procedure, or a remote stored procedure) and CmdExec (any command you can execute from the Windows NT DOS-prompt, including **.EXE**, **.COM** and **.BAT** files). The other three task groups are used for replication processes: the Log Reader task, the Distribution task and the Sync task.

Typical tasks you would schedule might include:

▲ **Database Maintenance** using **SQLMAINT.EXE** to run DBCC checks, dump databases and logs, update statistics, rebuild indexes, and to e-mail the resulting report to a specific operator. The *Database Administration Wizard* constructs a **SQLMAINT** task for you.

▲ **Data Imports**: You may need to import data from other systems. Task Manager can be used to schedule these events for after hours.

▲ **Data Exports**: Just as you might need to import data from other systems, you may need to send data out to other systems in ASCII format. You could accomplish this by scheduling a BCP task to run after hours.

▲ **Table Metrics**: You might run nightly stored procedures to check the growth of tables and indexes in your databases.

▲ **Replication**: You might need to push data out to other ODBC subscribers, or pull data in from other SQL Servers in your organization, for example. Replication tasks are frequently scheduled to run after hours, especially those that refresh entire tables or move large quantities of data.

Managing Scheduled Tasks

Now you have the idea behind the intended purpose of the task manager, but how do you use it? The next section will show you all the basic steps needed to configure and use tasks.

There are two ways to call the Manage Scheduled Tasks window within the Enterprise Manager: by clicking on the Manage Scheduled Tasks button on the main toolbar or by selecting the Server menu >> Scheduled Tasks option.

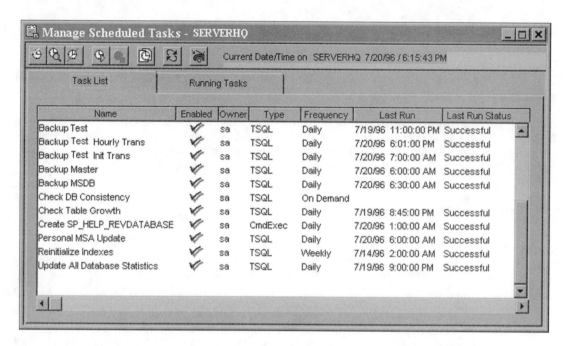

When you call the Manage Scheduled Tasks window, you will only be able to Add Tasks if tasks already exist on the server. Calling the New Tasks window, enables you to define the properties and schedule of a new task.

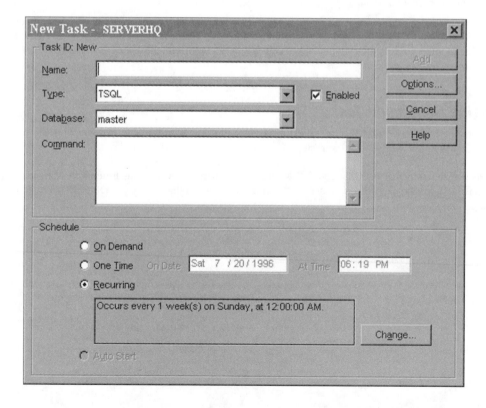

When defining a new task, you must enter a *name,* of up to 30 characters in length, that will be unique to the server. A *task type*, usually TSQL or CmdExec, is required. The replication tasks are available, but should be used with care. If you selected a TSQL task type, you must then enter the *database* where the TSQL will execute. This has the equivalent functionality of the **USE database_name** TSQL command. You must be particularly careful when calling stored procedures, since they're database specific. The CmdExec task type doesn't have a database property. Finally, you must enter a valid TSQL string or command-line executable in the *command* field. Once you've completed the rest of the set up of the task, you can toggle the Enable button to make sure the task's activated.

> **If you specify a CmdExec task, ensure that the command doesn't require any user interaction since it's executed on a virtual desktop and is invisible to the user.**

Only two steps are left now: setting the schedule of the task (the default schedule is to run the task once per week on Sundays at noon) and setting the options for the task.

You've set up your task. Now you need to confirm the schedule of the task. If you only want to run the task occasionally or if you want manual control of the task, then toggle the On Demand radio button. The task will only be executed when you click the Run Task button or when the task is called by the **sp_runtask** stored procedure. To run the task just once, toggle the One Time radio button and then specify a date and time of the task in the adjacent On Date and At Time fields. This feature is particularly useful for long-running tasks that you want to execute only once, such as **CREATE DATABASE** or **ALTER DATABASE**. You have just a little more work to do if you want the task to operate on a recurring schedule. Toggle the Recurring radio button, then click the Change button to call the Task Schedule window:

The Task Schedule window gives you absolute control over the time, frequency and duration of activity for any given tasks. For example, you can set a task to occur Weekly on Monday, Wednesday and Friday every 3 hours from 7 AM to 8 PM. You can even set a range of dates where the task will be active. When the End Date is reached, SQL Server will automatically disable the task. Just about any permutation in scheduling is possible.

Users can only review and edit tasks they've created, but the sa can view all tasks. You can also further adjust the behavior of a task on the Task Options window:

This window allows you to control how the task behaves after it's executed. The Notifications block on the Task Options window enables you to direct e-mail to an *operator*, that is, an e-mail user specified in the Operator window (discussed in a few moments). You can also direct the results of the task to the Windows NT event log. Both the operator and the event log can be contacted after the task completes successfully, after the task fails, or both. The Retry block allows you to specify, for CmdExec and Replication tasks, the number of times to retry a failed task and the amount of time to elapse before the next retry.

The Replication block allows you to specify the remote target server and the remote target database for logreader and distribution tasks.

> Note that tasks that are designed to respond to alerts now support the following parameters: SVR (server name), DBN (database name), ERR (error number), SEV (severity level) and MSG (message text).

Reviewing Task History

Once you have set up and
enabled a task, you will often
need to check up on it. You can
get a quick status check on the
task by looking in the Manage
Scheduled Tasks window itself
in the Last Run and Last Run
Status columns. When you look
in these columns, you can
immediately know when the task
was last run, and if it succeeded
or failed. Failures are especially
easy to spot in version 6.5
because the Last Run and Last
Run Status columns are
highlighted in red and a bold
'stop sign' icon appears next to
the Last Run Status of Failure:

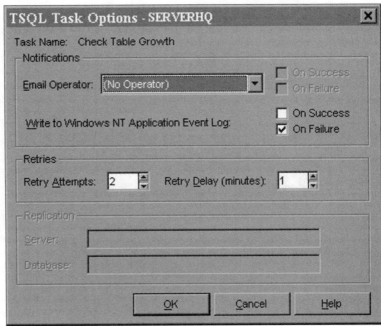

You can display an extensive history of the task in the Enterprise Manager by highlighting a given task
and clicking the Task History button, or by calling up the task in the Edit Task window and clicking the
History button. In either case, the Enterprise Manager queries the table syshistory in the *msdb* database and
the Task History window appears. The Task History window tells you the last date and time the task was
run, its success or failure status, the e-mail operator, if any, who was contacted, and the duration the task
ran for. The Task History window also shows the last message issued by the task on that particular run
date and time. If you scroll through the tasks to earlier ones, you'll see that the last message issued by the
task on that given run date and time will also be shown.

> When coding a TSQL script to be run by the task manager, remember that the last
> PRINT command or error message output of the script will be shown in the Last
> Message field of the Task History window, up to 230 characters in length.

You can also use the Refresh button on the Task History window to update the display at any time. If
you're tired of wading through all the entries in the Task History window, you can truncate the listing by
clicking the Clear All button. You can also set SQL Server to automatically truncate the Syshistory table
when it reaches a predefined length by clicking on the Task Engine Option button on the Manage
Scheduled Tasks toolbar.

Managing E-mail Operators

In the section on Managing Scheduled Tasks, you read that you can configure your tasks to automatically e-mail a specified user, or operator, when a given task fails or even when it's successful. The first step in this process is to create a definition for the operators in your organization. There are a number of ways to reach the Operators tab of Managing Alerts and Operators window. You can select Server menu >> Alerts/Operators selection or by clicking on the Manage Alerts and Operators toolbar button. From there you click on the Operators tab to see a list of operators and information showing when they were last e-mailed or paged. Click on the Add Operator button on the toolbar to add a new operator:

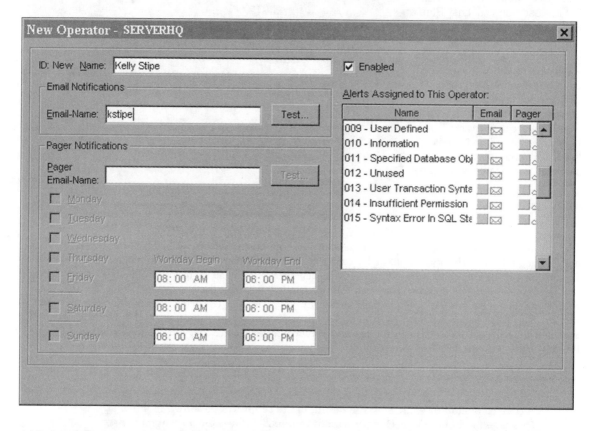

Adding e-mail operators is very easy. Adding pager operators is somewhat more complicated. In either case, SQL Server retains information about operators in the table **msdb..sysalerts**. To add a new e-mail operator, simply add their real name in the New Name field and enter their e-mail name in the Email-Name field. You can also construct lists of e-mail operators by entering a group name in the New Name field, and then selecting all of the desired e-mail operators by clicking the [...] button adjacent to the Email-Name field. You may click the Test button to send a sample message to the operator. Instead, you could use the Send Mail button to invoke the e-mail client and compose an e-mail message to the operator. This is particularly useful if you're changing the responsibility of an operator and want to notify them of the change while it's still fresh on your mind.

SQL Server allows you the added convenience of scheduling pager duty among a group of pager operators. Thus you can control which operators are on call for any given day of the week, with weekend days given special consideration. Unfortunately, you can only schedule days of the week. So, if your organization rotates beeper duty on a weekly basis, you'll be out of luck, particularly when that beeper goes off at 3AM!

> Your best bet for trouble-free pager functionality is to install MS-Mail Server because it utilizes the Microsoft Mail gateway to TAPI, the Telephone API. Other MAPI and TAPI enable products will work, but it takes much more work to integrate them with SQL Server.

Paging functionality must also be configured through the Alert Engine Options window >> Pager-Email tab. This tab retains all important pager and e-mail information relating to phone numbers and telephone prefixes and suffixes:

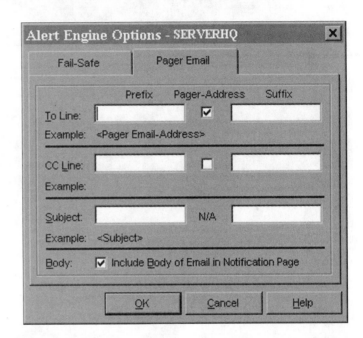

Managing Messages and Alerts

You've seen how to create automated tasks to run on a scheduled basis, and you've seen how to contact an e-mail operator or even a pager operator should your scheduled task run afoul. What happens if SQL Server encounters a more serious error—one that is unrelated to any specifically configured task? The answer to that worry is a SQL Server **alert**. An alert is a SQL Server notification that an predefined event has occurred. SQL Server integrates alert into its exception handling process, so that alerts can instigate e-mail and/or pager notifications or even react to the alert with a TSQL or CmdExec task.

This feature is one of the strongest benefits in SQL Server version 6.5. The integration of user-defined exception handling and error detection with the SQL Server engine itself enables DBAs to build reactive and proactive solutions for common (or even uncommon but catastrophic) problems directly into the server. In this way, you can enable SQL Server-based applications to detect troublesome situations, correct them and notify you in the process without any reliance on custom-built, client-side applications.

That isn't to say that client-side applications can't take advantage of the alert engine in SQL Server. You can utilize the **RAISERROR** or **RAISERROR WITH LOG** commands in your applications to invoke all the standard SQL Server error messages stored in sysmessages. If a custom message is more to your taste, you can use the stored procedure **sp_addmessage** to create a new message in the Sysmessages table. A particular benefit of the **RAISERROR WITH LOG** command is that you can now explicitly log SQL Server system (and application) errors directly to the Windows NT Event Log. You can create your own messages in the Enterprise Manager by clicking the New button in the Manage Messages window, reachable by clicking the Manage Messages button on the Alert toolbar.

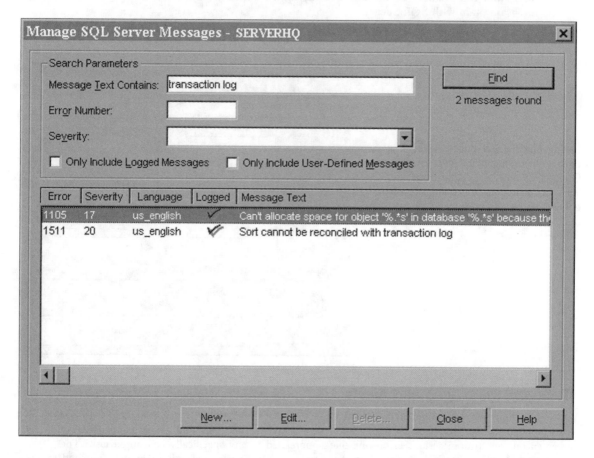

You can do a search of the Sysmessages table by entering criteria into Severity, Error Number or Message Text Contains... field then clicking the Find button. If you then discover that no message adequately meets your needs, you can add one by clicking the New button.

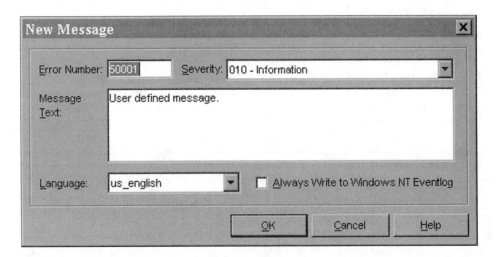

You can enter an error number that equals or exceeds 50001, a severity level and message text. You can also indicate whether the message should be automatically logged to the Windows NT Event Log, though the message's severity level can't exceed 18 to have this functionality. Click OK when you've completed adding your new message.

Once you've created any messages you might need for your alert, you can go about the business of adding alerts. To add an alert using the Enterprise Manager, click the Manage Alerts and Operators icon on the Server Manager toolbar >> click the Alerts tab >> click the New Alert icon on the Manage Alerts toolbar.

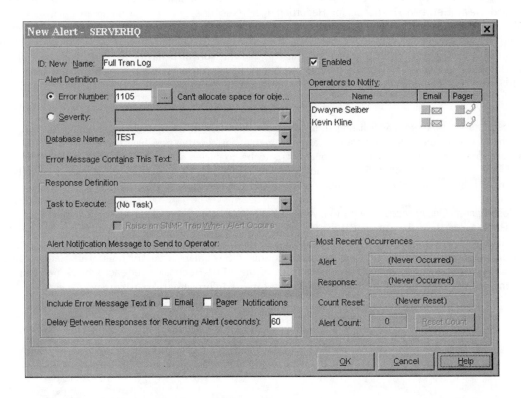

The Add Alert window is divided into four blocks, besides the Name and Enable fields, each containing a different set of information: the Alert Definition block, the Response Definition block, the Operator list box, and the Most Recent Occurrences block.

The four fields of the Alert Definition block are Error Number, Severity, Database Name and Error Message Contains This Text. You can set the alert to respond to a single error message. If you don't remember exactly which message you want the alert to respond to, you can click the Locate button, [...], to find the specific message. If you're less concerned about the message and would rather have SQL Server respond one way to an entire severity level, you can toggle the Severity field, and select a severity level from the drop-down list box. You can optionally assign the alert to a single database by entering a database name in the Database field. You can also alter the behavior of the alert by telling it to occur only if the text you enter into the Error Message Contains This Text is encountered. This field, which is optional, is particularly useful when combined with the Severity field, so that you can filter processing on a given severity level.

Once you've defined the event that will trigger the alert in the Alert Definition block, you can then construct a response to the alert in the Response Definition block. The Response Definition block contains these fields: Task to Execute, Alert Notification Message to Send to Operator, as well as the switches Raise SNMP Trap, Include Error Message in ... Notification and Delay Between Response for Recurring Alert (seconds). When an alert is raised, you might want to execute a task by selecting a pre-existing task from the Task to Execute drop-down list box. If you need to create a new task, you can select (New) from the list box and immediately create a new task. The task you specify must be a non-replication task that's scheduled to execute *On Demand*. You may optionally send a text string (up to 255 characters in length) to the operator, in addition to any error messages, by entering a message in the Alert Notification Message to Send to Operator. The Include Error Message in switches allows you to forward any error messages to the operator via e-mail or pager notification. You can raise a condition with SQL Server's SNMP agent by enabling the Raise SNMP trap switch. The last field of the Response Definition block, and Delay Between Response for Recurring Alert (seconds), deserves a bit more discussion. Alerts are all processed in parallel. Thus, if 12 users encounter the dreaded 1105 error (that is, transaction log is full) and you've configured an alert on that error, then you could potentially receive 12 notifications of the error within a few seconds of each other. You can alleviate this sort of behavior by entering a value for Delay Between Response for Recurring Alert (seconds). So, if you enter a value of 30 in this field for the 1105 error and 14 instances of the 1105 error are encountered in 30 seconds, you'll only be notified once.

The Operators list box contains a listing of all available operators. If no operators are listed, you can still create the alert but you'll probably want to add an operator as soon as possible. Two columns, email and pager, are shown to indicate whether the operator is to be contacted via an e-mail or pager notification. If either of the icons for the notification are shown as simple outlines, then you haven't provided enough information in the definition of the notification to contact the operator.

The Most Recent Occurrences block displays information about the alert. The Alert, Response and Count Reset fields show the date and time when the alert was last raised, when a response to the alert was initiated and when an operator reset the Alert and Response fields, respectively. The Alert Count field shows the number of times the alert has been raised since the counters were last reset. The Reset Count button allows an operator to reset all the other fields of the Most Recent Occurrences block once an alert has been resolved, enabling the Edit Task window to capture information about the newest alerts.

Behind the Scenes

Although the SQL Server alert engine provides some extremely potent capabilities to the DBA, it has some behavior that needs to be explained. First of all, all tasks execute within a 'virtual desktop'. This means that if an error with an associated alert occurs for 5 different users at once, SQL Server will activate a response for each of the errors based on the alert. Thus, you as the DBA might get 5 e-mails or pager notifications for essentially the same error. Additionally, alerts can generate their own errors that might have alerts associated with them. If you're not careful in the design and deployment of alerts, you could actually be constructing a system of alerts that will loop infinitely and could even crash the system. It's not common, but it could happen.

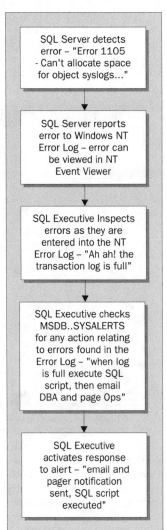

Also note that *msdb* by default is a small database. Since all data relating to events and alerts are stored in *msdb* tables like Syshistory and Sysnotifications, you may have to keep an eye on the size and growth rates of some of these tables. Notice in the chart below the way in which the SQL Executive exception-handler inserts records into the *msdb* database tables.

As you can see from the diagram, the entire alert capabilities of SQL Executive are tightly integrated with the Windows NT Event Log. Because the SQL Executive continually checks the Windows NT Event Log for new errors reported by SQL Server, any SQL Server error found in the event log can be handled by an alert. As you've seen from the section above, you can reactively manage your database through automated alerts and tasks. For example, you could create alert/task routines that would help minimize transaction log downtime by:

▲ Creating a 'transaction log handler' task that would DUMP the full transaction log. If the DUMP failed, you could then instruct the task to increase the size of the transaction log.

▲ Creating an alert to notify the DBA of the 1105 error (transaction log is full) plus the status of the transaction log after your 'transaction log handler' task complete.

Using SQL Performance Monitor for Proactive Management

Although the alert/task capability provides you with enormous flexibility that was unheard of a few years ago, it still has one major flaw: the error occurs *before* you can react to it! What if you wish to be more *proactive* and try to deal with problems before they happen? SQL Server has addressed this question too–through the integration of the SQL Performance Monitor with SQL Executive.

SQL Performance Monitor

SQL Performance Monitor (PerfMon) is a separate utility under the Windows NT program group Microsoft SQL Server 6.5. It doesn't run on a Windows 95 console. This utility enables you to graphically monitor the behavior of SQL Server and a dizzying array of behaviors. You can gain significant insight into the processing of *tempdb*, utilization of memory, CPU overhead of varying operations, and dozens–even hundreds–of other aspects of SQL Server and Windows NT. Refer to the *SQL Server Administrator's Companion* for a full discussion on the objects and counters available in PerfMon. The screenshot shows the default settings of the PerfMon.

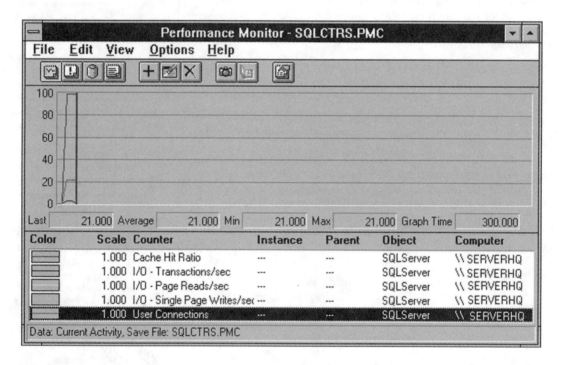

PerfMon uses the concept of a *counter*, a graph line depicting the current activity of a SQL Server or Windows NT process, to display performance information. When invoked, PerfMon starts up with some default counters already running: Cache-hit Ratio, I/O Transactions per Second, I/O Page Reads per Second, I/O Page Writes per Second and the total number of User Connections.

Each of these counters (and indeed every counter found in PerfMon) monitors a specific behavior that may at times be important to the DBA. The default counters usually consider the 'snapshot of health' of a database. At startup, Cache-hit Ratio should be very high (around 98% or more) because this counter shows the percentage of time that requests for data are read from the data cache and not the disk. If this number is less than 98%, SQL Server isn't getting access to enough data cache memory. The three I/O settings gives an idea for the number of TSQL transactions processing and the number of page reads and writes occurring to support those TSQL transactions. And finally, you are shown how many user processes (not actual users though) are connected to SQL Server.

A wise DBA might suggest that the use of SQL Performance Monitor will generate too much overhead when compared with the information it provides, but this isn't true. PerfMon incurs almost a 5% CPU hit on a single CPU server, but is almost negligible on a multiple CPU server. Besides, if you're using PerfMon properly, the information it provides is invaluable.

> The Windows NT Resource Kit has a service version of Performance Monitor which can be installed to start automatically with a predefined set of counters whenever the server is booted. In a production environment, this version of SQL Performance Monitor is preferable.

In a standard or mixed security environment, PerfMon uses the **probe** user id to monitor SQL Server, so be careful not to delete this user ID. In an integrated security environment, PerfMon must have sa privileges to access SQL Server.

You can actually use PerfMon to trigger alerts and thus tasks within SQL Server. The following section walks you through the process of creating a PerfMon *threshold*, or point at which PerfMon initiates its own alert, and integrating it with SQLALRTR.EXE, the event logging utility for PerfMon.

Summary

This chapter has covered a lot of ground, but you should have come away with several key points of knowledge. First, you should have a basic understanding of how to create databases in the Enterprise Manager and through the use of TSQL commands. You should understand what happens behind the scenes when you manage databases and should know how to get information about databases and transaction logs. You should be familiar with renaming, resizing and dropping databases and transaction logs. The database options should be clear to you, as should the ways in which you can disable and enable the various options. You should understand the benefits and implementation methods of removable databases. You should have at least some understanding about the uses and implementation of the SQL Executive to schedule tasks, automate processes and monitor servers and databases. And finally, you should have an idea about how to proactively monitor servers and databases using SQL Performance Monitor and the **SQLALRTR.EXE** event logging utility.

6.5

Create Table and Data Integrity

While looking at the problems involved in the management and creation of databases in the previous chapter, you might have noticed that we avoided discussing tables. This is because tables pose an entirely different set of problems for the DBA and merit separate consideration. Tables are the collection of records that make up your data. By properly structuring and maintaining your tables, you will enable the data to transcend itself and become something far more valuable–information.

However, information is of little use if it's inaccurate. One of the most important roles of a multiuser database is to safeguard the accuracy and consistency of the data. This is done by checking that columns contain valid values, checking that Foreign Keys match Primary Keys across tables and checking that the data in related tables is successfully updated. This is known as **data integrity**. The processes of table creation and ensuring that the database has integrity go hand in hand. This chapter covers:

- ▲ Storage Structure
- ▲ Datatypes
- ▲ Creating, altering and dropping tables
- ▲ Types of Data Integrity
- ▲ Adding constraints to tables
- ▲ Programmed integrity enforcement
- ▲ Stored procedures
- ▲ Triggers

Storage and Theory Primer

In order to properly maintain tables, you have to have a little background in the fundamentals. In this section, we'll cover important issues like storage structure, datatypes, primary and foreign keys.

Storage Structure

When we look at SQL Server, the object hierarchy is clearly laid out.

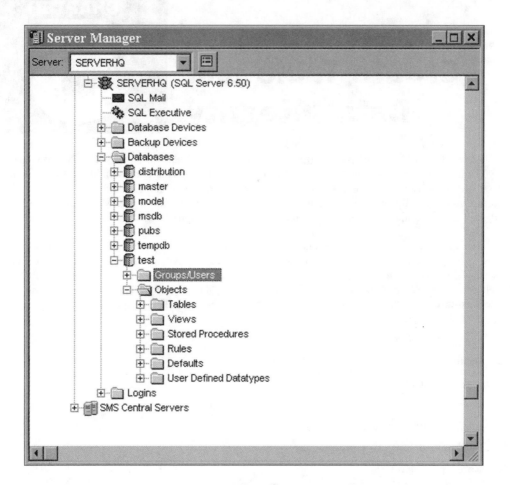

The Server Manager window, makes the hierarchy clear: devices hold device fragments, device fragments hold databases, databases hold objects like tables, and tables hold records. Internally, however, SQL Server takes a different perspective: devices hold databases, databases hold page allocations, pages hold tables and associated structures in 2K blocks. The big difference you may have noticed are **pages**. SQL Server stores all information at the page (i.e. 2048 block) level, in five different forms. The different types of pages in SQL Server are shown:

Page Type	Description
Allocation	Pages are grouped into 256 blocks equal to 512K or 0.5 megabytes. This is called an *allocation unit*. An allocation unit is also subdivided into 32 extents, a group of eight 2K pages or 16K total. The first of each 256 pages is used to keep pointers, called *links*, to all the others in the allocation unit.
Data/Log	The main storage unit in SQL Server. All other page types are variations of the data page. A data page is composed of a 32-byte header, a 54-byte log segment, and 1962-byte data segment. The 1962-byte data segment is also the max length of a record in a SQL Server table. Data pages also maintain links to prior and next page, these links in turn create a page *chain*. If variable-length fields exist in the page, additional overhead space will be consumed by a *row offset table*.

Table Continued on Following Page

Page Type	Description
Distribution	This type of page is created when you run Update Statistics. It is a data page, of sorts, that tells the query optimizer about the distribution of data in a given table based on its indexes. One distribution page exists per index.
Index	SQL Server uses two main types of indexes, clustered and non-clustered. Index pages store pointers to the widespread data pages, speeding access to the data pages and links that chain the index pages together. The amount of overhead for a clustered and non-clustered index page differ.
Text/Image	Pages used to store Binary Large Objects (BLOBs) up to 2GB in size are called text/image pages. These pages use an additional 112-bytes of space for overhead, so the maximum storage on a text/image page is 1800-bytes. All BLOBs are composed of a 'header' data page with metadata about the object and pointer information, and text/image pages that store the actual binary code.

Datatypes

When constructing tables, you have a number of SQL Server-defined datatypes to choose from. Each column or variable you create in SQL Server must have an assigned datatype. Datatypes impact the kinds of data that can be stored in the column (for example, numbers or characters), the acceptable range of values (date), and the maximum size of the column (binary). Here's an example of the way datatypes are used in a **CREATE TABLE** statement:

```
CREATE TABLE TEST_FIELD_DATA
    (test_id        INT           NOT NULL,
    tester_id       CHAR(9)       NOT NULL,
    instrument_id   INT           NULL,
    description     VARCHAR(50)   NULL,
    date_of_test    DATETIME      NOT NULL,
    results         VARCHAR(75)   NULL)
```

Unfortunately, you can't change the datatype of a column after you have created the table. The only way to change the datatype of a table is to create a new table with the desired datatype and move data from the old table to the new. As fundamental as datatypes are to the behavior and performance of your application, they are difficult to change once set into place. Here is a brief table, that explains the basics about the SQL Server default datatypes:

Datatype	Description
	Binary Datatypes
Binary	Stores fixed-length binary strings
Varbinary	Stores variable-length binary strings
Image	Stores large binary strings up to 2GB in size. Always separate text/image data into a table by itself with a key linking it to the originating table.
Timestamp	A binary representation of the current time and data. SQL Server handles inserting values to this datatype. Only one is allowed per table.

Table Continued on Following Page

Datatype	Description
	Character Datatypes
Char	Stores fixed-length character strings, including trailing blanks.
Varchar	Stores variable-length character strings, truncating trailing blanks. Never use a varchar(1). Less efficient than char and uses more overhead, but more flexible.
Text	Stores long character strings up to 2GB in size.
	Date Datatypes
Smalldatetime	Date-storage type with acceptable range of January 1, 1990 to June 6, 2079, precision to the minute, and a storage size of 4 bytes.
Datetime	Date-storage type with acceptable range of January 1, 1753 to December 31, 9999, precision to 3 milliseconds, and a storage size of 8 bytes.
	Logical Datatype
Bit	Stores only 1 or 0, equating to On/Off or True/False. Bit columns can't be indexed and they can't be NULL.
	Monetary Datatypes
Money	Stores exact values with four decimal places. Can store very large values, but uses 8 bytes storage.
Smallmoney	Stores exact values with four decimal places between -214,748.3647 and 214,748.3647. Uses 4 bytes storage
	Approximate Numeric Datatypes
Float	Stores enormous numbers with an accuracy up to 15 decimal places. Takes 8 bytes of storage.
Real	Stores enormous numbers with an accuracy up to 7 decimal places. Has a smaller range than float. Takes 4 bytes of storage.
	Exact Numeric Datatypes
Numeric	Stores exact numbers with a user-specified number of digits and decimal places. Synonymous with the decimal datatype.
Int	Stores exact, integer values between -2^{31} and 2^{31} and takes 4 bytes of storage.
Smallint	Stores exact, integer values between -2^{15} and 2^{15} and takes 2 bytes of storage.
Tinyint	Stores exact, integer values between 0 and 255 and takes only 1 byte of storage.

You can also create user-defined datatypes, but that functionality is basically the process of tacking on characteristics to an existing datatype. User-defined datatypes are the same as SQL Server datatypes in terms of storage and retrieval behavior.

NULL/NOT NULL

Datatypes also possess the characteristic of **nullility**, as shown in the sample code above. Every new column should be defined in the **CREATE TABLE** process as either allowing null values and not allowing null values. Nullable columns allow null values, but have some additional overhead and are treated behind the scenes like a variable-length column.

> It's important to note that, by default, SQL Server does not follow the ANSI standard if you don't specify nullility. If you leave out the NULL or NOT NULL property, SQL Server assumes NULLS are <u>not</u> allowed. There are SET commands, database options and, in 6.5, a server configuration option that change this behavior. But it's safest to be explicit and specify how you want each column to behave.

The *numeric* and integer datatypes (int, smallint and tinyint) may also possess the *Identity* property, though smallint and tinyint are probably bad choices for this property because of the small range of values they allow. Identity columns are columns where SQL Server automatically increments the value each time a new **INSERT** is executed on the table. The are basically 'counter' fields. Only one column in a table can have the *Identity* property. It is great for creating artificial keys since it is managed by the system.

Primary and Foreign Keys

A primary key (PK) is a column(s) that uniquely identifies one row in a table from all the others. For example, many human resource applications use Social Security Number as the PK of those tables containing information about personnel. A foreign key (FK) is a column in one table that is the primary key in another table. For example, an automobile tracking table might have a column called Owner_SSN that is a foreign key to the human resources table.

You declare a PK or FK in the constraint clause of the **CREATE TABLE** or **ALTER TABLE** commands. Primary keys can't be null and are automatically treated as unique indexes. Foreign keys are for documentation purposes.

> In version 6.0, tables that had foreign keys experienced erratic behavior with any triggers associated with the table.

Creating a Table

You've seen some of the fundamental concepts behind creating a table. You can create tables with SQL Enterprise Manager, Transact-SQL or VBA. You will ultimately want to have the Transact-SQL statements in case you need to recreate, restore, or modify the existing table. If you create a table with SQL Enterprise Manager or VBA, you can use SQL Enterprise Managers Script facilities to produce the appropriate Transact-SQL statements.

Creating a Table with Enterprise Manager

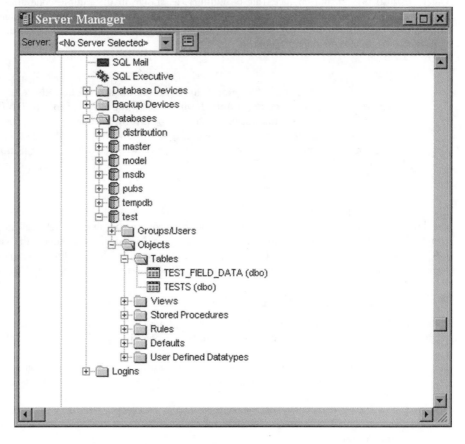

Select the server to be modified in the Server Manager window. Open the Database folder, then the Objects folder, and then the Table folder:

Right-click any table or the Table folder and select New Table. The Manage Tables window will appear:

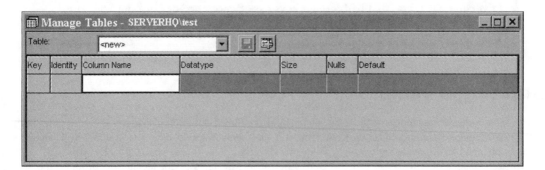

Enter the name of the first column in the Column_Name field. It should be 30 characters or less. Press Tab or click in the next field. Select a datatype from the drop-down list. The default is INT. If appropriate for the datatype, enter the size of the column. Toggle the Nulls characteristic on or off by clicking in the field or pressing the SpaceBar.

Key	Identity	Column Name	Datatype	Size	Nulls	Default
		Tester_ID	int			
		Tester_Last_Name	varchar	20	✓	
		Tester_First_Name	varchar	20	✓	

Enter a default value, if one exists, for the column. For example, you might want an employee's department to default to 'TEMP' or you might cause a Hire_Date column to default to the current date by using the **GETDATE()** function, if the user doesn't supply one.

Key	Identity	Column Name	Datatype	Size	Nulls	Default
		Tester_ID	int			
		Tester_Last_Name	varchar	20	✓	
		Tester_First_Name	varchar	20	✓	
		Tester_Hire_Date	smalldatetime		✓	getdate( )

Press the Down Arrow or click in the next blank record to add an additional column.

Adding Identity Properties

You can only add the identity property to a column while the table is being created. You can't add the identity property to an existing column by altering a table, although you can use alter to add a new column which has this property. To add an identity column, open the Manage Tables with Advanced Features window as shown on the following page. Add a new not-null numeric column, like INT or NUMERIC, then click on the Identity drop-down list. Your new column should appear in the list. Select it. SQL Server then defaults the value of the SEED, or starting value of the counter, and INCREMENT, the rate at which the counter increases, to 1. If, for instance, you want the Identity to start counting at 100 and every value to increase by 5, you would enter a Seed of 100 and an Increment of 5.

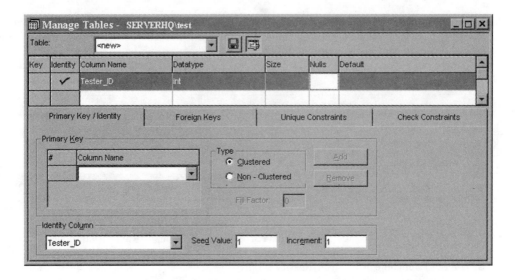

You may only have one identity field in a table. The column with the identity property may not be a NULL allowed column. You can only assign the Identity property to columns with the following datatypes:

- ▲ tinyint
- ▲ int
- ▲ decimal
- ▲ numeric

When you are ready to save the table definition to the database, click the Save Table button.

You may alter any of your column definitions prior to saving the table.

Creating a Table with Transact-SQL

To create the same basic table using Transact-SQL, you would use the **CREATE TABLE** command as shown below:

```
CREATE TABLE [database_name.[database_owner_name].]table_name
   (column_name1    properties1    constraint1,
    column_name2    properties2    constraint2,
    ...)
```

For example:

```
CREATE TABLE dbo.TEST_FIELD_DATA
   (test_id int NOT NULL ,
    tester_id char (9) NOT NULL ,
    instrument_id int NULL ,
    description varchar (50) NULL ,
    date_of_test datetime NOT NULL ,
```

```
       results varchar (75) NULL )
 GO
```

To add an identity to the **CREATE TABLE** statement for the **TEST_FIELD_DATA** table,

```
CREATE TABLE dbo.TEST_FIELD_DATA
   (test_id int identity(1,1) NOT NULL ,
    tester_id char (9) NOT NULL ,
    instrument_id int NULL ,
    description varchar (50) NULL ,
    date_of_test datetime NOT NULL ,
    results varchar (75) NULL )
 GO
```

you merely add the **identity (seed, increment)** clause to the column properties portion of the **CREATE TABLE** statement.

Creating a Table with VBA

To create a table with VBA, first you declare a new **Table** object. Then, for each column, you declare a new **Column** object and set its properties appropriately. Use the **InsertColumn** method of the **Table** object to add the column to the table. When you have added all the columns, you can then add the **Table** object to the **Tables** collection of the appropriate Database.

Dropping a Table

The simplicity of dropping a table can be a welcome relief from the intricacies and issues of properly creating a table. To drop a table in Transact-SQL, you simply issue the command:

```
drop table table_name
go
```

It's equally simple to do in SQL Enterprise Manager. Open the Server Manager window. Then drill down through the Database folder, Object folder and Table folder. Select the table(s) to be deleted, then right-click the table. Select the Drop option. SQL Server will display the Drop Objects prompt window as shown:

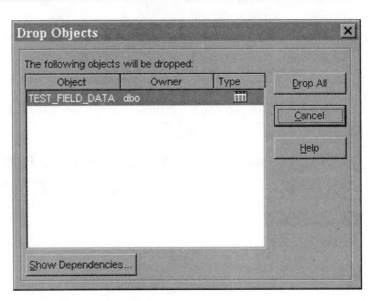

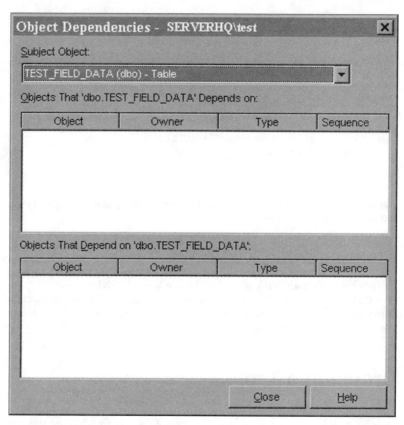

You may want to ensure that no triggers, views, or stored procedures use the table you want to drop. SQL Server will allow you to drop a table that other objects reference. This is called a **dependency**. You will only encounter an error when you attempt to utilize the dependent object. To confirm that your table is free of dependencies, click the Show Dependencies button. The Object Dependencies window will appear as shown:

When you are satisfied that you have resolved all the dependencies issues, you can click Close to return to the Drop Objects window. When ready to drop the table, click the Drop All button. To drop a table with VBA, you use the **Remove** method of the appropriate **Table** object.

Altering a Table

When altering tables, you have a limited number of choices. You can rename tables and columns, add columns to the table, and add or drop keys and constraints. You can't change column datatypes or properties, nor can you remove a column once added to a table. Once a column is added to a table, you're stuck with it until you drop it and recreate.

Altering Columns or Properties of a Table

In SQL Enterprise Manager, table alterations (except for renaming the table itself) are limited to the Manage Tables with Advanced Features window. Here is a quick overview of the means of altering a table using SQL Enterprise Manager:

Operation	Description	Transact-SQL Equivalent
Rename Column	Click on the column name and type in a new one. Click the Save button.	`Sp_rename old_name,` `new_name [, COLUMN]`

Alter Primary Key, Foreign Key, Unique Constraint or Check Constraint	Open the appropriate Advanced Feature tab. Remove the object and click the Save button. Create a new object to suit your needs.	`Alter table`
		`table_name drop`
		`constraint`
		`constraint_name ... then`
		`alter table table_name`
		`add constraint`
		`constraint_name ...`

Add a Column	Open the Manage Tables window and select the table to be altered. Move to the last open row and define a new column. Click the Save button.	`Alter table`
		`table_name add`
		`column_name1`
		`column_properties1`
		`column_constraints1, ...`

As you can see, in most cases you have to undo the work you've done to correct it. In most cases, it's worth spending a little extra time up front properly defining a table rather than taking a guess and risking mixed results.

Renaming a Table

In SQL Enterprise Manager, drill down to the table and right-click on it. Select the Rename button to call the Rename Object window. Enter the new name and click OK.

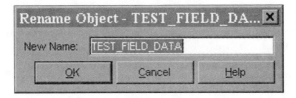

You may alter tables in Transact-SQL using the **command sp_rename oldname, newname**.

> **As with dropping tables, it's wise to check any dependencies on a table prior to renaming it since triggers, views, and stored procedures may explicitly reference the old table name.**

145

Data Integrity

As mentioned earlier, information stored within a database is of little use if it's inaccurate. The method of safeguarding the accuracy and consistency of the data is known as **data integrity**. There are two general ways to implement data integrity in SQL Server: declarative and programmed.

Declarative integrity enforcement refers to the ability to add constraints at the table or column level, as defined by the ANSI SQL-92 standards. This allows the DBA to add restrictions to tables as well as the relationships between tables within the **CREATE TABLE** and **ALTER TABLE** statements. The advantage to this type of enforcement is that the constraints are automatically enforced at the time the table is created/altered. The disadvantages are that constraints can only reference data in the current database and, in many cases, don't provide the flexibility offered by other SQL Server options.

Programmed integrity enforcement refers to the various extensions that SQL Server makes available to DBAs. These include user-defined datatypes, rules, defaults, triggers and stored procedures. The advantages to using these extensions are that you can code complex business rules directly into the database, they are reusable and can be programmed to interact with the server and/or operating system.

Both of these methods take place at the level of the server, rather than the client and, indeed, there are good reasons why this should always be so.

Why Enforce Data Integrity at the Server Level?

First of all, enforcing data integrity at the server level guarantees that business rules are enforced. Rules are bound to data objects in the server, not in applications spread throughout the organization. This guarantees that no matter which tool is used to update the data, the business and data rules are being enforced.

Secondly, it can cut development costs. If the applications which modify the data don't contain business or database rules, the programming time can be decreased. In addition, as business rules change, you may not need to modify client applications.

When you define data integrity at the server level rather than spread it throughout the organization, all of the rules that define and enforce data integrity are in one place. Thus, as business rules change, you only need to make modifications once at the server level. In effect, once you've changed the server rules, the client applications 'automatically' use them.

One of the problems of enforcing integrity at the client level is that you can never be sure that all data modifications are using the business and data integrity rules needed to keep your data accurate and consistent. We can illustrate this with a diagram:

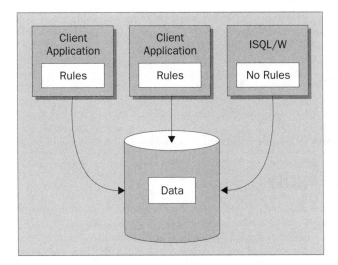

However, this isn't the case if integrity is enforced at the server level:

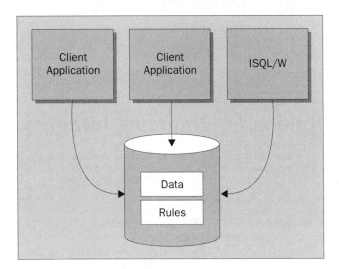

Types of Data Integrity

Data integrity falls into four general categories. We'll now briefly define each of the different types.

Domain Integrity

Domain integrity restricts the values that can appear in a column to a specified set. At the lowest level, SQL Server enforces domain integrity by datatype. For example, you can't put letters in a numeric field. We can enforce higher levels of domain integrity with defaults, rules or **DEFAULT** constraints.

Domain integrity is useful to prevent data entry errors or to guarantee that data will consistently be in a particular format. For example, it may be important that a column doesn't allow NULLS or that a value falls within a particular range.

Entity Integrity

Entity integrity preserves the uniqueness of Primary Keys in a table. This is generally enforced through **PRIMARY KEY** constraints or unique indexes. For example, it may be important for each row in a table or entity containing customers to be unique so that invoices are sent to the proper address and so on.

Referential Integrity

Referential integrity ensures that each Foreign Key matches some Primary Key, using declaratives, constraints or triggers and stored procedures. For example, it won't let you delete customers who have open invoices or delete all customer records when just one customer is removed from the system. These types of constraints ensure that no 'orphaned' records are created by data modification, or ensure that data changes in one table are 'cascaded' through all related tables.

User-defined Integrity (Business Rules)

User-defined integrity ensures that complex business rules are enforced, using rules, triggers and stored procedures. These extensions to SQL Server are often employed so that complex data and security issues can be managed in a central location. For example, if an insert to one of a series of related tables is unsuccessful, all the transactions to all the tables could be disregarded (this could be done with triggers).

SQL Server Options for Enforcing Integrity

SQL Server 6.5 has a lot of constraints and properties for enforcing data integrity. These options make life a lot easier for the DBA. The following table breaks down each of the SQL Server options into the different types of integrity they enforce:

Integrity Type	SQL Server Options
Entity	**PRIMARY KEY** constraint **UNIQUE** constraint Identity property Unique indexes
Domain	Datatypes Defaults Rules **DEFAULT** constraint **CHECK** constraint **NOT NULL** constraint
Referential	Triggers **FOREIGN KEY** constraint **REFERENCES** constraint

Table Continued on Following Page

Integrity Type	SQL Server Options
User-defined	Rules Triggers Stored procedures **WITH CHECK OPTION** on **VIEWS**

Declarative Integrity Enforcement

As we mentioned earlier, SQL Server provides many restrictions which we can add to tables and views using the Data Definition Language (DDL). These restrictions are collectively known as **constraints** and **properties**. In this section, we'll discuss all of the constraints and properties available to DBAs when you're creating or altering tables and when you're creating views.

Creating a Sample Database

To illustrate the declarative features available, let's look at a sample database consisting of seven tables: Customers, Products, Salesperson, Orders, Sales_region, Terms_code and State_code. The database is used to keep track of a company's products, salespeople, customers and customer purchases. Each of the tables is closely related (much as they are in any business). Below is a bullet list of the relationships depicted in the sample database, followed by an entity relationship diagram of the database. Note that the integrity of the data in this database is enforced solely through the use of constraints.

- ▲ Order – Product relationship: you can't sell something that doesn't exist.
- ▲ Customer – Order relationship: you can't sell to someone who doesn't exist.
- ▲ Salesperson – Order relationship: someone must sell the product to the customer.
- ▲ Salesperson – Sales_Region relationship: salespeople belong to sales regions.
- ▲ Customer – Terms_code relationship: customers must pay for goods based on their ability to do so.
- ▲ Customer – State_code relationship: customers belong to (live in) a state.

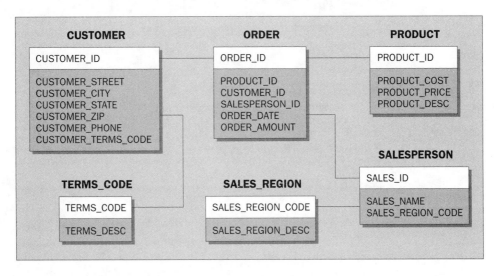

We can use the SQL **CREATE TABLE** statement to create the tables and constraints in our sample database:

```
CREATE TABLE TERMS_CODE
(
TERMS_CODE      INTEGER      NOT NULL IDENTITY(1,1)
                CONSTRAINT PK_TERMS_CODE PRIMARY KEY CLUSTERED,
TERMS_DESC      CHAR(30)
)
GO
```

```
CREATE TABLE SALES_REGION_CODE
(
SALES_REGION_CODE   INTEGER      NOT NULL IDENTITY(1,1)
                CONSTRAINT PK_SALES_REGION_CODE PRIMARY KEY CLUSTERED,
SALES_REGION_DESC   CHAR(30)
)
GO
```

```
CREATE TABLE STATE_CODE
(
STATE           CHAR(02) NOT NULL
                CONSTRAINT PK_STATE_CODE PRIMARY KEY CLUSTERED,
STATE_DESC          CHAR(25)
)
GO
```

```
CREATE TABLE CUSTOMER
(
CUSTOMER_ID         INTEGER      NOT NULL IDENTITY(1,1)
                        CONSTRAINT PK_CUSTOMER PRIMARY KEY CLUSTERED,
CUSTOMER_STREET         CHAR(35),
CUSTOMER_CITY       CHAR(25),
CUSTOMER_STATE      CHAR(02)     NOT NULL
                        REFERENCES  STATE_CODE(STATE),
CUSTOMER_ZIP        CHAR(5)
                        CHECK (CUSTOMER_ZIP LIKE
                        '[0-9][0-9][0-9][0-9][0-9]'),
CUSTOMER_PHONE      CHAR(10)
                        CHECK (CUSTOMER_PHONE LIKE
            '[0-9][0-9][0-9][0-9][0-9][0-9][0-9][0-9][0-9][0-9]'),
CUSTOMER_TERMS_CODE INTEGER          DEFAULT 1
                        REFERENCES  TERMS_CODE(TERMS_CODE)
)
GO
```

```
CREATE TABLE PRODUCT
(
PRODUCT_ID              INTEGER      NOT NULL IDENTITY(1,1)
                        CONSTRAINT PK_PRODUCT PRIMARY KEY CLUSTERED,
PRODUCT_COST        DOUBLE PRECISION  DEFAULT 0.00,
PRODUCT_PRICE       DOUBLE PRECISION  DEFAULT 0.00,
PRODUCT_DESC        CHAR(50)
)
GO
```

```
CREATE TABLE SALESPERSON
(
SALES_ID              INTEGER      NOT NULL IDENTITY
                        CONSTRAINT PK_SALESPERSON PRIMARY KEY CLUSTERED,
SALES_NAME                CHAR(35),
SALES_REGION_CODE    CHAR(2)
                      CHECK (SALES_REGION_CODE LIKE
                      '[NE],[SE],[MW],[NW],[SW]'),
)
GO
```

```
CREATE TABLE ORDERS
(
ORDER_ID              INTEGER          NOT NULL IDENTITY(10000,1)
                        CONSTRAINT PK_ORDER PRIMARY KEY CLUSTERED,
PRODUCT_ID               INTEGER              NOT NULL
 REFERENCES PRODUCT(PRODUCT_ID),
CUSTOMER_ID           INTEGER            NOT NULL
 REFERENCES CUSTOMER(CUSTOMER_ID),
SALESPERSON_ID        INTEGER            NOT NULL
 REFERENCES SALESPERSON(SALES_ID),
ORDER_DATE              DATETIME        DEFAULT GETDATE()
                      CHECK NOT FOR REPLICATION (ORDER_DATE => GETDATE()),
ORDER_AMOUNT          DOUBLE PRECISION   DEFAULT 0.00
)
GO
```

Adding Constraints using the CREATE TABLE Statement

The example database provides a look at all of the properties and constraints available in SQL Server. Let's look at each of them in more detail and see how we can use them to enforce the integrity of the database.

PRIMARY KEY

In the sample database, the four main tables have a Primary Key. In each case, the key is based on the identity columns **CUSTOMER_ID**, **PRODUCT_ID**, **SALES_ID** and **ORDER_ID**. The seed parameter in the orders table, **ORDER_ID**s in this table will start at '10000'.

UNIQUE

UNIQUE provides integrity for a column or columns. A unique column is like the Primary Key in that it ensures that each row in a table has a unique value in the column. Unlike **PRIMARY KEY**, however, a table can contain multiple **UNIQUE** constraints and columns within **UNIQUE** constraints can be NULL. A **UNIQUE** constraint will allow one row in the database with a NULL value in that column or set of columns.

To enforce **UNIQUE** constraints, SQL Server creates a unique index on the column or columns. By default, the indexes created for the **UNIQUE** constraint are non-clustered unless otherwise specified.

In the sample database, we didn't use the **UNIQUE** constraint as it wasn't necessary, but if, for example, we needed to ensure that each combination of **ORDER_ID** and **PRODUCT_ID** were unique, the code would be as follows:

```
CREATE TABLE ORDERS
(
ORDER_ID        INTEGER        NOT NULL IDENTITY(10000,1)
                        CONSTRAINT PK_ORDER PRIMARY KEY CLUSTERED,
PRODUCT_ID          INTEGER           NOT NULL
 REFERENCES PRODUCT(PRODUCT_ID),
CUSTOMER_ID         INTEGER           NOT NULL
 REFERENCES CUSTOMER(CUSTOMER_ID),
SALESPERSON_ID      INTEGER           NOT NULL
 REFERENCES SALESPERSON(SALES_ID),
ORDER_DATE          DATETIME      DEFAULT GETDATE(),
ORDER_AMOUNT        DOUBLE PRECISION   DEFAULT 0.00
CONSTRAINT U_ORDER UNIQUE NONCLUSTERED (ORDER_ID, PRODUCT_ID)
)
```

DEFAULT

Defaults allow you to specify a value that SQL Server assigns a column during an insert when no value is given. A **DEFAULT** constraint can contain constants, functions and built-in functions that don't require arguments or NULL. You can't create **DEFAULT** constraints on timestamp columns or on columns with user-defined datatypes that have a created default bound to them.

The advantages to using a **DEFAULT** constraint instead of a default (created with the **CREATE DEFAULT** statement) are that it requires no binding or unbinding and it's removed when the table is dropped. The disadvantage is that you must define the same default value for each column that will be using it.

In the sample database, there were several examples of the use of **DEFAULT** constraint. In the product table, **PRODUCT_PRICE** and **PRODUCT_COST** all default to 0.00. In the orders table, **ORDER_DATE** defaults to the current system date by using the system-supplied function, **GetDate()**.

> **During an insert, you can override the default by using an implicit NULL if the column allows.**

CHECK

The keyword **CHECK** enforces domain integrity by limiting the possible values that can be entered into a column. The expression can't contain subqueries and must evaluate to a TRUE or FALSE. **CHECK** constraints are automatically bound to the columns for which they are defined. You can only define one **CHECK** constraint per table column. If you define a check for multiple columns, you must define it as a table-level constraint. If a **CHECK** constraint and a rule exist for a column, both will be evaluated. (We'll take a look at rules later in the chapter.) In the sample database, we use **CHECK** in several different ways.

Let's look at each example, starting with the customer table. Here, it's used to ensure that **CUSTOMER_ZIP** consists of five numeric digits and **CUSTOMER_PHONE** is ten numeric digits:

```
...
CUSTOMER_ZIP          CHAR(5)
                      CHECK (CUSTOMER_ZIP LIKE
                             '[0-9][0-9][0-9][0-9][0-9]'),
CUSTOMER_PHONE        CHAR(10)
                          CHECK (CUSTOMER_PHONE LIKE
                 '[0-9][0-9][0-9][0-9][0-9][0-9][0-9][0-9][0-9][0-9]'),
...
```

In the salesperson table, it's used to validate **SALES_REGION_CODE** against a list of values:

```
SALES_REGION_CODE     CHAR(2)
                      CHECK (SALES_REGION_CODE LIKE
                      '[NE],[SE],[MW],[NW],[SW]'),
```

In the orders table, **CHECK** is used to ensure the **ORDER_DATE** is never greater than the current server date:

```
ORDER_DATE                  DATETIME        DEFAULT GETDATE()
                      CHECK NOT FOR REPLICATION (ORDER_DATE => GETDATE()),
```

If you don't want the **CHECK** constraint to be enforced during the distribution process used by replication, you can use an optional **NOT FOR REPLICATION** clause. This allows the distribution process to violate the given constraint, but the check will be enforced for all other users. (See Chapter 11 for more information on replication.) In the sample database, the **ORDER_DATE** check isn't enforced if the 'user' making the change is a replication process.

References (Foreign Key)

This constraint allows you to ensure that Foreign Keys in a child table match the Primary Key of the parent table. If you recall from earlier in this chapter, the customer table is related to the order table due to a business rule which states: 'You can't sell a product to someone who isn't a customer'. In our sample database, the **CUSTOMER_ID** is a Foreign Key in the order table. As you can see from the figure, the order table references the customer table to ensure only valid **CUSTOMER_ID**s are assigned to an order record:

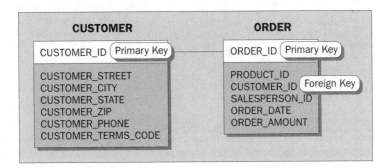

When defined, the number of columns and datatypes of each column specified in the **FOREIGN KEY** clause must match the **REFERENCES** clause.

In the sample database, this constraint may be the most important. The orders table relies heavily on this constraint to ensure that an order entered into the system has a valid **PRODUCT_ID**, **CUSTOMER_ID** and **SALESPERSON_ID**.

153

> It's a good idea to use the ALTER TABLE statement to create Foreign Keys. If you
> don't, creating tables can be a problem because a referenced table may or may not
> already exist when the database is first created. This is often referred to as the
> 'chicken and egg' problem.

Adding and Dropping Constraints using the ALTER TABLE Statement

The **ALTER TABLE** statement also provides several options which allow you to add and drop constraints. There are also check options which govern the addition of constraints to a table and data modifications within a view.

ADD

This adds a column or table-level constraint to an existing table. The syntax is similar to the **CREATE TABLE** syntax. Below are a few examples demonstrating this. The first example adds a Primary Key to the table **TABLE_ORDERS** on the column **ORDER_ID**. The name of the key is **PK_ORDER**. The index created to enforce this key will be clustered. (We added this constraint to the table as we created it.)

```
ALTER TABLE ORDERS
ADD
CONSTRAINT PK_ORDER PRIMARY KEY CLUSTERED (ORDER_ID)
```

The next example adds a Foreign Key to the orders table on the column **PRODUCT_ID**. This key will ensure that all values in the **PRODUCT_ID** column exist in the **PRODUCT_ID** column in the product table. The name of the key is **FK_PRODUCT_ID.**

```
ALTER TABLE ORDERS
ADD
CONSTRAINT FK_PRODUCT_ID  FOREIGN KEY (PRODUCT_ID) REFERENCES PRODUCT(PRODUCT_ID)
```

The final example adds the default of the current date to the column **ORDER_DATE** in the orders table. Like our first example, we added this property when we first created the orders table.

```
ALTER TABLE ORDERS
ADD
DEFAULT GETDATE() FOR ORDER_DATE
```

DROP

DROP removes a column or table-level constraint from an existing table. To drop a constraint, you must know its name. If you didn't enter the name of the constraint when you created it, you'll need to use **sp_help** or **sp_helpconstraint** to retrieve the system-generated constraint names. Here's an example.

```
ALTER TABLE ORDERS
DROP
CONSTRAINT U_ORDER
```

This dropped the **UNIQUE** constraint **U_ORDER** which we added earlier using an **ALTER TABLE** statement.

WITH NOCHECK

This allows you to add **CHECK** or **FOREIGN KEY** constraints to a table without verifying existing data for constraint violations. **PRIMARY KEY** and **UNIQUE** constraints are always checked. For example, on May 1st, a new business rule will go into effect stating that orders must be greater than $10.00, but any orders prior to this date can be of any amount. On May 1st, a DBA could run the following command to comply with this new rule:

```
ALTER TABLE ORDERS
WITH NOCHECK
ADD
CONSTRAINT CK_ORDER_AMOUNT CHECK (ORDER_AMOUNT >= 10.00)
```

WITH CHECK OPTION on VIEWS

This forces all data modifications executed against the view to adhere to the criteria set within the **SELECT** statement defining the view. When you modify a row through a view, the **WITH CHECK OPTION** guarantees that the data will remain visible through the view after the modification has been committed. Here's an example of a view created with this option:

```
CREATE VIEW SALESPERSON_1001
AS
SELECT ORDER_ID, PRODUCT_ID, ORDER_DATE, ORDER_AMT, SALESPERSON_ID
FROM ORDERS
WHERE SALESPERSON_ID = 1001
WITH CHECK OPTION
```

This shows a view, named **SALESPERSON_1001**, which will only allow data to be modified for **SALESPERSON_ID 1001**.

Using SQL Enterprise Manager to Add Constraints and Properties to Tables

We can assign all of the table and column level declaratives described above through the Manage Tables window in SQL Enterprise Manager. We'll briefly describe how to use the Manager to add data integrity to your tables. For this example, let's look at the customer table in our sample database:

Use this window to add columns and their defaults and to state whether or not NULLs are allowed. To add table constraints, press the advanced options button on the toolbar. The following figures show what the Advanced options tabbed interface looks like:

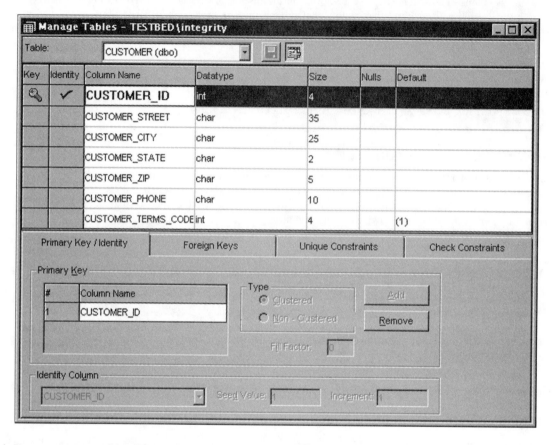

As you can see, to add a Primary Key to a table, simply select the columns and click the Add button. Similarly, to make a column the identity column, choose the column from the drop-down list and enter the Seed Value and the Increment.

> **If you add identity columns with Enterprise Manager 6.0, the Identity property is lost.**

To add Foreign Keys, specify the key columns and choose the Primary Key in a related table. In this example, the column **CUSTOMER_STATE** references the column **STATE** in the state table:

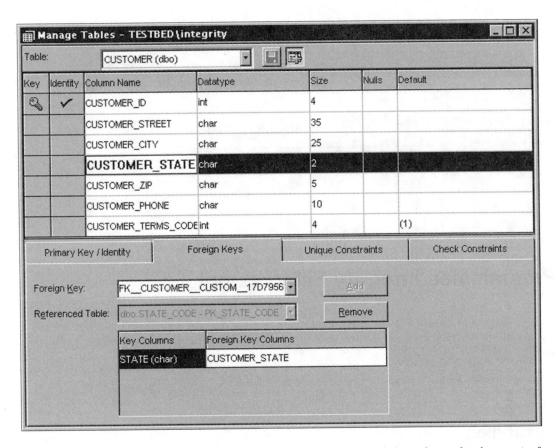

To add **UNIQUE** constraints to a table, choose the column or columns and if no clustered indexes exist for the table, choose the type of index to be created in order to enforce uniqueness. As you can see, the customer table doesn't have a **UNIQUE** constraint:

You can add **CHECK** constraints to tables by specifying a name and an expression:

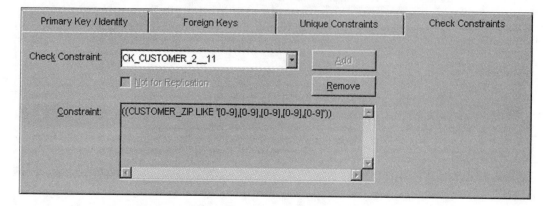

Programmed Integrity Enforcement

So far, we've learned how to declare data integrity within the Data Definition Language. Although this is a powerful method available to DBAs, it has limitations. Creating database objects such as rules, triggers and defaults allows the DBA to create reusable and complex methods of enforcing data integrity at the server level.

In this section, we'll discuss all of the objects that can be bound to columns and tables in an effort to ensure the consistency and accuracy of your data.

Datatypes

Datatypes determine what kind of information can be stored in a column, and are used as stored-procedure parameters or as local variables. In SQL Server, all system datatype names are case-insensitive. This allows table definitions, variables and procedure parameters to include upper- or lower-case datatype definitions.

System-supplied Datatypes

Datatype	Range	Sample
char(n)	<= 255 characters	'Mr. Jones'
varchar(n)	<=255 characters	'Garcia Electronics'
text	BLOB <= 2,147,483,647 characters in multiples of 2K	'Mr. Garcia'
binary(n)	<=255 characters	0xa2f1
varbinary(n)	<=255 characters	0xb3d1
image	BLOB <= 2,147,483,647 characters in multiples of 2K	0xa2f1 …
bit	0 or 1 (False or True)	1
int	-2,147,483,647 to +2,147,483,647	278

Table Continued on Following Page

Datatype	Range	Sample
smallint	-32767 to +32767	5890
tinyint	0 to 255	12
float(precision)	N/A	523.45890
double precision	N/A	345.67843
real	N/A	566.233
numeric (precision, scale)	-10^{38} to $+10^{38}$	523.45890
decimal (precision, scale)	-10^{38} to $+10^{38}$	523.45890
money	-$922,337,203,685,477.5807 to +$922,337,203,685,477.5807	$100.23
smallmoney	-$214,748.3647 to +$214,748.3647	$100.23
datetime	Jan 1, 1753 to Dec 31 9999 (accurate to 3 milliseconds)	'Apr 16, 1965 14:23.12'
smalldatetime	Jan 1, 1900 to Jun 6, 2079	'Apr 16, 1965 14:23'
timestamp	N/A	N/A

User-defined Datatypes

You can also define your own datatypes to supplement those supplied by the system. For example, we could define a **us_state_code** datatype as 2 characters **(char(2))**. Once we've defined it, we can use it to define columns in any table. The advantage of user-defined datatypes is that we can bound rules and defaults to them and use them in multiple tables. This ensures consistency across tables and also eliminates the need to have these checks done by front-end applications. Because datatypes are case-insensitive, you can't use identical user-defined datatype names with different capitalization.

Using Transact-SQL to Create a New Datatype

This is the code for creating a new datatype:

```
sp_addtype us_state_code, 'char(2)', NULL
```

> Note that the type is enclosed in quotation marks. This is because there's punctuation in the definition. The same goes for spaces.

In this example, **us_state_code** is allowed to be NULL. The next example creates the same datatype but doesn't allow NULL. This time, NOT NULL also has to be enclosed by quotation marks:

```
sp_addtype us_state_code, 'char(2)', 'NOT NULL'
```

To drop a user-defined datatype, use the system-supplied stored procedure **sp_droptype**. You can't drop a datatype if it's referenced anywhere in the database, whether it be as a variable or a parameter to a stored procedure. This example drops the datatype **us_state_code**:

```
sp_droptype us_state_code
```

We can also rename a user-defined datatype. To rename the datatype **us_state_code** to **us_states**, the code is as follows:

```
sp_rename us_state_code, us_states
```

> If a system-supplied datatype is found within a table, view or procedure definition that conflicts with a user-defined datatype, the user-defined datatype will be ignored.

Using Enterprise Manager to Create a New Datatype

To add user-defined datatypes using SQL Enterprise Manager, use the Manage User-Defined Datatypes window shown:

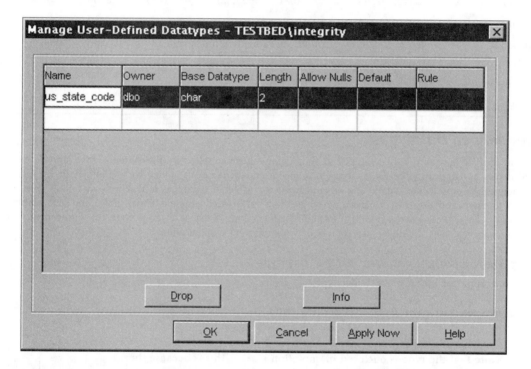

Defaults

Defaults allow you to specify a value that SQL Server inserts into a column when no value is given, be it any constant, built-in function, mathematical expression, or global variable. A default can't reference a database object. For example, the current date could be set as the default value for an **order_date** column. If a value for **order_date** isn't specified during an insert operation, SQL Server automatically sets the column equal to the current date. The code for creating this default is:

```
CREATE DEFAULT date_default AS getdate()
```

Getdate() is a SQL Server function that returns the current date and time. Once we've created the default, we need to bind it to a column. The code to bind it to the **order_date** column in the orders table would be as follows (this has already been done in the **CREATE TABLE** statements):

```
sp_bindefault date_default, 'orders.order_date'
```

Creating a Default using the SQL Enterprise Manager

Rather than writing these create and bind statements, you could do the same work using SQL Enterprise Manager. If you select the Defaults option from the Manage menu, you can first create the default:

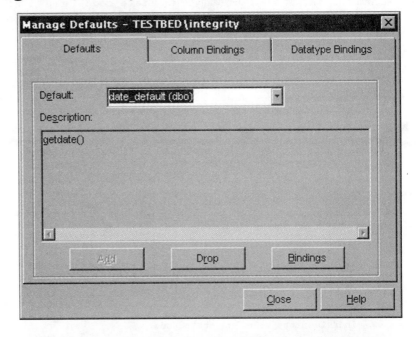

And then, from the same dialog, bind it to a column:

Here, we've again bound the default to the ORDER_DATE column in the orders table. An optional parameter of the stored procedure **sp_bindefault** is **future only**. Existing columns of the user-defined datatype inherit the new default unless they have a default bound directly to them or unless the **futureonly** option is used. New columns of the user-defined datatype always inherit the default.

We can also associate a default with a user-defined datatype. For example, we could associate a default value of **NY** with the datatype **us_state_code**. Doing this automatically binds the default **NY** to any column in the database where the datatype **us_state_code** is used. A default must be compatible with the column it's bound to and can't violate any rules that may be bound to the column.

Rules

Whereas datatypes define the type of data which can be inserted into a column, rules ensure that the value meets a set of criteria. Rules can require that a value falls within a range, matches a particular pattern or matches one entry in a list of values.

A rule can contain any expression that's valid in a SQL **WHERE** clause (but can't refer to column names). We can bind one rule to more than one column or user datatype and, once we've bound it, it's used automatically.

For example, in our state table, we decide that 'a customer can only be located in the states of Arizona, California, Illinois, Texas or Washington'. We can bind this rule to the **Customer_State** column in the customer table in our database. Here's the code for this rule:

```
create rule state_rule as @state in ('AZ','CA','IL','TX','WA')
sp_bindrule state_rule, 'Customer.Customer_State'
```

You can also bind rules to user-defined datatypes:

```
sp_bindrule state_rule, us_state_code
```

As there was with the stored procedure **sp_binddefault**, there is also an optional **FUTUREONLY** parameter of **sp_bindrule.** We can only use this option when we're binding a rule to a user-defined datatype. It prevents existing columns of a user-defined datatype from inheriting the new rule. If specified, any existing rule bound to that datatype will be bound to any existing columns of that datatype that don't already have a rule bound to them. To bind the rule **state_rule** to any columns with the datatype **us_state_code** that are created in the future, we would use this code:

```
sp_bindrule state_rule, us_state_code, FUTUREONLY
```

We can unbind a rule from a column or a user-defined datatype at any time. The code for unbinding the rule **state_rule** from the column **Customer_State** is:

```
sp_unbindrule 'Customer.Customer_State'
```

To unbind a rule from a user-defined datatype the code is as follows:

```
sp_unbindrule us_state_code
```

> **You don't have to unbind a rule from a column or datatype in order to bind another rule to that object. The new rule will automatically replace the old one.**

To drop a rule, use the **DROP RULE** statement. You can't drop a rule that is bound to any column or datatype in the database. If a rule is bound when you try to drop it, SQL Server will display an error message. This is the procedure for dropping a rule:

```
sp_unbindrule us_state_code
go
DROP RULE state_rule
```

First, this unbinds the rule from the datatype **us_state_code**, then drops it. Once again, we can do all this from the SQL Enterprise Manager and the Manage Rules dialog:

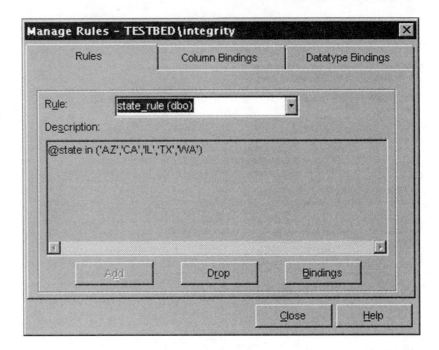

Stored Procedures

Stored procedures are precompiled SQL statements stored on the server. This means that they are checked for syntax and compiled only once, which makes them faster than dynamic SQL queries. They can be a powerful tool for enforcing data integrity for several reasons:

- ▲ They can contain complex business logic which can be shared by all applications to ensure that data is modified consistently.

- ▲ Users can be granted execute permission to a stored procedure even if they don't have permissions to the tables and views the procedure reference, thus adding another level of security to the database.

- ▲ As business rules change, the DBA can be sure that all applications which access the data are using the same set of rules, because these rules are stored at the server level, not at the application level.

Creating Stored Procedures

We create stored procedures using the **CREATE PROC** statement. Here's is the syntax:

```
CREATE PROC [owner.]procedure_name [;number]
    [@parameter1 [,@parameter2 ] … [@parameter255]]
[[FOR REPLICATION | WITH RECOMPILE] | WITH ENCRYPTION]
AS sql_statements
```

The following statement would create a procedure that would extract information about a specific customer, based on the customer ID provided:

```
CREATE PROC Get_Customer @cust_id integer
AS
SELECT CUSTOMER_ID, CUSTOMER_STREET, CUSTOMER_CITY, CUSTOMER_STATE,
       CUSTOMER_ZIP
  FROM CUSTOMER
 WHERE CUSTOMER_ID = @cust_id
```

Let's step through the basic structure of this stored procedure.

; number

;number is an optional integer used to group procedures of the same name so that you can drop them together with a single **DROP** statement. For example, two procedures used in one application could be called **update_cust;1** and **update_cust;2**. To execute the first procedure in the group, the code would be:

```
EXEC update_cust;1
```

The disadvantage of using the **;number** option is that you must drop the entire group of stored procedures at the same time.

WITH ENCRYPTION

This option encrypts the SQL statements of the stored procedure as it stores them in the Syscomments table on the server. When a stored procedure is compiled, the actual text or source code used to create the procedure is stored in the Syscomments table in the database the procedure was created in. You can then select this code back out of the table by using the stored procedure's *object_id* (the unique number assigned each database object). If, however, the stored procedure is compiled with the **WITH ENCRYPTION** option, the source is encrypted and can never be retrieved from the database (in a readable format) again. For this reason, it's very important to save the stored procedure's source to a text file prior to compiling with this option.

WITH RECOMPILE

This option tells SQL to not save an execution plan for this procedure and recompile it each time it's executed. You would only use it when the tables the stored procedure references are constantly changing is such a way that the execute plan the server chooses the first time it executes the stored procedure will be drastically different than subsequent executes or when the parameters being passed to the procedure may change the optimal execution plan. You should use this option sparingly.

FOR REPLICATION

This creates a stored procedure that can only be executed by replication. You can't use the **RECOMPILE** and **REPLICATION** options together.

Parameters

We have the option of declaring one or more parameters for a stored procedure. This is the syntax for defining a parameter:

@parameter_name datatype [= default | NULL] [OUTPUT]

Parameters can be passed in and out of stored procedures.

Passing Parameters In

As this is an important topic, we'll now look at it in greater detail, first considering how to pass a parameter into a stored procedure. To enable a stored procedure to accept parameters, we must declare the parameters at the top of the procedure. We need to preface all parameters with a **@** symbol and give them a datatype and length (if needed). Here's an example of a stored procedure that has one input parameter, **@orderdate** which is a **SmallDateTime** parameter.

```
CREATE PROC GET_DAILY_ORDERS @orderdate SmallDateTime
AS
SELECT SUM(ORDER_AMOUNT)
  FROM ORDERS
 WHERE ORDER_DATE = @orderdate
```

This is the statement to run this procedure:

```
EXEC GET_DAILY_ORDERS '12/1/96'
```

You must supply the value of each parameter to the procedure when it's executed. You can omit parameters where defaults were defined, but you can't interrupt the sequence. In other words, if the procedure has four parameters and all the parameters have defaults, you can't skip the 2nd parameter if you need to supply the 3rd and 4th.

We can make **@orderdate** an optional parameter in **GET_DAILY_ORDERS** by assigning it a default. The following example assigns today's date to the parameter. If no value is passed in when the procedure is executed, the procedure will use the current date as the value for **@orderdate**.

```
Drop Proc GET_DAILY_ORDERS
GO

CREATE PROC GET_DAILY_ORDERS
@orderdate SmallDateTime = NULL
AS
If @orderdate = NULL
  SELECT @orderdate = getdate()

SELECT SUM(ORDER_AMOUNT)
  FROM ORDERS
 WHERE ORDER_DATE = @orderdate
```

165

You can run this procedure either with or without the date:

```
EXEC GET_DAILY_ORDERS '12/1/96'
```

Passing Parameters Out

As we mentioned earlier, we can also return parameters from a stored procedure. The syntax is the same as for input parameters with the addition of the **OUTPUT** keyword. This feature can be extremely useful if you need to analyze and/or act upon data retrieved using a stored procedure. Let's rewrite this stored procedure so that the daily order amount is placed into an output variable to see how this parameter can be used in a batch:

```
Drop Proc GET_DAILY_ORDERS
GO

CREATE PROC GET_DAILY_ORDERS
@order_amt money OUTPUT,
@orderdate SmallDateTime = NULL

AS
If @orderdate = NULL
  select @orderdate = getdate()

SELECT  @order_amt=SUM(ORDER_AMOUNT)
   FROM ORDERS
  WHERE ORDER_DATE = @orderdate
```

The procedure could be run as follows and just the order amount would be retrieved:

```
DECLARE @order_amt money
EXEC GET_DAILY_ORDERS @order_amt OUT, '12/1/96'
SELECT @order_amt
```

Alternatively, we could set up a simple condition which would result in a message depending on the value of the parameter:

```
DECLARE @order_amt money
EXEC GET_DAILY_ORDERS @order_amt OUT
IF @order_amt > 1000
    PRINT 'Great day!'
ELSE
    PRINT 'We need to do more marketing!'
```

Notice that the execute statement must first declare a variable of the same datatype as the output parameter and the keyword **OUTPUT** must be included so that SQL Server knows to make the parameter value available. This may seem relatively trivial, but we can now use this parameter passing to start trapping errors.

Returning a Status from a Procedure

All stored procedures automatically return a **status code**. A status code is an integer which SQL Server makes available to the calling batch. The code indicates whether the stored procedure was executed successfully and, if it wasn't, what error was detected. SQL Server status codes range from 0, a successful return to -99. The table shows the status codes currently used by SQL Server:

Status Code	Meaning
0	Successful
-1	Object missing
-2	Type mismatch
-3	Process chosen as deadlock victim
-4	Permission error
-5	Syntax error
-6	User error
-7	Resource error
-8	Non-fatal internal inconsistency
-9	System limit was reached
-10	Fatal internal inconsistency
-11	Fatal internal inconsistency
-12	Corrupt table or index
-13	Corrupt database
-14	Hardware error
-15 to -99	Reserved for future use

In addition to these status codes, you can use your own codes.

To use status codes, you need to define conditions within the stored procedure and then associate codes to those conditions. It's important that any user-defined codes are known by both the procedure and any batches that call them so that the proper actions can be taken. The stored procedure must also use the keyword **RETURN** so that the status code is made available to the calling batch.

Let's rewrite the **GET_DAILY_ORDERS** procedure to include return codes:

```
Drop Proc GET_DAILY_ORDERS
GO

CREATE PROC GET_DAILY_ORDERS
@order_amt money OUTPUT,
@orderdate SmallDateTime = NULL

AS
DECLARE   @stat_code integer

SELECT @stat_code = 0

IF @orderdate = NULL
  select @orderdate = getdate()
ELSE
```

```
    SELECT @stat_code = 100

  SELECT @order_amt=SUM(ORDER_AMOUNT)
    FROM ORDERS
  WHERE ORDER_DATE = @orderdate

  IF @@error = 0
    RETURN @stat_code
  ELSE
    RETURN @@error
```

Here, the status code is first initialized to 0 (success). If the user specifies an **@orderdate** other than today (it's assumed that no one will pass in today's date), set that status code to 100. Before that status code is returned from the procedure, the global variable **@@error** is checked to make sure that no errors were encountered. If there was an error, the status code is set equal to that error and returned.

We can run the procedure like this:

```
DECLARE @order_amt money
DECLARE @ret_code int
EXEC @ret_code = GET_DAILY_ORDERS @order_amt OUT, '12/1/96'

IF @ret_code > 0
  BEGIN
    If @order_amt > 1000
       print 'Great day!'
    else
       print 'We need to do more marketing'

    If @ret_code = 100
       print 'Important: This data is NOT today's sales.'

  END
ELSE
    print 'An Error was encountered, Please Try Again!'
```

Notice that, to use the status code, we must declare a variable (**DECLARE @ret_code int**) to accept the code. We can also create stored procedures from the Enterprise Manager via the Manage Stored Procedures option in the Manage menu.

Dropping Stored Procedures

To remove a stored procedure from the current database, use the **DROP** statement. If it can't find the procedure in the current database, SQL Server attempts to drop it from the *master* database.

You can drop a procedure group (procedures with the same name but a different number) using a single **DROP PROC** statement. You can't drop one procedure in a group without dropping the whole group (**DROP PROC update_cust;2** isn't allowed). Here's the syntax for this statement:

```
DROP PROC [owner.]procedure_name
```

This example statement would drop a stored procedure:

```
DROP PROC Get_Customer
```

You can also do this directly from the Enterprise Manager:

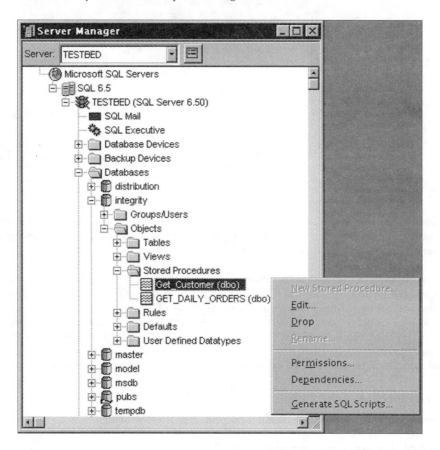

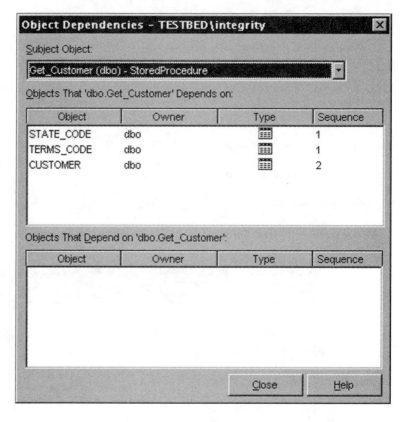

You should be careful to first check on any dependencies that might prevent you from dropping the stored procedure. You can do this via the Object Dependencies dialog:

Triggers

Triggers are nothing more than specialized stored procedures. The primary difference between the two is that stored procedures must be called to be executed, whereas triggers are automatically executed (triggered) when you try to modify data.

Triggers can prevent incorrect or inconsistent changes to data. They do this by performing an action when a change is attempted to data. We can use triggers to cascade a data modification across related tables, rollback transactions and even issue messages to users via e-mail. The key advantage of triggers is that we can use them to bind complex business rules to table columns. No matter who or what is attempting to modify the data, the DBA can be sure that data integrity and business rules are being enforced.

The maximum number of triggers allowed on a table is three (insert, delete and update).

Creating Triggers

You create triggers using the **CREATE TRIGGER** statement. Here's the syntax:

```
CREATE TRIGGER [owner.]trigger_name
ON [owner.]table_name
FOR { INSERT | UPDATE | DELETE }
[WITH ENCRYPTION]
```

```
AS
[IF UPDATE (column_name)…]
sql_statements
```

Here's an example of a delete trigger which checks to ensure that a product isn't deleted when there is an order for it in the order table. If an order exists, disregard the delete statement.

```
CREATE TRIGGER Delete_PRODUCT
ON ORDERS FOR DELETE
AS
IF EXISTS (SELECT * FROM ORDERS, deleted
   WHERE ORDERS.PRODUCT_ID = deleted.PRODUCT_ID)
BEGIN
   ROLLBACK TRANSACTION
   PRINT "Cannot delete this product, an order exists!"
END
```

This trigger first checks to see whether an order exists for the deleted product. It does this by joining **ORDERS** with the deleted table. Deleted is a logical table that is only available from within the fired trigger. If the join is successful, the transaction is rolled back and the user receives an error.

Insert

An insert trigger is executed (fired) when you try to insert rows into a table. When the insert trigger is executed, the new rows are added to the table and into the logical table inserted at the same time. The inserted table can only be referenced from inside the trigger.

The rows in the inserted table are always duplicates of the rows inserted into the table. This allows the user to compare the two sets of rows and perform any necessary actions.

```
CREATE TRIGGER Order_Insert
ON ORDERS
FOR INSERT
AS
UPDATE PRODUCT
SET PRODUCT_QTY = 0
FROM PRODUCT, inserted
WHERE PRODUCT.PRODUCT_ID = inserted.PRODUCT_ID
```

Delete

A delete trigger is executed or fired when you try to delete a row or rows from a table. When the delete trigger is executed, rows are deleted from the table and inserted into the deleted table. The deleted table can only be referenced from inside the trigger.

```
CREATE TRIGGER Product_Delete
ON PRODUCT
FOR DELETE
AS
IF EXISTS (SELECT * FROM ORDERS, deleted
        WHERE ORDERS.PRODUCT_ID = deleted.PRODUCT_ID)
BEGIN
   ROLLBACK TRANSACTION
   PRINT "Cannot delete this product, it has open orders!"
END
```

171

> The delete trigger doesn't execute for the TRUNCATE TABLE statement. This is because the statement removes all the rows from the table without logging the information to the transaction log.

Update

An update trigger is fired when you try to **UPDATE** a row or rows in a table. When the trigger is executed, the original rows are moved to the deleted table and the new updated rows are moved to the inserted table.

```
CREATE TRIGGER TermsCode_Update
ON TERMS_CODE
FOR UPDATE
AS
UPDATE CUSTOMER
   SET CUSTOMER_TERMS_CODE = inserted.TERMS_CODE
FROM CUSTOMER, deleted
WHERE CUSTOMER.CUSTOMER_TERMS_CODE = deleted.TERMS_CODE
```

This example ensures that the **TERMS_CODE** column in the customer table always references a valid record in the **TERMS_CODE** table. It does this by updating the **TERMS_CODE** column in the customer table with the new **TERMS_CODE** where **CUSTOMER.CUSTOMER_TERMS_CODE** is equal to the old value.

Other Options

There are a couple of useful options that you can use within triggers:

▲ **WITH ENCRYPTION**: This option encrypts the SQL Statements of the trigger when storing them in the Syscomments table on the server.

▲ **IF UPDATE**: This option tests for an **INSERT** or **UPDATE** action to one or more specified columns.

Creating Triggers with the Enterprise Manager

We can create triggers from the Enterprise Manager, once again from the Manage menu:

```
Manage Triggers - TESTBED\integrity                              _ □ X

Table:   PRODUCT (dbo)        ▼   Trigger:   ⬚X Product_Delete (dbo)   ▼   ▷  ⬚

if exists (select * from sysobjects
        where id = object_id('dbo.Product_Delete')
        and sysstat & 0xf = 8)
        drop trigger dbo.Product_Delete
GO

CREATE TRIGGER Product_Delete
ON PRODUCT
FOR DELETE
AS
IF EXISTS (SELECT * FROM ORDERS, deleted
                WHERE ORDERS.PRODUCT_ID = deleted.PRODUCT_ID)
BEGIN
        ROLLBACK TRANSACTION
        PRINT "Cannot delete this product, it has open orders!"
END
```

Nested Triggers

If a trigger performs an **INSERT**, **UPDATE** or **DELETE** on another table that has a trigger defined for that action, that trigger will also fire. This is called a **nested trigger**. Triggers are limited to 16 levels of nesting. To avoid exceeding this limit, we can check a system-provided variable, **@@nestlevel**. There's a couple of points worth remembering about nested triggers:

- A trigger can't see the contents of other triggers' inserted or deleted tables.
- We can disable nesting using the system-provided stored procedure **sp_configure**.

Dropping Triggers

To remove a trigger from the current database, use the **DROP** statement. Here's the syntax:

```
DROP TRIGGER [owner.]trigger_name
```

An actual example would be as follows:

```
DROP TRIGGER TermsCode_Update
```

Triggers and Data Integrity

As we saw above, triggers can enforce data integrity by cascading changes to tables throughout the database. We also saw that we can use triggers to enforce referential integrity by validating Foreign Keys and ensuring that appropriate actions are taken when cascading data modifications need to occur.

> **A trigger will not fire if a constraint has been violated.**

Multiple Uses of Triggers

We can use a single trigger for **Insert**, **Update** and **Delete**. This is useful if a business requirement is needed to log all modifications to a table. In such a case, the trigger could insert a record to a log or notify someone that a change has been made. Here are two such examples:

```
CREATE TRIGGER SendMessage
ON PRODUCTS
FOR INSERT, UPDATE,  DELETE
AS
xp_sendmail 'BigBrother', 'A user has modified the table Products.'


CREATE TRIGGER WriteMessage
ON PRODUCTS
FOR INSERT, UPDATE,  DELETE
AS
INSERT INTO LOGTABLE VALUES (GETDATE(), USERNAME(), inserted.PROD_ID)
```

Summary

In this chapter, we started by looking at how tables are physically stored within databases. We then considered the large amount of datatypes SQL Server provides to create tables with. We looked at how tables could be created, altered and dropped with either Enterprise manager, Transact-SQL and VBA.

We then moved on to discuss the importance of data integrity and the various options that SQL Server makes available to database developers to enforce integrity. It became apparent that it's preferable to enforce data integrity at the server level so that no matter what tool or application modifies the data, the rules of the database are consistently enforced.

Finally we looked at how data integrity can be buillt directly into tables and views via declaratives or programmed into the database by creating data objects such as rules, datatypes, stored procedures and triggers.

6.5

Database Backup
and Recovery

In this chapter, we'll look at database backup and recovery. Now, we grant you, this isn't the most exciting topic in the world. It's one of those things that you don't need to know as long as everything works, but you'll desperately need when something goes wrong. If you're lucky, you'll never have to recover a database. Of course, if you're really that lucky, you should probably buy a lottery ticket. You'll win big, be able to retire and never have to think about databases anymore! But the other 99.9% of us won't, so we'll have to cover:

▲ Some underlying backup concepts

▲ Defining and using dump devices

▲ Developing a backup strategy

▲ Performing backups

▲ Recovering databases and devices

Backup Concepts

You may ask yourself why you should bother with back up. Well, this is sort of like asking "Why brush your teeth twice a day?". You back up to protect yourself from disasters. A well-managed backup strategy will ensure that you can recover from:

▲ Media failure

▲ System software failure

▲ Inadvertent or malicious use of deletion statements

```
DELETE  prod_table
DROP DATABASE  ProdDB
FORMAT C:
```

▲ Accidental or malicious updates

```
UPDATE  Employee  SET  Salary = $50000
```

▲ Destructive viruses

▲ Disasters (fire, flood, earthquake, etc.)

▲ Man-made disasters (theft, trashing equipment, etc.)

In this section, we'll cover what you can back up, as well as what you want to consider when you're developing an overall backup strategy.

Dynamic Backups

SQL Server databases can be backed up while the databases are being used. A backup is a picture of the database taken at the time the backup was begun. SQL Server takes a checkpoint record (see below) in the transaction log. Then it starts at the beginning of the database, copying pages to the backup medium in sequence, starting at the first page. If the database spans multiple devices, the devices are backed up in alphabetical order of their logical names. Transactions performing updates while the backup is running are allowed to change pages that have already been copied. Transactions which want to change pages that haven't been copied are queued. During the backup, the process checks at regular intervals to see if transactions are waiting. If so, the backup process dumps those pages so that the transactions can continue.

Because backing up a database is a disk-intensive process, overall system performance will be degraded if you run backups while there are active users. If you're running a 24 hour 7 days a week shop, try to schedule the backups during the periods of lowest activity.

What You Can Back Up

In an SQL Server database, there are two different things to back up:

▲ Database

▲ Transaction Log

Of course, you can only back up the transaction log if you've put the data and log on separate devices. A typical backup schedule will use a combination of database backups and transaction log backups.

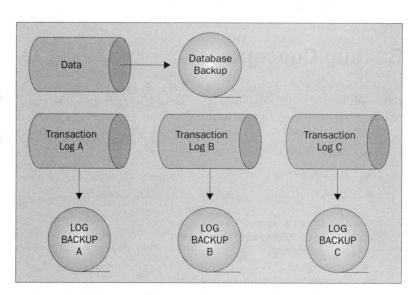

With SQL Server 6.5, you can also back up individual tables (we'll look at that later).

When you plan to make transaction log backups, it's important that you understand how SQL Server checkpoints work. Normally, SQL Server takes a checkpoint at the interval necessary to meet the recovery interval goal that you specified when you configured the server. Database owners can also issue a **CHECKPOINT** statement to force SQL Server to take a checkpoint. Checkpoints guarantee that completed transactions are written to the database. Remember that SQL Server writes committed transactions to the transaction log *first*, then records them in the database either when it's convenient or when it needs to flush a page from a buffer. When a checkpoint is taken, all dirty pages are written to the database.

One of the database options you can set is Truncate log on checkpoint. In general you shouldn't set this option for production databases, because doing so means that committed transactions are removed from the log at each system-generated checkpoint (but not from those checkpoints taken with the **CHECKPOINT** statement). When you set this option, recovery is possible *only* from a full database backup, which is why you should set it only for test databases or databases in development.

> Note that the master database does *not* have a separate transaction log and the TRUNCATE LOG ON CHECKPOINT option is set to TRUE in that database. You must always perform full database backups of the master database.

Backup Devices

SQL Server gives you a wide range of choices in backup media. You can back up databases onto tape, disk, a remote disk or diskettes. SQL Server backups are done to a named object called a **dump device**. A dump device is a logical name used by SQL Server to refer to a physical storage location. When you create a dump device, space isn't immediately allocated to it. Space won't be allocated until the device is actually used for a backup.

> With SQL Server 6 and later versions, you can create a dump device on the fly by providing its name as part of the command used to back up the database.

When you install SQL Server, the installation creates a dump device named **diskdump** that points to the NUL device. In previous versions of SQL Server, two additional devices for dumping to diskette were created for compatibility with the OS/2 versions of SQL Server. You'll create others as you need them. There are six different kinds of dump devices:

Device Type	Sample Logical Name	Sample Physical Name
Disk	TLOGDUMP	`c:\sql60\data\tlog.dmp`
Disk (network)	DATADUMP	`\\lmserver\backups\data.dmp`
Tape	TAPEDUMP	`\\.\TAPE0`
Diskette	DISKETTEDUMPA	`a:\mydata.dmp`
Named Pipe	PIPEDUMP	`\\.\pipe\sql\dump`
Null	NULLDUMP	`NUL`

Disk Devices

Diskdump devices can be local or network drives. If you're creating a dump device on a network drive, its physical name must be its **UNC** (Universal Naming Convention) name. If you want to back up to a network drive, the SQL Server account needs to be able to write to that drive. With SQL Server 6.5, Microsoft recommends that SQL Server, like the SQL Executive, run under a domain user account (see Chapter 2 for details). That account must have write privileges to the directory or directories where the dump files are to be written. If SQL Server is running as LocalSystem (which it will be if you haven't changed it), you'll need to modify the registry and add the share of the remote dump device to the **NullSessionShares** registry key.

> You'll often find it easier to back up a database onto a disk device and then use other backup programs or NT commands, such as COPY, to transfer the backup to tape. SQL Server has historically not supported direct-to-tape backups well and, although it's considerably improved, the disk backup is still easier to manage.

Tape Devices

Tape devices must be local devices. Tape backups will have an ANSI standard label together with the database name, the date and time of the backup and whether the backup is a database or log backup. You must install the tape drive under NT before you can create a device on it. NT controls the names of the tape drives and assigns them to each drive in succession. This gives you names like **\\.\Tape0**, **\\.\Tape1**, etc. Don't compromise on tape quality. Use the recommended tape for the drive. If you're backing up to DAT tapes, you should use computer-grade tapes. SQL Server won't back up to multiple tapes if you don't. Also, you should reserve specific tapes for SQL Server dumps; it doesn't work to put NT backups and SQL Server dumps on the same tape.

Diskette Dump Devices

The ability to back up to diskette is included for compatibility with previous versions. You can't create or manage diskette devices with SQL Enterprise Manager. If you're backing the database up to diskette, you'll need to have the console command line utility running before you start the backup.

> It's not a good idea to back up databases directly to diskette. Back them up to disk first, then copy the backup to diskette.

Named Pipe Dump Device

The ability to back up to a named pipe device provides a way for third party vendors to build specialized backup and restore tools.

The NUL Device

The NUL diskdump device is created each time SQL Server is started. If you back up a database to this device, you send it to the 'bit bucket' (a.k.a. Wastebasket, Dustbin, etc.). You can't use these backups for recovery. You may find this useful in a development environment if you run out of transaction log space.

Creating Dump Devices

You can create dump devices with SQL Enterprise Manager, with a Transact-SQL command and with VBA.

Creating Dump Devices with SQL Enterprise Manager

In SQL Enterprise Manager, you create a new device either by:

- Selecting a server, choosing Backup/Restore from the tools menu and clicking the New button under the list of devices.

- Right-clicking on the Dump Devices folder in the Server Manager display and selecting New Dump Device from the drop-down menu.

You provide the logical and physical names of the device and specify whether it's on tape or disk. For a tape device, you can choose to skip the header. Selecting this option means that SQL Server will ignore the ANSI standard label on the tape. SQL Server will always write the ANSI label whether or not this option is checked.

Creating Dump Devices with Transact-SQL

To create dump devices with Transact-SQL, you use the **sp_addumpdevice** system procedure. The syntax for the procedure looks like this:

```
sp_addumpdevice {'disk'|'diskette'|'tape'},
'logicalname', 'physicalname'[, {{cntrltype
[,NOSKIP|SKIP[,media_capacity]]} |
@devstatus={NOSKIP|SKIP}}}]
```

181

NOSKIP|SKIP   says whether you want to ignore ANSI labels (**SKIP**) or not (**NOSKIP**). **NOSKIP** is the default. It has meaning only for tape backups. If you want to specify **SKIP**   or **NOSKIP** without providing the **cntrltype** and **media_capacity** values, use the **@devstatus=** form.

> The **cntrltype** and **media_capacity** parameters are not used in SQL Server version 4.2 and above, but are still in the syntax for compatibility. They will be removed in a future version, so don't write new code using them.

To create a diskdump device named **MyDumpDevice**, you would use the following code:

```
sp_addumpdevice 'disk', 'MyDumpDevice',
    'c:\sql65\data\mydump.dat'
```

If you want to create a tape dump device, the command would look like this:

```
sp_addumpdevice 'tape', 'MyTapeDevice',
    '\\.\tape0', @devstatus=NOSKIP
```

Creating Dump Devices with VBA

The **DEVICE** object is a member of the devices collection of the **SQL SERVER** object. To create a new dump device, you must first create a **DEVICE** object, set its properties, then add it to the devices collection of the appropriate SQL Server. A dump device must have its **SQLOLE_DEVICE_TYPE** property set to one of the following:

- ▲ **SQLOLEDevice_DiskDump**
- ▲ **SQLOLEDevice_FloppyADump**
- ▲ **SQLOLEDevice_FloppyBDump**
- ▲ **SQLOLEDevice_TapeDump**

Dropping Dump Devices

When you've finished with a dump device, you can delete it with SQL Enterprise Manager by either right-clicking on the device in the Server Manager Display and choosing Delete or by choosing the Edit option from the Database Backup/Restore dialog box. Once you've deleted the device, use the NT command shell, File Manager or Explorer to delete the underlying operating system file if it's no longer needed.

> Remember that the underlying file holds a database or transaction log backup!
> Make sure that it's no longer needed before you delete it!

You can also get rid of a dump device by using the **sp_dropdevice** system procedure. The following command will drop **MyDumpDevice** and delete the underlying operating system file:

```
sp_dropdevice MyDumpDevice, DELFILE
```

To drop a device with VBA, simply remove it from the devices collection of the appropriate SQL Server object.

Developing a Backup Strategy

Developing and implementing an appropriate SQL Server backup strategy is one of the most important tasks that you will have as a system administrator because it's one component of your organization's overall disaster recovery strategy. Many organizations develop a complete corporate disaster plan and test it under some scenario, such as a fire which guts the corporate headquarters, so that they can answer two critical questions:

- How long will it take your organization to be back in business?
- How much money will you lose in the interim?

Your backup strategy is a critical component of putting an application into production. You need to consider backup as part of each application's design process and test it as part of putting each application into production. Remember that an application may actually use several databases and that your backup strategy will need to include whatever is necessary to keep these databases 'in sync'. Also, keep in mind that a SQL Server application involves components other than the database itself, so you need to consider these as well. For example, if the application uses extended stored procedures implemented by code that is external to the database, prudent backup procedures will make certain that those procedures are backed up on the same schedule as the stored procedures that reside in the database.

As you develop your backup strategy, you'll have to answer a lot of questions, including:

- How often do you need to back up?
- What will be backed up when?
- How will you recreate activities performed that are not recorded in transaction logs or other incremental backups?
- Online or after hours?
- Where will backups be stored and for how long?
- Manual control or automated scheduling?
- How long will it take to restore and is that acceptable?
- Who is responsible?
- What backup medium will you use?

Once you've defined your backup strategy, you need to test it. In this test, you should simulate as many different kinds of failures as possible. For example, can you recover from:

- A disk crash that destroys your database or your transaction log.
- Loss of the computer (fire, water, theft) that SQL Server is running on.
- Viruses or sabotage.

During these tests, measure how long it takes to recover and make sure that this time is acceptable.

Developing a Backup Schedule

In this section, we'll give you a few pointers about what to backup when and then review a typical backup schedule.

When Should You Backup What?

While we can't give you complete instructions for your backup schedule without knowing about your organization's particular requirements, we *can* give you a few hints.

Backing up the Master Database

You should back up the *master* database any time you:

▲   **CREATE** or **ALTER** a database

▲   Create, resize or drop a device or dump device

▲   Use DBCC to change the size of a database

▲   Change mirroring options

▲   Add or drop logins

The transaction log for the *master* database is on the same device as the database, so you must always do a complete database backup.

Backing up the msdb Database

You should backup the *msdb* database any time you

▲   Schedule tasks

▲   Set up replication

You'll decide when to backup *msdb's* transaction log and when to back up its database using the same guidelines as you use for backing up user databases.

> If you have to rebuild the *master* database, you'll have to restore the *msdb* database as well. For this reason, you may want to backup *master* each time you backup *msdb*, even if there haven't been any changes that have affected it.

Backing up a User Database

You should back up a user database after:

▲   It has been created.

▲   You've performed a non-logged operation, such as a bulk copy or **SELECT INTO**.

▲   You've created an index.

You must do other database and transaction log backups on a regular basis. The schedule for these will depend on the volatility of the data, the interaction of the particular database with other databases in your organization and the time you have available for recovering from a database disaster.

A Typical Backup Schedule

In this section, we'll look at a backup schedule for a database which has data and log files on separate devices. The database is available for update 24 hours a day, 7 days a week, but activity is light in the evenings and on weekends. An appropriate schedule might call for the following:

Friday Midnight	Friday Midnight	Saturday Midnight	Sunday Midnight	Monday Noon	Monday Midnight	Tuesday Noon	Tuesday Midnight	Tuesday Midnight
Backup Log	Backup DB	Backup Log	Backup Log	Backup Log	Backup Log	Backup Log	Backup Log	Backup DB

Suppose the system crashes at 10am on a Tuesday. At that point, the administrator must:

- ▲ Attempt to back up the transaction log so that committed transactions since the Monday midnight log backup can be preserved. If this isn't possible, those transactions will be lost. Call this the 10:01 log backup.

- ▲ Restore from Friday's DB Backup.

- ▲ Restore log backups from Saturday, Sunday, and Monday (2).

- ▲ Restore from Tuesday 10:01 log backup.

With this schedule, the most work that can possibly be lost is 24 hours, which is the interval between the Friday and Saturday and Saturday and Sunday backups. Most of the time, the risk is only 12 hours.

When you develop your own backup schedule, you'll balance the time it takes to actually perform the backup (and its potential impact on concurrent operations) with the time it takes to recover and the amount of work that could potentially be lost. This isn't an easy problem to solve. With the SQL Server 6.5 release, Microsoft has provided a Database Maintenance Wizard that will guide you through this task. We'll cover that tool after we look at the process of backing up the database.

Backing Up a Database

Before you can begin the process of backing up a database and its associated transaction log, you'll need to set some configuration options specific to backup and recovery.

Backup and Recovery Configuration Options

There are several SQL Server configuration options that apply to backup and recovery. You set these options in the same way that you set other configuration options.

Backup Buffer Size

You can set the backup buffer size which defines the size, in 32 page increments, of the buffer used in backup and restore operations. Increasing the size of this buffer can increase speed of these operations. This is a dynamic option and part of the standard set of options.

Striped Backups

SQL Server 6.0 supports striped backups. With a striped backup, you can improve the speed of a backup by writing it to multiple devices. SQL Server allows you to write a backup on up to 32 different devices simultaneously. If you're using this feature, you can also specify the number of backup threads which should be reserved for striped dumps and loads. If you set this value to 0, you turn off striped dumps. This is a static option and part of the standard set.

Recovery Flags

Set the recovery flags option to control what SQL Server records in the error log during recovery. A value of 0 (the default) records only the database name and a message that recovery is in progress. If you set this value to 1, information will be recorded about each transaction, including whether it was rolled back or committed. This is a static option and part of the standard set.

Media Retention

The final option is media retention which allows you to specify the default number of days each backup tape or disk file should be kept. The initial default is 0. If you set this option to a non-zero value, SQL Server issues a warning message if time has not elapsed

Before You Backup

There's no point in backing up a bad database! If your database is physically damaged, those problems will be recorded in the backup. You won't be able to restore from a backup that contains errors. To make sure that your database is healthy, you'll want to run a program named **DBCC** (Database Consistency Checker) to ensure that the database is logically and physically consistent. There are four things you need to run:

- ▲ DBCC CHECKDB
- ▲ DBCC NEWALLOC
- ▲ DBCC CHECKCATALOG
- ▲ DBCC TEXTALLOC

DBCC isn't directly available in SQL Enterprise Manager but the commands can be issued in the Query Tool. When you run **DBCC**, you may find that it reports errors. Don't panic. First of all, it sometimes reports spurious errors, particularly if you haven't put the database into single user mode. Some of these reported errors are in fact bugs; these are listed in the knowledge base. You can fix others by running **DBCC UPDATE_USAGE** which will clean up the information about indexes. You can always ignore complaints about bad index pages for *syslogs*. If you run **DBCC** while transactions are active, you'll also get misleading messages. Also, you need to be careful of running it against removable media databases, since it may report errors that don't exist, particularly if the database isn't in single user mode.

DBCC can have a noticeable effect on performance, even in SQL Server 6.0 or 6.5 where it has been enhanced so that it uses parallel threads. You may find that the time to run all of these checks may make it infeasible to do all of them with every backup. If so, you may want to set up so that you do one of them with one backup and then the next with the next backup, and so forth. Instead of **CHECKDB** you could also use **CHECKTABLE**, which will check specific tables rather than all the tables in the database.

DBCC CHECKDB

This command checks to see that the index and data pages are properly linked for each table and that index pages are in proper sorted order. It also verifies that pointers are consistent and that page offsets are reasonable. This is the syntax:

```
DBCC CHECKDB (database_name [, NOINDEX])
```

If you specify the **NOINDEX** option, only the clustered index will be checked. To check the health of a single table, use this command:

```
DBCC CHECKTABLE (table_name [, NOINDEX | index_id])
```

To perform the equivalent function with VBA, you use the **CheckTables** method of the database. You can check a single table by using the **CheckTable** method of that table.

DBCC NEWALLOC

DBCC NEWALLOC checks the data and index pages against the corresponding extent structure.

> This command is called NEWALLOC because it replaces an older version called CHECKALLOC.

The syntax for **DBCC NEWALLOC** is:

```
DBCC NEWALLOC (database_name [, NOINDEX])
```

To perform this function with VBA, you use the **CheckAllocations** method of the target database.

DBCC CHECKCATALOG

The final check you need to run is **CHECKCATALOG**. This will check for consistency in and between the system tables. For example, it will make sure that every table listed in *sysobjects* has at least one column in *syscolumns*. The syntax for the **CHECKCATALOG** command is:

```
DBCC CHECKCATALOG (database_name)
```

To perform this function with VBA, you use the **CheckCatalog** method of the target database.

DBCC TEXTALLOC

This command checks the allocation of text and image columns for a table and verifies that the linkage of the text chains is correct. The syntax of this command is:

```
DBCC TEXTALLOC [({table_name | table_id} [, FULL | FAST])]
```

If you choose **FULL**, the process looks at all allocation pages in the database, checks the linkage of the text chains and verifies that the pages in the chain are in fact allocated. If you choose **FAST**, only the last two checks will be performed.

If you want to check all of the tables in the database that have text or image columns, use the **TEXTALL** form of the command. Its syntax is:

```
TEXTALL [({database_name | database_id}[, FULL | FAST])]
```

In VBA, you can check the text and image columns of a single table with the **CheckTextAllocsFast** and **CheckTextAllocsFull** methods of the **TABLE** object. You can check all of the tables that have text and image columns with the **CheckTextAllocsFast** and **CheckTextAllocsFull** methods of the appropriate database object.

Doing a Back Up

Backing up a SQL Server database is traditionally referred to as **dumping** the database because the command used to make a back up is **DUMP**. In Version 6 of SQL Server, Microsoft introduced a striped backup capability and you can dump a database to as many as 32 different devices.

Remember that in SQL Server we have the option of backing up databases and backing up the transaction log. In this section, we'll show you how to do both.

Backing up Databases

You back up databases with SQL Enterprise Manager, Transact-SQL or with VBA. When you back up a database, the transaction log is also backed up.

> Be sure to do a full database backup after you perform any non-logged operations such as **SELECT INTO**, bulk copy, **WRITETEXT**. Otherwise, you won't be able to do any transaction log backups.

Backing up Databases with SQL Enterprise Manager

Select a server in the Server Manager window, then choose Backup/Restore from the Tools menu. You'll then see the following dialog box.

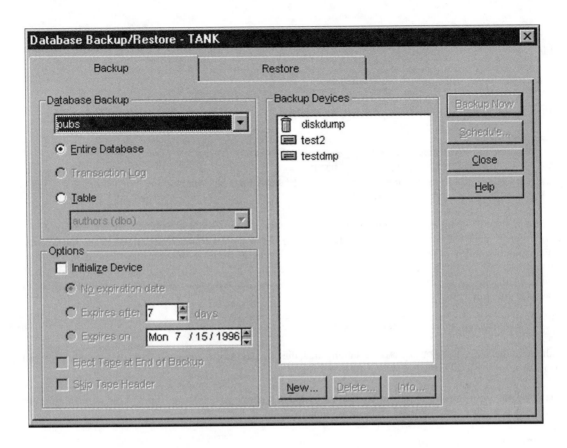

You must select a device (or devices, if you're trying to create a striped backup) from the device list. You can create new dump devices or modify them from this dialog box; you don't need to go back to the Server Manager window to do that.

> Note that you can write multiple backups to the same device. To do so, uncheck the Initialize Device box if it's checked. However, if this is the first dump that you're writing to the device, you must check the Initialize Device box. Otherwise, you'll get an error message. This error only occurs with SQL Enterprise Manager.

To do the backup immediately, click on the Backup Now button. You'll have the opportunity to confirm the label and, if appropriate, to confirm overwriting previous files on the dump device. Once the backup starts, you'll see a progress bar which tells you how far along the backup is. We'll look at the scheduling of backup tasks later in this chapter.

Backing up a Database with the DUMP Command

This syntax of this command has a lot of pieces, but is basically straightforward:

```
DUMP DATABASE {dbname | @dbname_var}
 TO dump_device [, dump_device2 [ … , dump_device32]]
 [WITH options [[,] STATS [= percentage]]]

dump_device =
      {dump_device_name | @dump_device_namevar
        | {DISK | TAPE | FLOPPY | PIPE} =
                     {'temp_dump_device' | @temp_device_var}}
      [ VOLUME = {volid | @volid_var} ]
```

You have a lot of flexibility in specifying the dump device. In the simplest case, it's just the name of a device you created with **sp_addumpdevice**. You can use a local variable (**@dump_device_namevar**) which makes it much easier than it used to be to build general purpose stored procedures to handle the backup tasks. With this command, which was introduced in SQL Server 6.0, you can create the dump device on the fly by providing its type (disk, tape, etc.) and the full path name of the output file. For example, you can write.

```
DUMP DATABASE PUBS TO DISK='C:\MyDumps\PUBSDUMP.DMP'
```

without predefining **PUBSDUMP.DMP** (assuming that the **C:\MyDumps** directory already existed). You can also use a local variable instead of the quoted string.

The **VOLUME** keyword allows you to specify the **volid** (volume ID) for the dump. This is most commonly used with tape files and is part of the ANSI standard label.

```
options =
    [[,] {UNLOAD | NOUNLOAD} ] (tape devices only)
    [[,] {INIT | NOINIT } ]
    [[,] {SKIP | NOSKIP } ] (tape devices only)
    [[,] {EXPIREDATE = {date | @date_var}
        | RETAINDAYS = {days | @days_var}}]
```

The **STATS** option reports on the progress of the dump at the interval specified by **percentage**. The default **percentage** is 10.

The following example assumes that **MyDumpDev** was created with SQL Enterprise Manager or **sp_addumpdevice** as **c:\sql65\dumps\mydump.dmp** and that we want to retain the backup for one month.

```
DUMP DATABASE Pubs to MyDumpDev
    WITH INIT,EXPIREDATE = '1996/08/17', STATS
```

As the backup progresses, the **STATS** option provides the following report:

```
Msg 3211, Level 10, State 4
10 percent dumped
...
```

Msg 3211, Level 10, State 1
100 percent dumped

The report is shown in the results window of either ISQL/W or the Query tool or in the isql output.

Backing up a Database with VBA

The **BACKUP** object has properties which correspond to the elements of the **DUMP** statement. Set these properties appropriately, then pass the **BACKUP** object to the **Dump** method of the appropriate database object.

Backing up Transaction Logs

If you perform any non-logged operations (**SELECT . . . INTO**, bulk copy, **UPDATETEXT**, **WRITETEXT**), you won't be able to back up the transaction log until you have done a database dump. When you're doing this kind of operation, either back up the database before you perform the non-logged operation and again afterwards, or dump the transaction log before you do the non-logged operation and then dump the database after.

> As we mentioned earlier, you can back up the transaction log separately from the database if you've placed the log on its own device. You can back up the transaction log with SQL Enterprise Manager, Transact-SQL or VBA.

Backing up the Transaction Log with SQL Enterprise Manager

You can back up the transaction log with SQL Enterprise Manager as long as you *haven't* set the truncate log on checkpoint option to True.

> Note that the printed documentation for SQL Server 6.0 says that you must have this option set on. This is incorrect.

The process is identical to backing up a database, except that you check the Transaction Log box. When you use SQL Enterprise Manager to back up the transaction log, the **TRUNCATE_ONLY**, **NO_LOG** and **NO_TRUNCATE** (see below) options are not available to you. However, you can to use SQL Enterprise Manager to truncate the transaction log. To do so, you need to choose Edit Database, then click the Truncate button.

Backing up the Transaction Log with Transact-SQL

We also use the **DUMP** command to back up the transaction log. The syntax is almost the same as the syntax for dumping a database:

```
DUMP TRANSACTION {dbname | @dbnamevar }
  TO [dump_device [,dump_device2, [ …, dump_device32]]
  [WITH {TRUNCATE_ONLY | NO_LOG | NO_TRUNCATE } {options} ]
```

However, you should note that there are three important options which apply only to dumping a transaction log:

▲ When you specify **TRUNCATE_ONLY** for a transaction log dump, you don't get a copy of the log. This option makes the dump behave as if the truncate log on checkpoint database option were set. You use this option to truncate the log (purge the inactive portion) when you're depending on full database backups as your only back up. Even if you're keeping a sequence of transaction log backups, you might use this option prior to backing up a database to clear out the log and decrease the total time required to back up the database. After you issue this command, you should immediately back up the database. You won't be permitted to dump the transaction log until you've done so.

> **Personally, I'd rather have the transaction log actually dumped! What if my database backup should fail?**

▲ If your database is inaccessible, you may be able to recover the contents of the transaction log by using the **NO_TRUNCATE** option. This option uses a pointer to the transaction log in the *master* database to find the transaction log. It provides up-to-the-minute media recovery when the *master* database and the log portion of the user database reside on undamaged database devices and when only the data portion of the user database is damaged.

▲ You dump the transaction log with the **NO_LOG** option only when you've run out of space in the database and can't use **TRUNCATE_ONLY** to purge the log. This option removes the inactive part of the log without making a backup copy of it and saves space by not logging the operation. If the transaction log of a published (replicated) database becomes full and absolutely must be truncated, you must unsubscribe all subscriptions to the publications of that database. This allows you to truncate past the oldest distributed transaction. When you've dumped a log with the **NO_LOG** option, you should dump the database immediately to ensure recovery. This option is commonly used with test or development databases and rarely used in a production environment.

> **You can be pro-active in monitoring the fullness of the transaction log so that you don't find that you must dump it with no_log. We'll show you some tools for doing that in Chapter 10.**

Backing up the Transaction Log with VBA

To dump the transaction log, create a **BACKUP** object with the appropriate device, etc. properties, and then pass that object to the **Dump** method of the database's **TRANSACTION LOG** object. To truncate the transaction log, pass a **BACKUP** object to the **Truncate** method of the **TRANSACTION LOG** object.

Purging the Inactive Portion of the Transaction Log

When you back up a transaction log, the inactive portion of the log will be purged.

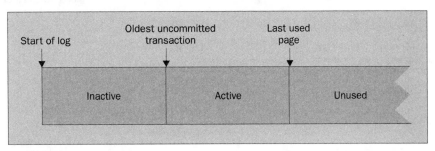

There is always a finite amount of disk space available, so it's useful to 'clean up' the transaction log periodically. Dumping the database doesn't remove the inactive portion of the transaction log. A typical sequence is to dump the database, then dump the log with **truncate_only**. However, once you've done this, you can't dump the transaction log until you again dump the database. Depending on your level of paranoia, you may find it more convenient to dump the transaction log with or without the **truncate_only** clause before you dump the database. This reduces the size of the log that will be copied with the database and leaves the log nice and clean for subsequent use.

> It's possible that the transaction log won't purge. Usually, this is the result of a transaction which has failed to commit. There's a DBCC command you can use to explore whether such transactions exist; we'll take a look at in Chapter 10.

Typical Backup Schedule Revisited

By now, you've probably gotten the picture that you're creating database and transaction log back up 'tapes'. You need to develop some sort of retention schedule or your 'tapes' will build up rapidly. Of course, how far back you save the backups depends entirely on how nervous you are. In this business, there's almost no such thing as being too nervous! The next table shows you when you can scratch a 'tape'. At this point, you have a new copy of all the prior information.

WHEN	'Tape' Name	Command	At Completion, OK to Scratch	Generation
Friday 1 Midnight	FRILOG2	DUMP TRAN		
Friday 1 Midnight	FRIDB	DUMP DATABASE	WEDSLOG1, WEDSLOG2, THURSLOG1, THURSLOG2, FRILOG1, FRILOG2	Grandfather
Saturday 1 Midnight	SATLOG	DUMP TRAN		
Sunday 1 Midnight	SUNLOG	DUMP TRAN		

Table Continued on Following Page

WHEN	'Tape' Name	Command	At Completion, OK to Scratch	Generation
Monday 1 Noon	MONLOG1	DUMP TRAN		
Monday 1 Midnight	MONLOG2	DUMP TRAN		
Tuesday 1 Noon	TUESLOG1	DUMP TRAN		
Tuesday 1 Midnight	TUESLOG2	DUMP TRAN		
Tuesday 1 Midnight	TUESDB	DUMP DATABASE	SATLOG, SUNLOG, MONLOG1, MONLOG2, TUESLOG1, TUESLOG2	Father
Wednesday 1 Noon	WEDSLOG1	DUMP TRAN		
Wednesday 1 Midnight	WEDSLOG2	DUMP TRAN		
Thursday 1 Noon	THURSLOG1	DUMP TRAN		
Thursday 1 Midnight	THURSLOG2	DUMP TRAN		
Friday 1 Noon	FRILOG1	DUMP TRAN		
Friday 2 Midnight	FRILOG2	DUMP TRAN		
Friday 1 Midnight	FRIDB	DUMP DATABASE	WEDSLOG1, WEDSLOG2, THURSLOG1, THURSLOG2, FRILOG1, FRILOG2	Son
Saturday 2Midnight	SATLOG	DUMP TRAN		
Sunday 2 Midnight	SUNLOG	DUMP TRAN		
Monday 2 Noon	MONLOG1	DUMP TRAN		
Monday 2 Midnight	MONLOG2	DUMP TRAN		
Tuesday 2 Noon	TUESLOG1	DUMP TRAN		
Tuesday 2 Midnight	TUESLOG2	DUMP TRAN		
Tuesday 2 Midnight	TUESDB	DUMP DATABASE	SATLOG, SUNLOG, MONLOG1, MONLOG2, TUESLOG1, TUESLOG2	Scratch Grandfather (who is now a Great-grandfather!)

For many years, it has been customary to retain grandfather, father and son backups. The last column of the table shows you the generations for this backup schedule. Some people like to keep extra, long-term backups or backups made before and after a particular event. Depending on your application, you might choose to keep backups made after, for example, month-end and year-end closings of ledgers or backups made before installation of a new database version for a longer time than you normally save backups.

Scheduling a Backup Task for SQL Executive

With SQL Enterprise
Manager, you can schedule
the back up tasks as a part
of the definition of the back
up. After you have defined
the backup, click the
Schedule button on the
Backup/Restore dialog:

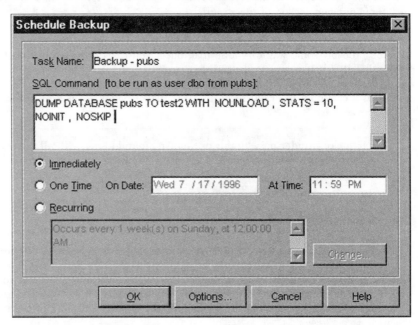

To set up a recurring backup schedule, click the Change button. You'll have the same scheduling options as you do with any scheduled task. You can monitor, modify and cancel scheduled backup tasks from the Task Scheduling window and view the history or a backup task just as you can for any other scheduled task

Once you've created a backup task, you can modify it by selecting it and clicking the Edit Task button. You can change the schedule in the same fashion as you set it up. If you want to change the nature of the backup, you must modify the text of the **DUMP** command shown in the SQL Command text box.

> If you don't want to use the **DUMP** command, delete your backup task and then create a new one using SQL Enterprise Manager.

Using the Database Maintenance Plan Wizard

At the beginning of this chapter, we talked about some of the questions you need to answer as you develop an appropriate backup schedule for your SQL Servers. In the 6.5 release of SQL Server, Microsoft have included a Database Maintenance Plan wizard that will guide you through this task. It will generate a daily and a weekly set of things to do.

Unfortunately, the wizard isn't magic. Like most of the Microsoft wizards, it gets you started but it doesn't finish the job! It won't, for example, notice that you have scheduled two backups of two different database to the same device at the same time! You should also note that the wizard is going to do things on an 'all or nothing' basis. You don't get to choose to run **NEWALLOC** on Tuesday, Thursday and Saturday, **CHECKDB** on Monday, Wednesday and Friday and **CHECKCATALOG** on Sunday! You'll see the same thing in the optimization section of the wizard.

You can't use the wizard twice on the same database–it wants to over-write what it did the first time! (There's probably some way to finesse that, but if you can do that, you probably don't need the wizard anyway!) But, if you're new to the business, it gives you a great jumping-off point. Also, if you only have one database to deal with, it may do everything you need. You'll find the Database Maintenance Plan wizard as a choice on the Help Menu and also a tool button for it on the button bar.

> If you're wondering why this option isn't found along with all the other backup and recovery options, you're not alone–it's a complete mystery to me as well!

It works in much the same way as most Microsoft wizards: you fill in information, click the next button and it leads you through everything.

The wizard develops a backup schedule for you based on your answers to questions about the volatility of your data. It allows you to select some or all of the DBCC checks that we mentioned earlier and to specify whether you want them run daily or weekly. The wizard will also allow you to include updating statistics and recreating indexes as part of the scheduled maintenance. You have all the scheduled task flexibility, including being able to send e-mail reporting on the success or failure of tasks with the tasks generated by the wizard.

If you look at the task generated by the wizard, you'll see that it uses a new command line utility that is supplied with SQL Server 6.5, called **SQLMAINT**:

```
SQLMAINT.EXE -D MyTestDB -CkDB -CkAl -CkTxtAl -CkCat -UpdSts -RebldIdx 10 -BkUpDB
C:\MSSQL\BACKUP -BkUpMedia DISK -DelBkUps 4 -Rpt C:\MSSQL\LOG\MyTestDB_maint.rpt
```

You can run this utility yourself by providing the parameters that are detailed in SQL Server Books On Line.

> The SQL Server Books On Line that shipped with the first release Version of SQL Server 6.5 doesn't have the documentation quite right. It has merged the discussion of the parameters CkAl and CkTxtAl, leaving out all discussion of CkAl.

SQLMAINT isn't automatically installed when you install the client software; you need to copy it from the CD yourself. If you want to run it on a machine where you haven't already installed the SQL Server or a SQL Enterprise Manager, you'll need to register the SQL-DMO on the target machine by issuing the following command:

```
regsvr32 c:\mssql\binn\sqlole65
```

Backing up Tables

In SQL Server 6.5, Microsoft introduced the ability to selectively back up and restore a table or set of tables. You should use this feature with caution because there's no guarantee of proper referential integrity if it gets screwed up. Table backup and restore is useful in situations such as:

▲ The table has no dependencies on other tables and you want to move it from one database to another.

▲ A table with no dependencies on other tables has become corrupt.

▲ You want to perform the kind of activity done in previous versions with deleting all the rows of a table (or issuing a **TRUNCATE TABLE** command) and inserting new rows.

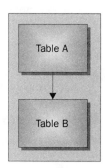

Backing up a table doesn't guarantee that all Primary and Foreign Key relationships are maintained. When you back up a table, a lock is placed on that table and a snapshot is taken of the contents of the table at that time. If you have in your database the following tables:

and you back up TableA, it will be locked and the back up made. If you subsequently back up TableB, it may contain records related to rows in TableA that were inserted after TableA was backed up. Restoring this data will result in an inconsistent database. You can back up a table using SQL Enterprise Manager or the **DUMP** command. There's no way to dump a table using VBA.

> **If you're working with large tables, the lock required may interfere with other operations.**

Recovering Devices and Databases

You'll no doubt back up far more often than you recover. In fact, if you're very lucky, you'll never have to use the recovery tools except when you test your backup plan. However, if you didn't buy that winning lottery ticket, you'll need to know how to:

▲ Recover a lost user database.

▲ Use special recovery options, including tables and point-in-time recovery.

▲ Recover a lost master database.

▲ Move a database to a new server using the **DUMP** and **LOAD** commands.

Recovering a Lost Database

There are two situations that will require you to recover a lost database:

- ▲ System failure
- ▲ Media failure

System Failure

When you experience a system failure, the database isn't physically damaged. This can happen when the system fails, leaving data in the data cache which hasn't been recorded in the database, or data has become corrupted as a result of application error. When you lose the database because of system failure, you'll need to take several steps:

- ▲ Attempt to dump the transaction log.
- ▲ Restore from the available transaction log and database dumps.
- ▲ Apply any changes made since the last backup.

Media Failure

When you experience media failure, such as a disk crash, the database is physically damaged. If you need to recover from media failure, you'll have to recreate the lost devices and lost databases before you can restore from the transaction log dumps. We'll describe what to do to recover from system failure first, then we'll talk about recreating lost devices and databases.

Dump the Current Transaction Log

If the device holding your transaction log is still accessible, you should try to dump the log. This log contains the committed transactions up to a point just before the crash. If the transaction log of the damaged or inaccessible database is on an undamaged device, dump it with **NO_TRUNCATE**. You can only dump the transaction log by using Transact-SQL; the **NO_TRUNCATE** option isn't supported by SQL Enterprise Manager. Depending on what state your database is in, this command may not work. If it doesn't succeed, all work performed since the last backup is lost.

Restore from the Database and Transactions Logs

When you're ready to restore from your backups, you shouldn't have the database to which you're restoring open. This means that it can't have any users in it at the time of the restore, including you, so you must be in the master database. You'll have to tell any active users to disconnect and kill any processes that remain in the target database after all users have disconnected from the database. First, you restore your most recent database backup.

> As you're restoring the database, if you get a message that the database has been marked 'suspect', you'll need to follow the procedures for recovering a lost device.

Then you begin restoring your transaction logs. Each of these restores rolls back any uncommitted transactions and replays committed transactions. You must be very sure to restore the transaction logs in the order that you made them. You can restore database and transaction log dumps with SQL Enterprise Manager, Transact-SQL commands and VBA.

> **If you've used the technique of dumping to disk and then copying or backing up the dump file to tape, you must restore the copy to an appropriate disk device before you can restore from it.**

Restoring Dumps with SQL Enterprise Manager

Select the appropriate server in the Server Manager display, then choose Backup/Restore from the Tools menu and open the Restore tab:

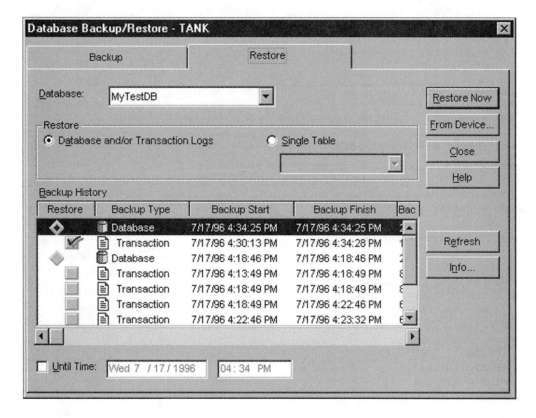

Select the files you want to restore and then click the Restore Now button. In this example, the database dump and one transaction log will be restored. If you want to see more information about a particular dump, select it and click the Info button:

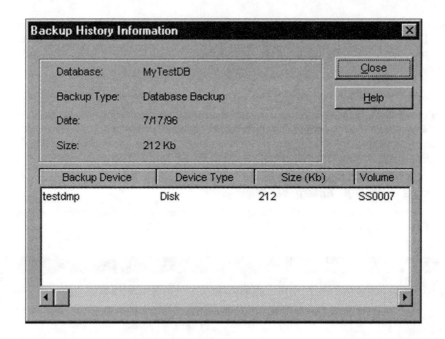

This shows you information about the contents of the header labels for each backup.

Restoring Dumps with Transact-SQL

To restore a dump with Transact-SQL, you use the **LOAD** statement:

```
LOAD DATABASE {dbname | @dbname_var}
  FROM dump_device [, dump_device2 [ ..., dump_device32]
  [WITH options
    [[,] STATS=percentage]]]
where
dump_device =
{dump_device_name | @dump_device_name_var}
|{DISK | TAPE | FLOPPY | PIPE} =
      {'temp_dump_device' | @temp_dump_device_var}
[VOLUME = {volid | @volid_var}]
options =
[[, ] {UNLOAD | NOUNLOAD}]
[[, ] {SKIP | NOSKIP}]
[[, ] FILE = fileno]
[[, ] STATS [= percentage]
```

Most of the values for dump device and options are the same as they are for the **DUMP** command. **VOLUME** specifies the volume ID of the backup device, a 6-byte character string. If you're dumping to a new tape, this value is the name of the ANSI VOL1 label. For SQL Server, the default is SQL001. For subsequent dumps, this value is used to validate the volume name of the dump device. If specified as a variable **@volid_var**, the volume name can be specified as a string or as a char or varchar variable. In general, you don't need to provide this value. If the dump device contains multiple dumps, you must give the file number of the file to be loaded in the **FILE** option. If you omit this option, the first file will be restored.

```
LOAD DATABASE Production FROM MyDumpDev, STATS
```

You also restore a transaction log by using the **LOAD** command:

```
LOAD TRANSACTION {dbname | @dbname_var}
 FROM dump_device [, dump_device2 [ …, dump_device32]
 [WITH options]
```

If you want to see the header information for the dump, use this version of the **LOAD** command:

```
LOAD HEADERONLY FROM MyDumpDev
```

Restoring Dumps with VBA

The **BACKUP** object has properties which correspond to the elements of the **LOAD** statement. Set these properties appropriately, then pass the **BACKUP** object to the **LOAD** method of the appropriate database object.

To restore the transaction log, create a **BACKUP** object with the appropriate device, etc. properties then pass that object to the **LOAD** method of the database's **TRANSACTION LOG** object.

Apply any Changes Made Since the Last Successful Backup

Hopefully, you were able to dump the transaction log before you started to restore the database. If so, you now have the last committed transaction back in the database and there's little more that you can do. The users will know what they were working on when the system crashed and can resume where they left off. If you weren't successful, unfortunately there aren't any magic tricks for you. You'll have to tell the users the point to which you were able to restore. They'll have to research what work was lost and recreate it. Anything that was set up as a batch job with input files may be available for re-running, but, in general, recapturing lost work will be a tedious manual process.

Recovering Lost Devices

When you've had a media failure, you'll have to recreate the device(s) and the database(s) before you can restore. The first thing you need to do in this case is to gather information, because you're going to have to recreate the devices and databases with exactly the same structure as they had before the crash. Prior to SQL Server 6.5, this was often a black art. Now there's a system procedure, named **sp_help_revdatabase**, that will make your life much easier.

Using System Procedures to Recreate Databases

This stored procedure will produce a script that creates the database fragments exactly as they were created initially. There's a companion procedure you may want to use, called **sp_coalesce_fragments**. If you've altered a database several times on the same device, you can collapse any contiguous fragments into a single one. When you need to recreate a database, first run **sp_coalesce_fragments**:

```
sp_coalesce_fragments pubs
go
```

This procedure will return a message about the number that sysusages fragments was reduced by. Next, you should run **sp_help_revdatabase**:

```
sp_help_revdatabase pubs
go
```

This creates the script by analyzing the existing database. You can then use the script to recreate the database structure.

```
/*********1*********2*********3*********4*********5*****6**
Reverse generated at 1996/07/20  17:50:37:770
Server / Database / Default sortorder ID :
LMSERVER / pubs / 51
DBName                  FromLPage   ToLPage   segmap
----------------------- ----------- --------- ----------
pubs                    0           511       7
pubs                    512         1535      7

@@version:  Microsoft SQL Server  6.50 - 6.50.201 (Intel X86)
*********1*********2*********3*********4*********5*****6**/
go
USE master
go
----------------- Space and Log allocations  -------------
CREATE  Database  pubs
      on  master  =  1  -- 512  of two Kb pages
go
ALTER   Database  pubs
      on  master  =  2  -- 1024  of two Kb pages
go
-------------------- DB Options  -------------------
EXECute sp_dboption  pubs ,'ANSI null default'
                          , false
EXECute sp_dboption  pubs ,'dbo use only'
                          , false
EXECute sp_dboption  pubs ,'no chkpt on recovery'
                          , false
/***
EXECute sp_dboption  pubs ,'offline'
                          , false
***/
/***
EXECute sp_dboption  pubs ,'published'
                          , false
***/
EXECute sp_dboption  pubs ,'read only'
                          , false
EXECute sp_dboption  pubs ,'select into/bulkcopy'
                          , false
EXECute sp_dboption  pubs ,'single user'
                          , false
/***
EXECute sp_dboption  pubs ,'subscribed'
                          , false
***/
EXECute sp_dboption  pubs ,'trunc. log on chkpt.'
                          , TRUE
```

```
go
------------------ sa is dbo --------------------
go
```

Both stored procedures take a database name or a pattern using wildcards (as is the case with the **LIKE** operator). There are no facilities in SQL Enterprise Manager or VBA for accomplishing the tasks performed by these stored procedures. You should get in the habit of running s**p_help_revdatabase** every time you increase the size of a database. That way, you'll have the information if you ever need it.

> If you aren't running 6.5 yet, you'll have to do some exploration. Fortunately, the information you need is in *master*. You'll need to find the VDEVNO and size for each device used by the database and the size and device assignment of databases. You must recreate the device exactly as it was created originally, and must make sure the database fragments are created in a fashion that is identical to the original ones. This can be a time-consuming process. See the *Administrator's Companion* for detailed instructions for finding the necessary information and for recreating the devices and databases.

Once you've gathered the information you need to recreate the devices and databases, you should start SQL Server in single user mode with this command:

```
sqlservr /c /dmasterdevice /m
```

For example, if your master device is in the directory **d:\sql65\data**, your command would look like this:

```
sqlservr /c /dc:\sql65\data\master.dat /m
```

Then you'll need to drop each damaged databases with:

```
DBCC DBREPAIR (db_name, DROPDB)
```

or with the **sp_dbremove** system procedure. Next, you must drop all of the affected SQL Server devices with the **sp_dropdevice** command. Issue the **CHECKPOINT** command and restart SQL Server in normal mode. Now you can recreate the devices with **DISK INIT**, using the original **VDEVNO** and size. Next you can recreate the database with the appropriate sequence of **CREATE DATABASE** and **ALTER DATABASE** commands. Once you've done this, you can restore from the backups as we've described.

> It's usually a good idea to save the ISQL scripts used to create devices and databases. While it's appealing and easy to create devices and databases with SQL Enterprise Manager, that tool doesn't create scripts of the DISK INIT and CREATE DATABASE commands you would need to recover a lost device. We recommend that you bite the bullet and create devices and databases the 'old way'.

If you don't get the database created with the correct fragments, you won't receive any messages until you run **DBCC NEWALLOC**. It takes a good while to restore a database, so the last thing you want to do is to immediately have to run DBCC to see whether the allocations are correct!

Restoring a Table

With SQL Server 6.5, Microsoft have added selective table back up and restore capability. You can restore a table from a table dump or from a full database backup. If you're planning to restore a table, there are some important things to be aware of:

- ▲ You can't restore a table that has text or image columns.

- ▲ You can't restore a table that has been published (i.e. the source of data being replicated).

- ▲ Triggers, rules, defaults and declarative referential integrity (DRI) are not enforced for table restores.

- ▲ Source and target table schema must be identical in their nullity, length and base-system type. User-defined types can be different, but the base types must be the same.

- ▲ You must set the **SELECT INTO/BULK COPY** option to **TRUE** before you can do a table restore.

- ▲ Once you've restored a table, you can't do transaction log backups until you do a full database backup.

Although you can restore a single table from a database dump, you should only load tables from table dumps. A table dump file is generated from a locked table and provides an up-to-date snapshot of the table. If you load a table from a database dump file and that table had outstanding transactions in the associated transaction log file, you won't see those transactions. A table load from a database dump looks only at the database portion of the dump. It doesn't replay the transaction part of the dump.

You can restore a table with SQL Enterprise Manager or with Transact-SQL. There's no VBA support for restoring a table.

> Don't depend on this selective table backup and restore as the major component of your backup strategy. It's fraught with peril. Restoring a table is useful in a disaster recovery situation where restoring the entire database may be a poor solution. Full database and transaction log backups remain the basis of a proper backup strategy.
>
> You should only use selective table backup and recovery in situations where they are completely safe. For example, if you have one table in your data base that has been damaged and that table has no Foreign Keys and no columns that are based on other tables, you could save time by restoring only this table.

To restore a table with SQL Enterprise Manager, you choose the single table option, then select the device containing the backup in the Restore dialog box. If you're restoring one table from a full database backup, you'll be able to select the desired table from the drop-down list of tables in the database.

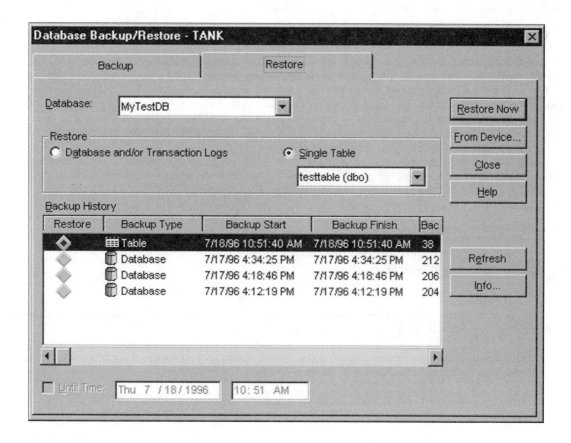

If you select a backup of type table, it will default to a table restore. Note that you can't restore from one table into a table of a different name using SQL Enterprise Manager. To restore a table using Transact-SQL, use the **LOAD** statement:

```
LOAD TABLE  [[database.]owner.]table_name
    FROM dump_device [, dump_device2 [..., dump_device32]]
[WITH options]
```

There are two options which apply only to table restores:

```
SOURCE = source_name
APPEND
```

Use **APPEND** when the data in the table backup should be added to a table that already contains data. If you want to load the data into a table which doesn't have the same name as the table that was backed up, use the **SOURCE** option to specify the name of the source table.

Point-in-time Recovery

Microsoft have added the ability to recover transactions up to a certain point in time starting with SQL Server Version 6.5. This option only applies to transaction log restores. With point-in-time recovery, you can recover from a badly-behaved application. For example, suppose a new release of some program was put into production at noon. The database was backed up before the new release was put into production. At 2pm, it turns out that the application is putting incorrect data into the database. At that point, you could dump the transaction log. Then you could restore from the latest database dump and use the point-in-time recovery capability to restore transactions that were committed before noon and roll back all transactions (committed or uncommitted) after that time. SQL Server doesn't provide a way of browsing the transaction logs to determine the time; you'll have to figure out the appropriate time based on other information, such as the last time a user ran the misbehaving application.

> Keep in mind that all transactions that took place after the specified time are rolled back. This also applies to any correct work performed concurrently with the misbehaving application.

You can perform point-in-time recovery with SQL Enterprise Manager or with the **LOAD** statement. This capability isn't provided in VBA

The SQL Enterprise Manager Restore dialog gives you an opportunity to specify the target date and time. Any transactions committed after this time will be rolled back.

The **LOAD** statement has an option, called **STOPAT**, which allows you to specify a date and time. Any committed transactions before this time will be recovered; the remainder will be rolled back.

```
STOPAT = date_time | @date_time_var
```

If you use a variable for **STOPAT**, it should be a varchar or a char.

Recovering a Lost Master Database

When you lose the master database, you effectively lose SQL Server's world. Prior to Version 6, you had to use a separate stand-alone utility to restore the master database, but now you use SQL Server Setup. Since the master database doesn't have (and doesn't permit) a separate transaction log, you'll always be restoring *master* from the last database dump. All changes since that dump are lost and must be reapplied. This is why we've stressed the need to back up master after all changes that affect its contents. You can perform the restore operations either with SQL Enterprise Manager or with Transact-SQL commands.

> Also remember that the Truncate Log On Checkpoint option is set to TRUE in *master*. This only increases the importance of backing up master whenever you make any change to its contents.

To recover a damaged *master* database, you must perform the following steps in this order:

1 Run SQL Server setup and choose the Rebuild Master Database option.

2 Select the same Sort order and character set as you selected when you installed SQL Server.

3 Expand the master device size if you expanded it when you installed SQL Server or subsequently extended it.

> Remember that you must do the expansions in the same order and amounts as you did originally. You should use `sp_help_revdatabase` each time you extend the master database so that you have a record of what you've done.

4 Add a dump device.

5 Copy your most recent backup of master to this device if it isn't already there.

6 Restart SQL Server in single user mode.

7 Restore *master* from the most recent backup.

8 Restart SQL Server in your standard mode.

9 Apply any changes since the most recent dump.

10 Restore the *msdb* database. Note that the process of rebuilding master destroys the existing *msdb* database. You'll need to expand the MSDBDATA device if you had extended it. You'll also need to alter the *msdb* database if you made it larger than the default. Once you've done all this, you can restore the latest *msdb* database dump and replay its transaction log dumps.

> Rebuilding *master* will take anywhere from 30 minutes to an hour, depending on your hardware and the size of your master device.

Moving a Database with Dump and Load

There are times when you'll want to move a database from one server to another. For example, you may need to move a version from test into production or from a development site to a client site. As long as the databases are on the same hardware platform, the quickest way to move them is with **DUMP** and **LOAD**. If they are on different platforms, you'll have to use the Transfer Management feature of SQL Enterprise Manager (SQL Server 6.5) or Transfer Manager (SQL Server 6.0). You'll quite often move a database from one SQL Server version to another using this technique. The following table shows you when you can accomplish this migration using backups.

Source DB	4.2	6.0	6.5
4.2	YES	YES	YES
6.0	NO	YES	YES
6.5	NO	With SQL Server 6.0 service pack 3	YES

> Note that the character set and sort order of the source and target server must be the same.

When you're creating a database which you're immediately going to load with a database dump, you can use the **FOR LOAD** option of the **CREATE DATABASE** statement (or check the For Load option on SQL Enterprise Manager's New Database dialog). When you create a database for **LOAD**, database pages are not initialized. The database you create with this option will be set to DBO Use Only and will only permit you to use the **LOAD** and **ALTER DATABASE** statements. This can save some time if the bulk of the source database is used. If you create a 100 megabyte database **FOR LOAD**, then restore a 5MB database dump into it, the remaining database pages will be initialized and it will take just about as long as if you had created the database without this option.

```
CREATE DATABASE database_name
[ON {DEFAULT | database_device} [= size]
     [, database_device [= size]]
FOR LOAD
```

> You can use the FOR LOAD option any time you create a database. For example, if you're recreating the database for a lost device, using this option might save you quite a bit of time.

When you're creating a **FOR LOAD** database, you must make sure that it's at least as large as the database whose dump you plan to restore into it.

> You should also create a FOR LOAD database with the same fragments as the source database from which you are restoring it. This is another time when it's good to have sp_help_revdatabase.

You shouldn't put the log on a separate device when you create the **FOR LOAD** database; you can move it after you have restored the database dump. If you're creating a new database on the same server, remember that its name must be unique. Once you have created the new database, you can:

▲ Dump the old database

▲ Load the new database

▲   Clear the DBO Use Only option

▲   Move the transaction log if appropriate

▲   Drop the old database if appropriate

If you're moving the database to a different server, you can follow the same procedure. However, you'll need to make sure that if the syslogins are different on the new server, then you set up aliases to map these to the user IDs on the old server. You could also drop users of the database, drop logins, recreate logins and then recreate database users to ensure that the mappings are correct.

> In early versions, stored procedures, views and triggers used internal identifiers for objects. As these may differ in the move to a different server, you need to rebuild these objects. It's not a bad idea to do so, in any case.

Alternatives to Using SQL Server Backups

When we talked about devices, we pointed out that the devices are, in fact, simply files from the point of view of the operating system. One question that this always raises is "Why can't we just use NT's backup facilities to back up the devices? That way we won't have to worry about all these fragments and other issues. After all, if you lose a device, you should just be able to put in a new one and restore the image of the old one and all should be well." There are four alternatives to doing SQL Server backups:

▲   Operating system file copy

▲   bcp

▲   Database transfer utility

▲   Replication

There are pros and cons to each of these; I'll talk about each of them in the next few sections.

Operating System File Copy

This technique includes using both the file copy (with File Manager or at the command prompt) and NT's backup program or third-party file backup programs. The first drawback to this approach is that you must shut down the SQL server before you can copy (or back up) the files since SQL Server has them open.

> Do not attempt to use file copy techniques if you have multiple databases on the same device or if your databases span devices. In both cases, you risk having copies out of sync. The time you may save isn't worth it, believe me.

The copy technique can be useful when you're maintaining a decision support database or when you have one server that needs to be identical to another server but can only be shut down for a brief time.

When you're using this technique, the databases on the source and target servers must be identical in size and composed of the same segment structures (see above). To copy device files from one server to another you must:

1 Stop the source server.

2 Copy the device files to the appropriate directories on the target server but use different names.

3 Stop the target server.

4 Rename or delete the device files on the target server.

5 Rename the new device files so that they are back to their original names.

6 Restart the target server.

> It's crucial that you copy all device files, including the transaction log, and that you understand the mapping of database segments to devices if you're using this technique.

Note that this method won't get rid of corruption that may exist. An SQL Server dump may get rid of corruption if it's on unused pages, since those won't be backed up by the **DUMP** command.

> If you have a damaged database, you may want to copy the device files and save them for subsequent analysis and data retrieval before you restore from a backup. This is perfectly safe.

Using bcp for Backups

This is a slow approach to backup. The bcp program is great for moving data across different platforms and for getting database data out for use by other applications, but it's not a tool for backup. First of all, as well as copying out all the data, you must also be prepared to recreate the schema. Second, you'll have to recreate all of the clustered indexes, which will need time and disk space. Third, even if you run a 'fast' (non-logged) bulk copy, you'll need enough space in the transaction log to record all of the new extents that will be created as you add data. Finally, you'll really need to shut down the database being backed up with bulk copy to be sure that tables don't get out of sync with each other.

Using Database Transfer Utility

This one (and the same is true for the Transfer Manager of previous versions) has all the drawbacks of bulk copy with the added requirement that the two servers involved must be physically connected to each other! This solution may work well for you for a small database, but isn't a good choice for a large production database.

Using Replication

You can use replication to keep two databases in sync, so it would work to keep a backup copy of a database. This is a slow solution, however. With replication, you're doing your backup one transaction at a time, and usually across the network to boot! If you want a warm backup server, it's much quicker to do it with data base dumps (I'll talk about that in the next section).

Warm Backups and FallBack Servers

Finally, there are two methods which effectively involve running backup servers to take over if one of them fails.

Maintaining a Warm Backup

While this approach requires two servers, it may give you the quickest recovery in the case of a major disaster. This approach is similar to the one discussed for moving a database. Assume you have two servers named 'Production' and 'Waiting'. Waiting and Production have identical logins, devices and databases. Each time you dump a database on Production, you restore the dump into Waiting. You do the same thing with each transaction log dump. If Production fails, you simply point your applications at Waiting and you're back in business. If you want to be super-safe, you would put the warm backup in a different location from the production server. This last approach increases WAN traffic and introduces a performance degradation, but at least people can keep doing their work.

> Ideally, your applications will allow the user to specify the name of the server to connect to. If the applications are connecting with ODBC, however, the name of the server may be buried away in some `.INI` file on the user's desktop. You can still accomplish the switch by changing the name of the SQL server with `sp_addserver`.

Fallback Support

This feature is new in SQL Server 6.5 and takes advantage of the ability of hardware and/or an operating system to 'adopt' the file system of a failed server. Setting up fallback support is similar to setting up remote servers. You need to tell the primary server who its fallback server is, using **sp_addserver**. The fallback server's sa needs to be added to the primary server as a remote login with **sp_addremotelogin**, and the fallback server needs to know who it's providing fallback support to.

On the primary server, execute the following:

```
exec sp_addserver 'SVRFALLBACK' ,'fallback'
exec sp_addremotelogin 'SVRFALLBACK' ,'sa' ,'sa'
```

On the fallback server, run this:

```
exec sp_addserver 'SVRPRIMARY'
```

Next, you must tell the fallback server what databases it may have to support:

```
exec sp_fallback_enroll_svr_db 'SvrPrimary' ,'DabSales'
exec sp_fallback_enroll_svr_db 'SvrPrimary'
                        ,'DabProduct'
```

The primary server name must be a srvname in the Sysservers table on the fallback server.

> **Please note that the databases DabSales and DabProduct that are being configured for fallback must be on a switchable disk for fallback to work.**

When the fallback server takes over a switchable disk from the primary server and assigns a new drive letter to the disk, you need to do several things. In this example, the fallback server will see the disk as drive letter **H:**. The disk was seen by the primary server as drive letter **D:**. You need to tell the fallback server this and to tell it that it is now in charge of all databases from the primary server, with the following:

```
exec sp_fallback_upd_dev_drive 'SvrPrimary' ,'D:' ,'H:'
exec sp_fallback_activate_svr_db 'SvrPrimary', '%'
```

If you're planning to use fallback support, make sure that you don't have any databases that are sharing devices. If you want to provide fallback support for replicating servers, the publisher and the distributor should reside on the same server.

Summary

In this chapter, we've taken you through the backup and recovery process in detail. We first introduced the different devices on which you can do a backup. We've discussed how to create a sensible and safe backup schedule and showed you the process involved in backing up a database, from setting the necessary configuration options to the backing up of the database and transaction log and how to go about just backing up single tables. We've also considered briefly how the Database Maintenance Plan wizard can help you do this.

The second part of this chapter was concerned with the recovery of lost devices and databases. In particular, we discussed how to restore databases, transaction logs, separate tables and even information added up to a certain point in time. We discussed what to do if the worst happens and the master database is lost and ended the chapter with a look at the dump and load features and how to move a database to a different device or server. In the next chapter, you'll switch to a completely different topic: managing security.

6.5

Managing Security

As a SQL Server System Administrator, you will find that security is one of your major concerns. Microsoft SQL Server has a rich security model and there are a variety of actions you can take to make certain that your data isn't subject to unauthorized access. You can also set up SQL Server so that it uses NT's logon security. This makes it possible to give users a single logon which is often convenient. In this chapter, we'll discuss:

- Implementing integrated, standard and mixed security
- Using SQL Security Manager
- Object ownership
- Object and statement privileges
- Using views as a security mechanism
- Setting up remote servers

The SQL Server Security Model

SQL Server provides security at four levels:

- Login–who is allowed to log in to a particular server
- Database–who is allowed to use a particular database
- Object–who is allowed to read, update or use a particular database object
- Command–who is allowed to issue a particular command

As System Administrator, you will be responsible for managing security at all of these levels. Although there are four levels, we're going to cover them in two parts. In the next section, we'll discuss login and database security.

Login and Database Access

Before users can do anything with a SQL Server, they must be able to log in to the server and use at least one database on that server. You'll need to create a login id for each user and give each user rights to the databases which support the applications the user will run. In a database, it's also possible to put users in groups. This feature is often used to make it easier to manage privilege assignments.

Login Security

You have a choice of three kinds of login security for a SQL Server:

- ▲ **Integrated security:** the user logs in to NT not to the SQL Server. Authentication is done with NT mechanisms. This requires what are called 'trusted connections'.

- ▲ **Standard security:** the user logs in to the SQL Server as a separate activity from logging in to NT. SQL Server authenticates the user.

- ▲ **Mixed security:** in a mixed security environment, some of the users connect to the SQL Server with trusted connections and others login directly with standard security.

Regardless of the login security mode you choose, every SQL Server user has a login id. This is the name by which a user is known in SQL Server. A login id has an associated password and an optional default database and default language.

If you're using integrated security, the login id for each user will be created automatically when you add the NT user to the server. (See the discussion of implementing Integrated Security later in this chapter.) If you're using standard security, you must create the login id yourself.

Special Logins

Two ids are created when SQL Server is installed. Others will be created when replication is set up (see Chapter 11). The most important of these is sa, the System administrator login. Also created is probe, a special login id used as the security context for some administrative applications (notably the performance monitor). Users shouldn't log in as probe. The probe account has no password and, if you try to give it one, the performance monitor won't work if you're using standard security. If you're using integrated security, you might want to delete this account.

The System Administrator (sa) login operates outside the SQL Server privilege system. This login represents a role that's usually responsible for:

- ▲ Installing SQL Server
- ▲ Creating devices and databases
- ▲ Managing and monitoring
- ▲ Disk space use
- ▲ Memory
- ▲ Connections
- ▲ Performance
- ▲ Creating logins
- ▲ Backing up and restoring databases
- ▲ Diagnosing system problems
- ▲ Tuning SQL Server

As you might imagine, individuals who have this role must walk on water and leap tall buildings. This isn't a role to be granted lightly. The sa has some privileges that can't be transferred to others. When you install SQL Server, the sa account is created with no password; one of your first acts should be to add a password.

> If you don't add the sa password, you leave your system wide open. Since sa operates outside the privilege structure, if you don't change the password you risk inadvertent or malicious changes to your environment.

You can create a default login id that can be used for integrated and mixed security. This is used for authenticated NT users who don't have a corresponding SQL Server login id. This is customarily given the name **guest**. If there is no default login, then access will be denied.

Database Security

Creating a login id for a user simply permits that user to log onto the SQL Server. It doesn't grant any particular privileges to that user enabling them to use a database. Anyone who needs access to a particular database must be made a user of that database. You grant access rights to a database to a login id by making that login id a user of the database. Each database user can have a name in the database which is different from the login id. It isn't necessary to give the user a different name.

Users in the database can be organized into **groups**. Object and statement privileges can be given to users or groups. It's usually easier to manage these privileges with groups than by granting them to individuals.

> User privileges often go along with organizational structure. That is, some individuals, all of whom have the organization title clerk, have the same set of privileges inside a database. If you create a group structure that models your organizational structure, you will often find that the assignment of privileges is simplified. For example, if someone is promoted from clerk to manager, simply move that individual from the clerk group to the manager group. Whatever privileges are given to a manager are now automatically given to the promoted individual.

The Public Group

There's a public 'group' that exists in all databases and all users are members of it. Any user can be a member of *only one* additional group.

> If you're working in Transact-SQL, create groups before users, so that you can put users in groups when you add them to the database.

You can add a guest user as a member of the public group. If you do this, people who are not users in the database will be able to access it with all of the privileges granted to the public. The user name must be guest and there's no mapping to a login id.

> The guest database user isn't the same as a guest login id although it functions in a similar fashion. It's a good idea to have a guest login in training databases such as Pubs and others that you create for people to learn with. In general, you won't want a guest user in any databases for which you want to control access.

Creating Login ids

You can define login ids with SQL Enterprise Manager, with Transact-SQL and with VBA. We'll briefly look at how you can achieve this using all three methods.

> The login id is what's returned by the Transact-SQL function `suser_name()`. Its internal identifier is returned by `suser_id()`.

Using Enterprise Manager to Create Login ids

It is easy to create logins with SQL Enterprise manager. To do this, use the Manage Logins dialog (found on the Manage menu or in the logins folder in the Server Manager display).

Manage Logins - LMSERVER

Login Name: `MyNewUser`

Password: `xxxxxxxx`

Default Language: `<Default>`

[Add] [Drop] [Close] [Help]

Database Access

Database	Permit	Default	User	Alias	Group
master					
model					
msdb					
pubs					
tempdb					

Notice that you can assign the user to a database and to a group at the same time as you create the login. To add a user to a database, simply check the Permit column. The first database you do this for will be assumed to be the user's default database, but you can change this by unchecking the default column. The login id will be placed in the User column and is the user's name in the database unless you type over it. The user will be placed in the public group; if you've defined other groups you can select the desired one from the drop-down menu that will appear when you set the focus to the group field. We'll cover aliases later in this chapter. Note that when you permit a user to a database with this dialog, the user is *automatically* added as a user of the database.

Creating Logins with Transact-SQL

You add logins to the SQL Server with the **sp_addlogin** procedure.

```
sp_addlogin login_id [, password [, defdb [, deflang
    [, login_suid] ]]]
```

- ▲ *defdb* is the user's default database; if not specified, default database is *master*.
- ▲ *deflang* is the user's default language; if not specified, the SQL Server default language is assumed.
- ▲ *login_suid* is a login suid in the Syslogins table. If *login_suid* is NULL the suid isn't affected. Use this parameter only when a database user in the Sysusers table is an orphan to the Syslogins table. This parameter is only available in version 6.5.

You can change the default database later, with the **sp_defaultdb** procedure, and the default language with the **sp_defaultlanguage** procedure.

Note that **sp_addlogin** doesn't add the login id as a user of the default database. Unless there's a guest user, the user will see an error message when logging in. If you're creating logins with **sp_addlogin**, you must add the user to the default database with the **sp_adduser** procedure as follows:

```
sp_addlogin MyNewUser, password
```

To review the logins you've created, use **sp_helplogins** (version 6.5 only).

Creating a Login id with VBA

To create a login id with VBA, create a new login object. Set its properties appropriately, then add this object to the logins collection for the SQL Server.

Dropping Login id

There may come a time when you want to get rid of a login id. To do this, you need to drop it. You can drop the login id with SQL Enterprise Manager by simply selecting it in the Server Manager display, clicking the right mouse button and choosing Delete from the drop-down menu.

To drop a login id using Transact-SQL, use the **sp_droplogin** procedure.

```
sp_droplogin login_id
```

You can drop a login with VBA. Use the **Remove** method of the login object. You can't drop a login which owns objects or is a user in any database.

Creating Groups

You can create groups with SQL Server Enterprise Manager, Transact-SQL or VBA.

Creating Groups with SQL Enterprise Manager

In the Server Manager display, select a database, then right-click on Groups/Users and select New Group from the drop-down menu or choose Groups from the Manage menu.

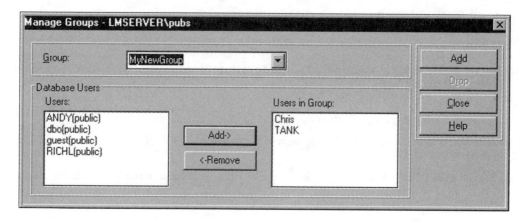

You can create a group and simultaneously put any database users into it. Note that the only users that will show in the User list are those that have already been added to the database. You won't see a list of all logins on this screen.

Creating Groups with Transact-SQL

To create a group with Transact-SQL, use the **sp_addgroup** procedure.

sp_addgroup *group_name*

To see the groups that you've created, use the stored procedure **sp_helpgroup**.

Creating Groups with VBA

To create a group with VBA, create a new group object. Set its properties appropriately and add it to the groups collection of the appropriate database.

Adding Users to a Database

You can add users to a database with SQL Enterprise Manager, Transact-SQL and VBA. Note that the login ids have to exist before you can add the user to a database. When you add a user to the database, you can specify a name for that user within the database. This name need not be the same as the user's login name.

> The name in the database is what you get if you use the niladic function USER or the Transact-SQL function user_name().

Adding Users to a Database with SQL Enterprise Manager

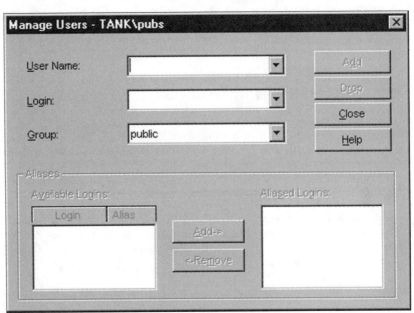

To add a user to the database with SQL Enterprise Manager, select a database in the Server Manager display, then either choose Users from the Manage menu or right-click on Groups/ Users and choose New User from the drop-down menu.

Once you've done this you'll see one of the more confusing screens SQL Enterprise Manager has! The focus is in the user name text box, but this isn't really where you want to be. Instead, tab down to the login list box. Drop down the list and select the user you want to add. At this point, you've chosen a login id to add to the current database. You would expect the login name to appear in the User text box, but it won't, even when you tab to some other field on the form. You must enter the name you want this login to have in the database yourself! Since this is usually the same as the person's login name, it's a mystery to me why Microsoft has set this screen up this way! If you do drop down the list of names in the User text box, you'll see users that are already in the database. As you select them, their login names will show up in the next box.

Once you have the user name and login entered, you can select the group for the user as well.

Adding Users to a Database with Transact-SQL

To add a user to a database with Transact-SQL, use the **sp_adduser** procedure.

sp_adduser *login_id* [, *name_in_db* [, *group_name*]]

To see the users of a database, use the stored procedure **sp_helpuser**.

Adding Users to a Database with VBA

To add a user to a database, create a new user object and set its properties appropriately. Note that the Group to which the user belongs is one of its properties. If you set this property to a group other than public, the group must already exist. Once the properties are set, add the user object to the database's user collection.

Dropping Users and Groups

At some point, you may want to remove a user from a group or change the group to which it belongs, or you may want to drop a user or a group from the database. You should remember that when you remove a user from a group, the user becomes a member of the public group. Removing a user from a group doesn't remove the user from the database.

Removing a User from a Group

In SQL Enterprise Manager, open the Groups/Users folder then double-click the desired group or right-click on the group and choose Edit from the drop-down list. Once you see the group membership screen, select the name in the Users in Group list (the list on the right) and click the Remove button. The user is still in the database but in the **public** group.

To remove a user from a group using Transact-SQL, use the **sp_changegroup** procedure.

```
sp_changegroup group_name, Name_in_db
```

To remove a user from a group with VBA, set the group property of the appropriate user object to **public** or some other group.

Removing a Group from the Database

You can get rid of a group with SQL Enterprise Manager, Transact-SQL or VBA. In SQL Enterprise Manager, open the Groups/Users folder, then either select the group you want to delete and press the delete key or right-click on the group and choose Drop from the drop-down menu. If there are users in the group, SQL Enterprise Manager transfers them to the public group before dropping the group.

To get rid of a group with Transact-SQL, use the **sp_dropgroup** procedure.

```
sp_dropgroup group_name
```

If there are any users in the group being dropped, the request will fail. You will need to move the users to some other group with **sp_changegroup**, SQL Enterprise Manager or VBA.

To get rid of a group using VBA, select the appropriate member of the groups collection and use its **Remove** method.

Deleting a User from a Database

You can remove a user from a database with SQL Enterprise Manager, Transact-SQL or VBA. Note that you can't drop a user who owns objects. After you remove the user from a database, the SQL Server login still exists.

To remove a user with SQL Enterprise Manager, open the Groups/Users folder, then select the user you want to delete and either press the delete key or right-click on the user and select Delete from the drop-down menu.

To remove a user with Transact-SQL, use the **sp_dropuser** procedure.

```
sp_dropuser  name_in_db
```

To remove a user with VBA, select the appropriate member of the users collection and use its **Remove** method.

Implementing Integrated, Standard and Mixed Security

The various types of security require similar methods of implementation. We'll consider the integrated security implementation in depth and then look briefly at how the standard and mixed ones differ.

Implementing Integrated Security

Integrated security is based on NT's per user security. This security is administered for a domain and there's a common accounts database shared by all computers on the domain.

The Primary Domain Controller (PDC) maintains this security database and, at a regular interval, sends copies to all of the Backup Domain Controllers (BDC) for the domain. Should the PDC fail, a BDC can be promoted to a PDC so that the security can still be ensured. Other computers are simply members of the domain. Because the PDC and BDC are busy with the authentication processes, SQL Server is usually installed on a member computer and not on a PDC or BDC. Integrated security provides multiple layers of protection:

- NT domain security
- NT computer-level security
- SQL Server login security
- Database permissions

Integrated security requires trusted connections. This means that the underlying network protocol must support authenticated connections between client and server. The SQL Server supported network protocols that provide this are named pipes and multiprotocol. You must use one of these protocols if you want to have integrated security.

With integrated security, a user's network security attributes are established at network login time. When a network user tries to connect to a SQL Server, SQL Server uses NT facilities to determine network name of user and permits or denies access based on that name alone.

With integrated security, a network user name maps into a SQL Server login name. Once the trusted connection is logged in, SQL Server database permissions still apply. Trusted connections are available for:

- Windows NT Workstation clients
- Windows 95 clients

▲   Windows for Workgroups clients

▲   Microsoft LAN Manager clients running

▲   MS-DOS

▲   Windows 3.x

▲   Windows 3.1 clients using Novell software (the user must provide NT with user name and password when connecting to SQL Server)

When you want to implement integrated security, there are three basic steps. Two of them must be performed by the SQL Server sa and the third must be performed by a Windows NT Administrator, Domain Administrator or Account Operator.

What	Who
Set login security to integrated and choose other security options	SQL Server system administrator
Create Windows NT users and groups	Windows NT administrator, domain administrator, or account operator
Authorize NT users to SQL Server	SQL Server system administrator

Setting Integrated Security Options

You set integrated security options with SQL Enterprise Manager or SQL Server Setup.

Request integrated security by checking the box. Here's where you can specify a default login that will be used when there's no SQL Server login that maps to the users network name. Note that you must actually create this login using **sp_addlogin**, SQL Enterprise Manager or VBA. Simply specifying it as the default login doesn't accomplish anything.

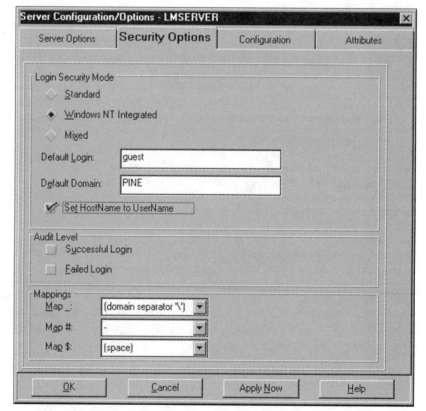

You should also specify a default domain. This is the NT domain name that's the default for matching network user names to SQL Server login names. You need to do this because the same network user name can be defined in two different domains for two different users and both can be authorized to access SQL Server. SQL Server needs to be able to distinguish between the two names in the login process for a trusted connection.

For network user names defined in domains other than the specified default, SQL Server adds the domain name and a map character such as an underscore (_) to the network user name before attempting the lookup in Syslogins. For example, we've chosen PINE as the default domain. That means SQL Server will assume PINE as the domain for users who attempt to log in. If there's a user RICH in the PINE domain and one in the ARCH domain, SQL Server will assume that RICH in Syslogins means PINE\RICH. If RICH from the ARCH domain tries to log in, SQL Server will look for ARCH_RICH in Syslogins in order to authenticate that person.

If you choose set HostName to UserName, the network user name (NT login name) will be used instead of the standard host name (usually the computer name) by tools such as **sp_who**, which display active user info. This applies to standard and mixed security as well as integrated security.

You can set up auditing of login attempts. This feature is available in standard, integrated and mixed security modes. The audit records go to the error log. You can log successful logins, failed logins or both.

Mappings

The Mappings part of the dialog applies only to integrated security. What you're doing here is specifying how characters that are legal in NT user names but illegal in SQL Server user names should be handled. For example, NT names allow hyphens, spaces, domain separator and periods but these aren't permitted in SQL Server. In this section, you say which legitimate SQL Server characters should be substituted for NT characters.

Map _   default mapping for domain separator \
Map #   default mapping for hyphen -
Map $ default mapping for <space>

An example would be:

DOMAIN\John-Boy Doe maps to **DOMAIN_John#Boy$Doe**

> This is another very confusing interface! It seems quite backwards! You need to read it as "when I see the domain separator (a \\), map it to an underscore (_)". It would be much clearer if the columns on the display were reversed! And, you only get 3 characters–but there are 9 that might appear in an NT name! Your life will be simplest if your NT user and group names conform to SQL Server's rules!

Creating NT Groups and Users

Create two or more local Windows NT groups on the SQL Server computer using User Manager. At a minimum, you must have a group for people who are going to have sa privileges and a different group for people who have only user privileges. Then you add members to these groups. Members can be:

▲ Locally defined users

▲ Users defined in the domain

▲ Global groups defined in the domain

When you create users and groups, use names that are valid SQL Server identifiers and, since SQL Server allows users to be in only one group, you should avoid placing users in more than one NT group if you're planning to have your NT groups map into database groups.

Authorize NT Users to SQL Server

You map NT Users into SQL Server users with the SQL Security Manager. This is a very confusing tool. Although there was some hope that it was going to be improved with the 6.5 release, it appears to be no different from its earlier versions. When you start it, you are presented with the following, relatively ambiguous, screen.

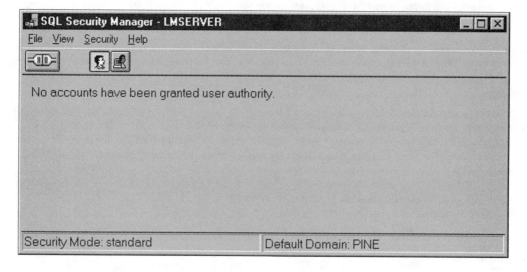

The button with a person on it, which is pressed when you first see the screen, is the user button. The other button is the administrator button. That's the one that shows the beleaguered administrator with a monitor on his back! Each NT group you want to map to SQL Server must be either a user group or an administrator group. Let's assume we've created two NT groups: SQLUsers and SQLAdministrators and start off by mapping the members of SQLUsers into SQL Server IDs. To do this, choose Grant New from the Security menu and you'll see the following dialog box:

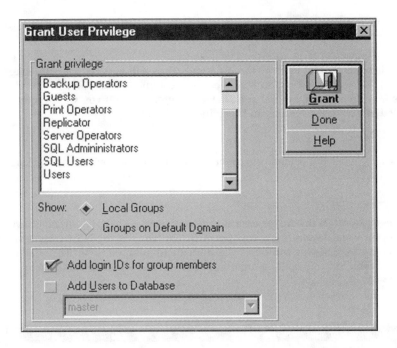

If you don't see the groups you want, check the Groups on Default Domain box. Highlight the group you want to add. Then you have two choices. The first is to add login ids for everyone in the group. You'll usually want to do this. If you don't do it and you have a default id, all the people in this group will be mapped to that! If you do it and any of the users in the group already have a SQL Server login id with the same name, they will be rejected. You can also ask that the users be added to a specific database. If you do this, a group with the same name as their NT group will be created and the users placed in it for you. After you click the Grant button, you can see the users that have been added by double clicking on the group that will appear.

Although it appears that everything is ready for the users to log in, you will have to stop the SQL Server and restart it before you can begin using integrated security.

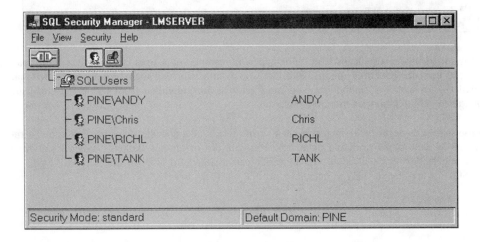

This figure shows their domain name on the left and their SQL Server login id on the right.

> If you subsequently add users to the NT group, they will automatically be mapped
> into SQL Server as a guest. You will need to select the new user, choose **Account**
> **Details** from the **Security** menu and click the **Login** button if you want the user to
> be added as a SQL Server user in his or her own right.

You perform a similar series of operations to grant sa privileges, but you start by clicking the Administrator
button.

> When you first select the Administrators, you will notice that you already have
> some! When you selected Integrated Security, everyone in the NT administrators
> group on the SQL Server computer was added and mapped to sa. This may not be
> what you want, but you can't do anything about it until you take some group and
> map *it* to sa.

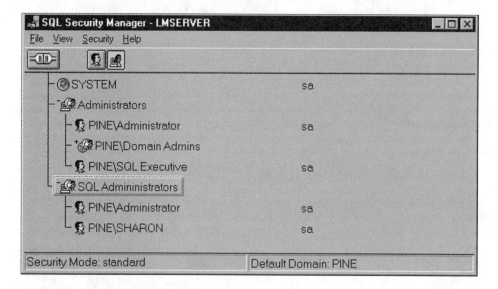

When you want to revoke privileges from either an administrator or a user group, select the group and
choose Revoke from the Security menu. Note that you're only working with groups, not individuals. To
revoke privileges for a specific individual, you must remove the individual from the NT group using the
User Manager or User Manager for Domains.

You can also use SQL Security Manager to review the details of a specific account. You can see the
mapped name as well as the available databases. You can add or change database usage from this screen.
There's a search facility that will allow you to verify permissions and also to find 'Orphan' SQL login ids.
These are SQL logins that no longer map back to NT network users.

Implementing Standard Security

When you want to implement standard security, you only have two tasks to perform:

▲ Set security options

▲ Create a login id for each user who is allowed access to the server

You set security options for Standard security with SQL Enterprise Manager or SQL Server Setup. The procedure is similar to that outlined for integrated security. Check the Standard Security box. Then supply a default login and default domain if you want. These will be used only by applications which request trusted connections: they will be of no interest to most users. The audit log works in Standard security just as it does in integrated security. You don't need to bother with the mappings since they only apply to NT network names and you're going to define your own SQL Server logins which, by definition, will conform to the rules!

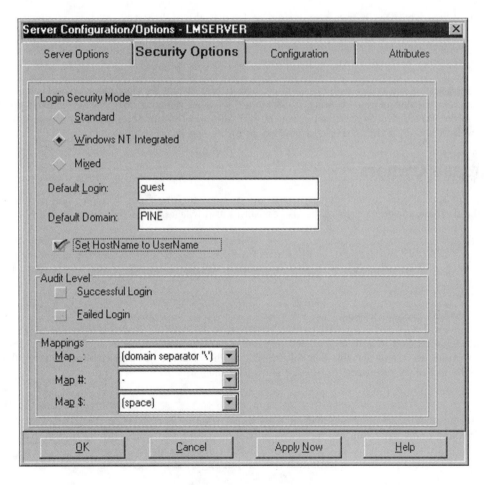

After you've set security options, create login ids following the procedures outlined at the beginning of this chapter.

Implementing Mixed Security

As you might expect, implementing mixed security requires you to do all the steps for integrated security and all the steps for standard security. The only thing that's different is that you check the Mixed security box under security options. Then you follow these steps:

▲ Create NT users and groups

▲ Use SQL Security Manager to authorize users and administrators who will be using trusted connections

▲ Define login ids for the users who won't be using trusted connections

Object and Command Permissions

At this point, you have seen how to permit users to login to the SQL Server and how to allow them access to specific databases. But your task isn't done yet. The users can make a database their current database, but they can't see a single bit of data yet! To let the user actually *do* something with the database, you need to grant object and statement permissions.

We need to start this section by defining another special role: that of the database owner. Then we'll discuss object ownership in general, since it determines who has rights to objects when explicit privileges have not been granted. Finally, we'll show you how to allow users to perform actions on objects they don't own, as well as how to grant or restrict a user's right to use specific commands.

Database Owners

There is one 'special' user in each database–dbo: the person who 'owns' the database. The person who creates the database is automatically dbo. The dbo has full privileges inside the database and

▲ Allows other users access to the database

▲ Grants users permission to create objects and execute commands within the database

▲ Creates groups

▲ Assigns users to groups

The database owner logs in with an assigned name and password but in the database that they own, they're known as dbo. Note that this is a role specific to the database the person owns. In any other databases the individual has access to, they're known by their user name.

> It's important to remember that the 'real world' identity of dbo is lost if you are making audit trails. You can have several people who perform the role of dbo. If you want to know who actually did something, remember that you need to use suser_name() to get the login id. USER and user_name only give the name in the database.

sa is the owner of master and therefore has dbo rights to all databases.

When SQL Server is installed, only sa has the privilege of creating databases. The sa can grant this permission to others. Often, because the sa is custodian of disk resources, they don't grant this privilege. Instead, the sa creates the database and then transfers ownership to a responsible owner.

To transfer the database ownership, you use **sp_changedbowner**.

sp_changedbowner *login_id* **[, TRUE]**

TRUE transfers all existing aliases (see below) to the new owner (***login_id***). When you issue the **sp_changedbowner** command, you must be in the database whose ownership is to be changed. The ***login_id*** can't already be a user in the database.

Aliases

An alias is a database user name shared by several login ids. Inside the database, the login id isn't visible, only the database user name to which the logins are aliased can be seen. For example, assume that Mary and Joe have SQL Server login ids MARYJ and JOEQ. There's a user in the database named *helpdesk* (this is a database user name, not necessarily a login id). If Mary and Joe are aliased to *helpdesk*, they still login with their server ids but things like **sp_who** will simply show their name as *helpdesk*.

Should you ever need to see the list of users that a specific login id is aliased to, select that id in the Server Manager display and edit it. You will see the following display.

Aliases are quite often used to allow several people to share the database owner role. You can create aliases with SQL Enterprise Manager, Transact-SQL or VBA.

Creating an Alias with Enterprise Manager

Creating aliases with SQL Enterprise Manager again takes us to the confusing Manage Users dialog.

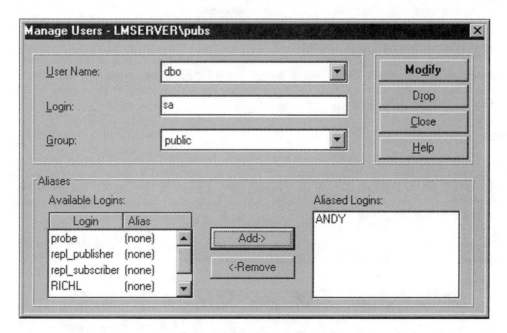

What you need to do this time is select the target database user name from the User Name drop-down list. Then, at the bottom of the screen, find the login id you want to alias to the user name. Highlight it and then click Add. In the screen above, ANDY is already aliased to dbo. Any of the names in the list of available logins could be added as an alias, though it wouldn't be customary to alias probe or the special logins for replication to another user.

Creating an Alias with Transact-SQL

To create an alias with Transact-SQL, use the **sp_addalias** procedure.

sp_addalias *login_id, name_in_db*

For example, to make Andy an alias for dbo (thus giving him dbo privileges)

```
use pubs
sp_addalias Andy, dbo
```

Creating an Alias with VBA

To create an alias using VBA, create a delimited list of logins (type **MultiIdentifie**r) and pass it to the **AddAlias** method of the appropriate member of the SQL Server Databases Users collection.

Object Ownership

Users can be given privileges to create objects (this is done with the statement privileges that we'll discuss in the next section). When a user other than dbo creates an object, they become the owner of that object. An object owner has full rights to objects it owns. Object owners must grant permissions before any other user (except *sa*) can access the object. Note that even the dbo can't access an object without its owner giving permission. There's no way to transfer object ownership.

SQL Server has some rules for determining which object you're talking about when there are multiple objects with the same name and different owners in a database. When you refer to an object by name, SQL Server looks for:

- An object with that name that you own
- An object with that name owned by dbo that you have permission to access

If neither can be found, it issues an error message. To refer to an object that someone else owns, you must qualify the reference by including the owner name:

- ownername.objectname

When you own an object and want to refer to one owned by dbo with the same name, you must also qualify the reference:

- dbo.objectname

The fact that different users can own objects creates what are called 'ownership chains'. These chains are created because some objects depend on other objects. For example:

- Views depend on tables or other views
- Procedures depend on procedures, tables and/or views

Typically, the owner of the highest level object also owns all the objects it depends on. In this case, SQL Server assumes a user with permission to access the top-level object can access all the lower level objects and doesn't check further when it's developing a query plan. When there are different owners in the chain, the chain is said to be 'broken'. In this case, SQL Server checks permissions on each lower level object owned by a different user.

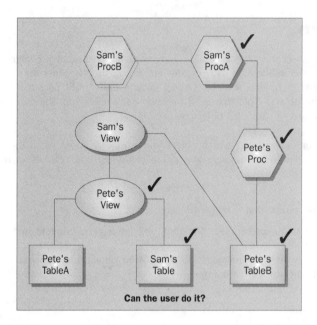

Can the user do it?

When a user executes Sam's ProcA, SQL Server must recheck permissions at each break in the chain, i.e. at each of the points marked with a check mark in the preceding illustration.

Impersonation

We've said that even dbo needs permission to access objects owned by others. Clearly this could create a messy situation if the individual who created an object is no longer around to grant these permissions. There is another tool available to the dbo, however. This is **impersonation**. A dbo can impersonate any user in the database he or she owns and sa can impersonate any user in any database. This allows dbo and sa to grant and revoke permissions on objects owned by others. And, although there's no way to transfer object ownership, this allows the sa to create objects to be owned by others.

To impersonate another user, issue the **SETUSER** statement

```
SETUSER ['username' [WITH NORESET]]
```

To stop impersonation, just issue the **SETUSER** statement without a user name. If you use the **WITH NORESET** option, this won't set your identity back to dbo or sa. If you are dbo or sa, you can drop objects owned by others without needing to impersonate the user.

Statement Permissions

Some Transact-SQL statements aren't available to all users. Instead, specific permission to use these statements must be granted to users or groups. The privileged statements are:

```
CREATE   DATABASE          CREATE   TABLE
CREATE   DEFAULT           CREATE   VIEW
CREATE   PROCEDURE         DUMP   DATABASE
CREATE   RULE              DUMP   TRANSACTION
```

CREATE DATABASE permission can be granted only by the sa and only to users in *master*. This means that if you want to give someone the privilege of creating databases, you must first add that user's login ID to *master* as a user of that database. All other statement permissions can be granted by sa or dbo. Statement permissions are granted for a specific database; giving someone **CREATE TABLE** privilege in database A doesn't have any bearing on whether they have that privilege in database B.

Note that, if you grant privileges to a group, everyone in that group gets the privilege unless you explicitly revoke it. Since everyone is effectively a member of the group *public*, any privileges granted to *public* are granted to everyone. You can grant statement privileges with SQL Enterprise Manager, Transact-SQL and VBA.

Using SQL Enterprise Manager to Grant Statement Permissions

To grant statement permissions with SQL Enterprise Manager, open the Edit Database dialog box and choose the Permissions tab.

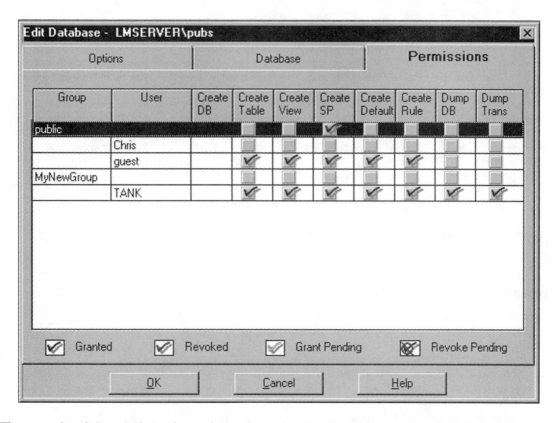

This is another dialog which can be confusing. In version 6.0, if a privilege was revoked, it was indicated with a red check mark! Hardly what you'd expect since a check mark usually means OK! In version 6.5, there's no indication that a privilege has been revoked. That is, there's no difference between never having had the privilege and having had it revoked.

To grant a privilege, click the box. You'll see a green check mark. When you have granted everything you want to, click OK. If you want to review your work, you will have to bring this dialog back from the Server Manager display.

> In previous versions of SQL Server, both the grants and revokes were saved in a table called Sysprotects. In SQL Server 6.5, it appears that only the grants are being saved, at least for statement permissions. This means we're losing some information that might be useful.

Using Transact-SQL to Grant Statement Permissions

To grant statement permissions with Transact-SQL, use the **GRANT** statement.

```
GRANT {ALL | statement_list } TO {PUBLIC | name_list }
```

> **statement_list**
>   **CREATE DATABASE, DEFAULT, PROCEDURE, RULE,**
>   **TABLE** and/or **VIEW**
>   **DUMP DATABASE** and/or **TRANSACTION**
> **name_list**
>   list of user and group names, separated by commas

To give TANK the right to create tables, defaults, procedures, rules and views, you would use the following statement:

```
GRANT CREATE TABLE, CREATE DEFAULT, CREATE PROCEDURE, CREATE RULE, CREATE VIEW TO TANK
```

This statement gives all the members of the Developer group the right to create stored procedures:

```
GRANT CREATE PROCEDURE TO Developers
```

To allow the Night Operator group to do backups, you issue the following statement.

```
GRANT DUMP DATABASE, DUMP TRANSACTION TO NightOperator, Chris
```

To review the privileges that you've granted, use the stored procedure **sp_helprotect**.

Using VBA to Grant Statement Permissions

To grant statement privileges with VBA, prepare a delimited list of one or more users or groups. This is a **MultiIdentifier** type. Pass this list, together with the privilege which is one of the following:

```
SQLOLEPriv_CreateTable
SQLOLEPriv_CreateDatabase
SQLOLEPriv_CreateView
SQLOLEPriv_CreateProcedure
SQLOLEPriv_DumpDatabase
SQLOLEPriv_CreateDefault
SQLOLEPriv_DumpTransaction
SQLOLEPriv_CreateRule
SQLOLEPriv_AllDatabasePrivs
```

to the **GRANT** method of the appropriate member of the Databases collection.

Object Permissions

Object permissions say what a user is allowed to do with various database objects.

Action	Associated Object(s)
SELECT	Table, view, column
UPDATE	Table, view, column
INSERT	Table, view
DELETE	Table, view
REFERENCES	Table (primary key)
EXECUTE	Stored procedure

Object permissions can be granted and revoked by the object owner. With version 6.5, it's possible to grant a privilege with the right to grant that privilege to others. Note that you must explicitly grant the **REFERENCES** privilege; it isn't implied by granting **SELECT** privileges. You can grant and revoke object permissions with SQL Enterprise Manager, Transact-SQL and with VBA.

Using SQL Enterprise Manager to Grant Object Permissions

To grant or revoke object permissions with SQL Enterprise Manager, you select a database in the Server Manager Display, then select Permissions from the Object menu. You can also get to the permissions dialog by selecting an object and choosing Permissions from the drop-down menu.

SQL Enterprise Manager lets you work from either a user point of view or an object point of view, as shown below. You can choose the method that suits you best and flip back and forth between them.

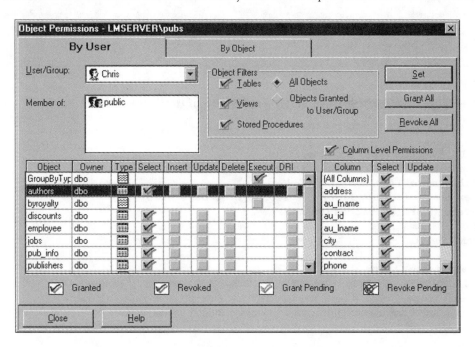

The Object Filters options allow you to reduce the amount of information that's displayed. DRI stands for Declarative Referential Integrity; if you check this box, you're granting **REFERENCES** permission.

This dialog is similar to that used for granting statement permissions. After you've chosen the privileges you want granted, click on Set to apply them.

Note that it isn't possible to use the 'grant with grant' option with SQL Enterprise Manager.

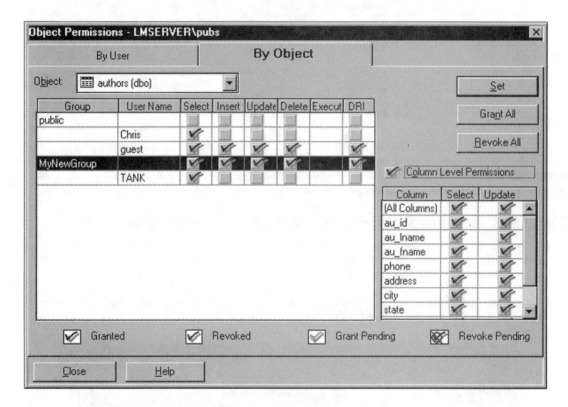

Granting Object Permissions with Transact-SQL

You grant object privileges with the **GRANT** statement.

```
GRANT {ALL [PRIVILEGES] [column_list] |
    permission_list [column_list] ON
    {table_name [(column_list)] |
    view_name [(column_list)] | stored_procedure_name |
    extended_stored_procedure_name}
TO {PUBLIC | name_list}
WITH GRANT OPTION

    permission_list
        SELECT, INSERT, DELETE, UPDATE, REFERENCES, EXECUTE
    name_list
        a list of user names and/or group names delimited by commas.
```

The **WITH GRANT OPTION** allows the user who's granted a permission to grant it with others. You can't use the **WITH GRANT OPTION** if you've granted a privilege to a group. This example grants several privileges on the Authors table, to the group MyNewGroup.

```
GRANT SELECT, INSERT, DELETE, UPDATE, REFERENCES
ON authors TO MyNewGroup
```

Granting Object Permissions with VBA

Each of the database objects has a **GRANT** method. You select the target object, build a delimited list of users and groups (type **MultiIdentifier**) and invoke the **GRANT** method with the list and the appropriate value from:

```
SQLOLEPriv_Select
SQLOLEPriv_Insert
SQLOLEPriv_Update
SQLOLEPriv_Delete
SQLOLEPriv_Execute
SQLOLEPriv_References
SQLOLEPriv_AllObjectPrivs
```

Revoking Permissions

In SQL Enterprise Manager, revoke either statement or object privileges by clicking on a check box that shows a granted permission.

In Transact-SQL, use the **REVOKE** statement.

Statement permissions
```
        REVOKE {ALL | statement_list}
        FROM {PUBLIC | name_list}
```
Object permissions
```
        REVOKE [GRANT OPTION FOR] {ALL [PRIVILEGES] |
         permission_list} [(column_list)]
        ON {table_name [(column_list)] |
        view_name [(column_list)] | stored_procedure_name |
        extended_stored_procedure_name}
        FROM {PUBLIC | name_list}
        CASCADE
```

GRANT OPTION FOR revokes the ability to confer the permission to another user but leaves the user with the permission still granted.

CASCADE revokes **WITH GRANT** privileges that were granted by the specified user, including those of the specified user.

To revoke privileges with VBA, pass the appropriate **SQLOLE_PRIVILEGE_TYPE** and a delimited list of users and/or groups to the **REVOKE** method of the object.

Views as a Security Mechanism

You can create views that limit the user to:

- A particular subset of the rows of a table
- A particular subset of the columns of a table
- To summary data only

> In some cases, you may find creating views preferable to granting column privileges. If you grant column privileges and a user issues a SELECT * command, the user will see an error message. To see an example of this, login to SQL Server as some one other than **sa** and issue SELECT * FROM master..syslogins. If you create a view that includes only the columns the user is allowed to see, the user can issue SELECT * with impunity.

You can also use views to limit user access to data based on the user's identity. This is the only way to get context-based security in a SQL Server database. Here's a simple example that limits the user to rows that are identified as belonging to the user:

- Add a column named *who_owns_me* to the table
- Fill in *who_owns_me* with the user's **login** name (not the name in the database)
- Create a view with a **WHERE** clause that tests the column in the table against the login name of the user, e.g. **WHERE who_owns_me = SUSER_NAME()**

Of course, you can make the view condition much more complex than the one shown here. Using views will allow you to extend greatly the already robust privilege scheme that's built into SQL Server.

Remote Servers

SQL Server supports the concept of remote servers. A remote server is another SQL Server on the network. Rather than logging in to the remote server explicitly, users access it through their local server. Users can execute stored procedures on remote servers. Remote servers underlie both replication and the distributed transactions that are available in version 6.5, although you won't have to worry about setting them up for those features. If you use replication or distributed transactions, the remote servers will be automatically set up for you.

Remote servers are set up in pairs and each server must be configured so that it recognizes the other. Let's look at the following scenario.

A user is logged in on a server named Vegetable and wants to run a procedure named WhatsForDinner which is in the MeatRecipes database on a server named Animal:

```
declare @Recipe varchar(30)
exec Animal.MeatRecipes.dbo.WhatsForDinner
    "Hamburger", @Recipe OUTPUT
```

To make this possible, you need to set up the Animal and Vegetable servers so that they know about each other.

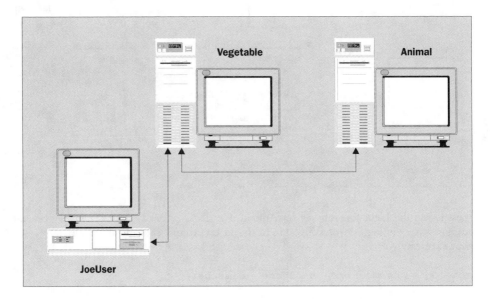

You can set up remote servers using Transact-SQL, SQL Enterprise Manager or VBA. We'll will look at the process with Transact-SQL first, then the SQL Enterprise Manager approach, as it's clearer that way.

To set up remote servers using Transact-SQL, you connect to Vegetable and add Animal as a remote server with the **sp_addserver** procedure.

```
sp_addserver Animal
```

Then you connect to Animal and add Vegetable as a remote server.

```
sp_addserver Vegetable
```

You should check the **remote access** configuration (using SQL Enterprise Manager or **sp_configure**) and make sure it's set to 1 (the default).

You also should check the **remote login timeout**, which is the number of seconds to wait before returning from an attempt to login to a remote SQL Server. Its default value is 5 seconds; if you set it to 0, you're requesting an infinite wait. You should also check the **remote query timeout**. This option specifies the number of seconds to wait before returning from processing a remote query. The default is 0, an infinite wait. If you don't see these options, make sure Show Advanced Options is turned on. If you change either of these options, restart the server.

Once the servers know about each other, you need to set up the remote users. In this process, you're providing the information shown in the following diagram.

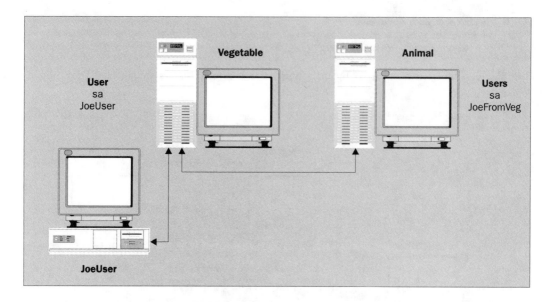

First, you must create the login JoeFromVeg on Animal if it doesn't already exist. Then, logged into Animal, you must map the login id on Vegetable to the id on Animal. You do this with **sp_addremotelogin**.

sp_addremotelogin *fromserver, namehere, namethere*

You should also set the remote login option for the user by using the **sp_remoteoption** procedure.

sp_remoteoption [*remoteserver, loginame, remotename, optname,* {TRUE | FALSE}]

Currently, there's only one value for optname: **TRUSTED**. This specifies whether the password will be checked for the remote user. The default is **FALSE**, which means the password will be checked.

```
sp_remoteoption Vegetable, JoeFromVeg, JoeUser,
     TRUSTED, TRUE
```

In SQL Enterprise Manager, you set up remote servers by selecting Remote Server from the Server Menu. You will get a single dialog box that allows you to set up the servers and manage the logins.

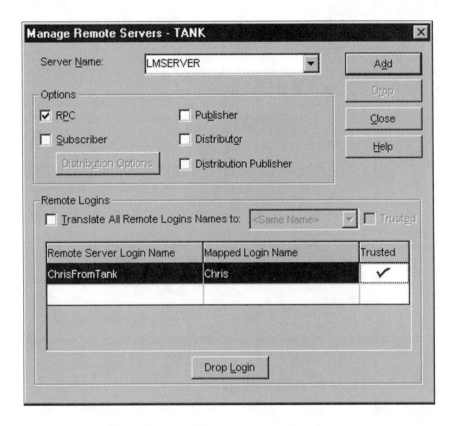

In this example, the remote servers are being configured only for Remote Procedure Calls (RPC). The other options deal with replication and we'll cover that in Chapter 11. The top part of the dialog accomplishes what was done with **sp_addserver**; the bottom half accomplishes what was done with **sp_addremotelogin** and **sp_remoteoption**. You will still need to check the configuration values if you use SQL Enterprise Manager to set up remote servers.

To set up remote servers using VBA, you must first create a remote server object, set its properties appropriately and add it to the SQL Server's remote server collection. When you have done that, you can create a remote login object for each user and add these to the remote login collection of the remote server you've just created.

Summary

In this chapter we've covered the SQL Server security model, showed you how to add logins, database users and groups. Then we went on a tour of integrated, standard and mixed security. After that, we looked at how to grant and revoke object and statement permissions and gave you a sample of how you might use views to implement context-based security. The chapter was wrapped up with a discussion of remote servers and showed you how to set them up.

6.5

Transaction Management and Locking

If you've heard the marketing buzz or read the press releases stating that the latest benchmarks have reached unprecedented transactions per second with concurrent users, you might have been led to believe that this kind of phenomenal performance was achieved by merely installing the newest version of the DBMS. The truth is that many hours were spent just analyzing and examining the way the benchmarking application retrieves data and processes transactions. Just as the fastest highway is of no benefit if all the access roads are blocked off, the fastest database and hardware platform are of limited use to an application that inefficiently locks its resources or can't ensure data integrity.

SQL Server automatically enforces a practical model for locking, but this is probably not sufficient for a large, multiuser application, at least not without considerable tweaking and tuning. As a DBA, it will be up to you to provide the basic understanding of transaction management and to offer insight into implementing performance gains in your application's locking behavior. This chapter discusses the major issues involving transaction locking and management in a multiuser application that's designed to provide excellent transaction throughput and maximize user concurrency.

The Basics of a Transaction

To understand how SQL Server controls access to its data resources, you have to understand the basics of a **transaction**. In its simplest form, a transaction is merely the act of adding, altering or deleting data within the server. Change one value with a single command—that's a transaction. Change the value of 50,000 records with a single command—that too is a transaction.

Most SQL Statements, no matter how many rows of data they affect, are implicitly defined transactions (there are a few exceptions to this rule like **SELECT...INTO** or **TRUNCATE** commands). As you'll see later in this section, we can also group SQL statements into explicit transactions using the transaction delimiters **BEGIN TRAN** and **COMMIT TRAN** or by changing session or server-level user options. We'll also discuss the behavior of these keywords when we use them in stored procedures and triggers.

But first, let's cover the basics characteristics of a transaction as posed by the ACID Test. Although it sounds more like a weapon of mass destruction or a trip into the psychedelic, all this test requires is that the DBMS ensures that all of its transactions are:

- **Atomic**: provide an all or nothing characteristic to the transaction. Either the transaction succeeds and writes to the database, or fails and is reversed.

- **Consistent**: a consistent transaction preserves the state of the data that is unaffected by the transaction. Conversely, a consistent transaction alters only the data effected by the transaction. The actions of users don't interfere with one another.

- **Isolated:** isolated transactions don't affect other transactions in process. Isolated transactions impose no change in behavior on other incomplete transactions that affect the same data.

▲ **Durable:** a durable transaction has effects that persist despite a system failure. In SQL Server, transaction durability is maintained through the recovery process.

To ensure the ACID nature of the transaction, the front-end application can explicitly commit or terminate the transaction or SQL Server itself can implicitly **commit** or **rollback** the transaction. *Commit* means to write the data to the database. *Rollback* means to fully reverse the effect of the transaction.

Using the Transaction Statements

As we mentioned earlier, the vast majority of SQL statements are implicit transactions, so you might think reasonably enough that SQL statements are treated identically by SQL Server. Indeed, the following two batches of statements are equal:

```
UPDATE MYTABLE
SET COLUMN1 = NewValue
WHERE KEY_COLUMN = KeyValue
GO
```

```
BEGIN TRANSACTION
    UPDATE MYTABLE
    SET COLUMN1 = NewValue
    WHERE KEY_COLUMN = KeyValue
COMMIT TRAN
GO
```

However, the default SQL Server configuration doesn't treat the following SQL statements in the same way. The first batch of SQL statements are treated as two implicit transactions. The second batch of statements is delimited by **BEGIN TRAN** and **COMMIT TRAN** and are thus considered a single unit of work or transaction.

```
UPDATE MYTABLE1
SET COLUMN1 = NewValue
WHERE KEY_COLUMN1 = KeyValue
GO
UPDATE MYTABLE2
SET COLUMN2 = NewValue
WHERE KEY_COLUMN2 = KeyValue
GO
```

> Note that a block of TSQL code punctuated with a GO statement is considered a batch. The batch above contains two transactions, while the batch below contains only one.

```
BEGIN TRAN
    UPDATE MYTABLE1
    SET COLUMN1 = NewValue
    WHERE KEY_COLUMN1 = KeyValue

    UPDATE MYTABLE2
    SET COLUMN2 = NewValue
    WHERE KEY_COLUMN2 = KeyValue
END TRAN
GO
```

This is a very good reason why you should always try to use explicit commands to define the bounds of a transaction within your application. Although SQL Server has implicit transaction behavior in its front-end tools like ISQL and SQL Enterprise Manager, your application isn't likely to get the exact same treatment due to variations in the front-end tool. For example, Microsoft JET (used in MS-Access) sends multirow updates as singular update statements. Since a transaction can involve one or one million data modifications, you should tell SQL Server where to start a given transaction and where to end it. In general, the best kinds of transactions are short (code-wise), brief (in CPU time) and properly delimited.

> New to SQL Server 6.5 is a `user_option` called `IMPLICIT_TRANSACTIONS`. When this option is turned on, the above SQL statements are treated equally. Turning on this option places your session in 'transaction context'. Any transaction open must then be closed with a `COMMIT` or `ROLLBACK`. To determine whether this option is turned on, use the `sp_config 'user_options'` command.

So let's take a close look at the commands that define transactions and how they affect database behavior.

The Begin Transaction Command

This command denotes the beginning of an explicitly defined transaction. All SQL statements from this statement to a **COMMIT TRAN** statement are considered one unit of work, thus a transaction. You can uniquely identify a transaction by naming it. This is the syntax:

```
BEGIN TRAN[SACTION]   transaction_name
```

The transaction name is entirely optional, but can be quite useful if you're opening multiple transactions in one batch process or are nesting transactions. In nested transactions, the transaction name is only useful on the outermost **BEGIN..COMMIT** or **BEGIN..ROLLBACK** pair. You can't use inner nested transaction names, since only the outermost transaction name is registered with the system. You will, however, receive an error if you don't an equal number of **COMMIT** and **BEGIN TRAN** statements. Also, a global variable **@@trancount** is incremented each time SQL Server finds a nested transaction within a batch.

The Commit Transaction Command

This command denotes the end of an explicitly defined transaction. When it meets a **COMMIT**, SQL Server finalizes any data modifications which took place in the transactions and frees any locks taken due to the modifications. The syntax used for this is:

```
COMMIT TRAN[SACTION] transaction_name
```

Here again, the transaction name is entirely optional and only needed if the **BEGIN TRAN** statement has a transaction name associated with it. If you're working with nested transactions, you must remember that none of the transactions are committed until the outermost transaction is committed. Conversely, if the outermost transaction is rolled back, the same goes for all inner nested transactions.

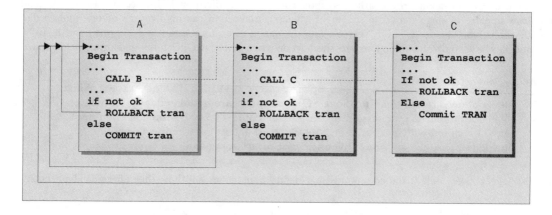

The Rollback Transaction Command

This command rolls back or undoes all data modifications. From undoing a single-row insert to rolling back the update statement that made all of the firm's top managers hourly employees, **ROLLBACK** is the first word off of the DBA's lips when data modifications go awry. The syntax looks like this:

```
ROLLBACK TRAN[SACTION] transaction_name savepoint_name
```

The transaction name and savepoint name are optional. If you don't specify a savepoint, the transaction is rolled back to the beginning (the first **BEGIN TRAN** Statement in the transaction). Note that **ROLLBACK TRAN** will fail if you've already issued a **COMMIT TRAN** command. **ROLLBACK TRAN** will also fail within a nested transaction if you attempt to rollback to any other transaction besides the outermost transaction.

The Save Transaction Command

This command allows you to mark places in a transaction where you can rollback without having to undo the entire transaction. The syntax for issuing a savepoint midway into your transaction is:

```
SAVE TRAN[SACTION] savepoint_name
```

A savepoint is nothing more than marker within a transaction. Even if you rollback to a savepoint, you must still complete the transaction with a **COMMIT** or abort it with a full rollback. In fact, rolling back to a savepoint doesn't release any of the locks the transaction has acquired to that point. Here's an example of how we can use a savepoint to allow users to reverse only a portion of a transaction:

```
BEGIN TRAN MyTran

    SAVE TRAN Tran1

        UPDATE MyTable
        SET MyColumn = 'aaaa'
        WHERE KEY_COLUMN = MyKey

    If @@ERROR > 0 THEN
        ROLLBACK TRAN Tran1

    SAVE TRAN Tran2

        UPDATE MyTable2
        SET MyColumn2 = 'bbbb'
        WHERE KEY_COLUMN2 = MyKey2

    If @@ERROR > 0 THEN
        ROLLBACK TRAN Tran2

COMMIT TRAN
```

Without savepoints in this transaction, the successful updates to the tables **MyTable** and **MyTable2** would both have to be successful for either update to be committed to the database. By using savepoints, the transaction allows for all, one or both tables to be updated.

At first glance, this example might seem no different than using no transaction control statements at all. After all, without them, the updates would occur independently and locks would be freed quicker. However, there are two key advantages to using the above savepoint approach. First, other users won't see any of the data changes until all the modifications have been completed. Second, we can easily undo the entire transaction by issuing a **ROLLBACK MyTran** statement.

> Warning: SQL will allow duplicate savepoint names within a transaction. Using the savepoint name **Tran1** for both savepoints in the above example won't generate an error. If the second update statement fails, however, both update statements will be rolled back. SQL Server only uses the first occurrence of a savepoint name when performing a rollback.

Transactions and @@trancount

We mentioned earlier that a global variable, **@@trancount**, is incremented each time SQL Server finds a nested transaction, so you can probably deduce that **@@trancount** holds the number of pending transactions for a given connection. This table illustrates the effect that different SQL statements have on the **@@trancount** variable:

Statement	Effect
BEGIN TRAN	@@trancount = @@trancount + 1
COMMIT TRAN	@@trancount = @@trancount - 1
ROLLBACK TRAN	@@trancount = 0
ROLLBACK TRAN savepoint_name	@@trancount = @@trancount (no effect)
SAVE TRAN	@@trancount = @@trancount (no effect)
UPDATE	@@trancount = @@trancount (no effect)
INSERT	@@trancount = @@trancount (no effect)
DELETE	@@trancount = @@trancount (no effect)
SELECT	@@trancount = @@trancount (no effect)

You can inspect the current value of **@@trancount** by selecting it. For example:

```
SET NOCOUNT ON              -- turns off the '(n rows affected message)'

SELECT 'Transactions before =', @@trancount

BEGIN TRAN
   ...TSQL Code...
   SELECT  'Transactions during =', @@trancount
COMMIT TRAN
GO

SELECT 'Transactions after =', @@trancount
```

Here's the result set for this query, assuming that **@@trancount** is zero when it's executed:

Transactions before = 0

Transactions during = 1

Transactions after = 0

As you can see, **@@trancount** can be very useful for determining the state of a transaction during a stored procedure or other lengthy process.

> **Data is never committed to the server until @@trancount equals 0. This means that locks aren't released on database objects until @@trancount is equal to 0.**

Nested Transactions

Although SQL Server allows transactions to be nested, the inner transactions have no effect on the committal of data. In fact, nesting transaction does little more than increment the **@@trancount** variable. SQL only recognizes the outermost **BEGIN TRAN** and **COMMIT TRAN** statements. SQL will, however, generate an error if the number of **COMMIT TRAN** statements doesn't match the number of **BEGIN TRAN** statements in a batch, stored procedure, or trigger. For example, this batch:

```
BEGIN TRAN MyTran1
    UPDATE MyTable ...
    BEGIN TRAN MyTran2
        UPDATE MyTable2 ...
        ROLLBACK MyTran2
    COMMIT TRAN MyTran2
    UPDATE MyTable2
COMMIT TRAN MyTran1
```

will generate the following error:

Cannot rollback MyTran2 - no transaction or savepoint of that name found.

The previous batch will, however, cause **@@trancount** to be incremented by two. Similarly, nested **COMMIT TRAN** statements have don't effect when data is committed in a transaction. For example, issuing the following batch won't generate an error, neither will it commit data until the outermost **COMMIT TRAN** is reached:

```
BEGIN TRAN MyTran1
    UPDATE MyTable1...
    BEGIN TRAN MyTran2
        UPDATE MyTable2
    COMMIT TRAN MyTran2
    UPDATE MyTable3...
    ROLLBACK TRAN MyTran2
COMMIT TRAN MyTran1
```

This example will result in all data modifications to **MyTable1**, **MyTable2** and **MyTable3** being rolled back to the Transaction **MyTran1**. The innermost **COMMIT TRAN** statement is ignored and thus never committed. In other words, the outermost commit is the only commit that has an effect on the data.

Transactions and Stored Procedures

It's always a good idea to put transaction control commands in stored procedures. They generally execute faster, thus holding locks for less time, and provide better error trapping when things go wrong. There are, however, a few important things to consider when you're using transactions in stored procedures, particularly when the stored procedure itself is called from within a transaction.

Let's look at a simple stored procedure which inserts a row into a table. If the stored procedure encounters an error, it undoes the insert:

```
CREATE PROC MyProc1 @MyParm int
AS
BEGIN TRAN


   CREATE TABLE #MyTable (col_1 int)

   INSERT INTO #MyTable (Col_1) VALUES (@MyParm)

 If @@error > 0

   begin
      raiserror 99999 "Sorry, there is a problem"
      ROLLBACK TRAN
      return 99999
   end

 Else

   begin
      COMMIT TRAN
      return 0
   end
```

Run by itself, this stored procedure will work without a problem.

```
EXEC MyProc1 65
```

If this stored procedure is called from within a transaction and the rollback is executed, you'll receive an error stating that the **COMMIT TRAN** has no corresponding **BEGIN TRAN**.

```
BEGIN TRAN
EXEC MyProc1
COMMIT TRAN
```

The reason for this error is simple: **ROLLBACK TRAN** always resets the **@@trancount** variable to 0. When SQL Server encounters a **COMMIT TRAN**, it tries to decrement the **@@trancount** by 1. When **@@trancount** is 0, there are no pending transactions, so an error is generated.

To get around this problem, your stored procedures must be aware of the current transaction nesting level, or the calling batch must use the stored procedure's return code to determine the appropriate action. In either case, it's important that you ensure that your stored procedures will work as designed, regardless of the outcome. The next example is same as the previous sample stored procedure, except that it contains conditional transaction statements:

```
CREATE PROC MyProc1 @MyParm  int
AS
DECLARE @tcount int

SELECT @tcount = @@trancount

if @tcount = 0
   BEGIN TRAN MyTran1
else
   SAVE TRAN MyTran1
```

```
INSERT INTO MyTable (Col_1) VALUES (@MyParm)
If @@error > 0
begin
    raiserror 99999 "Sorry, there is a problem"
    ROLLBACK TRAN MyTran1
    return 99999
end
Else
begin
    if @tcount = 0
    begin
       COMMIT TRAN MyTran1
       return 0
    end
end
```

> Transactions executed on remote servers through remote stored procedures are beyond the scope of ROLLBACK and COMMIT. Coding must be included in the RPC and not in the local stored procedure to properly handle how the transaction is terminated. Alternatively, you might use the new Distributed Transaction Coordinator (DTC) to enable two-phase commit functionality. Refer to Appendix B on Microsoft DTC for more information.

Transactions and Triggers

Triggers are special Transact-SQL programs associated with a specific table and a specific kind of transaction: **INSERT**, **UPDATE** or **DELETE**. They differ from stored procedures in that they are considered a part of the transaction that caused them to fire. Thus, a delete trigger on the table Pubs.authors issues a delete against the Pubs.titleauthor table. Although they seem like distinct **DELETE** statements, they are both part of a single transaction. Although a trigger increments **@@trancount** by 1, the commit or rollback is considered part of the data modification that 'fired' it.

In addition, when a trigger rolls back a data modification, all components of the transaction are rolled back, including the calling transaction, data modifications in the trigger itself, and any subsequent SQL code in the trigger. It's for this reason that **@@trancount** is of limited value in trigger code.

> Also note that SQL Server considers triggers as if they were implied transactions, so all transactions within a trigger behave as if they were nested one level deep.

Important Reminders for Transactions

Finally, there are several commands that are off-limits within an explicitly defined transaction. These include,

```
ALTER  DATABASE
DISK  INIT
DUMP  TRANSACTION
LOAD  DATABASE
LOAD  TRANSACTION
RECONFIGURE
UPDATE  STATISTICS
```

where **<object>** is any type of database object, such as **DATABASE**, **INDEX**, **TABLE**, or **VIEW**. We recommend that you *don't* use system stored procedures inside a transaction unless you're willing to perform additional testing to ensure proper performance.

One last note for you: local variables can't bridge transactions. So, if you define the value of a local variable within one **BEGIN..COMMIT TRAN** block of a stored procedure, it will lose that value in another **BEGIN..COMMIT TRAN** block of the same stored procedure. For example:

```
DECLARE @xyz varchar(30)
SELECT @xyz = "I am here"

BEGIN TRANSACTION
    INSERT INTO temptbl values("v1", "value one")
    INSERT INTO temptbl values("v2", "value two")
    PRINT @xyz      — displays "I am here"
GO            — end of batch

PRINT @xyz    — Msg 137, Level 15, State 2  Must declare variable @xyz'.
COMMIT TRANSACTION  — works fine
SELECT * FROM temptbl   — "value one", "value two" are displayed
```

Remember the golden rule as you create or evaluate transactions in your applications: short and sweet. Always commit transactions as soon as you have completed them and avoid relying on implicit commits. Long running transactions negatively impact concurrency and can hamper recovery time, promote blocking and contribute to deadlocks (all discussed later in the chapter).

SQL Server Locking

In a single-user or read-only database, a user can read and write data without worrying that other users are making changes to the same data at the same time. In a multiuser environment, however, it's possible for many people to simultaneously attempt to access the same record. It's wise, therefore, to ensure that a database has a method of ensuring that data remains consistent and data access is coordinated. This is done by placing a lock on a record or group of records when they are accessed by users.

To better illustrate the importance of coordinating data access in a server, let's look at a two simple scenarios in which users access data concurrently and examine the potential effects.

Scenario 1: Coordinated Data Access Problem

Bob works in Accounts Receivable (AR) and Jerry works in Accounts Payable (AP). Bob opens Mr. Garcia's customer invoice record to post that Mr. Garcia's account is paid in full. While Bob is in the record, Jerry also opens it to place a Past Due notice on it. Bob saves the record and a few moments later Jerry does the same. Poor Mr. Garcia, who has paid off his account (or so he thinks), has a past due account.

This example illustrates one of several problems you can encounter when records aren't properly locked: a **lost update**. A lost update is a situation in which one user should have a lock on a record, but, for some reason, another user is able to update the record, negating the effects of the first user's transaction. Other common problems include **dirty reads**, where users read data that hasn't yet been committed to the database (discussed next) and **phantoms**, where users access records that are deleted while they're still working with them and without their knowledge.

Scenario 2: Consistent Data Access Problem

Bob and Jerry work in a bank. Bob is a teller and Jerry works in data entry. Jerry opens Mr. Garcia's account and adds a $100.00 deposit to an account currently with a balance of $0.00. Jerry's application has a method of making changes, but not committing them until he's sure all the information is correct. While Jerry is making these changes to Mr. Garcia's account, Bob opens Mr. Garcia's account and, seeing Mr. Garcia has a balance of $100.00 dollars, allows Mr. Garcia to withdraw it. In the interim, Jerry realizes he has opened the wrong record and cancels the transaction.

If Bob hadn't been allowed a dirty read, Mr. Garcia's request would have been denied and this entire problem could have been avoided.

How Locking Works

You've been presented with some common problems with locking. The next sections explain the fundamentals of locking and how problems like lost updates, dirty reads and phantoms can be avoided.

When Locking Works

Whenever a transaction is initiated, SQL Server uses its internal locking manager to ensure the ACID properties of the transaction. (The two problem scenarios shown earlier discussed transaction management systems that didn't guarantee the ACID properties of a transaction.) The SQL Server lock manager takes a snapshot of the required data resources (data pages, tables, indexes and so on) at the time the transaction is initialized in order to guarantee the successful completion of the transaction. If the required data resources are in use by other users or processes at the time the transaction is initiated, the transaction may encounter **blocking**, a situation where one user waits for the other to release their locks on data, or **deadlocking**, where two users wait on each other, causing SQL Server to automatically rollback one of the two transactions. Once blocking and deadlocks have been resolved, the lock manager is able to issue the appropriate locks on the database resource to complete the transaction and then SQL Server commits the transaction. As you can see, locking and transaction processing go hand-in-hand. One can't occur without the other.

> We can influence some of the behavior of the locking manager by using the optimizer hints that we'll discuss later in this chapter, but the default lock handling will usually take place.

Types of Locks

SQL Server will issue a lock any time it reads or modifies data. The SQL Server lock manager has several different options available when you're issuing locks on database resources. The type of lock issued is usually determined by the SQL Server query optimizer (though you can affect this processing by issuing optimizer hints or setting advanced isolation levels). When it's determining how locking will occur, the lock manager evaluates two factors: the number of records affected by the transaction and whether the transaction will read or modify data. Depending on the answer to these two questions, the lock manager will use one of the following lock types:

- ▲ **Shared**: under shared locks, multiple **SELECT** statements can access the same data concurrently without being blocked by any other, while ensuring no dirty reads have occurred. Shared locks are taken when the query is submitted to the server and is released a page at a time as the pages are read. For example, a query such as **SELECT * FROM TITLES** would lock all the pages in the table **TITLES**. After the first page had been read, the lock on that page would be released and so on until the last page was read. This allows data consistency, yet allows the greatest concurrency for that table.

- ▲ **Exclusive**: exclusive locks, typically issued for DML statements like **UPDATE**, **INSERT** or **DELETE**, hold the database resource for the sole use of the transaction. Exclusive locks are often responsible for any blocking or deadlock problems you may encounter. Exclusive locks not only block any other transaction trying to alter the database resource, they also block any other process merely trying to read the database resource.

- ▲ **Update**: update locks are used by the lock manager to indicate that a database resource is about to be modified, as soon as SQL Server can promote the lock to an exclusive lock. Update locks are usually used for **UPDATE** and **DELETE** transactions and **INSERTS** into a table with a clustered index. Update locks are also compatible with shared locks.

- ▲ **Intent**: there are three kinds of intent locks: intent share, intent exclusive, and share with intent exclusive. As the name implies, intent locks show the future intentions of the lock manager for a given transaction. SQL Server uses intent locks to queue shared locks (intent share) or exclusive locks (intent exclusive) on a data resource, thus preventing any other transaction from acquiring an exclusive lock on the same resource. Intent locks queue transactions in such a way as to allow read-only transactions to proceed while blocking write transactions that arrive later in the queue (share with intent exclusive).

Lock Compatibility

We can use these locks in conjunction, although their basic nature makes some of the locks incompatible with others. Here's a table of the lock compatibility of the possible combinations of locks issued by the SQL Server lock manager:

Lock Type	Shared	Update	Exclusive
Intent Shared	Yes	Yes	Yes
Intent Exclusive	No	No	No
Shared with Intent Exclusive	Yes	No	No
Shared	Yes	Yes	No
Update	Yes	No	No
Exclusive	No	No	No

Scope of Locking

So far, we've looked at the types of locks that are used, but not at how SQL Server determines how much of the database it needs to lock. Locking in SQL Server is a resource-intensive process. Each lock that SQL Server issues consumes the same amount of overhead, no matter what the scope of the lock. Therefore, when processing a transaction, SQL Server attempts to lock the smallest scope (sometimes called granularity) of data resources at any given time.

- ▲ **Page**: page locks acquire a 2K data page or index page at a time. Page locks are the most common form of lock. It's not unusual for a transaction to acquire locks on many pages before escalating to a table lock. Page locks are most often used for shared locks where the optimizer has chosen an index for the transaction.

- ▲ **Extent**: you would only use extent locks when you're de-allocating or allocating additional space for a table or index. An extent is a contiguous group of eight 2K data pages or index pages. Extent locks typically occur during **CREATE** transactions, **DROP** transactions or **INSERT** transactions that require the creation of new data or index pages. The use of extent locks frees up lock resources and cuts down on 'lock starvation', a situation where there aren't enough lock resources available for all the processes running simultaneously on the server.

- ▲ **Table**: an entire table, including all data and indexes are locked. Table locks are frequently found when an index is being created on a table, the optimizer can't find an index to use for the transaction, or the lock manager has decided the transaction has exceeded the page lock escalation threshold.

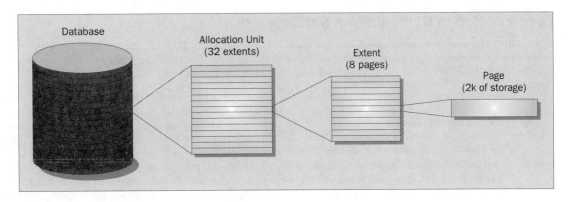

Lock Escalation

Whenever SQL Server requests a lock, it attempts to use page locks unless the table is very small. By default, SQL Server allows a process to hold 200 page locks before it escalates all the way to a table lock. Lock escalation provides an excellent mix between low overhead, high performance and properly ensured ACID properties for transactions. However, lock escalation isn't always desirable and if a transaction exceeds the lock escalation threshold, it can have a negative effect on performance.

To demonstrate this, we'll look at an example using the **PUBS** database, but envisaging that the database has grown significantly in size over the years. Imagine, there's now several thousand entries in the authors table, and you're starting to experience concurrency problems in the front-end application. After doing some investigation with the Current Activity Window, you find that a key maintenance stored procedure (one that inserts and deletes various records) used by several users in the organization is no longer issuing page locks, but is instead locking the whole table. What can you do to stop these table locks?

You could do a few things. You could alter the server's basic lock escalation level. You could examine the indexes and fill factors on the affected tables and perhaps increase the padding offered by a larger fill factor. Or, if you're feeling a little more daring, you could alter your front-end application to issue transactions with the **NOLOCK** hint.

In general, lock escalation (LE) levels are set low to make table scans and other operations against large tables more efficient by reducing locking overhead. However, the default is often far too low a number on large look-up tables in an OLTP application with tens of thousands of data pages. If many processes are attempting to pull data from the look-up table at the same time, SQL Server could be prematurely escalating to table locks, thus blocking other processes. So, if you wish to alter this, you'll need to change the configuration settings.

> In the early days of SQL Server 6.0, one of our key replication processes persistently failed, sometimes crashing the server. I later discovered that the problem was due to premature escalation to a table-level lock. I set the LE maximum setting to 40000 (the number of pages in the table), up from a default of 200, and tried the operation again. This time, it was successful.

Lock Escalation Configuration Settings

SQL Server allows you to adjust three configuration settings that affect how the server processes lock escalation: LE threshold maximum, LE threshold minimum and LE threshold percentage. Settings with an asterisk beside them are advanced settings and can only be viewed with the setting Show Advanced Settings = True.

▲ **LE threshold maximum*** establishes the maximum number of page locks on a specific table before SQL Server escalates to a table lock. If a transaction attempts to lock a greater number of page locks than the LE threshold maximum, SQL Server will escalate to a table lock. LE threshold maximum takes precedence over LE threshold percentage, so a table lock will still occur if the LE threshold maximum is exceeded while the LE threshold percentage is not. LE threshold maximum has a default value of 200. If you decide to increase this number, make sure you increase the locks configuration setting proportionally.

▲ **LE threshold minimum*** sets the minimum number of page locks on a specific table before escalating to a table lock, when used in conjunction with the LE threshold percentage setting. When these two settings are set together, SQL Server will issue a table lock only when the LE threshold minimum and LE threshold percentage are exceeded. You can use the LE threshold minimum, which has a default of 20, to prevent table locks on small tables where the LE threshold percentage is very quickly reached.

▲ **LE threshold percent*** causes page locks to be escalated to a table lock when the specified percentage of pages become locked. If the LE threshold percentage is set to 0, SQL Server ignores this configuration.

▲ **Locks**, which defaults at 5000, sets the exact number of locks available on the server. If all open processes hold more locks than are allowed by this configuration parameter, the processes attempting to acquire locks in excess of this setting will fail with an error message. You can monitor the exact number of locks in use through the TSQL system stored procedure **sp_lock** or through the Enterprise Manager Current Activities window.

If you decide to increase the LE threshold maximum, you should also consider increasing the number of available locks. For example, if your analysis shows that many users might need to simultaneously acquire 685 page locks on one of your main look-up tables, you could increase the LE threshold maximum to 700. Now, your users will be able to acquire all the data resources they need without locking the whole table and blocking other users. But if you have 12 users acquiring 700 locks each, you'd better have a Locks setting of at least 9000 (12 * 700 = 8400, plus 600 for other processes). Note that each lock requires 32 bytes of memory, so make sure you have enough RAM available for any increase.

Troubleshooting Locking Problems

Even though SQL Server does an excellent job of handling transactions under the default behavior of the lock manager, problems still arise. Locking problems increase dramatically as the number of users accessing the application rise. Other factors that can strongly affect locking are usually related to a weakness in table design, indexing or query construction. The most common kinds of transaction problems are **blocking** and **deadlocking**.

Blocking

Blocking is a situation where one transaction must *wait* for another transaction to release its locks on a data resource. The keyword to remember with blocking is **wait** and you know how much users like to do that. Blocking typically occurs because a transaction has gained an exclusive lock on data resources, forcing all subsequent transactions to wait for the resource to be released.

For example, it's actually fairly common to experience blocking in well-designed and properly tuned applications. Since SQL Server's default lock allocation is a 2K page, you can easily hold several rows in a single 2K page, particularly if the table in question is a very narrow, highly normalized design. So, if this table is a frequently used lookup or validation table, it's quite possible for multiple users to attempt to access the data on a single 2K page at the same time. Whenever this happens, a block occurs and the users wait.

> **An excellent way to reduce the possibility of blocking is to increase the fill factors on a table's clustered index. The higher the fill factor of a clustered index, the fewer records stored on a data page, which leads to a lower chance of locking any given data page.**

Hot Spots

Another common occurrence is called the **hot spot**. Hot spots usually occur on tables designed as serially updated data files, where each record is written in chronological or alphanumeric order. For example, a record is keyed on date or has an incrementally increasing value, such as that provided by the Identity property. Thus, when multiple users attempt to insert data at the same time, they compete for an exclusive lock on the final 2K page of the table causing a hot spot to occur. Hot spots frequently develop in applications where table serialization is used and one of these additional conditions exist:

▲ The table doesn't have an index.

▲ The table has only a non-clustered index.

▲ The table has a clustered index built on an incremental key.

Attending to these conditions will usually greatly reduce your exposure to hot spots. If it doesn't, try Insert Row-level Locking (IRL)–we'll look at this later in the chapter. There are reasons why even if you have ensured that the table has an index, hasn't only a non-clustered index or hasn't a clustered index built on an incremental key, you won't always completely remove the possibility of a hot spot. For example, tables with a non-clustered key can still encounter hot spots on the index pages. If you get hot spots in this scenario, even IRL won't solve your problem because it can only be implemented on tables with their clustered index built on a unique index.

Deadlocks

The good news about deadlocks is that SQL Server automatically detects and breaks them. The bad news is that deadlock resolution means that someone's transaction will be automatically rolled back. A deadlock is where two transactions have exclusive locks on separate objects and are waiting to obtain a lock on the other's object. Think of deadlocks as two users blocking each other with each one waiting for the other to release their locks.

Deadlock Example

If you think back to our coordinating server access example at the bank, only one user can have an exclusive lock on a page or table and a user can't take an exclusive lock until all the shared locks have been exhausted. So, Bob could hold a shared lock on the titles table and then request an exclusive lock on the Authors table. At the same time, Jerry takes a lock on the Authors table and requests an exclusive lock on the Titles table.

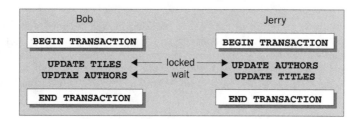

This situation can't be resolved without intervention. Bob must wait for Jerry's process to complete and vice versa. If a system wasn't in place to recognize and resolve circular conflicts like this one, both users would wait indefinitely and a 'chain' could stack up behind them, eventually blocking everyone attempting to access these two tables.

Fortunately, SQL Server can detect and resolve issues like these. It detects and automatically resolves it by rolling back the first transaction that will break the deadlock for all other pending transactions (if there are more than two). In this way, the remaining transaction(s) obtains the required lock and is free to continue. When SQL Server breaks a deadlock, it also notifies the deadlock victim via message 1205 that their process was aborted, as shown below:

Msg 1205, Level 13, State 2
Your server command (process id 34) was deadlocked with another process and has been chosen as deadlock victim. Re-run your command

Either Bob or Jerry gets the dreaded message 1205, while the other is allowed to continue. The deadlock victim's only recourse is to restart the transaction. Note that deadlocks (and blocking for that matter) can occur not only on data pages, but also on index pages.

Preventing Deadlocks

Here are a few tips to help reduce deadlocks. Note that some of these guidelines aren't good as a general practice, but are useful for reducing blocking and deadlocking problems.

Transaction Design Tips

Keep transactions and transaction times as brief as possible. Carefully design stored procedures so that any user interaction takes place either before a transaction is opened or after a transaction is concluded, otherwise, a transaction may wait for a user to respond to a prompt, thus blocking other pending transactions.

Partitioning and Performance Tips

Isolate as many of your transactions in stored procedures as is reasonable. Stored procedures generally execute faster than dynamic SQL statements and thus hold locks for shorter periods of time.

Application Design Tips

These tips could be of help when you encounter blocking or deadlocking problems:

Include in your application code that will intercept 1205 (deadlock victim) messages and resubmit the transaction.

If your application is encountering severe locking or deadlocking problems (which is usually a strong hint to consider redesigning the system), you can use the **NOLOCK** hint in **SELECT** statements. This will ensure the users writing to those tables will have a better chance of taking an exclusive lock without conflict. However, there are some intrinsic risks with this approach, though, since the **NOLOCK** hint allows dirty reads. Conversely, you should avoid using the **HOLDLOCK** hint in SQL statements, to reduce blocking problems.

Because deadlocks are bound to happen in any multiuser environment, always test for deadlock errors. In most cases, if the statement is resubmitted, it will be successful because the process that caused the deadlock has completed. Long running transactions are the most common instigator of deadlocks. You can use the **SET DEADLOCK PRIORITY** command (described later in this chapter) to help control the impact of SQL Server's automatic deadlock resolution.

If your application throughput is experiencing extreme degradation caused by excessive locking, you can also do a little detective work using **sp_lock** during general operation and DBCC trace flags on specific transactions. The DBCC trace flags 1204, for cursory detail, and 1205, for heightened detail, return a significant amount of information about current processes and their locking behavior. However, they only return this information in the event of a deadlock. You should set these trace flags when you're starting the server. Look at Chapter 10 for more detail on syntax and usage of DBCC trace flags.

Insert Row-level Locking

There is a new method for helping to prevent blocking, called **Insert Row-level Locking** (IRL), an optional feature in SQL Server 6.5. IRL can help to significantly reduce the amount of blocking encountered in an application, particularly those applications that perform high-volume inserts. However, IRL isn't a panacea, so you should evaluate it carefully before you use it.

Compared to other major relational databases such as Oracle or Informix, one of the few things you could really complain about in SQL Server was that it lacked row-level locking. SQL Server 6.5 is now beginning to answer this deficiency by introducing Insert Row-level Locking. However, it probably takes more analysis to properly implement IRL than regular page-level locking.

The benefits of IRL can be quite profound, particularly on **INSERT** transactions: greatly reduced contention for data resources, diminished risk of blocking, and minimal possibility of deadlocks. The greatest benefit of IRL is usually in the greatly reduced possibility of encountering hot spots.

On the other hand, IRL has a dark side. You'll find that row-level locking produces more overhead than page-level locking, so transaction logs must typically be enlarged. You'll find that IRL can also introduce deadlocking problems where they didn't previously occur (if you haven't done a careful study of the application). There's a problem that IRL only encompasses the **INSERT** statement, though it does influence the behavior of other types of transactions. All other SQL DML statements, such as **DELETE** or **UPDATE**, still use page-level locking.

In fact, if you're upgrading from an earlier version of SQL Server, we recommend that you don't automatically implement IRL. In most well-designed OLTP and DSS applications, the default page-level locking will be sufficient. If, after careful analysis and monitoring, your application is still not adequately addressing locking and transaction management, you should implement and test IRL. It may provide that extra boost you need.

There are a few situations where row-level locking can really save the day, say, in the hot spot scenario that we've just described. The big performance gain now available with IRL is found in applications that make heavy use of multiuser inserts.

Implementing Insert Row-level Locking with Stored Procedures

You can implement IRL in your database using the system stored procedure **sp_tableoption**. IRL is installed on a table-by-table basis and is **OFF** by default. Each time you create a table, you must explicitly turn on IRL if you want it for that table. The syntax for IRL is based on the system stored procedure **sp_tableoption,** as shown below:

```
sp_tableoption tablename, 'insert row lock', ['true' / 'false']
```

This example activates IRL for the Authors table:

```
    sp_tableoption 'authors', 'insert row lock', 'true'
    go
```

sp_tableoption allows the use of wildcard characters in the table name value in the same format as you would use with the **LIKE** operator. You must use the quote marks (') if you use a wildcard, however, you don't need to use quote marks when you're specifying a single table. For example, this example disables IRL for all tables in the database:

```
    sp_tableoption '%.%', 'insert row lock', 'false'
    go
```

If you use a fully qualified table name including the database name, it must be the current database. If you leave the option value NULL, **sp_tableoption** will report on the current settings of any tables matching the table name value. IRL takes effect immediately after executing this stored procedure.

Because IRL locks records and not pages, SQL Server 6.5 has introduced a couple of new types of locks that you'll only meet if you're using **INSERT** row-level locking: **INSERT_PAGE** and **LINK_PAGE**. They're described below:

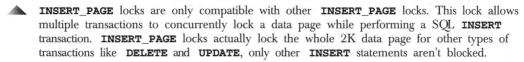

- **INSERT_PAGE** locks are only compatible with other **INSERT_PAGE** locks. This lock allows multiple transactions to concurrently lock a data page while performing a SQL **INSERT** transaction. **INSERT_PAGE** locks actually lock the whole 2K data page for other types of transactions like **DELETE** and **UPDATE**, only other **INSERT** statements aren't blocked.

- **LINK_PAGE** locks are used whenever page splitting occurs, i.e. when new records are inserted to the point of filling the 2K data page, a new data page must be allocated to the table. This is called a **page split**. When the lock manager detects that the next insert is going to cause a page split, the **INSERT_PAGE** lock is promoted to a **LINK_PAGE** lock. Subsequent **INSERT_PAGE** locks are blocked until the processes that started **LINK_PAGE** lock is able to complete and link a newly allocated data page to the current one.

The table shows the compatibility of the new IRL locks with the regular page-level locks:

Type of Lock	Shared	Update	Exclusive	Insert_Page	Link_Page
Shared	Yes	Yes	No	No	No
Update	Yes	No	No	No	No
Exclusive	No	No	No	No	No
Insert_Page	No	No	No	Yes	Yes
Link_Page	No	No	No	Yes	Yes

You must pay close attention to the initial size and subsequent growth of your database's transaction log. We recommend that you use SQL Performance Monitor to track the size of the logs and to alert you to any unusual growth patterns. If you discover that the log is growing quickly, you should increase the size of the log, dump the log more frequently, or both.

The best approach to take with IRL is to be aware of the benefits and weakness of this locking method. If your application utilizes high-volume **INSERTS** to specific tables, install IRL and monitor the application's behavior. Watch for excessive deadlocking, transaction log growth and any unusual blocking behavior. If these problems appear minimal, you can permanently implement IRL into your application.

Tuning Locking Behavior

While SQL Server processes locking automatically, version 6.5 provides the DBA with a great deal of control over locking. You can control locking behavior at three levels: the transaction level, the session level, and the server level. You can control transaction locking behavior using optimizer hints, but remember that they only affect locking behavior for the duration of their single transaction. Session locking behavior is implemented through the **SET** command. Session level behavior continues for all transactions issued by a single user until the user logs off the server or changes the locking behavior with another **SET** command. Server level locking behavior is put in place for all transactions being processed on the server. Server locking behavior can be controlled by adjusting the lock escalation (LE) configuration settings and by implementing Insert Row-level Locking (IRL) on a table-by-table basis. We'll discuss each of these options in greater detail in the following sections.

> We recommend you control locking behavior first with optimizer hints because of the limited scope and impact to other users and process. Next, use SET options, which apply to a single user connection. Finally, you can alter locking behavior at the server level. This is usually my last choice, since any change at this level affects all locking behavior on the server and should usually be tempered with a good deal of analysis.

Optimizer Hints

Optimizer hints are non-ANSI SQL syntax that give you direct control over what indexes are used and what if any locks are issued. You can use optimizer hints in both **SELECT** statements and **UPDATE** statements. Optimizer hints provide you with a lot of power, but you should use them judiciously. In most cases, the access methods chosen by the optimizer will be more than sufficient. Each optimizer hint is fully described below.

NOLOCK

This hint allows dirty reads. This can result in quicker response times, but these **SELECTs** can be problematic. When you use this hint, there's a chance that uncommitted or rolled back transactions will be read. If this happens, the **SELECT** clause will cause an error. You can usually resolve the error by resubmitting the **SELECT** statement.

HOLDLOCK

This hint holds a lock until the completion of a transaction (instead of releasing the shared lock as soon as the required table or data page is no longer needed, whether or not the transaction has been completed). You can't use **HOLDLOCK** in a **SELECT** statement that includes the **FOR BROWSE** option. This option is very useful if you want to ensure that no other users can alter the record (page) until you've committed your transaction (others can still read the record). This example selects the record using the **HOLDLOCK** option, then updates the record:

```
BEGIN TRANSACTION
SELECT * FROM TITLE (HOLDLOCK)

UPDATE TITLE SET …
WHERE …
COMMIT
GO
```

UPDLOCK

This is similar to the **HOLDLOCK** option, except it takes update locks rather than shared locks while reading the table and holds them until the end of the transaction. You would use this option to ensure that no other users can take update or exclusive locks on the selected rows until the transaction has been completed.

```
BEGIN TRANSACTION
SELECT * FROM TITLE (UPDLOCK)

UPDATE TITLE SET …
WHERE …
COMMIT
GO
```

TABLOCK

This takes a shared lock on the entire table until the end of the transaction. If **HOLDLOCK** is also specified, the shared lock is held until the end of the transaction. This option is used to ensure that no other users can modify the selected table until the transaction has been completed.

```
BEGIN TRANSACTION
SELECT * FROM TITLE (TABLOCK, HOLDLOCK)

UPDATE TITLE SET …
WHERE …
COMMIT
GO
```

PAGLOCK

This takes shared page locks on a table where a single shared table lock would normally be taken. This can be extremely useful in ensuring that only the pages that you'll be accessing will get locked, rather than the entire table due to lock escalation.

TABLOCKX

This takes an exclusive lock on the table that is held until the end-of-command or end-of-transaction. This option will lock the table and all of its indexes from being accessed in any manner. Although this option can be very useful if it's imperative that you keep a table from being read from or written to, you should use it sparingly as it will call blocking issues.

```
BEGIN TRANSACTION
SELECT * FROM TITLE (TABLOCKX)
…
COMMIT
GO
```

As you can see, using hints can drastically change locking behavior in SQL Server. For this reason, it's important you use them with caution. Forcing SQL Server to hold locks or take locks it wouldn't normally take can cause concurrency issues and may lead to blocked processes, particularly with running long transactions.

> Hints override any session-level options which may have been specified with the **SET** statement or through server configuration settings like LE values.

You can sometimes use optimizer hints in conjunction with one another, such as **TABLOCK** and **HOLDLOCK** on a **SELECT** statement, though the more restrictive hint will preempt less restrictive ones. Hints also prevail over session-level behavior specified by the **SET** command. This example uses a **PAGLOCK** hint to force a shared page lock when updating the author's table and uses **NOLOCK** when executing a subquery against the Titleauthors table.

```
UPDATE authors
    SET au_lname = 'Whitt'
    FROM authors(PAGLOCK)
WHERE au_lame = 'White'
   AND au_id in
   (SELECT au_id FROM titleauthor (NOLOCK))
```

PAGLOCKX

This takes exclusive page locks on a table where a single exclusive table lock would normally be taken. Like **PAGLOCK**, this hint can be extremely useful in ensuring that only the pages that you'll be modifying will get locked, rather than the entire table due to lock escalation, thus increasing concurrency without affecting data consistency.

The SET Command

The **SET** command provides session-level control for locking behavior. Session-level control means that the setting will remain in effect as long as the user is logged on and the setting hasn't been changed with a subsequent **SET** command. The **SET** command remains in effect for the entire duration of a running trigger or stored procedure. This is the syntax for **SET** options that affect locking:

```
SET  CURSOR_CLOSE_ON_COMMIT  [ON/OFF]
  /  DEADLOCKPRIORITY  [LOW/NORMAL]
  /  IMPLICIT_TRANSACTIONS  [ON/OFF]
  /  TRANSACTION  ISOLATION  LEVEL  [READ  COMMITTED
      /  READ  UNCOMMITTED
      /  REPEATABLE  READ
      /  SERIALIZABLE]
  /  XACT_ABORT  [ON/OFF]
```

> An alternate syntax for all of these **SET** commands is to use: `sp_configure 'users options', 'setting name', '[on/off]'`. Refer to the command **SP_CONFIGURE** for more information.

When it's set to **ON**, **CURSOR_CLOSE_ON_COMMIT** enforces ANSI-NIST standard behavior. This tells SQL Server to close a cursor once its transaction has been committed or rolled back. The **COMMIT** and **ROLLBACK** commands close any open cursors.

DEADLOCKPRIORITY, when set to **LOW**, tells SQL Server that any transactions initiated in this session should be the preferred deadlock victim. When set to **NORMAL**, deadlocks are resolved automatically by killing the transaction with the lowest CPU count.

IMPLICIT_TRANSACTIONS, when set **ON**, sets the ANSI standard behavior that tells SQL Server to open an implicit transaction requiring an explicit **COMMIT** or **ROLLBACK** for any of the following statements:

```
ALTER  TABLE
CREATE
DELETE
DROP
FETCH
GRANT
INSERT
OPEN
REVOKE
SELECT
TRUNCATE  TABLE
UPDATE
```

If this setting is issued while transactions are still open, they must still be explicitly committed or rolled back. However, if no transactions are currently open, every subsequent ANSI SQL statement will start an implied transaction.

TRANSACTION ISOLATION LEVEL alters the default locking behavior for all SQL statements issued during the user's session.

Transaction Isolation Levels

Transaction isolation levels (TIL) are categories of locking behavior as defined by ANSI. The higher the level, the more pessimistic the locking and, thus, the more consistent your data at the expense of concurrency.

You can set the TIL in SQL Server to four different levels, using the **SET** command. As with all other **SET** options, the change is made for a single connection and is reset when the connection is terminated. The syntax for doing this is as follows:

SET TRANSACTION ISOLATION LEVEL READ UNCOMMITTED | READ COMMITTED | REPEATABLE READ | SERIALIZABLE

- ▲ **READ UNCOMMITTED** (TIL 0) allows dirty reads. Users can read from uncommitted pages.

- ▲ **READ COMMITTED** (TIL 1) is the default TIL in SQL Server. Users can only read from pages where no transactions are pending. Unlike TIL 0, dirty reads are prohibited.

- ▲ **REPEATABLE READ** (TIL 2) ensures that a record read several times within a transaction is guaranteed to be identical. You can get the same effect on a transaction basis by using the **HOLDLOCK** optimizer hint.

- ▲ **SERIALIZABLE** (TIL 3) disallows a transaction from reading a row that has been changed and then rolled back (a phantom record).

> **Under SQL Server, TIL 2 and TIL 3 are identical. Setting either option will enable both.**

When it's set **ON**, **XACT_ABORT** aborts a transaction if it encounters any errors, even if it contained multiple SQL statements. When set **OFF**, the transaction only aborts the SQL statement that raised the error while allowing the transaction to complete any other SQL statements remaining.

Locks and Cursors

Although cursors act on a single row of data at a time, the locks they acquire are still at the page level. Because of this, it's important to understand how locks behave inside cursors. In particular, if you don't design them properly, **UPDATE** cursors can cause concurrency problems.

FOR READ ONLY Cursors

SQL Server uses a shared lock on the page it's currently reading. The lock will remain on the page containing the row being fetched for the duration of the **FETCH** and will then be released.

FOR UPDATE Cursors

SQL Server takes an update lock on the page containing the row for the duration of the **FETCH** operation. If the fetched row is modified, the lock is upgraded to an exclusive lock. The exclusive lock is then held for the duration of the transaction. If the transaction isn't explicitly defined, the lock is released as soon as the update is complete, otherwise it's held until the transaction is committed or rolled back.

FOR UPDATE Cursors with SHARED

You can instruct SQL Server to used a shared lock instead of an update lock by using the **SHARED** keyword. The lock is upgraded to an exclusive lock when the row is modified. The exclusive lock is held for the duration of the transaction. The **SHARED** keyword is very useful if your cursor uses a join in the SQL statement. You can flag all the tables which won't be updated as shared. This will allow greater concurrency without compromising data consistency.

> Cursor actions often take significantly longer to complete when compared to ordinary SQL statements or stored procedures. For this reason, locks taken in cursors are generally held longer, so can cause concurrency issues.

Finally, you should always beware of updating a table's Primary Key using a cursor with the **UPDATE** option. You can inadvertently create an infinite loop where the cursor will never end, as in the following example:

```
CREATE TABLE abc
  ( primkey int NOT NULL,
    descript varchar(20) NULL,
    PRIMARY KEY (primkey) )
go
SET nocount ON

INSERT abc VALUES(1, "First Record")
INSERT abc VALUES(2, "Second Record")
INSERT abc VALUES(3, "Third Record")
go


SET nocount ON
DECLARE @primkey int,
  @descr varchar(50),
  @ct int
SELECT @ct = 10 -- counter to reassign primary key value
DECLARE updateabc cursor for
SELECT primkey, descript FROM abc
FOR update

OPEN updateabc
FETCH next FROM updateabc INTO @primkey,@descr

WHILE @@fetch_status = 0
  BEGIN
    SELECT @descr = @descr + " has a key of " + str(@primkey,3,0)
    PRINT @descr

    SELECT @ct = @ct + 1
```

```
     UPDATE abc SET primkey = @ct WHERE current of updateabc

     FETCH next FROM updateabc INTO @primkey,@descr
    end

  CLOSE updateabc
  DEALLOCATE updateabc
```

This would produce the following output:

```
First Record has a key of   1
Second Record has a key of   2
Third Record has a key of   3
First Record has a key of  11
Second Record has a key of  12
Third Record has a key of  13
First Record has a key of  14
Second Record has a key of  15
etc.
```

Pessimistic vs. Optimistic Concurrency Management

As we've seen, SQL Server provides a robust set of options with which data consistency can be managed, some of which can be used in ways that vary the restrictions of lock management. We've also seen that there's no such thing as a free lunch when it comes to this management. The less restrictive your locking scheme, the greater the user concurrency, but the greater the opportunity for data consistency problems. The more restrictive the locking scheme, the more consistent your data becomes, but the greater the risk of blocked processes and locking related slowdowns.

These differing styles of lock management are often referred to as **pessimistic** and **optimistic lock management**. Pessimistic is the most restrictive and optimistic is the least restrictive.

A very pessimistic scheme assumes that many people will often attempt to access records simultaneously, so, when a user accesses a record, it will lock it until he or she has finished using it. People can neither read nor write to records currently being accessed. Using the **HOLDLOCK** option in a query is a good example of this. The downside to such a technique is that other users must wait for the user to finish the transaction before they can proceed. Not only will this slow down the system, it will most likely cause blocking issues as well.

An extremely optimistic scheme assumes that the changes of multiple users accessing a record simultaneously are slim. Such a management system holds no locks on a record until it's in the process of being updated. Because of this, users will rarely have blocking issues. They will however, run the risk of reading dirty records and worse still, they will occasionally over-write another user's changes.

The job of system architects and administrators isn't to choose between the lesser of two evils, but to choose the mix of the two approaches that works best given the needs of the business. For example, in a read-only reporting tool, dirty reads are most likely an acceptable risk. On the other hand, in an invoicing system, data accuracy is most likely very important and a more pessimistic approach is probably better.

Generally speaking, transaction isolation level 1 is probably a good starting point for most applications. This level of isolation solves the most common problems with concurrent use of resources while allowing a reasonable amount of concurrent use.

Case Study

A company has a large table which is regularly downloaded to an ASCII file. This data is used in various supporting business processes and thus needs to be downloaded several times daily. Someone notices that, during the download process, users are being blocked from updating the table and, in many cases, are having problems accessing the table at all.

Should we:

▲ Consider server-level changes to the lock management scheme?

▲ Look into session-level parameters for the download process?

▲ Look at the query to see if it can be optimized or rewritten so that it either runs faster, or holds locks differently?

In most cases, start at the query and work your way up. The query or the way a client application is using the query is most likely the problem, not the way the server is currently configured.

Using Optimistic Concurrency Control

Optimistic concurrency control is easiest to implement with a timestamp, so we'll consider this method. The timestamp column is automatically updated when a row is inserted or modified. You can inspect the binary value of this column to determine whether the record has become dirty since you first selected it. With a little effort, you can simulate row-level locking to manage your updates while increasing concurrency.

It works as follows: instead of updating rows of data directly, when an application first selects the record, it stores the timestamp column value locally. When the application submits the update query to the server, the application adds a **WHERE** clause to compare the timestamp column with the timestamp value read from the column initially. If the two values are equal, the row hasn't been modified and the update can continue. If they're not equal, another user has modified the row since it was first selected and the update doesn't occur.

In order for this locking scheme to work, all client applications must use a technique similar to the one described below or data consistency will be compromised. The basic rules that all applications/developers must follow are:

▲ Never make updates to records without first selecting them.

▲ Never write data without comparing the selected timestamp value to the current value (e.g. "`WHERE tsequal(current_timestamp, previous_timestamp)`").

▲ All tables must include a timestamp datatype column.

▲ All tables must have a Primary Key with which any record can be selected individually given the proper where clause.

How to Simulate Row-level Locking in a Client Application

This example enables your application to simulate a very optimistic kind of row-level locking, but it isn't directly comparable to IRL. If you wish to use the timestamp datatype to simulate row-level locking, you need to implement three steps:

1   **READ**: The client selects a record from the database.

```
SELECT COL1, COL2, …, COLTIMESTAMP
FROM MYTABLE
WHERE KEY = x
```

2   **STORE**: The client stores the timestamp column locally.

```
MYTIMESTAMP_VAR = COLTIMESTAMP
```

3   **WRITE**: The client compares the stored timestamp value to the timestamp value in the record.

```
UPDATE MYTABLE
SET     COL1 = a,
        COL2 = b,
          .
          .
          .
WHERE KEY = x
AND TSEQUAL(COLTIMESTAMP,  MYTIMESTAMP_VAR)
```

> **TSEQUAL is a system supplied function which will compare any two timestamp values and return True or False.**

If the record hasn't changed, the **WHERE** clause finds a match (**TSEQUAL** evaluates True) and updates the record. If it doesn't find a match, the record has either been deleted or modified since it was selected in the first step.

Studying Locks

You've seen a lot about transaction and locking. In some cases, such as IRL, the success of the entire locking strategy is proven through good measurement of locking performance. In other cases, such as troubleshooting blocks or deadlocks, gathering information about the status of locks on your server is critical.

Monitoring Locking with Transact-SQL

You can get a quick and easy snapshot of the lock activity of any given server by executing the system stored procedure **sp_lock** in an ISQL windows. An example of the **sp_lock** report might look like this:

spid	locktype	table_id	page	dbname
11	Ex_extent	0	62608	distribution
11	Ex_extent	0	62616	distribution
11	Ex_extent	0	62624	distribution
11	Ex_intent	16003088	0	distribution
11	Ex_pag	80003316	153417	distribution
11	Ex_page	80003316	153418	distribution

11	Ex_page	80003316	153419	distribution
11	Sh_intent	176003658	0	distribution
11	Sh_page	176003658	1612	distribution
14	Sh_intent	640005311	0	master
14	Ex_extent	0	400	tempdb
16	Ex_table	8	0	distribution
19	Sh_table	16003088	0	pubs

The report is simple to read. Spid indicates the process id holding the given lock. Locktype indicates if the lock is shared (SH), exclusive (EX), or update, and the scope of the lock as table, page, or extent. Locktype also shows SQL Server's intent to acquire shared or exclusive locks as **Sh_intent** or **Ex_intent**, respectively. If any lock were blocking another transaction, Blk would appear by the blocking process in the Locktype column.

It's hard to tell exactly what data resource is being locked just by looking at the output from **sp_lock**. You can find out what the table is by issuing the use statement to make the target database current, then issuing a **SELECT** with the **OBJECT_NAME** function and the table id. For example:

```
SELECT object_name(16003088)
```

If you want to find out exactly who the user or process is behind a given Spid, use the system stored procedure **sp_who**. **sp_who** returns information about active processes, as demonstrated:

spid	status	loginame	hostname	blk	dbname	cmd
1	sleeping	sa		0	master	MIRROR HANDLER
2	sleeping	sa		0	master	LAZY WRITER
3	sleeping	sa		0	master	CHECKPOINT SLEEP
4	sleeping	sa		0	master	RA MANAGER
10	runnable	Kevin	KKLINE	0	pubs	INSERT
11	sleeping	sa	SERVERHQ	0	distributi	AWAITING COMMAND
14	runnable	sa	SERVERHQ	0	pubs	DBCC
15	sleeping	sa	TMORRI	0	pubs	AWAITING COMMAND
16	runnable	Kevin	KKLINE	0	master	SELECT
19	runnable	Dwayne	DSEIBE	10	pubs	UPDATE

Here's an explanation of the output columns of **sp_who**:

▲ Spid: the unique process id that can be killed.

▲ Status: shows if the spid is currently running.

▲ Loginame: represents the user id for this process id.

▲ Hostname: the name of the machine the user logged in from.

▲ Blk: the Spid of the blocking process. If the Blk column contains a 0, it isn't being blocked.

▲ Dbname: the database name the process id is logged onto.

▲ Cmd: the command the Spid is currently running (if any).

You could quickly find out what the exact activity of a given Spid is by issuing the command:

dbcc inputbuffer(spid)

In this example, **dbcc inputbuffer**, which can only be used by the SA, would return the results from Spid, which, from the description of Spid 19 in the previous example, appears to be some sort of query in the **PUBS** database:

```
dbcc inputbuffer(19)
go
```

Input Buffer

---

select * from pubs..authors

(1 row(s) affected)

DBCC execution completed. If DBCC printed error messages, see your System Administrator.

If Spid 19 had actually been blocking another critical transaction, you could kill the transaction that processes the entire connection by issuing the **KILL** command. Syntax for the **KILL** command is:

kill spid

> **System processes and processes running extended stored procedures can't be terminated.**

If **KILL** doesn't work, you're basically out of luck. You'll have to down SQL Server and restart it to kill the process. (If you frequently encounter Spids that can't be killed, you may need to reduce your Max Worker Threads SQL Server setting.)

Monitoring Locking with SQL Enterprise Manager

You'll often use the Current Activity Window within SQL Enterprise Manager to pull up a report of the current user and locking activity on a given server. You can access the Current Activity Window in one of two ways: by selecting the Current Activity choice from the Server menu or by clicking the Current Activity icon on the tool bar, as shown:

The Current Activity Window

Using the various tabs of the Current Activity window, you'll be able to view information on current users, process activity, and locks. The Current Activity windows utilizes a toolbar with five distinct buttons, as shown in: View Details, Send Message, Kill Process, Refresh and Display Legend.

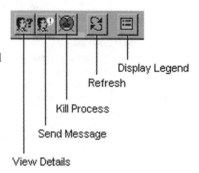

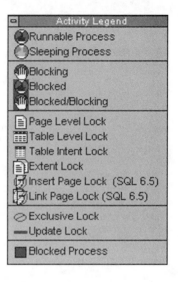

The Refresh and Display Legend buttons are available in all tabs of the Current Activity window. Clicking the Refresh button causes SQL Enterprise Manager to requery the Sysprocesses table and report on any new or changed processes. Clicking the Display Legend button reveals an explanation for all of the symbols used in the Current Activity window, as shown in the next screenshot. You'll need to become familiar with these symbols as you use the Current Activity window.

The View Details, Send Message, and Kill Process buttons are only available in the User Activity and Detail Activity tab. The buttons only become active if you have selected a specific process inside of the tab. We'll provide more information on these buttons later in this section. Only the SA can use the Kill Process button. It will confirm that you want to kill the process before actually terminating it. The View Details button and Send Message button both invoke pop-up windows that we'll describe in greater detail in a while.

The User Activity Tab

The Current Activity windows has three distinct tabs: the User Activity tab, the Detail Activity tab and the Object Lock tab. The User Activity tab shows you the login IDs currently connected, their activity, process id, the user name, status and the type of locks they currently hold, as shown:

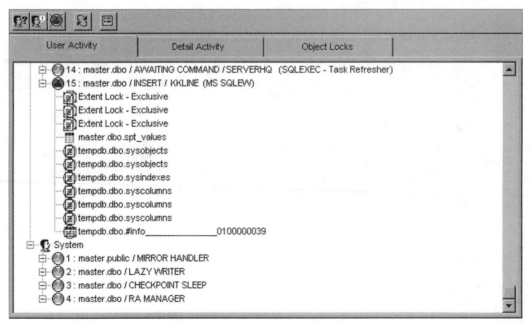

An item shown with a red background indicates that process is blocking other transactions. A globe in full color indicates an active process, while a globe in gray-scale indicates a sleeping process. You can expand or contract information associated with the login id by clicking the plus or minus symbol next to the process. As shown in the example, it's very common for a single process to hold many locks on several different data resources.

The Detail Activity Tab

The Detail Activity tab provides a great deal of extra information compared to the User Activity tab. Note that the example screen shots here are broken into a left and a right half. There's no reason for you not to display the whole Detail Activity tab at one time, assuming your monitor supports the required resolution. The next screenshot shows the first half of the Detail Activity tab:

	User Activity		Detail Activity		Object Locks		

Status	Process	Login ID	Database	User Name	Command	Host	Application	Blocked By
●	15	sa	master	dbo	INSERT	KKLINE	MS SQLEW	0
●	15	sa	master	dbo	INSERT	KKLINE	MS SQLEW	0
●	15	sa	master	dbo	INSERT	KKLINE	MS SQLEW	0
●	15	sa	master	dbo	INSERT	KKLINE	MS SQLEW	0
●	15	sa	master	dbo	INSERT	KKLINE	MS SQLEW	0
●	15	sa	master	dbo	INSERT	KKLINE	MS SQLEW	0
●	15	sa	master	dbo	INSERT	KKLINE	MS SQLEW	0
●	15	sa	master	dbo	INSERT	KKLINE	MS SQLEW	0
●	15	sa	master	dbo	INSERT	KKLINE	MS SQLEW	0
●	15	sa	master	dbo	INSERT	KKLINE	MS SQLEW	0
○	16	sa	master	dbo	AWAITING COMMAND	KKLINE	Microsoft ISQL/w	0
○	1	System	master	public	MIRROR HANDLER			0
○	2	System	master	dbo	LAZY WRITER			0
○	3	System	master	dbo	CHECKPOINT SLEEP			0
○	4	System	master	dbo	RA MANAGER			0

Information displayed in this portion of the screen includes:

- ▲ Status: the globe symbol indicates the current status of the process. Gray-scale if the process is sleeping and full color if the process is active.

- ▲ Process ID: the numeric Spid of the process.

- ▲ Login ID: The SQL Server login id of the user owning the process. A value of SYSTEM indicates a SQL Server internal process.

- ▲ Database: the name of the database where the process is active.

- ▲ User Name: the SQL Server username of the process.

- ▲ Command: the general TSQL command being executed. This column doesn't display a lot of detail on the command being executed by the process. For example, this column might say DBCC when the user is actually executing **DBCC CHECKTABLE(SYSLOGS).**

- ▲ Host: the computer name of the client computer executing the process.

- ▲ Application: the name of the application program. This value is passed by the application to the server and most by coded for custom applications.

▲   Blocked By: the Spid of another process that is blocking this one. Note that the blocked process is also designated by a red background behind the globe symbol. A 0 indicates the process isn't blocked.

The next screenshot displays the second half of the Detail Activity tab:

Blocking	Lock Type	Locked Object	Group Name	CPU Usage	Physical I/O	Host Process
	User Activity	Detail Activity	Object Locks			
0		Extent Lock - Exclusive	public	1893	37	fffa651d
0		Extent Lock - Exclusive	public	1893	37	fffa651d
0		Extent Lock - Exclusive	public	1893	37	fffa651d
0		master.dbo.spt_values	public	1893	37	fffa651d
0		tempdb.dbo.sysobjects	public	1893	37	fffa651d
0		tempdb.dbo.sysobjects	public	1893	37	fffa651d
0		tempdb.dbo.sysindexes	public	1893	37	fffa651d
0		tempdb.dbo.syscolumns	public	1893	37	fffa651d
0		tempdb.dbo.syscolumns	public	1893	37	fffa651d
0		tempdb.dbo.syscolumns	public	1893	37	fffa651d
0		tempdb.dbo.#info_____0100000039	public	1893	37	fffa651d
0		(No Locks)	public	10	4	fff86a91
0		(No Locks)	public	0	0	
0		(No Locks)	public	0	0	
0		(No Locks)	public	0	378	
0		(No Locks)	public	0	21	

Information displayed in this portion of the screen includes:

▲   Blocking: indicates whether this process is blocking another, also indicated by the hand covering the globe symbol. Any number beside a 0 means that the process is blocking another.

▲   Lock Type: this column displays a symbol for the various types of possible locks or if the process holds no locks. Refer to the Current Activity Legend for a description of each lock symbol.

▲   Locked Object: the name of the locked object in the format dbname.user.table (e.g. pubs.dbo.authors).

▲   Group Name: the name of the SQL Server group if you have created and assigned one, or Public if not.

▲   CPU Usage: this number is the cumulative CPU time for a given process. It's sometimes useful to frequently Refresh the Current Activity window to confirm that an active process is getting a reasonable amount of CPU. Though it's not as accurate as SQL Performance Monitor or the system stored procedure **sp_monitor**, it can give you the quick-and-dirty status of an active process.

▲   Physical I/O: this number represents disk reads and writes accumulated by the process since it began.

▲   Host Process: this value represents the process ID number of the client workstation.

The Object Locks Tab

Sometimes, you are less interested in finding out about the status of individual process or login ids, and are more interested in finding out the status of locks and objects on the server. You can find this information out by going directly to the Object Locks tab, as shown:

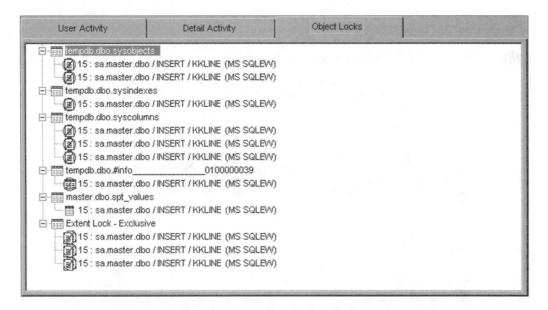

The report shown in the Object Locks tab is organized by database and table, with lock type, process id, user id and statement type shown below. As with the other tabs of the Current Activity window, a red background indicates a blocking process. You can expand or contract items by clicking the plus or minus symbol to the left of the database and table indicator.

Viewing Information on Specific Processes

From any of the tabs in the Current Activity window, you can view additional information about a specific process. Simply click the View Details icon on the Current Activity toolbar or double-click the process you want to see more about to get a display similar to the one depicted:

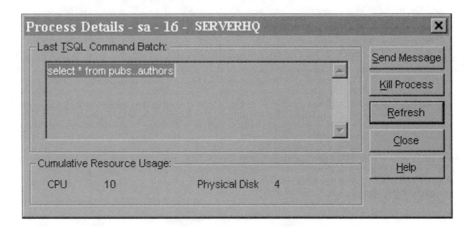

The Process Details pop-up window provides a lot of great tidbits about the process you're examining. The Last TSQL Command Batch displays the first 255 characters of the statement being executed by SQL Server for this process. The Cumulative Resource Usage block shows the current accumulation of CPU time and physical disk read and writes. Plus, if you are SA, you're given the option of killing the process by clicking the Kill Process button or sending an MS-Mail message to the user by clicking the Send Message button. If you think the process has moved on to another command or transaction, click the Refresh button to requery the status of the process.

Sending a Message to a Process Holder/User

As SA, you can send messages to users (or at least to their computers) assuming that you've properly set up SQL-Mail. To invoke the Send Message pop-up window, as shown in the next screenshot, select a process to e-mail, then click the Send Message button on the Current Activity toolbar. Alternatively, you may invoke the Process Details window and click the Send Message button there.

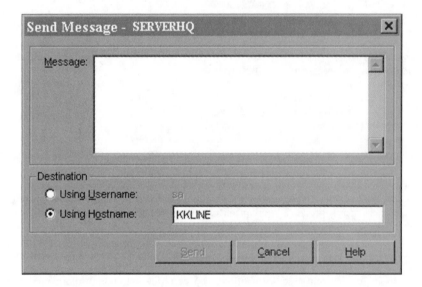

Once the Send Message window appears, type the text of your message in the Message block. In the Destination block, select either the Username or the Hostname radio button to choose between sending to the username or specific host computer. You can also send an e-mail to all users connected to the NT server (not just SQL Server) by typing an asterisk (*) in the Hostname box. Once you've completed your message and identified who to send the message to, click Send to release the e-mail. Since this is a real e-mail notification and not a Netware broadcast-style functionality, the e-mail message mail take a while to reach the user, depending upon the distance and type of LAN/WAN.

Summary

It's practical and wise for a DBA to understand all aspects of transaction locking and management. Few areas of database administration will provide you with more opportunities to tune and troubleshoot. You should, first of all, be thoroughly acquainted with the ACID characteristics of a transaction. You need to know not only the concepts behind, but also the syntax for **BEGIN TRAN**, **COMMIT TRAN** and **ROLLBACK TRAN** and how these commands work both with TSQL batches, triggers and stored procedures. You have to fully understand shared, exclusive and update locks, as well as intent locks. You need to have a good grasp on the scope of locking and the difference between page, extent and table locks. Knowing these fundamentals will enable you to deal with the problems that constantly arise as well as to tune the application for better performance.

To have a well-developed troubleshooting and tuning skill set, you must fully understand blocking, hot spots and deadlocks, as well as how to correct for these problems with ISQL or SQL Enterprise Manager. You should know how to get the details on specific processes and how to kill them, if needed. And you should know how to tune locking with optimizer hints, the **SET** command, LE threshold levels and, if absolutely needed, insert row-level locking. Learning all of these basics will put you well on the road to master-level DBA skills.

6.5

Managing SQL Server Performance

In this chapter we take a look at something which is dear to the heart of everyone involved in working with databases. Whether you're a manager who needs to justify expenditure on a database system, a developer entrusted with producing a database-centered solution, an administrator responsible for looking after a database or a user who needs to access one every day, one of your prime concerns will be performance. The manager wants to know whether she's getting value for money; the developer wants to know how much the database's performance will impact the perceived speed of the application; the DBA wants to know whether she can maintain the same response times as more and more data gets poured into the database; and the poor old user is just fed up with looking at an hourglass all day!

In terms of power–transaction throughput and price per transaction–SQL Server 6.5 is a market leader. Microsoft claim it's 50% faster than SQL Server 6.0 and TPC-C figures appear to back up this claim. But that doesn't mean that every database solution based on SQL Server 6.5 will be lightning fast. In this chapter we'll be looking at one of the key features which will determine whether your queries crawl, run or fly–indexes. We will also look at how you can analyze slow queries, work out what is slowing them down and then make them faster. The main strategies for managing and improving performance are:

- ▲ Indexing strategies
- ▲ Query optimization
- ▲ Tools for analyzing query performance
- ▲ Using the performance monitor to find bottlenecks
- ▲ Physical database design

Indexing Strategies

Indexes are simply structures which are created to facilitate the retrieval of data from tables. It's important for you to understand both the index structures supported by SQL Server and the way the Query Optimizer uses indexes if you're going to have high-performance database applications.

Basic Principles

Suppose you have a database with a Students table containing ten rows like this:

Rowid	Student	Course
1	Ian Smith	Woodwork
2	David Sussman	Home Brewing
3	Kyle Millar	Car Maintenance
4	Russell Morgan	Feminist Theory
5	John Meek	Investment Management
6	Mike Churchman	Home Brewing
7	Mark Fenton	First Aid
8	Stephen Farrell	Gardening
9	Tracey Parry	Shorthand
10	Lesley Weatherhead	Nursery Nursing

If you wanted to retrieve the names of students who were studying Home Brewing, you would look at every row in the table in turn, decide whether the value of the Course field was equal to Home Brewing and then return the name of the student for the rows which matched.

However, if the Course field were indexed, there would be a sorted list of values in that field together with a pointer to the actual data.

Course	Rowid
Car Maintenance	3
Feminist Theory	4
First Aid	7
Gardening	8
Home Brewing	2
Home Brewing	6
Investment Management	5
Nursery Nursing	10
Shorthand	9
Woodwork	1

Now if you want to find the names of all students who were studying Home Brewing, you would simply read the index until you find an entry for Home Brewing. Then you would use the value in the row column to find the first row in the table (row 2) which had a value of Home Brewing in the Course field.

You would read the next entry in the index and use it to find the next row in the data table which had a value of Home Brewing (row 6). Once you find an entry in the index which is greater than Home Brewing (Investment Management) you know you've finished. SQL Server, like all databases, allows you to create a variety of indexes on your tables.

B-trees in SQL Server

There are three methods in common use for indexes: B-trees, hash tables or ISAM structures. SQL Server uses B-trees for its indexes. The diagram below shows the constituent parts of a B-tree index.

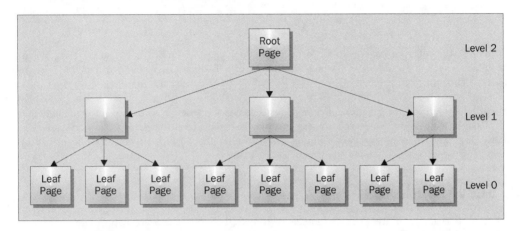

The top level is always called the **root level** and the lowest level (containing the data) is the **leaf level** or Level 0. The number of intermediate pages depends on the data being indexed. It's particularly important to note that with B-trees, the distance from the root to any leaf page is constant. When data is inserted, such that there's no room for it to fit within the current pages of a B-tree, the required page will split into two pages which are each the same distance from the root as the original page was.

The reason that the distance from root to leaf is important is that it represents the number of disk pages which will need to be read in order to read the data on the leaf page. Therefore, the fewer levels in the tree, the fewer disk pages that will need to be accessed in order to read the data. Although it's likely that the root of any index will be held in cache, it becomes less likely that a specific page will be cached the further away it is from the root.

Page Splitting

When a page at the leaf-level of an index becomes full it may have to be split. In the case of a non-clustered index this will be the leaf-level of the index, but in the case of a clustered index this will mean the data page as well. Page splitting is best illustrated with a diagram showing a simple example. Suppose we have a non-full intermediate page containing a pointer to a full leaf page.

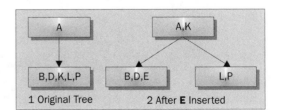

If a new record is inserted and the leaf page into which it's inserted is already full, the median key of the leaf page is migrated into the intermediate page. The full leaf page is then split into two non-full leaf pages.

You should notice that for this strategy to work, the intermediate page needs to have available space. This is guaranteed because full root pages will themselves split to form a new root. This can also be shown in a simple diagram.

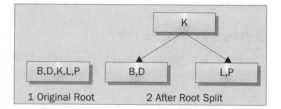

In this situation, the full root page splits to form a new root page (K) and a new leaf page (L, P). Splitting the root in this way is the only way in which the height of a B-Tree can grow. Note that the tree grows from the root and not from the leaf.

As you will have realized, the creation of new pages if necessary when records are inserted (and the removal of pages if necessary when records are deleted) is expensive in terms of CPU and more importantly disk I/O. To minimize page splitting you can alter the fill factor when creating or rebuilding the index.

SQL Server Indexes

Although SQL Server uses B-trees for its indexes, within SQL Server there are two different types of B-tree index. With a **clustered** index, the arrangement of the data pages corresponds to the order of the key upon which the index is built. A **non-clustered** index, however, implies nothing about the location of the data pages.

Clustered Indexes

We'd like to note, before we start, that the eagle-eyed among you will spot that the next example actually violates the B-tree rule that any node has between k and k/2 branches where k is the branching factor. However, the next example is used to demonstrate the difference between how clustered indexes work as opposed to non-clustered indexes and that's all we're concerned with here. We can see how SQL Server would store the data if a clustered index had been created on the Student field.

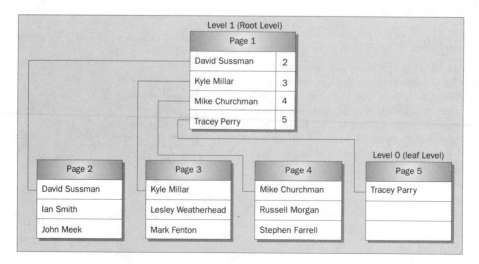

As you can see, in a clustered index, the leaf level (level 0) contains the actual data pages from the table itself. The data in the leaf pages is physically stored in index order. For this reason, you're only allowed to have one clustered index per table–and it's that index which determines the order in which the data in the table is stored.

Because there isn't an index entry for each data row (only the first row in a data page has a matching index entry) this type of index is sometimes referred to as a **sparse index**.

Non-clustered Indexes

Non-clustered indexes differ from clustered indexes in that they don't affect the order in which the data within a table is stored. Instead, they operate by maintaining at the leaf level a series of pointers to the actual data, So, if a non-clustered index was built on the Student field in our table, it would look like the diagram below.

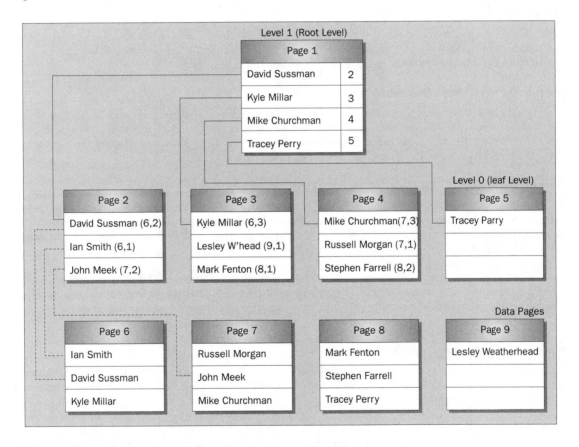

As you can see, with this type of index there's an index entry for every row in the data pages. For this reason, it's sometimes known as a **dense index**. Because records are generally smaller than pages, a sparse index will hold fewer keys than a dense index. So, the smaller the record size, the fewer pointers there are within the sparse index.

In practice, the tree for a sparse index will typically have one level less than the tree for a dense index. This, in turn, means that using a clustered index will generally result in one less disk access than a non-clustered index on the same key. For this reason, the decision as to which index should be clustered can be very significant.

The implication here, is that you should strive to make your indexes (whether clustered or non-clustered) as narrow as possible. Composite indexes (indexes based on multiple columns) tend to have a large key size which results in more pointers being stored within the index, which means more index pages and, therefore, more disk access.

Because they don't affect the physical ordering of the records within a table, you can have as many non-clustered indexes on a table as you want. (Actually, the limit is 249 indexes, but in practice you shouldn't ever get anywhere near this amount.)

Index Options

There are a whole variety of options available which allow you to save time when creating an index. You can use them to minimize page splitting or just to save time when data is being sorting. They can be altered from the Manage Indexes dialog in the SQL Enterprise Manager.

Sorted Data (Clustered Indexes Only)

You should check this box if the data in the column(s) being indexed is already in index order. If you check this box and SQL Server finds data which isn't in index order, the index creation process will terminate. Sorting the data in an index can be time consuming on large tables, so selecting this option can save you time if you know the data is already sorted.

Sorted Data ReOrg (Clustered Indexes Only)

This is similar to the Sorted Data option in that it checks whether the data is sorted by comparing each value against the previous value. However, it also physically rearranges the data and causes all non-clustered indexes on the table to be rebuilt. For this reason, an index built with this option will take longer than an index built with the Sorted Data option.

The Sorted Data ReOrg option is particularly useful if you suspect that page splitting is occurring. By rebuilding the index with a suitable fill factor and specifying the Sorted Data ReOrg option you can ensure that the data pages of the table are physically rearranged to allow an appropriate amount of space for future insertions and updates.

Ignore Duplicate Keys (Unique Keys Only)

Normally, when you try to add to a table a row with a key which contains identical values to an existing key value in that table and there's a unique index on that key, SQL Server will roll back the transaction of which that insertion is part.

If, however, you check the Ignore Duplicate Keys checkbox, the transaction will not be rolled back. Rather, the rest of the transaction will continue and the duplicate row will be ignored. However, a warning message will be displayed.

This feature isn't retroactive, so you can't create a unique index on a column which includes duplicate key values by simply checking the Ignore Duplicate Keys checkbox. Instead, you must remove the records with duplicate key values first.

The Ignore Duplicate Keys feature also affects updates. So if you attempt to update a row such that its new key value is equal to the key value of another row in that table, and that key has a unique index with Ignore Duplicate Keys on it, the updated row will be removed from the table. This is because the update is actually performed as a delete followed by an insert.

Ignore/Allow Duplicate Rows (Clustered Indexes Only)

This option is only used when you're creating a non-unique clustered index. If you select Ignore Duplicate Rows, SQL Server will prevent duplicate rows from being added to the table. Instead, all other (valid) rows within the operation will be added and a warning message displayed.

By contrast, selecting Allow Duplicate Rows will allow duplicate rows to be added to a table with a non-unique clustered index.

Although you can't select the Ignore Duplicate Keys option to eliminate duplicate keys when you build an index, you can select the Ignore Duplicate Rows to eliminate duplicate rows. If Ignore Duplicate Rows is set when you attempt to create an index and the table already contains duplicate rows, the duplicate rows are deleted, the index created and an error message returned.

Fill Factor

We saw earlier how specifying a fill factor allows you to dictate how full each index page (and data page for clustered indexes) will initially be. The effect of differing values of the fill factor are summarized in the table below.

Fill Factor	Non-leaf Page	Leaf Page
0%	One free entry, or two free entries if non-unique clustered index	100% full
1– 99%	One free entry, or two free entries if non-unique clustered index	<= fill factor % full
100%	100% full	100% full

Normally, when an index is created, space is left on the index pages for the insertion of one or two new rows. However, you can alter the amount of free space on the index pages (and on the data pages of a clustered index) by changing the value of the fill factor when you create the index.

For example, a fill factor of 50% leaves half of each page empty, whereas a fill factor of 90% would leave 10% of the page free. Decreasing the fill factor increases both the depth of the tree and the amount of disk space it takes up, because it will cause the tree to be spread over a larger number of pages. However, it will also increase the number of inserts possible on the underlying table before page splitting occurs with its associated performance degradation. For this reason, you should select a high fill factor for indexes which will see a lot of insert and update activity.

The fill factor isn't maintained after the index has been created. Instead the index pages (and data pages in the case of a clustered index) will fill or empty according to the data that's entered into the table. Consequently, if you feel that page splitting is occurring and causing a performance overhead, you should recreate the indexes on the tables concerned using the appropriate fill factor to restore the required amount of free space within the index pages (and data pages for a clustered index).

You should note that the fill factor acts differently on leaf and non-leaf pages. The fill factor specifies how full the leaf pages of the new index will be unless a fill factor of 0% is specified, in which case the leaf pages are completely filled.

In contrast, one free space is always left on the intermediate page of an index (or two if the index is clustered and non-unique) unless a fill factor of 100% is specified, in which case the intermediate pages are completely filled.

You should, therefore, only use a fill factor of 100% on read-only tables. Any insertion (and, possibly, update) on a table with an index with a 100% fill factor will cause a page split to occur.

The default value for a fill factor is 0%. If you wish to use a different default you can change it with the **sp_configure** stored procedure. For example, the following statement will change the default to 30%.

```
sp_configure fill, 30
```

This statement can only be executed by the system administrator and will not take effect until SQL Server has been stopped and restarted. However, it's unusual to change the default. This is because the choice of a suitable fill factor will vary from index to index and because the default can be overridden when a new index is created.

Creating Indexes with Enterprise Manager

To create an index on a table, you can either use the SQL Enterprise Manager or use a Transact-SQL statement. To create an index using the SQL Enterprise Manager, you should select Indexes... from the Manage menu, to get to the Manage Indexes dialog.

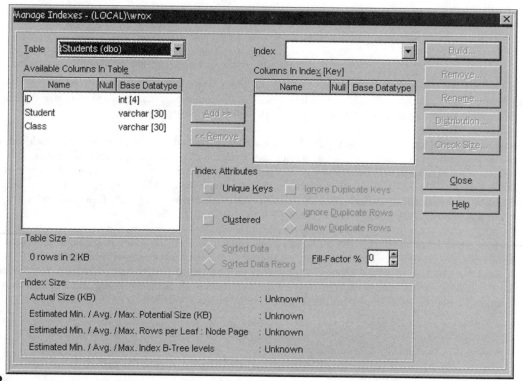

The following section describes the impact of selecting various options on the Manage Indexes dialog.

Unique Keys

If you check this box, the index you create will force uniqueness on the column (or columns, in the case of a composite index) forming the index. This includes NULL values, so you can't create a unique index on a column (or columns) where more than one row has a complete key of NULL.

Checking the Unique Keys check box will in turn enable the Ignore Duplicate Keys check box.

Clustered

Checking this box will cause the new index to be created as a clustered index. If you leave the box unchecked, a non-clustered index will be created. Checking this box will also enable the Ignore Duplicate Rows and Allow Duplicate Rows radio buttons.

Scheduling Index Builds

After specifying the appropriate index attributes, you click the Build... button to create the index. At this stage, you'll be asked whether you want to create the index immediately or schedule the creation for a later date. If you choose the latter option, a dialog will appear to allow you to add a task to the Task List.

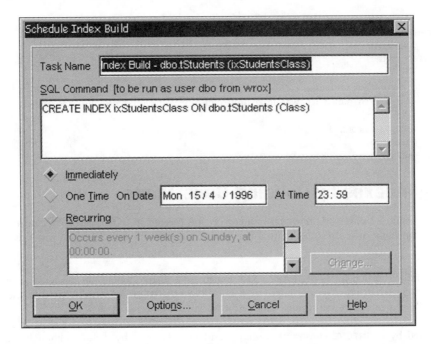

This option is particularly useful if you're creating (or rebuilding) an index on a large table and would like to do so after hours when everyone else has gone home for the night. Because clustered indexes affect the order in which data pages are arranged, creating a clustered index will lock all the records in the underlying table, and so you may prefer to build your clustered indexes out of hours when other people will not be using the tables.

Creating Indexes with TSQL

If you want to use Transact-SQL to create an index, you should use the following syntax.

```
CREATE
        [UNIQUE]
        [CLUSTERED  |  NONCLUSTERED]
INDEX   index_name
ON  [[database.]owner.]  table_name  (column_name [,  column_name]...)
        [WITH  [FILLFACTOR = x]
                [[,]  IGNORE_DUP_KEY]
                [[,]  {SORTED_DATA  |  SORTED_DATA_REORG}]
                [[,]  {IGNORE_DUP_ROW  |  ALLOW_DUP_ROW}]]
        [ON  segment_name]
```

The options to the **CREATE INDEX** statement correspond to the index attributes which you select in the Manage Indexes dialog in Enterprise Manager.

For example, if you wanted to create a unique clustered index on the **CaseID** field of the **tCase** table, and you knew that the data in the column to be indexed was already sorted, you would use the following statement:

```
CREATE UNIQUE CLUSTERED INDEX ixCaseID
ON tCase (CaseID)
WITH SORTED_DATA
```

If you wanted to rebuild an non-unique clustered index on the **RepCode** field of the **tCase** table and space the data so that each data page was now only half-full, you would use this statement:

```
CREATE CLUSTERED INDEX ixRepCode
ON tCase (RepCode)
WITH FILLFACTOR = 50, SORTED_DATA_REORG
```

Creating Indexes by Defining Constraints

Explicit creation isn't the only way in which indexes can be created in SQL Server. Whenever a **PRIMARY KEY** constraint or a **UNIQUE** constraint is placed on columns in a table, an index is created on those columns.

By default, the index created for a **PRIMARY KEY** constraint will be unique and clustered. However, if there's already a clustered index on the table, or if the **NONCLUSTERED** keyword is used in the creation of the constraint, then a non-clustered unique index will be created.

The index created by a **UNIQUE** constraint is unique and non-clustered by default, although this can be changed by using the **CLUSTERED** keyword when creating the constraint.

As well as deciding whether to make the index clustered or non-clustered, the following optional keywords are available to you when creating an index from a constraint:

```
WITH [FILLFACTOR=x],
     [ON  segment]
```

For example, to create a **PRIMARY KEY** constraint with an associated clustered unique index on the **au_id** column of the authors table and to fill each page 40% full, you would use the following statement.

```
ALTER TABLE authors
ADD CONSTRAINT pkauthorid
PRIMARY KEY (au_id)
WITH FILLFACTOR=40
```

The indexes generated by the creation of constraints can only be dropped by dropping the constraint which created them.

Rebuilding Indexes

A new DBCC option has been added to SQL Server 6.5 to allow the rebuilding of indexes which were created by the creation of constraints. The option is **DBREINDEX** and it has the following syntax:

```
DBCC   DBREINDEX
       (   tablename,
       [   indexname
       [,  fillfactor
       [,  SORTED_DATA  |  SORTED_DATA_REORG]]])
```

If 0 is specified as the fill factor, the index will be rebuilt with the fill factor originally specified when the index was created. This information is held in the Sysindexes table (see later). For example, the following statement will rebuild the index created by the **PRIMARY KEY** constraint **pkAuthorID** using the original fill factor.

```
DBCC DBREINDEX (authors, pkAuthorID, 0)
```

If no index name is specified, all the indexes on the named table will be rebuilt. For example,

```
DBCC DBREINDEX (authors)
```

Dropping Indexes

If you want to drop (i.e. remove) an index from a table, you can also do this from the Manage Indexes dialog. Simply select the name of the table and the index you wish to drop and hit the Remove... button. As with the index creation process, you'll be given the option of dropping the index immediately, or scheduling the removal of the index as a task.

The following syntax is used to drop an index using Transact-SQL:

```
DROP   INDEX   [owner.]table_name.index_name
```

For example, to drop the index **ixCaseID** on the table **tCase**, you would use the following syntax.

```
DROP INDEX tCase.ixCaseID
```

If you want you can drop more than one index in the same statement as in the following example:.

```
DROP INDEX tCase.ixCaseID, tPeople.ixPhoneType
```

If you drop a table with the **DROP TABLE** statement, any indexes on that table are automatically dropped as well. However, if you perform a non-logged deletion of the data in the table with the **TRUNCATE TABLE** statement, the indexes are left intact.

Statistics

One of the best innovations in SQL Server 6.0 was the inclusion of the index size and distribution statistics to the Manage Indexes dialog. I have a number of Excel spreadsheets on my computer at work which I used to use to calculate the size of indexes. Now all those complicated calculations are done for me by SQL Server!

Index Size

The Index Size statistics give an indication of the size of the currently selected index.

Index Size			
Actual Size (KB)	: 4		
Estimated Min. / Avg. / Max. Potential Size (KB)	: 4	4	4
Estimated Min. / Avg. / Max. Rows per Leaf : Node Page	: 48 : 42	74 : 64	288 : 182
Estimated Min. / Avg. / Max. Index B-Tree levels	: 1	1	1

As you can see from the figure above, the actual size of the index is displayed as well as the minimum, average and maximum potential size of the index. SQL Server also displays the minimum, average and maximum number of rows that are held on the leaf and node (i.e. non-leaf) pages of the index, as well as the minimum, average and maximum number of levels in the B-tree index. As we saw earlier in this chapter, the fewer levels in the B-tree, the faster you can expect the index to perform.

If the index is clustered, the number of rows in leaf pages aren't shown because with a clustered index the leaf pages contain the actual data. Instead SQL Server displays the minimum, average and maximum number of rows that are held on the (non-leaf) index pages.

Index Size			
Actual Size (KB)	: 4		
Estimated Min. / Avg. / Max. Potential Size (KB)	: 4	4	4
Estimated Min. / Avg. / Max. Rows per Index Page	: 48	78	401
Estimated Min. / Avg. / Max. Index B-Tree levels	: 1	1	1

These figures can be updated by clicking the Check Size... button.

Index Distribution

The Index Distribution Information gives you statistics about the cardinality of the index and, therefore, how suitable it is as an index.

```
┌─ Index Distribution Information ─────────────────────────┐
│                                                          │
│   Table Name              : dbo.tStudents                │
│                                                          │
│   Index Name              : ixStudentsClass              │
│                                                          │
│   Rows In Table           : 10 rows                      │
│                                                          │
│   Number of Steps         : 9 steps of type varchar [30] │
│                                                          │
│   Sampling Step Interval  : 1 rows                       │
│                                                          │
│   Average Row Hits        : 1                            │
│                                                          │
│   Date of Last Update     : Apr 15 1996 11:18PM          │
│                                                          │
└──────────────────────────────────────────────────────────┘
```

The statistics are gathered by SQL Server 'walking' through the table in a number of steps. At each step, SQL Server inspects the value of the indexed field and finally generates a figure for Average Row Hits. This represents the average number of rows which would be returned by an equality search on the indexed field. If the table displays optimal selectivity, as in the figure above, the Average Row Hits will be 1. In other words, each value in the indexed field is unique.

If the table has more than 200 rows, SQL Server will also display a rating indicating the selectivity of the index. It's calculated according to the following algorithm.

Avg. Row Hits	Rating
1 row	Optimal
More than 1 row, but less than 0.5% of rows	Very good
More than 0.5% of rows, but less than 1% of rows	Good
More than 1% of rows, but less than 2.5% of rows	Fair
More than 2.5% of rows, but less than 5% of rows	Poor
More than 5% of rows	Very poor

Remember, the more selective an index, the fewer pages will need to be read to satisfy a search on the index and consequently the faster the search will be. If the Average Row Hits is more than 2.5% of the rows, it probably isn't going to be worthwhile creating the index.

You can view the same information, albeit in a less attractively presented format, by using the **DBCC SHOW_STATISTICS** command with the table name and index name. For example, to view the statistics of the index **ixStudentsClass** on the **tStudents** table, you would use the following syntax.

```
DBCC SHOW_STATISTICS (tStudents, ixStudentsClass)
```

This would generate output similar to this:

```
Updated                  Rows      Steps      Density
--------------------     --------  ---------  -------
May 19 1996  8:41PM      10        9          0.08

(1 row(s) affected)
```

```
All density          Columns
----------------------  -----------------------------
0.12                 class
```

(1 row(s) affected)

```
Steps
------------------------------
Car Maintenance
Feminist Theory
First Aid
Gardening
Home Brewing
Home Brewing
Investment Management
Nursery Nursing
Shorthand
```

(9 row(s) affected)

DBCC execution completed. If DBCC printed error messages, see your System Administrator.

Two key figures in the **DBCC SHOW_STATISTICS** output are the Density and All Density values. These indicate the density of the index. In this situation, a dense index is one in which a large number of values in the indexed column(s) are identical. In other words, density is the opposite of selectivity. A highly selective index is one in which very few of the values in the indexed column(s) are identical. The more selective an index is, the more likely it is to be used by the query optimizer.

If you multiply the Density value by the number of Rows in the table, you can calculate the Average Row Hits which is displayed in the Manage Indexes dialog. This is the number of rows in the table which are likely to have the same value in the indexed column(s) as any other arbitrarily selected row. For a unique index this value will be 1.

The All Density figure is useful when the index is a composite index (i.e. it's composed of more than one column). In this case, it will display the density of each of the columns in the index.

```
All density          Columns
-------------------  -----------------------------
0.052665             au_lname
0.001039             au_lname, au_fname
```

This is useful for determining whether the whole index needs to be specified for the index to be used or whether the index will also be used if simply a prefix of the columns is used. In the example above, a search on **au_lname** will probably not use the index as the selectivity is low. However, if **au_fname** is also included in the **WHERE** clause, it's more likely that the index will be used as the composite index is highly selective and so will probably result in the retrieval of fewer data pages than a table scan would.

Updating Statistics

To update the index distribution statistics, simply hit the Update... button in the Index Distribution Statistics dialog in SQL Enterprise Manager. You can achieve the same effect in Transact-SQL by using the following command.

```
UPDATE  STATISTICS  [[database.]owner.]table_name  [index_name]
```

> If index_name is omitted, SQL Server will update statistics for all indexes in the named table.

The index distribution statistics are used by the SQL Server query optimizer when determining the optimal query plan for executing a query. Consequently, if the statistics are inaccurate because they haven't been updated, a sub-optimal query plan may be decided upon.

Suppose, for example, that you create a table and place ten rows of test data into it. Then you add an index to the table and update the index distribution statistics. Now let's suppose that over the period of 6 months some 500,000 rows are added to the table. If you don't update the index distribution statistics, SQL Server will still think that there are only 10 rows in the table and so will probably decide that a table scan is the best way to retrieve values from the table. Doing a table scan on half a million rows isn't fun and your users will soon let you know that!

The process of updating index statistics causes SQL Server to create a distribution page. This is a full data page which contains the information about the selectivity of the index. A distribution page is created for each index in a table when **UPDATE STATISTICS** is run for that index.

> Because the distribution page is just that–a single page–it follows that the larger the key, the fewer distribution values can be held on that page. What this means in practice is that the narrower the key on which the index is built, the more accurate the distribution data is, because more distribution entries can be fitted onto a single page.

Fortunately, there's now an even easier way to make sure that index distribution statistics are updated at regular intervals. If you use the Database Optimization Wizard, you will be prompted on the Data Optimization page to Update optimizer information.

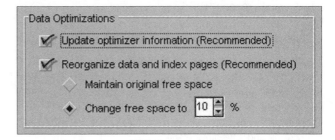

Selecting this option will cause all indexes in the database to have their distribution statistics automatically updated when the appropriate maintenance plan is executed. This is the same as running **SQLMAINT.EXE** with the **-UpdSts** argument.

The stats_date Function

If you want to know when the statistics for a particular index were last updated, you should use the **stats_date(tableid, indexid)** function. For example, if you wanted to determine when the statistics for the clustered index on the authors table were last updated, you would use the following query.

```
select stats_date (object_id('authors'), 1)
```

This information is also displayed when the **DBCC SHOW_STATISTICS** command is run for the selected index.

Keeping Your Tables in Trim

Even if you have rationalized the indexing of your tables and constructed your queries in such a manner to make optimal use of them, you may still find that your queries don't perform as quickly as you would expect them to. This may be caused by **fragmentation**.

Fragmentation occurs when a table has been subject to a great deal of insertions, updates or deletions. The amount of data on each data page–which was originally determined by the fill factor specified when creating the clustered index–begins to vary. Some pages are filled with data whereas others may be almost empty. The overall effects of this fragmentation are to reduce the efficiency of reads, especially where read ahead is being used,and sometimes to increase the amount of space taken up by the data.

In order to determine how fragmented a table is, you can use the **DBCC SHOWCONTIG** statement with the id of the table from the Sysobjects table.

```
DBCC SHOWCONTIG (1947812)
```

To determine if an index is fragmented and needs rebuilding, supply the object id of the table and the indid value of the index from the Sysindexes table.

```
DBCC SHOWCONTIG (1947812, 2)
```

The output of the **DBCC SHOWCONTIG** statement looks like this.

```
DBCC SHOWCONTIG scanning 'titles' table...
[SHOW_CONTIG - SCAN ANALYSIS]
-----------------------------------------------------------
Table: 'titles' (192003715)  Indid: 1   dbid:5
TABLE level scan performed.
- Pages Scanned............................: 3
- Extent Switches..........................: 0
- Avg. Pages per Extent....................: 3.0
- Scan Density [Best Count:Actual Count]...: 100.00% [1:1]
- Avg. Bytes free per page.................: 856.3
- Avg. Page density (full).................: 57.48%
- Overflow Pages...........................: 0
- Disconnected Overflow Pages..............: 0

DBCC execution completed. If DBCC printed error messages, see your System Administrator.
```

The key figures in this output are those for Scan Density and Avg. Page Density. The Scan Density indicates how contiguous the data is within the table. The amount by which this is less than 100% indicates how fragmented the table or index is. The Scan Density Best Count shows the number of extents that would need to be traversed if everything were contiguously linked, and the Scan Density Actual Count shows the actual number of extents that were traversed.

The Avg. Page Density indicates how full with data an average page is in the table. The higher the figure, the less space will be taken up by the data and the more efficient reads will be.

If your table appears to be fragmented, you can defragment it by rebuilding the clustered index for the table using **DBCC REINDEX** which was discussed earlier.

The Sysindexes table

No investigation of indexes in SQL Server would be complete without a look at the Sysindexes table. This table is part of the database catalog. In other words, there's a Sysindexes table in every database. The table contains one row for every index, clustered or non-clustered, within that database. It also contains an additional row for each table with text or image columns and a row for every table that has no clustered index.

The primary key for the Sysindexes table is formed of the id and indid columns. The id column contains the id (from Sysobjects) of the table to which the index belongs. The indid is a unique identifier for each index in the table referred to by the value in the Sysindexes.id column.

- If indid = 1, the row describes clustered index on the table referenced by id.
- If indid > 1, the row describes one of the non-clustered indexes on the table referenced by id.
- If indid = 255, it indicates that the table referenced by id contains text or image columns.
- If indid = 0, it indicates that it doesn't have a clustered index.

From this, you should realize that for every table in the index there will be, for any given value in the id column:

- One and only one row that has an indid of either 0 or 1
- Zero or more rows with an indid greater than one and less than 255
- Zero or one rows with an indid of 255

The following table lists the columns in the Sysindexes table and the meaning of the data it contains.

Column	Datatype	Notes
Name	varchar(30)	(indid = 0 or indid = 255) the name of the table, or (indid > 0 and indid < 255) the name of the index.
Id	int	(indid = 0 or indid = 255) the id of the table, or (indid > 0 and indid < 255) the id of the table to which the index belongs.
Indid	smallint	If 0, the row refers to a table. If 1, the row refers to a clustered index If >1 and <255, the row refers to a non-clustered index. If 255, the row refers to a table with text or image columns.
Dpages	int	(indid = 0 or indid = 1), the number of data pages in the table (indid > 1 and indid < 255), the number of leaf-level index pages (indid = 255), dpages is always 0.
Reserved	int	(indid = 0 or indid = 1), the number of pages allocated for all indexes on the table and data pages. (indid > 1 and indid < 255), the number of pages allocated for the current index. (indid =255), the number of pages allocated for text and image data.
Used	int	(indid = 0 or indid = 1), the number of pages actually used by all indexes on the table and data pages. (indid > 1 and indid < 255), the number of pages actually used by the current index. (indid =255), the number of pages actually used by text and image data.
Rows	int	The number of rows of data in the table. This value can only be guaranteed accurate where indid <2. For indid >1, the value may be inaccurate (see below).
First	int	A pointer to the first data page or leaf page.
Root	int	(indid = 0 or indid = 255), a pointer to the last page. (indid > 0 and indid < 255), a pointer to the root page.
Distribution	int	(indid > 0 and indid < 255), a pointer to the distribution page.
OrigFillFactor	tinyint	The fill factor which was used when the index was initially created. This value isn't amended as the amount of free space on pages alters with the addition, deletion or updating of data on those pages.
Segment	smallint	The index of the segment on which this object resides. This value refers to the segment column in Syssegments.
Status	smallint	This value is a bitmask indicating various attributes of the index. The following list details values and their meanings: 2^0 Abort command which attempts to insert duplicate keys 2^1 The index is unique 2^2 Abort command which attempts to insert duplicate rows 2^4 The index is clustered 2^6 The index allows duplicate rows 2^{11} The index enforces a **PRIMARY KEY** constraint 2^{12} The index enforces a **UNIQUE** constraint So a value of 18 ($2^1 + 2^4$) would indicate that the index was clustered and unique.

Table Continued on Following Page

Column	Datatype	Notes
Rowpage	smallint	The maximum number of rows that could fit onto a page.
Minlen	smallint	The minimum size of a row.
Maxlen	smallint	The maximum size of a row.
Maxirow	smallint	The maximum size of a non-leaf index row.
Keycnt	smallint	The number of keys.
Keys1	varbinary(255)	A description of the key columns.
Keys2	varbinary(255)	A description of the key columns.
Soid	tinyint	If there's character data in the index, the sort order id with which the index was created. If there's no character data in the index, this is 0.
Csid	tinyint	If there's character data in the index, the character set id with which the index was created. This refers to the id column in Syscharsets. If there's no character data in the index, this is 0.
UpdateStamp	varbinary	Used internally by SQL Server to monitor synchronisation of changes to row page counts.

Using Sysindexes

If you understand the meaning of the values held in Sysindexes, you'll find that you are able to determine just about all of the information that appears on the Manage Indexes dialog in Enterprise Manager. This can be useful if you want to determine information about an index from a client machine which doesn't have Enterprise Manager installed.

You can also use Sysindexes to quickly determine other information in an efficient manner. For example, if you want to know the location of all indexes and data for a particular table in a database, you can run the following query which makes use of the data held in the segment column of Sysindexes.

```
SELECT si.indid, 'Index/Table Name'=si.name, Location=ss.name
FROM sysindexes si, syssegments ss
WHERE si.segment = ss.segment
AND si.id = object_id('authors')
```

You can see that the data in this table is located on the default segment (because that's where the clustered index is located).

```
indid   Index/Table Name          Location
------  ------------------------  ------------------------
1       UPKCL_auidind             default
2       ixauthorname              default
3       ixauthorstate             seg_disk1

(3 row(s) affected)
```

The index **ixauthorname** is also on the default segment, but the index **ixauthorstate** is on the **seg_disk1** segment.

Another useful trick is to use the value of the rows column to determine the number of rows in a table. You might have thought that the quickest way to determine the number of rows would be to run a query such as this:

```
SELECT COUNT(*)
FROM orders
```

However, this query would have to count every row in the orders table before it could return its result. If the orders table were large, this could be quite a time consuming operation. However, if you ran the following query, only one row would need to be accessed which would be considerably quicker for large tables.

```
SELECT rows
FROM sysindexes
WHERE id = object_id('orders')
AND indid < 2
```

Note that we've had to restrict the search to where **indid** is less than 2. This is because the row count in rows is only automatically updated where the **indid** is 0 or 1. To update the value of rows for non-clustered indexes, you should use the **DBCC UPDATEUSAGE** command.

DBCC UPDATEUSAGE

Some of the values in the Sysindexes table are automatically updated. Others aren't and so can report incorrect values. To update these values, you should use the **DBCC UPDATEUSAGE** command. This command causes the rows, used, reserved and dpages columns to be updated with correct values. The syntax of the **DBCC UPDATEUSAGE** command is as follows.

DBCC UPDATEUSAGE (*databasename* [**,** *tablename* [**,** *indexname*]]**)**

The **DBCC UPDATEUSAGE** command can be used to update rows in Sysindexes for a specific index, for all indexes in a specific table or for all indexes in all tables in a specific database. If a 0 is used for the database name, updates are applied in the current database.

When this command is run, if any inaccuracies are found, the old and new values from Sysindexes are displayed.

```
DBCC UPDATEUSAGE: Sysindexes row for Table 'mytable' (IndexId=2) updated:
        ROWS count: Changed from (2) to (3) rows
DBCC UPDATEUSAGE: Sysindexes row for Table 'sysobjects' (IndexId=2) updated:
        DATA Pages: Changed from (1) to (2) pages
        USED Pages: Changed from (1) to (3) pages
        ROWS count: Changed from (13) to (70) rows
DBCC execution completed. If DBCC printed error messages, see your System Administrator.
```

If there are no inconsistencies, the only following text is displayed.

```
DBCC execution completed. If DBCC printed error messages, see your System Administrator.
```

Another way to update these values in the Sysindexes table is to use the **sp_spaceused** stored procedure with the **@updateusage** flag. For example,

```
sp_spaceused mytable, @updateusage=true
```

which would return something akin to the following:

```
DBCC UPDATEUSAGE: Sysindexes row for Table 'mytable' (IndexId=2) updated:
      ROWS count: Changed from (3) to (4) rows
DBCC execution completed. If DBCC printed error messages, see your System Administrator.
```

name	rows	reserved	data	index_size	unused
mytable	4	32 KB	2 KB	4 KB	26 KB

Index Placement (Segments)

The **CREATE INDEX** statement contains one option which isn't available through the Manage Indexes dialog: the ability to place the index on a specific segment.

Segments are a collection of device fragments and provide a method of distributing objects within the same database on separate devices. The chief reason for using segments is to increase performance. If the device fragments reside on separate disks, you can place a frequently used table on a separate disk to the remainder of the database objects. Alternatively, you could use segments to place the non-clustered indexes for a table on a separate segment to the data.

Because the leaf-level of a clustered index contains the actual data pages for the table, the location of the clustered index determines the location of the data. Therefore, if a table resides on one segment and the clustered index for that table is created on a different segment, then the table itself will normally move to the segment which contains the clustered index. The exception to this is when the **SORTED_DATA** option is also specified, in which case the B-tree of the index and any new data pages are created on the new index while existing data pages remain on the old segment.

If a segment isn't specified when an index is created, the index will be placed on the **DEFAULT** segment for that database. However, you can specify an index by using the **ON** segment option of the **CREATE INDEX** statement. The following examples illustrate the use of segments when creating indexes.

```
CREATE CLUSTERED INDEX ixCaseID
ON tCase(CaseID)
WITH SORTED_DATA
ON segDevelopment
```

This example will create a clustered index on the **CaseID** column of the table **tCase**. The index will be placed on **segDevelopment** and new data pages will be allocated from that segment. However, existing data pages will remain on their original segment.

```
CREATE CLUSTERED INDEX ixCaseID
ON tCase(CaseID)
WITH SORTED_DATA_REORG
ON segDevelopment
```

In contrast, the example above will move the entire table onto the segment **segDevelopment**. This is because the **SORTED_DATA_REORG** option causes the underlying data pages to be physically re-ordered, whereas the **SORTED_DATA** option merely checks that the data pages are in sorted order.

```
CREATE NONCLUSTERED INDEX ixCaseID
ON tCase(CaseID)
ON segDevelopment
```

This final example will cause the non-clustered index **ixCaseID** to be created on the segment **segDevelopment**. However, because there's a level of indirection between the leaf pages of the index and the data pages, the table itself isn't moved onto **segDevelopment**. In addition, any new data pages will be allocated from the table's existing segment.

Query Optimization

By mentioning the need to update index distribution statistics at regular intervals, we have touched on one of the subjects which is central to obtaining optimal performance from SQL Server. SQL Server contains what you'll often see referred to as an 'intelligent cost-based optimizer'. In this section we'll see what that phrase means, how the optimizer does its job and how we can make it easier for the optimizer to get it right.

Optimization methods

The vast majority of commercial DBMSs employ one of two optimization methods; cost-based optimization and syntax-based optimization.

Syntax-based

Syntax-based optimization derives the optimal execution plan for a query by analyzing the syntax used to generate the query itself. This allows the person writing the query to have much more control over the access pattern which the optimizer will suggest, but it also places greater demands on the user to know how the nuances of the SQL they produce will affect the final execution plan. This is highly effective in a static environment where indexes can be tuned to queries.

Cost-based

A cost-based optimizer, determines the different execution plans that could be used to execute a query and assigns to each of these execution plans a cost. This cost is based on the amount of CPU usage and, much more critically, the amount of disk access that will be required to execute the plan. This, in turn, is calculated by examining the internal statistics held for each table, which contain information about factors such as the number of rows in each table and the selectivity of the indexes (see above). The optimizer then compares these separate costs and puts forward as the optimal query plan the one which incurs the smallest cost. This is the type of optimizer which SQL Server uses.

Phases of Optimization

The cost-based optimizer employed by SQL Server, performs the optimization process in three distinct stages. These are:

- ▲ Query Analysis
- ▲ Index Selection
- ▲ Join Selection

Keep in mind that every query can be processed. Lacking any better approach, the required tables can be scanned from beginning to end. In fact, this may often be the appropriate approach. For example, when all the rows in a table are needed without ordering, it's cheaper to simply scan the table than to traverse the several levels of an index structure. It's the optimizer's job to determine whether there's a cheaper alternative.

Query Analysis

The first task is to look at the separate clauses which make up the query and to determine whether any of these are optimizable. The aim at this stage is to determine whether there's any possibility of using an index. For example, if a query contains a clause containing an exclusive operator, such as

```
...
  WHERE authors.au_id <> '7164'
```

the optimizer will be unable to determine the selectivity of the query until it's scanned every row in the table. However, if a clause contains an inclusive operator, such as

```
...
  WHERE authors.au_id = '7164'
```

the optimizer may be able to use an index to speed up the search for those rows.

Once the optimizer has determined which clauses of the query can be optimized and which can't, the execution plan uses table scans for the non-optimizable clauses and submits the optimizable ones for index selection.

Index Selection

During the index selection process, the optimizer looks to see whether there are any useful indexes which can be utilized to optimize the processing of each clause. If an index is comprised of multiple columns (i.e. it's a compound index) it will be considered if either:

- It contains all the columns mentioned in the clause being analyzed.
- The column(s) mentioned in the clause being analyzed match the initial column(s) in the index.

The situation in which all of the columns in the **SELECT** list and all of the columns in the **WHERE** clause of a query are contained in a non-clustered index on the table is called a **covered query**. In this situation, the optimizer will choose to use the index as there will be no need to read any data pages. Instead, all data can be read from the leaf pages of the non-clustered index. Although a covered query should execute quickly, you should think twice before creating exceptionally wide indexes specifically to 'cover' your queries as narrow indexes will generally provide better performance over a wider range of queries.

You'll find that with index selection that the clustered index tends to be favored. If you wish to estimate the number of accesses that it will take to find a appropriate row, then you can use the following criteria for each method:

Type of Index	Formula for Estimating Number of Accesses
No index	Number of data pages in the table
Clustered index	Number of levels + Number of data pages Number of data pages = Number of qualifying rows/rows per page
Non-clustered index	Number of levels + Number of qualifying leaf pages + Number of rows Number of qualifying leaf pages = Number of qualifying rows/rows per leaf page This assumes each row is on a separate page
Unique index, equality query	Number of accesses = number of levels + 1

If you wish to improve the effectiveness of an index then you should consider the following points, all of which the optimizer takes into account.

Index Distribution Statistics

In determining whether an index should be used, the optimizer looks at the index distribution statistics for that index to estimate the selectivity of the clause. The greater the selectivity of the clause, the smaller the number of data pages that will need to be retrieved from disk to satisfy the query. If the number of data pages which will need to be retrieved is estimated to be lower than the number of pages that would need to be retrieved if the table were scanned, then the index will be used.

The index distribution statistics used by the optimizer are updated in three instances:

- ▲ When the index is initially created or rebuilt with the **CREATE INDEX** statement and there's data in the table
- ▲ When the **UPDATE STATISTICS** statement is issued for that index
- ▲ When the **SQLMAINT.EXE** executable is run with the **-UpdSts** switch.

As an administrator, you should ensure that these statistics are kept updated at regular intervals so that the statistics used by SQL Server reflect the true number of rows in the table, and the actual distribution of values in the indexes.

Search Arguments (SARGS)

Another point you should consider is the fact that SQL Server can only use an index if the **WHERE** clause of a search condition is in a format known as a **search argument** or **SARG**. A SARG must have the following format:

Column	Operator	Expression
Author	=	smith
Books	=	2

Further, there's a list of valid operators that must be contained within the **WHERE** clause for it to be considered a SARG by the optimizer. These are:

▲ =

▲ >

▲ >=

▲ <

▲ <=

Also, **AND** (conjunction) is allowed, but all columns in the conjunction must be from the same table. To help avoid confusion, here's a list of some examples of some valid SARGS and some expressions that wouldn't be considered SARGS:

SARGS	Not SARGS
LastName = 'Baxter'	Employee.EmpID = HasSkill.EmpID
Salary > $30000	DeptNum != 300
3 < CostSharePercent	Datepart(day, HireDate)
Gender = 'M' AND Salary = $20000	DeptNum = 300 AND ProjectID = 3
UnionDues > $50	UnionDues * 2 > $100

You should think of a SARG as something that, if false, makes the entire query false. The optimizer doesn't throw everything out though. It recognizes that it's possible to convert some statements into SARGs, for example:

▲ `Salary BETWEEN $20000 AND $40000` is converted to

   `Salary >= $20000 AND Salary <= $40000`

▲ `LastName LIKE 'Sm%'` is converted to

   `LastName >= 'Sm' AND LastName <= 'Sn'`

▲ Can also deal with `LIKE 'Sm%h'` but can't make a SARG out of `'%m'`

▲ Can make SARGS out of constant expressions

▲ `Salary > $20000 * 2` is converted to `Salary > $40000`

You should be aware of the use of SARGS when creating indexes, because without them, you could have a negative impact on performance.

OR Strategy

When using an index to retrieve data, the best performance will be achieved when using the equality operator, such as

```
...
WHERE authors.au_id = '7164'
```

In contrast, suboptimal performance will be achieved when you use the disjunctive **IN** or **OR** operators against indexed columns, such as

```
...
WHERE authors.au_id IN ('7164', '7165')
```

or

```
...
WHERE authors.au_id = '7164' OR authors.au_id = '7165'
```

To achieve better performance, SQL Server may choose to employ what's known as the 'OR Strategy' in this situation. This involves making a pass through the table for each argument in the **OR** clause taking the page number and row number of the rows which satisfy the criteria and adding them to a worktable. After all of these passes have been made, the duplicates are removed from the worktable. This worktable is then considered to be a 'dynamic index' and can be scanned to retrieve the data rows from the underlying tables.

The 'OR Strategy' will be used if all of the following conditions apply.

- All of the rows in the **OR** clause are within the same table.

- For each part of the **OR** clause, the statistics indicate that use of an index is preferable to scanning the underlying table.

- There are no other access plans which will result in less physical disk I/O.

Index Cardinality

A final key factor which affects how much an index speeds up data retrieval is the **cardinality** (or selectivity) of the index. These two terms refer to the uniqueness of values within the index.

If an index is comprised of completely unique items, then SQL Server will only ever have to retrieve the index pages plus one data page to fetch all records which match that indexed value. In this case, the index is said to display high cardinality or good selectivity.

In contrast, if the values in the indexed field were all identical, SQL Server would have to read the index pages plus every data page to retrieve all matching values from the table. In this situation (where there's low cardinality or poor selectivity) using an index to perform a search would actually slow down the search. It would be a bit like looking up the word 'the' in the index of a book and using that to find the pages which contained the word 'the'.

In fact, if you index a column with poor selectivity, SQL Server's optimizer will choose to ignore the index and will just scan the table as if there were no index anyway. In this case, you would get no benefit from adding the index, but would suffer a performance penalty from the overhead involved in inserting, updating and deleting records.

When deciding which fields to index, you should consider the following:

- ▲ Columns on which you search by range
- ▲ Columns involved in joins
- ▲ Columns you order or group by
- ▲ Columns used with aggregate functions

Join Selection

The final stage in the optimization process, once individual clauses have been optimized and costs assigned to them, is to determine the optimal order in which the clauses should be executed. The join order which results in the least physical disk I/O is the one which is ultimately selected for the optimal execution plan.

It should be noted that the number of ways in which n clauses can be executed is the factorial of n. So, for one clause there's only one order in which that clause can be executed. Two clauses can be executed in 1 x 2 = 2 different orders. Three clauses can be executed in 1 x 2 x 3 = 6 different orders, four clauses in 1 x 2 x 3 x 4 = 24 different orders and so on. The efficiency with which an optimizer is able to determine the optimal join selection pattern for complex queries containing many optimizable clauses is key to the overall performance of the optimizer.

In fact, although there are mathematically n! ways in which n tables can be joined, SQL Server breaks up the list of tables in the **FROM** clause into more manageable clumps of four when determining the cost of joining the tables. This allows for more efficient analysis of the different join combinations that are available.

In order to illustrate this, let us suppose that a query has 5 tables in the **FROM** clause (which we will call a, b, c, d, e) and these tables are joined such that:

```
...
a.col1 = b.col2
AND b.col1 = c.col2
AND c.col1 = d.col2
AND d.col1 = e.col2
```

When SQL Server determines the cost of joining these tables, it will break the five tables into combinations of four tables. These five tables can be broken into 5 such combinations (abcd, abce, abde, acde, cdef). And within each of these 5 combinations, the four tables can be rearranged into in 24 permutations.

You can see this mechanism in more detail if you set Trace Flags 310 and 3605 before executing a query which joins more than four tables such as this:

```
SELECT a.au_lname
FROM authors a, titles t, titleauthor ta, publishers p, pub_info pi
WHERE a.au_id = ta.au_id
AND t.title_id = ta.title_id
AND t.pub_id = p.pub_id
AND p.pub_id = pi.pub_id
AND au_lname like 'S%'
```

This will cause trace output to be written to the error log detailing the combinations and permutations considered by SQL Server and the costs calculated for each of the costs.

Nested Iteration

The normal method used by SQL Server for joining tables is known as nested iteration. As the name might suggest, this method involves a series of loops, or iterations, first to select a number of rows from one table and then, as each is selected, to select corresponding rows from the 'joined' table.

Reformatting

In some situations, however, where there's no useful index on either side of the join and where the tables are large, SQL Server resorts to a method known as reformatting. This involves creating a temporary table into which SQL Server places the rows from the smaller of the two tables and then creating a clustered index on that worktable. SQL Server can then use the clustered index when performing the join to retrieve the corresponding records from the second table.

Obviously, reformatting is an expensive strategy in terms of the disk I/O that is required to create the indexes. It's only used as a last resort, and if you determine that SQL Server is using this method to execute a query, you should seriously consider putting an index on one side of the join to improve performance.

Using Query Analysis Tools

If a query is executing slowly, you will need to know what execution plan the optimizer is using before you can decide how you're going to improve the query's performance.

Fortunately, SQL Server provides a number of tools which allow you to analyze individual queries in order to allow you to determine how they can be tuned to run faster. These options are:

▲ **SHOWPLAN** (Textual)

▲ **STATISTICS IO** (Graphical and Textual)

▲ **STATISTICS TIME**

SHOWPLAN

Setting the **SHOWPLAN** option causes SQL Server to generate a description of the execution plan used to process the query. For example, let's assume that you have a query that looks like this:

```
SELECT a.au_fname, a.au_lname, t.title
FROM authors a, titleauthor ta, titles t
WHERE a.au_id = ta.au_id
AND t.title_id = ta.title_id
AND ta.royaltyper < 50
ORDER BY a.au_lname
```

To turn on the textual Showplan option, you can check the Show Query Plan tickbox on the Query Options dialog which appears when you select Set Options... from the Query menu in ISQL/W.

Query Options

Abort on Arithmetic Error	Parse Query Only
Ignore Arithmetic Error	Show Query Plan
No Count Display	Show Stats Time
No Execute	Show Stats I/O

Alternatively, you can execute the command **SET   SHOWPLAN   ON** in the ISQL/W window.

If the same query is executed with textual Showplan turned on, a textual description of the query execution plan is displayed in the Results panel of the ISQL/W query window.

```
STEP 1
The type of query is INSERT
The update mode is direct
Worktable created for ORDER BY
FROM TABLE
titleauthor ta
Nested iteration
Table Scan
FROM TABLE
authors a
Nested iteration
Table Scan
FROM TABLE
titles t
Nested iteration
Using Clustered Index
TO TABLE
Worktable 1
STEP 2
The type of query is SELECT
This step involves sorting
FROM TABLE
Worktable 1
Using GETSORTED Table Scan
```

As you can see from this example, the textual Showplan output reveals more information than the graphical Showplan output, but it's harder to decipher. For full details on the textual Showplan output, you should consult the *Understanding Showplan Output* chapter of the *Administrator's Companion* in SQL Server Books Online. However, some of the more useful outputs are described below.

STEP n

This indicates the number of the step in the query. A single query can require multiple steps. Each step corresponds to one page of output in the graphical Showplan output.

Index: index-name

This indicates that the optimizer decided to use a non-clustered index in order to process this part of the query. As was mentioned above, the optimizer will use a non-clustered index if doing so will result in less physical disk I/O than scanning the table.

Table Scan

This indicates that the optimizer has chosen to scan the table row-by-row. This can be an expensive option on large tables. To avoid this you should try to implement usable indexes on columns in the **WHERE** clause of your queries.

The type of query is

This indicates the type of clause which is being executed.

The update mode is

If the update mode is direct, SQL Server executed the query in one pass. This is also known as an **update-in-place** and only involves logging the modifications to the row.

If the update mode is deferred, it means that SQL Server has had to perform the update as a delete followed by an insert. This will always be slower than a direct update.

Some of the conditions causing deferred mode updates are:

- Attempts to modify a clustered index.
- Attempts to update a table with an update trigger.
- Attempts to update a table marked for replication.

The following conditions also apply depending on whether the update is a single- or multiple-row update. For a single-row update, the update mode will be deferred if:

- The new total row size doesn't fit on the same page as the old row.
- The updated column is part of a non-unique, non-clustered index and the index key isn't a fixed-width column.
- The updated column is part of a unique non-clustered index and the index key isn't fixed-width or the WHERE clause criteria doesn't have an exact match.
- The new row has differing bytes by more than 50 percent of the original row size, or the total number of discontiguous differing bytes is more than 24.

For multi-row updates, the update mode will be deferred if:

- The table contains a column with the timestamp datatype.
- The updated column is part of a unique non-clustered index.
- The updated column isn't fixed length.

This step involves sorting

This indicates that a worktable has been generated in order to sort the data in a query. This can be avoided by creating a useful index (or setting the **FASTFIRSTROW** optimizer hint).

Using Clustered Index

This indicates that the optimizer has decided to use a clustered index to retrieve the data.

Using Dynamic Index

This indicates that the optimizer has decided to implement the 'OR Strategy' (see above).

Using GETSORTED

This indicates that the optimizer is using a worktable for sorting data.

Worktable created for

This indicates that the optimizer has had to create a temporary worktable to process the data in the query. Worktables are often used when sorting and always used for **GROUP BY** clauses.

If you want even more detailed information, you can use Trace Flags. Details of how to use Trace Flags, together with the Trace Flag output for the above query, can be found in the chapter on Troubleshooting SQL Server.

STATISTICS TIME

The **STATISTICS TIME** option is used to display the time in milliseconds taken to execute each step of a query. This can be set either by issuing the **SET STATISTICS TIME ON** command in the ISQL/W window or by checking the Show Stats Time tickbox in the Query Options dialog.

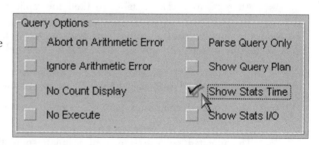

The output produced by this option for the query above would look something like this:

```
SQL Server Execution Times:
    cpu time = 0 ms.  elapsed time = 12177 ms.
SQL Server Parse and Compile Time:
    cpu time = 20 ms.
au_fname            au_lname
------------------- ----------------------------------------
Marjorie            Green
Burt                Gringlesby
Stearns             MacFeather Variations
Michael             O'Leary
Michael             O'Leary
```

Anne   Ringer
Akiko   Yokomoto

(7 row(s) affected)

SQL Server Execution Times:
    cpu time = 10 ms. elapsed time = 10 ms.
SQL Server Parse and Compile Time:
    cpu time = 0 ms.

Whenever you attempt to optimize a query it always makes sense to note down this output before and after optimization. This gives you an objective recording of the time taken for the query to execute, so you can determine whether your attempts at optimization have had the intended result.

Obviously, the time taken for the query to execute will be affected by other activities on the server. Therefore, if the server on which you're analyzing query performance isn't a dedicated SQL Server, you should either seek to minimize the other activities occurring on the server or run each query a large enough number of times in order to establish a higher degree of confidence that any changes you're making do have a positive benefit.

If you choose to run your query analysis on a server which isn't your production SQL Server, you should ensure that the performance gains you achieve in the test environment can be replicated in the production environment. In many cases, performance degradation is due to molecular rather than atomic influences. In other words, the degradation is the result of a combination of factors operating upon each other rather than a single factor.

STATISTICS I/O

This option displays the amount of I/O that was required to execute the query and comes in both a graphical and a textual form. Like the Showplan option, the graphical form can be set by selecting the Statistics I/O entry on the Query... menu bar. Alternatively, it can be set by clicking the Display Statistics I/O button.

When the graphical Statistics I/O option is set, the amount of logical and physical I/O generated for each table in the query is displayed on the Statistics I/O page of the query window.

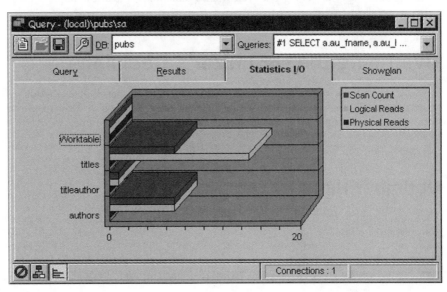

The scan count indicates the number of times the table had to be scanned during the processing of the query.

Logical Reads indicates the number of pages which needed to be accessed during the processing of the query.

Physical Reads indicates the number of pages which needed to be read from disk during the processing of the query. This number will be lower than logical reads if the data is already in cache. The physical reads figure can be impacted by other activities on the server and may vary between calls. For this reason, logical reads is a better metric to use when analyzing query performance as it will be invariant irrespective of other server activity.

In order to display textual Statistics I/O output, you can either issue the **SET STATISTICS IO ON** command in the ISQL/W window or check the Show Stats I/O tickbox in the Query Options dialog.

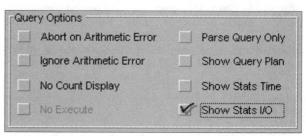

An example of the output displayed by the Statistics I/O option is shown below:

```
Table: authors   scan count 7,  logical reads: 7,   physical reads: 0,  read ahead reads: 0
Table: titleauthor  scan count 1,  logical reads: 1,   physical reads: 0,  read ahead reads: 0
Table: titles   scan count 7,  logical reads: 15,  physical reads: 0,  read ahead reads: 0
Table: Worktable   scan count 0,  logical reads: 0,   physical reads: 0,  read ahead reads: 0
```

As you can see, this displays the same information as the graphical Statistics I/O option except that it includes details of 'read ahead reads'. These are an indication of the number of buffers which were brought into the cache for a particular table during a read ahead. (Read ahead occurs when SQL Server detects that sequential pages are being retrieved from a table and so issues multiple separate threads to pre-fetch pages in parallel.)

Overriding the Optimizer's Decisions

If you wish, you can override the execution plan selected by the optimizer. Although this option is sometimes useful, you should be very careful about when you use it. Most of the time SQL Server will correctly devise the optimum execution plan for a query, and attempting to override it can lead to a serious degradation in performance. However, if you're sure that SQL Server is using a suboptimal execution plan, you can override it by using **optimizer hints**.

Optimizer Hints

These are placed in the **FROM** clause of a **SELECT** statement and force SQL Server to follow the strategy indicated by the hint.

```
SELECT   selection-list
FROM   tablename [(optimizer hint)],  tablename [(optimizer hint)]…
```

The optimizer hints listed below all affect the performance of a query.

INDEX = *index_name*

This instructs the optimizer to use the index named **index_name** when executing the query

INDEX =0│1

If an **index_id** of 0 is supplied, the optimizer is forced to scan the table. If an **index_id** of 1 is supplied, the optimizer is forced to use the table's clustered index if one exists.

FASTFIRSTROW

This option causes SQL Server to return the first row of the result set as quickly as possible. Often the optimizer will choose to scan a table and then sort it as a faster option than using a non-clustered index. However, although this strategy is faster at returning the entire result set, there may be a delay before the first row instead. By forcing the optimizer to use a non-clustered index (if one matches the column(s) in the **ORDER BY** clause), this optimizer hint secures fast retrieval of the first row of the result set with the possible cost of slower overall retrieval of the entire result set.

Set Forceplan On

Another way to override the optimizer is to set the **FORCEPLAN** option to **ON**. This forces the optimizer to join the tables in the query in the order that they appear in the **SELECT** statement. When you do this, you will want to place tables with high selectivity at the start of the list of tables in your **SELECT** statement, with tables with low selectivity towards the end of the table list.

As with all of the **SET** options, the **SET FORCEPLAN** option remains on until you turn it off. This means that all queries will be processed using the explicitly assigned join order until the option is turned off.

SQL Eye

There are also a number of third-party tools which can be used to monitor the performance of SQL Server. One of the more popular ones is called SQL Eye and you can obtain it from the Microsoft Development Library. It's an application which is based on Microsoft's Open Data Services architecture and sits between the client application and SQL Server. Client applications connect to SQL Eye and SQL Eye passes queries on to SQL Server. By intercepting queries in this way, SQL Eye is able to display the queries, results, error messages and timings. These can either be displayed on the screen in an MDI interface, written to a log file or stored in a SQL Server table.

As such, SQL Eye is useful for providing a high-level view of SQL Server activity to allow the user to:

▲ Determine what queries are being sent to SQL Server from client applications (although this can now be done just as effectively using the SQL Trace utility)

▲ View the data sent by SQL Server to multiple clients

▲ Monitor the time taken by each of these queries to execute

For further information on SQL Eye, you should consult the Microsoft Development Library.

Using SQL Server Performance Monitor

One of the most attractive features of SQL Server is its tight integration with the Windows NT operating system. On the one hand this leads to excellent performance benefits as it relieves SQL Server of many of the overheads which other database management systems need to handle for themselves–such as the management of load across multiple processors. On the other hand, it makes the real-time monitoring of SQL Server and Windows NT performance incredibly easy using the Windows NT Performance Monitor.

Using Counters

When you install SQL Server it installs various counters which incorporate themselves into the Performance Monitor. In fact, these counters are actually stored within separate DLLs which the Performance Monitor interrogates using standard published calls. By exposing these counters, SQL Server allows you to use Performance Monitor to track those elements of the system to which the counters relate.

On Demand vs. Direct Response

The default mode for retrieving the values of these counters is Direct Response mode. This means that the counter values are collected separately from their display in the SQL Performance Monitor. This allows the results to be displayed immediately in Performance Monitor; however, the results will be one period old.

In contrast, if the values are collected in On Demand mode, Performance Monitor will wait for the latest results to be collected before displaying them. This results in a slower response time in Performance Monitor, but the data is guaranteed to be up-to-date.

You can modify the collection mode for SQL Performance Statistics through the SQL Server Setup program.

Default Counters

By default, the Performance Monitor for SQL Server initially displays the following counters.

▲ **Cache Hit Ratio**
This counter indicates the percentage of time that data requested by SQL Server was found in cache rather than having to be retrieved from disk. Given the vast difference between the speed of reading from disk and from memory, you want the cache hit ratio to be as high as possible. If the cache hit ratio is consistently low, you may find that adding additional memory to SQL Server will remedy the situation.

▲ **I/O – Transactions/second**
This indicates the number of Transact-SQL command batches executed per second and is the key indicator of the throughput of SQL Server.

▲ **I/O – Page Reads/second**
This counter indicate the number of physical page reads which occurred every second. Disk i/o is very expensive and for this reason you will want to reduce the number of page reads as much as possible. This is typically done by either increasing the size of the cache, so that logical reads do not result in physical reads, or by adding unable indexes to tables in the database so that an entire table does not need to be scanned whenever a query needs data from that table.

▲ **I/O – Single Page Writes**
Writing to the disk is also expensive and so you will want to reduce the value of this counter as much as possible. Single Page Writes occur when either the log or the cache is flushed to disk. To reduce this, you should ensure that you always have free buffers in the buffer pool. You can determine the number of free buffers by monitoring the Number of Free Buffers counter of the Cache object.

▲ **User Connections**
This obviously indicates the number of connections to the SQL Server being monitored. Each connection uses up just under 40 Kb of server memory, so a high value for this counter may impact throughput by reducing the amount of memory available for other SQL Server usage.

Although these five counters are a very good starting point, you may well want to add some of the other counters available if you suspect that you have a performance problem. We will now look in turn at the three most frequently encountered bottlenecks and how you can use the Performance Monitor to isolate them.

CPU Bottlenecks

CPU bottlenecks are perhaps the easiest to identify. The primary counter used to identify CPU bottlenecks is the % Processor Time counter of the Processor object. This indicates the amount of time which the processor spends executing non-idle threads and therefore indicates the amount of time that the processor is doing useful work. If this figure is consistently high, (say, over 80–90%) you may find that performance will improve either by upgrading the processor to one of a higher speed, or by adding additional processors to the system to share the load.

You should generally consider upgrading to a faster CPU before you think about adding additional CPUs. This is because the extra work involved by Windows NT in managing the extra CPU will incur an overhead which will necessarily diminish the performance gain achieved by the additional processing power. However, once you've installed the fastest CPU available to you, you should then consider adding extra CPUs if performance is still suboptimal.

However, although adding extra CPUs will not provide a linear improvement in performance, the gains from adding up to four processors are considerable. The graph below illustrates the type of performance improvement that can typically be achieved by adding extra CPUs.

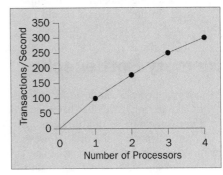

Note, however, that the curve soon begins to flatten and the extra return in terms of processing power becomes less and less as more processors are added.

Disk Bottlenecks

The importance of fitting a server running SQL Server with a fast disk subsystem can't be overemphasized. The bus, the controller and the disks themselves should all be of a high specification. As well as having high-performance components, the configuration of the components is key to implementing a fast disk subsystem. Disk striping and other levels of RAID control can be particularly effective methods for improving access speed, but the performance benefit needs to be weighed against the increased cost of purchasing 'redundant' drives.

As you might expect, the two primary objects to monitor when you expect a disk bottleneck are the I/O and Physical Disk objects. The counters for the Physical Disk object aren't enabled by default. In order to use these counters you need to run the following command from the command line and then restart the server.

```
diskperf -y
```

Once you've enabled the Physical Disk counters in this way, you should monitor % Disk Time and Disk Queue Length in particular.

The % Disk Time counter indicates how much of the time the disk is busy with read/write activity. If this figure is consistently high, then the disk subsystem may be the bottleneck. In other words, performance may be improved by speeding up the disk subsystem in some way.

The Disk Queue Length counter indicates how many disk I/O requests are pending. If this figure is consistently higher than 2, then it is again likely that the disk is a potential bottleneck.

Another useful object is the I/O object which has three counters: Outstanding Reads, Outstanding Writes and Log Writes/sec. The first two counters indicate the number of physical read/writes that are pending. Again, a consistently high figure for this counter is symptomatic of a disk bottleneck. The third counter, I/O – Log Writes/sec, indicates the number of log pages physically written to the disk every second. If this figure reaches the maximum throughput of the drive on which the log is located, you will have a bottleneck. In this case, you should move the log device to a disk with a greater throughput (such as a striped or RAID-controlled disk set).

Memory Bottlenecks

Memory bottlenecks can arise for one of two reasons. Either there isn't enough RAM installed in the server or the amount of RAM that has been assigned to SQL Server is too low or too high. The classic signal of insufficient memory is disk thrashing. At first sight, the high level of disk activity may lead you to think that the bottleneck is the disk. However, the following counters should enable you to recognize that memory is in fact the bottleneck. The counters are the Cache Hit Ratio and I/O – Lazy Writes/sec counters of the SQL Server object and the Page Faults/sec counter of the Memory object.

As mentioned above, the Cache Hit Ratio counter is displayed by default when the SQL Performance Monitor is loaded and indicates the amount of time that data was found in cache rather than having to be read from disk. If this figure is consistently around the 80% mark or higher, it's likely that you'll be able to improve performance by increasing the size of the data cache. You can do this in one of two ways. Either increase the amount of RAM available to SQL Server or increase the amount of memory that SQL Server allocates to the data cache as opposed to the procedure cache. To see how memory is apportioned between the data and procedure cache, you should execute the following statement.

```
sp_configure procedure_cache
```

This will indicate the proportion of SQL Server memory which is apportioned to procedure cache. Reducing this figure (using the **sp_configure** statement) will free more memory for use by the data cache. To see the actual amount of data available to the data (page) cache, execute the **dbcc memusage** statement.

The I/O – Lazy Writes/sec counter of the SQL Server object can also be used to detect a memory bottleneck. This counter registers the number of dirty aged pages which the Lazy Writer flushes every second. If this figure is consistently greater than 0, it indicates that the Lazy Writer is constantly having to flush pages to disk. This is generally an indication that the data cache is too small.

The Page Faults/sec counter of the Memory object indicates how frequently a virtual page was not found in memory and therefore had to be read from disk. Far from indicating a lack of memory for SQL Server, a consistent non-zero value for this counter indicates that the operating system itself has insufficient memory. In general, the best way to rectify this is to either add more RAM to the server or to assign more memory to Windows NT and less to SQL Server.

Physical Database Design

A final area to touch on when dealing with performance monitoring and optimization is the physical design of the database. In fact, this should probably be one of the first as this is one factor which can have a dramatic effect on the performance of your application. There are two significant areas to consider:

- Index Design
- Table Design

Deciding What to Index

When deciding which fields to index, you should consider the following:

- Columns on which you search by range
- Columns involved in joins
- Columns you order or group by
- Columns used with aggregate functions

Data Normalization

Everyone reading this book should know at least the first three normal forms. For those that don't, the most complete reference on this subject is probably *The Relational Model for Database Management Systems* written in 1990 by E. F. Codd. Adherence to these normal forms brings many benefits, such as an increase in consistency and maintainability, a reduction in data redundancy and better search performance from smaller tables with narrower rows. However, the down-side to all this is that these multiple small tables all have to be joined up again and multiple joins can mean slow performance. Your approach should always be to consider strategies that preserve the qualities of your data model. However, there are occasions when denormalizing ('pre-joining') is the right answer.

Denormalization

Although complete normalization of your data model makes perfect sense for your logical data model, when you come to implement the physical data model, you may find that adherence to 3NF is simply impractical in terms of performance. If this is the case, then you may determine a need to denormalize your data. It's a point well worth making that denormalization is a step in itself. I am of the opinion that it always pays to normalize initially to at least 3NF and then only denormalize in your physical implementation once you're convince that a completely normalized solution is unworkable. That way, when you finally summon up the courage to denormalize, you will have a more open mind as to the different ways that you can do this.

Coalescing Foreign Keys

This is perhaps the most obvious way to denormalize. Let's suppose that you have a students table, a courses table and a rooms table. A student attends a course and a course is held in a room. Normalized, it looks like this:

However, if you want to find out which building a student needs to go to, you need to implement a three-table join. However, if you denormalized the students table by adding the foreign key RoomID, then this query would be reduced to a two-table query.

Obviously, you now have to worry about maintaining the integrity of CourseID and RoomID, in the students table but if you determine that the enhanced performance of the new query outweighs the overhead of one or more triggers, then denormalizing in this way is an option.

Derived Data

Another time-consuming operation in a relational database is the aggregate query. What if we wanted to keep a tally of the number of bottles of wine our shop has sold? Each bottle of wine can feature in multiple orders, so our normalized database may look like this:

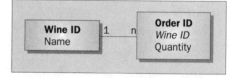

But if the orders table is very large and constantly being updated by dozens of users, we may decide that we want to forego the necessity of running an aggregate query against it, by keeping a running total of the number of bottles sold in the wines table.

Again, there need to be strict measures in place to ensure the integrity of the summary derived value, and the cost of enforcing this integrity needs to be weighed against the savings gained in the faster execution of the summary query.

Artificial Keys

Another mechanism for speeding up joins is to reduce the size of the primary key on the table. Narrower primary keys lead to more records per page and, therefore, smaller indexes. In addition, the smaller the key, the more accurate the data that will be held on the distribution page. This type of 'normalization' is usually employed to replace a multiple-field (composite) primary key with an artificial system-assigned key. The new key will generally be an identity column and its contents meaningless except for manufacturing joins with the foreign key in other tables.

Splitting Tables Horizontally

If you determine that some of the rows within a table are more frequently accessed than others, you might consider splitting the table horizontally. Thus, you could split your orders table according to the region from which the order came in. This might leave you with four tables (Orders_n, Orders_s, Orders_e, and Orders_w) all with an identical structure. This would allow you to place the most heavily used table on a separate, fast drive. Again, however, you'll need to balance the benefits of faster data retrieval (although this may not be significant if you're accessing the data via an index) against the overhead of performing union queries. A benefit, though, of horizontal splitting is that it can allow you to localize the effect of running expensive aggregate queries to one of the new smaller tables.

Splitting Tables Vertically

The alternative is to split the table vertically and construct a one-to-one join between the two tables. For example, we might decide to split up our wines table so that the price is held in one table and all the other attributes of the wine are held in another table.

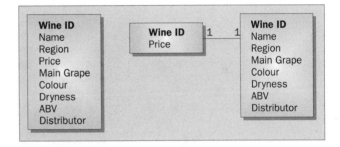

This sort of split isn't too cumbersome to maintain and can be used as a mechanism for reducing lock contention and improving the performance of table scans. Also, as with horizontal splitting, it can be used to localize the overhead of aggregate queries in environments where Data Entry and Decision Support are combined in the one database.

All of these methods of denormalization can introduce significant costs in terms of maintenance and of introducing extra measures to enforce data integrity. Clearly, these costs have to be borne in mind and weighed up against any potential benefits in terms of faster query performance. It makes sense, therefore, to consider denormalization only when you've determined that the normalized implementation of your logical model will not provide the required performance.

Once you've determined that (and in my experience users of database systems are never reluctant to draw performance problems to a DBA's attention!), then by using one or more of the tools described in this chapter, you should be able to determine where exactly the problem lies. Then you'll need to consider what solutions to the problem you can implement. This may involve the creation, modification–or even removal–of an index. Or it may require the reconfiguration or addition of some type of system resource. For each solution you consider, you should bear in mind the risk and the long-term cost of implementing that solution. Then, after thoroughly testing the proposed fix, you can implement it into the production system.

Never forget that databases are organic entities. They grow, they change, they move, they react to changes in the environment around them. And being aware of the potential for change will prepare you for the action you will need to take in order to manage the impact of that change.

Summary

In this chapter, we've looked at many different ways you can improve the performance of your database. You could devote a whole book to the topic so we've tried to summarize the methods that will have the most impact on performance. The first technique is that of indexing and we considered the advantages of clustered and non-clustered indexing. We considered what options are available from the Enterprise Manager to save time when creating an index or to minimize page splitting. We looked at how to create indexes with the Enterprise Manager and with Transact-SQL.

We also examined how to optimize queries so that they execute faster and how to analyze the performance of queries with different query analysis tools. The optimizer often plays a significant part in the speed of a query and if it's not doing its job properly then we considered how you'd go about overriding. We looked at how the performance monitor can be used to detect bottlenecks. Finally, we considered how you can improve performance when creating the physical design of the database.

6.5

Troubleshooting SQL Server

In the previous chapter, we showed you how you to monitor and improve the performance of SQL Server. The emphasis throughout the last chapter was on a proactive approach of planning and preparation. However, even with the best planning, unexpected problems can arise and you can bet your bottom dollar that it will be at the very moment that you can least afford them to. In this chapter, we'll give you some tools that you can use to fix these unexpected problems.

The chapter starts with the general approach you need to take when trying to identify and fix unexpected behavior in SQL Server. Many of these guidelines are simply common sense, but it doesn't hurt to spell them out. After that, we'll show you some of the many tools which are available to the SQL Server administrator to help identify where exactly the problem occurred and what precisely went wrong. Finally, we'll show you how you can actually solve problems once you have identified them.

Troubleshooting Strategies

Before we get into the nitty-gritty of solving problems that you may encounter as an SQL Server administrator, we'll review a few basics that you need to keep in mind as you go through the troubleshooting process. It's easy to jump to the wrong conclusions when a call comes in from a user to say that none of the applications which use the **SalesProd** server are functioning properly. If you don't adopt the right approach to correcting the problem, a five minute fix could turn into a five hour nightmare.

The ideas that we'll present in the coming sections are not necessarily great insights, but are rather the simple application of common sense, one of *the* most underrated tools in the identification and correction of problems.

> Above all, don't panic! Take a deep breath. Stay calm. Don't let anyone push you for answers to "When will it be fixed?" Move slowly, because actions you perform in haste, you may repent at leisure.

Verify that There is a Problem

I was going to call this section 'Don't take their word for it', but that seemed a little inflammatory! Obviously, one of the first things to do when a problem is reported to you is to verify that the problem actually exists. For example, you may get a call saying that when the users of the Sales application tried this morning to run their monthly mail merge, only half the customer details were retrieved. Before you take the server down and start poring over the Transact SQL in the mail merge stored procedures, just take a moment or two to ask yourself a couple of questions, such as:

▲ Has the printer run out of paper halfway through the mail merge, so that all the letters were merged but only half of them were printed?

▲ Did the user have the <u>K</u>ey Clients Only check box checked when they ran the mail merge?

I'm not suggesting that you should doubt everything a user tells you, but neither should you veer to the other extreme and suppose that the problem he or she has encountered is exactly as they've explained. This is particularly true when a user reports a solution rather than a problem. For example, you may receive a call from Fred, a user in the Sales department, who says,

"You're going to have to increase the size of the Transaction Log on the SalesProd database, because I just got an error 1105."

If you ever get a call like that, ignore everything except *"I just got an error 1105"*. Imagine you went to the doctor and said,

"Doc, I'm gonna need a tonsillectomy because I've got tonsillitis..."

What would you think of a doctor who performed the tonsillectomy without checking:

▲ Whether you actually have tonsillitis as you suspect?

▲ What your clinical history is?

▲ Whether a tonsillectomy is the most appropriate course of action?

You should show the same diligence and objectivity in matters of database administration that you would expect a doctor to show towards you in matters of health. Focus on the symptoms and work out the diagnosis for yourself.

Identify the Last Change Made...

When problems occur, they don't normally do so of their own volition. Invariably, when a problem appears to arise out of the blue, it's a reaction to something that has recently been altered. If you're not sure what has caused a problem, think back to the last thing you changed. Ask yourself whether that could possibly be the cause of the problem.

It helps to keep a log of all the changes you make to a database, to the server or to other areas of the system. This helps you to remember what you last changed and it helps others to identify what has recently been changed if you're not around.

...but Beware the Guilty Conscience

Although you should be aware that today's problem may have been caused by yesterday's fix, you should take care to avoid the opposite extreme of allowing your guilty conscience to cloud your objectivity. You put in a hasty bug fix last night. You thought at the time,

"I've tested it as much as time allows but, hey, these guys have got a business to run. They need this fix as soon as possible. I can't afford to hack them off by keeping the server down for another day. I am sure this will work fine... and in any case the ball game starts at eight tonight..."

So, when Fred phones and says that that he has had an error 1105, you suddenly think back to that quick bug fix. It doesn't occur to you that your bug fix could possibly not be the cause of Fred's problem. Your guilty conscience persuades you that deep down you *know* that last night's hasty bugfix is to blame.

That's no position to be in when you're trying to objectively determine the cause of Fred's problem. It's simple to avoid being in this 'guilty conscience' situation: don't give yourself the chance. Always test any bugfixes thoroughly, so you don't find yourself leaping to the wrong conclusions when something goes wrong.

In short, be aware that the most recent change may be the cause of your problems, but don't become obsessed with that change as being the *only* potential cause.

Check the Obvious First

Another trap we all fall into from time to time is that we fail to see the forest for the trees. Jane phones up to say that, this morning, she is unable to connect to the server. You immediately start running through various issues in your mind: does the client machine have the appropriate net library installed? Are there too may connections to the server? Has anyone modified the **ODBC.INI** file?

Once you've spent a good hour checking these through, it isn't very amusing (although your companions may disagree) for you to find that the reason why Jane can't connect to the server is that the cleaners were in last night and accidentally disconnected the network cable from her computer when they were dusting it.

Similarly, if you've written a stored procedure and, when you test it, you expect it to return 3 rows from a table of 100 rows and you find it returns no records at all, don't spend hours working through the nitty-gritty of the Transact SQL until you've checked that the data was in the base table to start with.

Think low-tech, simple causes first of all. Only when you've eliminated those should you begin to focus on the more obscure highly technical causes.

Change One Thing at a Time

Once you've isolated the area where the problem is occurring, you may think you have a few solutions you could try. If so, try them out, but try them *one at a time*. If you make lots of changes before you test the application again, you run a significant risk. If the problem does go away, you won't be sure which of the changes you made actually solved the problem. You run the risk of having made an unnecessary change which may in turn cause further problems to surface at a later date.

Document It

As you're trying to debug a problem, it's also important that you document any changes you make. The purpose of this is twofold. First, if you find that your debugging has led you down a blind alley, you'll be able to backtrack and return to a known position. Second, if your efforts are successful and you do manage to fix the problem, you'll have documentation for future reference in case the problem ever surfaces again. The relatively small amount of effort you put into documenting the solution at the time will reap manifold benefits later on.

Isolating the Problem

So far, we've looked at a general approach to the troubleshooting task. In this section, we'll cover various tools and methods that you can use to identify the particular causes of unexpected behavior in SQL Server.

SQL Server Error Log

When you're attempting to determine precisely what happened, one of the first places to look is the SQL Server Error Log. By default, this is located in **C:\Mssql\Log\Errorlog**. A new Error Log is created every time SQL Server is started and previous Error Logs are then archived with extensions of **.1, .2, .3,** etc.

The Error Log contains informational, warning and error messages generated by SQL Server. These may vary from critical messages, such as hardware errors and database integrity errors, to informational messages detailing the time that SQL Server was started and the current version of SQL Server.

Error Messages

SQL Server error messages are made up of four constituent parts:

- ▲ A unique message number
- ▲ A severity level
- ▲ A state number that identifies the source of the error
- ▲ A message indicating the nature of the problem and how it may be fixed

For example, if we try to drop a table, **authortable**, which doesn't exist, this error message will be generated:

```
Msg 3701, Level 11, State 1
Cannot drop the table 'authortable', because it doesn't exist in the system catalogs.
```

These error messages are stored within the **sysmessages** table in the master database. If you want, you can see the contents of this table by executing the following query in the ISQL/W window:

```
SELECT *
FROM sysmessages
```

Depending on the severity of the error message, the message may simply be returned to the client or it may also be recorded in the Error Log.

Severity Levels

An indication of the seriousness of an error is provided by its severity level. This varies from level 0 (trivial, informational messages) to level 25 (a fatal internal server error). The severity level of the error message is stored in the **severity** field of the **sysmessages** table.

Informational Messages

If a message has a severity level of 10 or lower then it's purely informational and doesn't require correction. An example is the confirmation message number **14025**, which has a severity level of 10:

The article was successfully updated.

User-correctable Errors

If a message has a severity level of 11 to 16, it indicates that the user can correct the error that has occurred. For example, if a user attempts to drop a non-existent table, the following message from **sysmessages** is displayed:

Msg 3701, Level 11, State 1
Cannot drop the table 'authortable', because it doesn't exist in the system catalogs.

Resource Shortage Errors

A message with a severity level of 17 indicates that there are insufficient resources to complete the requested action.

Msg 1118, Level 17, State 1
Database SALES_DATABASE is full. Cannot allocate space for object feerefunds. All available pages are held by other transactions. Try your command again.

Non-fatal System Errors

Messages with a severity level of 18 indicate that an internal error has occurred which has prevented the requested statement from being completed, but which hasn't caused the connection to the database to be terminated. An example of such an error is:

Msg 1520, Level 18, State 1
Sort failed because dpages in the Sysindexes row for table feerefunds in database SALES_DATABASE had an incorrect value. Please run DBCC CHECKTABLE on this table to correct the value, then re-run your command.

Fatal System Errors

If an error message has a severity level of 19 or higher, it indicates that a fatal system error has occurred. This will normally lead to the connection with the client application being aborted. Such an error is often associated with media failure and this is indicated by a severity level of 24.

Msg 902, Level 24, State 1
Hardware error detected reading logical page 1025510, virtual page 3024152 in database SALES_DATABASE.

> If you're generating a user-defined error with the RAISERROR statement, you should observe the following conditions: that user-defined errors should be allocated an error number of 50000 or higher and only system administrators can generate an error with a severity level greater than 18

Inspecting the Error Log

You can inspect the contents of the SQL Server Error Log in a variety of ways. From within the SQL Enterprise Manager, you can select Error Log... from the Server menu. This displays the Error Log for the current session in an MDI window.

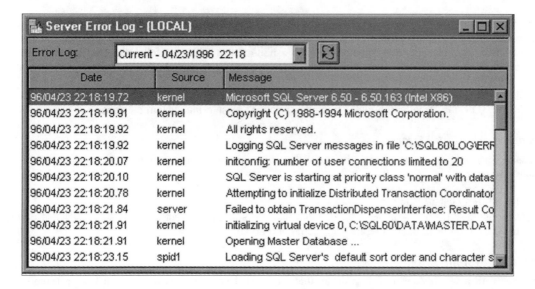

By using the drop-down box at the top of the window, you can select the archived logs from previous SQL Server sessions for viewing.

An alternative method of viewing the SQL Server Error Log is to open the file with a text editor, such as Windows Write or Notepad. However, both of these methods can prove rather laborious if you want to search the Error Log for specific messages. In this situation, you may find it more convenient to use the NT **findstr** utility, which allows you to search a file for specific text strings.

Event Log

When you're debugging erratic behavior in SQL Server, another area to look is the NT Application Event Log. You can browse this with the Event Viewer, a shortcut to which is placed by default in the Administrative Tools Program Group. SQL Server can write informational, warning and error messages to the NT Application Event Log, as well as to the SQL Server Error Log. However, browsing the NT Event Log has four advantages.

First, it contains messages from applications other than SQL Server. This can be useful if another application (or NT itself) is causing SQL Server to behave erratically. By looking at the sequence of events in the NT Event Log, you can monitor the chain of events that caused SQL Server to misbehave.

Secondly, the NT Event Log visually differentiates between errors of different severity levels. As you can see in the screenshot, errors, warnings and informational messages are identified by different icons:

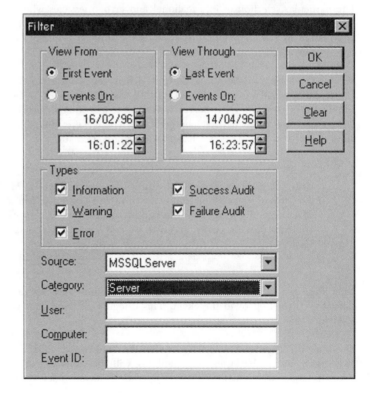

Thirdly, you can filter the NT Event Log to display only the events that you're interested in. To filter events in the Event Log, select Filter Events... from the View menu in the Event Viewer. In the dialog which then appears, you can select the type of events you wish to view.

The final advantage is that a person with administrative privileges can specify certain 'housekeeping' options to prevent the **Event Log** from growing too large. By selecting Log Settings... from the Log menu, it's possible to specify:

▲ A maximum size for the Event Log, so that the oldest events are automatically deleted when the Event Log reaches that size.

▲ A maximum age, so that all events over that age are automatically deleted.

> Although setting these options to lower values makes it easier to browse the Event Log, you should be aware that a single application misbehaving could easily write a great number of consecutive events to the Event Log, thereby causing details of older but still potentially useful SQL Server events to be deleted.

SQL Server Trace Flags

The particular selection of informational and error messages which are written to the Error Log is determined by what you might think of as a 'factory-set default'. SQL Server could record a lot more information in the Error Log, but, most of the time, it wouldn't be of interest to administrators and would only clutter the Error Log unnecessarily.

However, what about the 5% of the time when you would happily forego performance and disk space, just to see *exactly* what was going on inside SQL Server? Wouldn't it be good if you could fine tune the amount of information SQL Server would record, so that it recorded the real nitty-gritty when you were debugging some problem, but ignored it when you were operating in a production environment. The good news is that you can. That is what trace flags are used for.

> Trace flags are *not* part of the supported feature set of Microsoft SQL Server. They are provided as is and may vary in future versions. You should be aware that Microsoft might not provide support or answer questions about trace flags and their output. However, given those provisos, they can still be a very, very useful tool.

Trace flags generally serve one of two purposes. Some allow extra diagnostic information to be sent to either the Error Log or to the client. This category of trace flags is useful for identifying problems (such as why does this query take so long to execute?).

The second category of trace flags modify the behavior of SQL Server in other ways. These flags are often provided to ensure backwards compatibility with previous versions of SQL Server. They are useful for resolving issues which arise when you upgrade from an older version of SQL Server.

Setting Trace Flags

There are three ways to set trace flags. Whichever method you use, remember that you should only use trace flags for a short period of time. They can lead to a notable degradation of performance and may significantly increase the size of the Error Log.

Setting Trace Flags with DBCC TRACEON

If you want to set one or more trace flags during an SQL Server session without taking down the server, you can use the **DBCC** statement with the **TRACEON** argument. This should be followed with the identifiers for the trace flags listed later in this chapter.

```
DBCC TRACEON (trace1, trace2, …)
```

So, let's suppose you have a query which returns the names of all authors and books where the authors receive less than 50% of the royalties for the book; and let's suppose that you find that the query is taking longer to run than you expected. To examine the way in which SQL Server is performing the joins in the query, you could execute these SQL statements in the ISQL/W window:

```
DBCC TRACEON (302, 310, 3605, -1)
go

SELECT a.au_fname, a.au_lname, t.title
FROM authors a, titleauthor ta, titles t
WHERE a.au_id = ta.au_id
AND t.title_id = ta.title_id
AND ta.royaltyper < 50
ORDER BY a.au_lname
go

DBCC TRACEOFF (302, 310)
go
```

The first line sets four trace flags.

- ▲ The first two flags (**302** and **310**) record the actual information about the joins and their ordering.

- ▲ The third flag (**3605**) indicates that this information should be written to the Error Log. If we had specified **3604** instead, the trace output would have been sent to the client.

- ▲ The fourth flag (**-1**) indicates that these trace flags should apply to all current connections, as opposed to simply applying to the client connection on which the DBCC statement was executed. Note that any new connections to the server won't have their trace output recorded.

Then we execute the query itself. Finally, we turn off the trace flags. We only need to turn off the flags responsible for collecting the information, because the other two flags simply indicated what should happen while those two trace flags were set.

Setting Trace Flags at the Command Line

Another way to set trace flags is to do so when you start SQL Server from the command line by using the **-T** switch with each of the flags you wish to set. So, to start SQL Server with the trace flags specified above, you would type this at the command line:

```
sqlservr -T302, -T310, -T3605
```

You should note that we don't need to specify the fourth flag (-1). This is because trace flags set from the command line automatically apply to all connections. These trace flags will remain set for the active session, i.e. until SQL Server is shut down and restarted.

When setting trace flags from the command line, you should take care to use an uppercase **-T**. A lowercase **-t** will cause the required trace flag to be set, but it will also cause a number of undocumented internal flags to be set.

Setting Trace Flags in Setup

A third method for setting trace flags is to specify them as parameters via setup. Run the SQL Server Setup utility and select Set Server Options when prompted. In the Select Server Options dialog box which then appears, you should click the Parameters button.

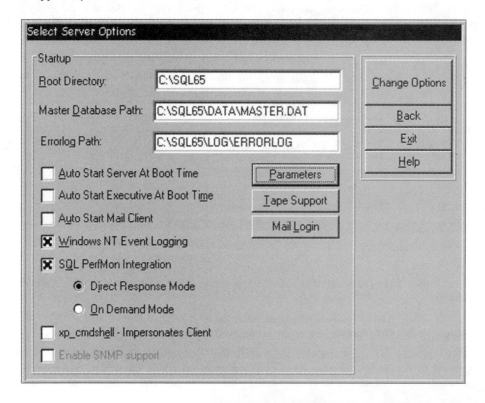

In the next dialog, you need to add the trace flag parameters as they would appear if typed at the command line. Then hit the OK button and exit the setup utility.

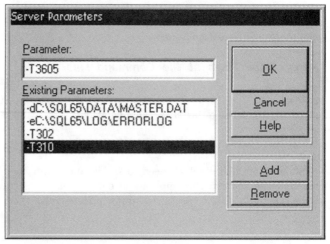

Now the trace flags you have specified will be invoked every time you start SQL Server.

We mentioned earlier that you should set trace flags only when you're debugging specific problems and unset them once the problem has been solved. For this reason, you should be very careful about setting trace flags via the setup utility–it's just too easy to forget they are there.

That's not to say that you should never set trace flags at start-up. The setup utility is more suited to the setting of the second category of trace flags we mentioned earlier, those which modify SQL Server behavior, often for compatibility with previous versions. An example of this is trace flag 243 which, when set, causes SQL Server 6.5 to treat nullity violations in the same manner as SQL Server 4.2x.

Informational Trace Flags

In the next sections, we'll detail the 'informational' trace flags and their effect. These can be very useful when you're attempting to debug SQL Server behavior.

302

This indicates whether the statistics page is used, the actual physical and logical I/O for the indexes and what SQL Server estimated this would be. Here's an example of the output produced by this trace flag:

```
Leaving q_init_sclause() for table 'titles' (varno 2).
The table has 18 rows and 3 pages.
Cheapest index is index 0, costing 3 pages per scan.
```

310

This prints information about join order. You can use it in conjunction with trace flag 302 to provide detailed information regarding the cost of various execution plans considered by SQL Server when executing a query. It lists the various permutations available for joining the tables in the query, together with the estimated cost of those joins.

325

This prints information about the cost of using a non-clustered index or a sort to process an **ORDER BY** clause.

326

This prints information about the estimated cost of sorts and the actual cost of sorts.

1200

This prints lock information (the process ID and type of lock requested). For example, executing the following statements with trace flag **1200** set,

```
BEGIN TRAN

SELECT t.title
FROM  titles t (HOLDLOCK)
```

```
ORDER BY t.title
go
```

might cause output similar to this to be written to the Error Log.

```
Process 11 requesting page lock of type SH_PAGE on 5 27
chaining lock onto PSS chain
Process 11 releasing page lock of type SH_PAGE on 5 27
Process 11 requesting table lock of type SH_TAB on 5 192003715
chaining lock onto PSS chain
```

1204

This prints information about deadlocks when they are detected. The information produced contains the process number (**spid**) of the blocked and blocking processes, the actual commands which caused the deadlock to occur, the types of lock held by each process, which process was selected as the deadlock victim and the **cputime** of the victim.

1205

When you use this in conjunction with trace flag 1204, it displays register information for each of the processes involved in the deadlock.

1704

This prints information when a temporary table is created or dropped.

3502

This prints a message to the log at the start and end of each checkpoint. The message will look something like this:

```
96/06/08 21:47:33.63 spid15   Ckpt dbid 5 started (0)
96/06/08 21:47:33.66 spid15   Ckpt dbid 5 phase 1 ended (0)
96/06/08 21:47:33.72 spid15   Ckpt dbid 5 complete
```

3503

This indicates whether the checkpoint at the end of automatic recovery was skipped for a database.

4030

This prints a byte and ASCII representation of the receive buffer. This can be very useful if you want to record what statements were being submitted by the server. Here's an example of the output:

```
96/06/08 21:51:35.77 15 LangExecBuffer, status 0, maxsize 4096, size 31:
   0: 0101001f 00000200 73656c65 6374202a   ........select *
  10: 2066726f 6d206175 74686f72 730d0a      from authors..
RecvByte: spid 15, status 0x2, RECV_EOM
```

Although SQL Server 6.5 now includes the SQLTrace utility to monitor statements received from clients and save them to a log file, nevertheless it may still be useful to set trace flag 4030. This is because you can use it with trace flag 3605 to record the contents of the receive buffer in the Error Log alongside the output of other trace flags.

4031

This prints a byte and ASCII representation of the send buffers. This is the converse of trace flag **4030** in that it shows data that the server returned to clients rather that received from them.

4032

This prints only an ASCII representation of the receive buffer. This is similar to trace flag **4030**, but because it only returns the ASCII representation of incoming statements, it's both easier to read and less expensive in terms of its overhead on query performance. The output would typically look like this:

```
96/06/08 22:08:17.30 15 LangExec: 'select * from authors..
```

3604

This indicates that trace output should be sent to the client. You should use this flag if you're debugging SQL Server from a client machine and so want to monitor the trace flag output through that connection.

3605

This indicates that trace output should be written to the Error Log. This provides a central repository for all trace flag output and contains other informational and warning messages generated by SQL Server. Seemingly erratic behavior is often caused at the molecular rather than atomic level. In other words, it's due not to a single event but to the interaction of a series of related events. By comparing the trace flag output in the **Error Log** with the other messages logged around it, you can establish the bigger picture and view events at the molecular rather than atomic level.

- 1

This indicates that trace flags should be set for all current client connections, rather than for the single client connection which invoked it. You don't need to specify this flag if you're setting trace flags when SQL Server starts up, as trace flags set at start-up automatically apply to all connections.

Compatibility Trace Flags

The next list details the trace flags which modify SQL Server 6.5 behavior, very often to emulate the behavior of previous versions of SQL Server. This is particularly useful when you're upgrading from a previous version of SQL Server and suspect that the problems you're encountering are due to the modified behavior of the new version.

If you determine that your problems are due to differences in behavior between the two versions, you can cause SQL Server to emulate the old behavior by placing the appropriate trace flag in the start up parameters for SQL Server. However, you should bear in mind that, because these trace flags have limited support from Microsoft and may change in future releases, they only provide you with a temporary solution. You should use the trace flags to allow applications to continue to function while they are being modified to take advantage of the new functionality in the current release of SQL Server.

107

Normally, SQL Server interprets numbers containing a decimal point as being of **decimal** datatype. However, setting this trace flag causes SQL Server to interpret them as **float** instead. The **float** datatype is an approximate datatype meaning that, unlike the **decimal** datatype which is accurate to the least significant digit, the accuracy of numbers with the **float** datatype can only be preserved as far as the binary counting system allows.

110

When set, this flag disables the behavior new to SQL Server 6.5 of disallowing duplicate table names in a **SELECT** statement. In previous versions of SQL Server, this statement,

```
SELECT *
FROM pubs..authors,pubs.dbo.authors
```

was interpreted as:

```
SELECT *
FROM authors a, authors b
```

This statement,

```
SELECT *
FROM authors,authors
```

was interpreted as:

```
SELECT *
FROM authors
```

However, SQL Server 6.5 generates an error for both of these statements. In order to return to pre-6.5 behavior, you should set trace flag **110**.

204

This trace flag allows SQL Server to perform various non-ANSI-compliant actions.

- ▲ It allows queries containing aggregates or a **GROUP BY** clause to have items in the **SELECT** list that are not in the **GROUP BY** clause and are not aggregate functions.

- ▲ It allows queries that contain sort columns in the **ORDER BY** clause that are not in the select list when the **DISTINCT** keyword is supplied.

This flag also causes SQL Server to ignore trailing blanks in the search pattern specified with a **LIKE** clause. By default, SQL Server from version 6.0 onwards will truncate trailing blanks in a search pattern to a single trailing blank. However, if you want trailing blanks ignored altogether, you should set trace flag **204**.

206

Prior to release 6.0 of SQL Server, the **SETUSER** statement didn't allow system administrators to restrict themselves to another user's privileges by using the **SETUSER** statement. In other words, they retained system administrative privileges at all times. Setting trace flag **206** reasserts this old behavior. (The new behavior now allows system administrators to restrict their privileges with **SETUSER**.)

237

In SQL Server 6.5, anyone creating a Foreign Key needs **REFERENCES** permission on the table containing the Foreign Key. When trace flag **237** is set, they only need **SELECT** permission in order to create the **FOREIGN KEY** constraint using **REFERENCES**, which is the behavior exhibited by SQL Server 6.0.

242

This provides backward compatibility for correlated subqueries where non-ANSI-standard results are desired.

243

This trace flag causes SQL Server to display the same for nullity behavior as version 4.2x. In versions 6.x of SQL Server all nullity checks are made at run time and a nullity violation results in the command terminating but the batch/transaction continuing to process.

In versions prior to 6.0, however, processing of the entire batch was terminated if the nullity error (for example, inserting NULL into a NOT NULL field) could be detected at compile time. If the error was detected at run time, the offending row was skipped but the command continued to execute. These two behaviors are those displayed by SQL Server 6.x if trace flag **243** is set.

244

Setting this flag prevents SQL Server from checking for allowable interim constraint violations. If SQL Server detects within a single statement and transaction a change causing a constraint violation followed by a second change which undoes the violation of the constraint, SQL Server will allow the statement to be processed. However, this checking for allowable interim constraint violations comes with the overhead of the creation of a number of worktables.

If you don't want the overhead of these worktables, you can disable the checking for allowable interim constraint violations by setting trace flag **244**. When this flag is set, any interim constraint violations will cause a statement to fail.

246

SQL Server 6.5 requires a column name to be explicitly supplied with the **CREATE VIEW** or **SELECT INTO** statements. For example, if the column is derived from a mathematical function or an aggregate function or where two columns could have the same name, SQL Server 6.5 will generate an error if a column name isn't explicitly supplied. To suppress the error and so ensure compatibility with version 6.0 and earlier, you should set trace flag **246**.

652

Setting trace flag **652** disables read-ahead at the server.

653

Setting trace flag **653** disables read-ahead for the current connection only.

1609

This turns on the unpacking and checking of RPC information with the execution of the **sp_sqlexec** extended stored procedure in Open Data Services. If possible, you should avoid using this trace flag and instead rewrite the application to use the **EXECUTE** statement.

2701

When set, this trace flag causes the global variable **@@ERROR** to be set to **50000** when **RAISERROR** is used to create messages with severity levels of **10** and under. This is SQL Server 6.0 behavior. The new default behavior in SQL Server 6.5 is for **RAISERROR** messages with severity levels of 10 and under to set the global variable **@@ERROR** to **0**.

3205

By default, SQL Server will automatically enable hardware compression when performing a DUMP to a tape drive which supports it. Setting trace flag 3205 prevents SQL Server from automatically enabling hardware compression. This can be useful when you wish to use tapes with a number of drives, some of which don't support hardware compression.

3607

This option disables automatic recovery for all databases.

3608

This option disables automatic recovery for all databases with the exception of the *master* database. You can set this flag if you receive error 1105 (Can't allocate space...on the model database). This would normally prevent SQL Server from starting.

After restarting SQL Server with trace flag **3608**, you should then set **no chkpt on recovery** for the **model** database and truncate the inactive portion of the log by dumping the transaction log for the **model** database with the **WITH NO_LOG** option.

3609

This flag skips the creation of the *tempdb* database. You can use this if the device on which *tempdb* resides is problematic or if problems exist in the *model* database.

3640

Setting this flag eliminates the sending of **DONE_IN_PROC** messages to the client for each statement in a stored procedure. These are short messages of no interest to the client and can kill network performance in a WAN.

4022

When set, this flag causes the execution of start-up stored procedures to be bypassed. This would be useful if, say, you had created a start-up stored procedure which generated an Access Violation causing SQL Server to crash and you wanted to disable the stored procedure to give you a chance to debug it.

Examining Trace Flag Output

So far, we've seen how to set trace flags and what each one does, but what does their output look like? We'll look at the output provided by the first example in this section. If you remember, we generated trace output by executing the following statements:

```
DBCC TRACEON (302, 310, 3605, -1)
go

SELECT a.au_fname, a.au_lname, t.title
FROM authors a, titleauthor ta, titles t
```

```
WHERE a.au_id = ta.au_id
AND t.title_id = ta.title_id
AND ta.royaltyper < 50
ORDER BY a.au_lname
go


DBCC TRACEOFF (302, 310)
go
```

Now, if you look in the Error Log via the SQL Enterprise Manager, you'll see that these unhelpful entries have been generated:

OK, so it's not particularly useful, especially because you can't scroll horizontally in the Error Log window! (Although you can resize to the first two columns to make room for the message.) However, you can either view the information in an editor, such as Write or Notepad or, if you apply trace flag 3604 then you send output straight to the results window of ISQL/W. The first few lines would look like this:

```
********************************

Leaving q_init_sclause() for table 'authors' (varno 0).
The table has 23 rows and 1 pages.
Cheapest index is index 0, costing 1 pages per scan.


********************************
```

Leaving q_init_sclause() for table 'titleauthor' (varno 1).
The table has 25 rows and 1 pages.
Cheapest index is index 0, costing 1 pages per scan.

****

Leaving q_init_sclause() for table 'titles' (varno 2).
The table has 18 rows and 3 pages.
Cheapest index is index 0, costing 3 pages per scan.

****

Remember, however, that trace flags are not part of the SQL Server supported feature set. Microsoft haven't documented them, don't provide support for them and can't guarantee consistency in future releases. Even so, there is a great deal of useful information that can be gleaned from their output if you're prepared to spend a little time working through it and use a modicum of common sense.

Tracing SQL Statements

Sometimes, you may find it useful to monitor the client requests which are coming into an SQL Server. Is the server running slowly because someone has submitted an aggregation query which scans every table ten times? And if someone is doing that, who is it?

Monitoring requests from the client-side is a relatively simple task. Some applications will allow you to log any SQL output they pass to a server. For example, the JET Engine used by Microsoft Access allows you to modify an **.ini** file setting,

```
SQLTraceMode=1
```

which will cause the output to a server to be logged in a text file (**Sqlout.txt**).

ODBC Tracing

Alternatively, if your application uses ODBC, you can use the ODBC Administrator (**ODBCAD32.EXE**) utility to log any ODBC API calls made by client applications. You do this by selecting the Trace ODBC Calls check box in the Options dialog box in the ODBC Administrator. By default, these calls are logged in a file called **C:\Sql.log**, although the same dialog gives you the option to change the name of the file if you wish.

When you're tracing ODBC API calls, be sure to check the Stop Tracing Automatically check box. This restricts ODBC Tracing to the next application launched on the client machine which uses ODBC. If you don't enable the Stop Tracing Automatically check box, ODBC API calls will continue to be logged for all client applications which use ODBC. This will lead to the output log file expanding quickly, leading to rapid deterioration of performance and loss of free disk space.

You can browse through the output file with a text editor, teasing out the SQL that your application sent and determining the answers to such questions as: how many connections did the client request? Were the queries executed asynchronously or synchronously? What was the last successful call before my application received an ODBC Call Failed error?

The contents of the text file logged by ODBC Tracing are the ODBC API calls made by the client application. However, this doesn't always make for very readable output. For example, the seemingly simple process of opening the authors table in the **pubs** database from Microsoft Access 7.0 for Windows 95 generates 350 lines of output.

In addition, the native ODBC API calls don't always make for easy reading. Consider, for example, this line of output taken from such a trace file:

SQLSetConnectOption(hdbc001799F0, 103, 00000014);

Now unless you either know by heart or have to hand the header files which define the ODBC **SetConnectOption** constants, you'll have little idea what this statement is doing.

ODBC Spy

For more informative output, you can use a utility such as ODBC Spy, which is one of a variety of useful utilities which comes with the ODBC SDK. Like ODBC Tracing, this utility intercepts ODBC API calls made by a client to a specific ODBC data source. However, it has two advantages over traditional ODBC Tracing.

Firstly, we can log the ODBC API calls to the screen as well as to a log file, which makes for faster debugging. Secondly, the ODBC Spy utility translates ODBC constants and makes them easier to understand. So, the API call we looked at above appears in ODBC Spy as:

```
SQLSetConnectOption
    0x001799F0
    SQL_LOGIN_TIMEOUT
    0x14000000
    SQL_SUCCESS
```

This not only translates the value **103** into the constant name **SQL_LOGIN_TIMEOUT**, but also indicates the return code of the call, **SQL_SUCCESS** indicating that the call succeeded. This does come at a price, however, as logging ODBC API calls to screen affects performance to such a degree that it slows opening the attached 23-row **authors** table in Microsoft Access v.7 for Windows 95 to almost a minute!

Another major problem with both of these methods is that they are client-centered. The configuration and collection of data is originated from the client machine. This both imposes an unwelcome performance penalty on each client machine and also makes administration and collection of the results a very complicated task. Far better would be a tool which allows you to browse information about all client requests simultaneously from the server. That's just what the new SQL Trace utility in SQL Server 6.5 allows you to do.

SQL Trace

When you start SQL Trace, you begin by specifying the SQL Server to which you wish to connect. Thereafter, you choose which SQL statements you wish to capture. You do this by means of filters. To specify a new filter, you should select New Filter... from the File menu. Alternatively you can hit *CTRL+N* or click the New Filter button on the toolbar.

Next, specify the criteria to filter the statements you wish to capture. These criteria can include:

- Specific logins
- Specific applications
- Specific host machines

▲ Specific SQL keywords

▲ Connect and disconnect statements

▲ Remote procedure calls

▲ Attention events

You can also choose how you wish to capture the results. If you want, they can be:

▲ Displayed in a window on the screen

▲ Saved into a file displaying just the SQL

▲ Saved into a log file (giving details of time, connection, etc....)

You can also specify whether the output from separate clients should be displayed in separate windows or combined in a single window.

The SQLTrace utility is new to SQL Server 6.5. In previous releases of SQL Server, client input could be monitored by using the trace flags 4030 or 4032, or by using the **DBCC INPUTBUFFER(*processid*)** command. This option is still available and may prove useful if you want to log the incoming SQL statements in the **Error Log** alongside other diagnostic trace output.

Finding a Cure

Once you've located the source of your problem, you can start to find a solution. The most obvious place to turn for help is the documentation which comes with SQL Server. SQL Server Books Online is an excellent tool and will probably solve the majority of your problems.

Commercial Resources

A further tool is the Microsoft Developer Network Development Library. This comes in CD format and, as well as containing the product documentation for almost all Microsoft products, also contains technical articles, white papers, knowledge bases and sample code for those products. It uses the same application for displaying its information as Books Online (**Infoview.exe**), but where it scores over Books Online is that it's updated and redistributed quarterly, which means that you get to find out about late-breaking bugs which were only discovered after the release of your version of SQL Server.

Microsoft also do the monthly TechNet CD which is oriented towards the support professional. It's a very useful resource for the administrator, often including detailed information on tuning and troubleshooting. It also comes complete with a current knowledge base.

Resources Online

If you don't want to pay the subscription costs to the Microsoft Developer Network Development Library and you have an Internet connection, you can find an even more up to date list of articles relating to SQL Server at Microsoft's site on the Internet. The best starting point is probably the Support Online site, which allows you to search for articles by keyword. This is located at **http://www.microsoft.com/KB** and contains bug notices, tips and hints, all updated on a regular basis. The search engine isn't as elegant as that in **INFOVIEW** and response time over the Internet can be poor at certain times of the day, but it's free and very extensive.

Also free on the Internet are the Microsoft public newsgroups. If your browser supports it, you can access these newsgroups by pointing to **Msnews.microsoft.com** as your news server. This server contains well over two hundred forums with six currently dedicated to SQL Server covering areas such as programming, replication, connection issues, etc. As with all newsgroups, you take the rough with the smooth, but we have found the content for the most part well-informed and up-to-date.

These are not the only sources of information on SQL Server. There are plenty of magazines and, of course, a whole host of newsgroups and bulletin boards available through access providers such as CompuServe and America OnLine.

Your Own Documentation

Another source of useful information should be your own notes. Towards the start of this chapter, we said that you should keep a note of any problems that you come across and the steps that you took to resolve them. The reason for this, of course, is that this will give you your own ready-made knowledge base of articles relevant to your site. I guess when I come across a problem with my own SQL Server installation, over half the time I will have come across the same problem before. I know just how annoying it is when I remember what the problem was, but not how I fixed it! So when you fix a problem, write down how you did it and keep your notes safe.

Solving Common Problems

Finally, we'll end this chapter with the solutions to what I have found to be the two areas which yield the most problems that befall SQL Server DBAs. In each case, the problems are fairly simple to solve if approached in a methodical manner. Nonetheless, they can be confusing (and frustrating) if you haven't come across them before.

Debugging Connection Problems

Finding that a client application can't connect to SQL Server is a particularly annoying experience. The problem is that there are so many links in the chain, how do you determine which one is broken? Well, as with all debugging, the secret is to take a structured approach. This checklist details the steps to follow, in order, when you're attempting to debug a connectivity problem.

Can You Connect Locally?

The first step is to go to the server and attempt to log on to the server locally, using a tool such as ISQL. If you can't connect locally, this will indicate either:

- ▲ You're supplying the wrong user name or password.
- ▲ There's a problem with SQL Server itself.

Is the Correct Client Net Library Loaded?

If your client is MS-DOS-based, the Net Library will be a DOS TSR (Terminate and Stay Resident program). You can determine which TSRs are loaded by running the **mem /d** command from the DOS prompt.

If your client isn't MS-DOS based, you can determine the client Net Library by running the Client Configuration Utility. The correct Net Library depends on the network that you're running on. The table details the libraries appropriate to each operating system and network.

Network	Windows NT or Windows 95	Windows	MS-DOS
Named Pipes	`Dbnmpntw.dll`	`Dbnmp3.dll`	`Dbnmpipe.exe`
NWLink IPX/SPX	`Dbmsspxn.dll`	`Dbmsspx3.dll`	`Dbmsspx.exe`
Banyan VINES	`Dbmsvinn.dll`	`Dbmsvin3.dll`	`Dbmsvine.exe`
TCP/IP Sockets	`Dbmssocn.dll`	`Dbmssoc3.dll`	Not available
Multiprotocol	`Dbmsrpcn.dll`	`Dbmsrpc3.dll`	Not available

Can You Make a Network Connection?

The method of testing whether you can make a network connection to the server depends on the type of network that you're running. Methods of testing connections via named pipes, TCP/IP and IPX/SPX are detailed below.

Named Pipes

The first step is to determine whether you can connect to the server's named pipe by trying to connect to the hidden **IPC$** share on the server. To do this, run the following command from the command line:

```
net use \\server\IPC$
```

If this is successful, but you still can't connect to the server, you should test the connection with the **makepipe** and **readpipe** utilities. The **makepipe** utility, which is installed by default in the **\Mssql\Bin** directory, is run from the server and creates a named pipe to which the client can connect. When you run this, you should see output at the command line like this:

```
Making PIPE:\pipe\abc
read to write delay (seconds):0
Waiting for Client to Connect...
```

To make the connection from the client, you should run the **readpipe** connection from the command line on the client machine. This executable is located by default in the **\Sql\Bin** directory for DOS clients, in the **\Sql\Binn** directory for NT clients and in the **\Sql\Binp** directory for OS/2 clients. Win16 clients have a version, called **readpipw**, which is located in the **\Sql\Bin** directory. The syntax of this command is:

```
readpipe /Sservername
```

For example:

```
readpipe /SRob@Home
```

When you run **readpipe**, the client attempts to send the string shutdown on the named pipe. If it's successful, you should see the following output:

```
SvrName:\\Rob@Home
PIPE   :\\Rob@Home\pipe\abc
DATA   :shutdown
Data Sent: 1 :shutdown
Data Read: 1 :shutdown
```

If the connection is unsuccessful, you should note the error code returned and terminate **makepipe** on the server by hitting *CTRL+C*. The following table indicates the meaning of the various status codes returned by the **readpipe** command:

Status	Description	Possible Cause
3	Path not found	Named pipes not installed correctly.
5	Access denied	Permissions not granted on named pipes.
6	Invalid handle	Network layer problem. Check hardware.
13	Invalid data	Wrong version of **Netapi.dll**.
53	Network name not found	Network layer problem.
65	Network access denied	Permissions not granted on named pipes.
84	Out of structures	Configuration settings.
109	Broken pipe	Network layer problem.
110	Open failed	Possible protocol incompatibility.
206	Filename exceeded range	Server name more than eight characters.
231	Pipe busy	Pipe isn't available.

TCP/IP

To check the network connection when you're using TCP/IP to connect the client and server, you should use the **ping** utility by typing the following at the command line on the client machine:

ping *ip_address*

where ***ip_address*** is the IP address of the server you wish to connect to. For example:

```
ping 192.130.115.108
```

If the connection can be made, the **ping** command will indicate the amount of data transmitted and the time taken for the round trip of the data packet sent.

If you're using name resolution, you can specify a host name in place of the IP address.

IPX/SPX

The first thing to check is that the client is connected to the network. If it is, you should see the message Attached to server servername after **Netx.com** is loaded on MS-DOS and Windows-based clients. For Windows NT -based clients, check the Event Viewer to ensure that the NWLink network support software was properly loaded.

Next, check that the server is connected to the network. Under Windows NT, check the **Event Log** for a message containing the text **ODS: server-side**.

The next step is to attempt to make a local connection to SQL Server with Novell NetWare as the default Net Library. If you can connect locally using named pipes but can't connect locally using the Novell NetWare Net-Library, SQL Server isn't registered properly on the network.

If you can connect locally but can't connect from a client across the network, check that the server is accessible to the client. You do this by typing the following command at the command line on the client:

```
isql /L
```

This lists the servers available to the client. If the server name doesn't appear in this list, the client won't be able to connect to it.

Is the Hardware or NOS Faulty?

If you can't make the network connection using the methods described above, you'll need to rectify this problem before you attempt to connect to SQL Server. The key areas to check are:

- ▲ Are all cables plugged in securely?
- ▲ Are any cables faulty?
- ▲ Is the network card faulty?
- ▲ Does the client computer recognize its network command?
- ▲ Are there interrupt problems?
- ▲ Is all intermediate hardware (e.g. bridgers, routers) operative?
- ▲ Is the network operating system running on both machines?

Curing (and Preventing) a Full Transaction Log

The second problem can be just as frustrating to debug. All operations in SQL Server are logged. You can't turn off the transaction log if you want. Everything is logged, even if the amount of information that is logged is sometimes reduced, such as when you issue the **TRUNCATE TABLE** or **SELECT INTO** commands. Even when you run 'fast' (non-logged) bulk copy, extensions to the database are logged.

If you've been using or administering SQL Server for any length of time, it's a fairly safe bet to assume that you've seen the following error text at one time or another:

Can't allocate space for object syslogs in database SALES_DATABASE because the logsegment is full. If you ran out of space in Syslogs, dump the transaction log. Otherwise, use ALTER DATABASE or sp_extendsegment to increase the size of the segment.

This is error **1105** and it indicates that the **Transaction Log** is full. What makes it a particularly frustrating error is that most of the methods that you initially use to try to resolve the problem are thwarted by SQL Server, resolutely telling you that you can't take that course of action because the **Transaction Log** is full in the first place.

When this error occurs, your only recourse is to dump the **Transaction Log** for the affected database using the **WITH NO_LOG** option. When the **Transaction Log** is full, SQL Server can't write the checkpoint record required if you run **DUMP TRANSACTION**. This is a last gasp solution and, immediately after you do this dump, you should back up the database. You may want to consider expanding the size of the **Transaction Log** unless you have clear evidence that this was a one-time occurrence.

Why the Transaction Log Fills Up

There are a couple of reasons for why the **Transaction Log** might fill up more quickly than expected. We'll take a look at them now.

Large Atomic Transactions

Any bulk operation such as a bulk **INSERT, DELETE** or **UPDATE** will be regarded as composing a single transaction that must be applied completely or not at all. As a result, even if the **truncate log on checkpoint** option is set, the checkpoint handler won't attempt to truncate the **Transaction Log** during one of these operations. Clearly, the longer such an operation takes, the more times the checkpoint handler will be unable to truncate the log and the more the log will fill up. For this reason, if you know that a database is likely to undergo a large atomic transaction, you should cater for this expansion when you're sizing the **Transaction Log** to handle the transaction.

Uncommitted Transactions

Obviously, it's not only implicit transactions like those described above which prevent the log from being truncated. The same applies to an open transaction of any size. This may occur because a client application has terminated execution of a statement ungracefully, or simply because a client application has been poorly designed so that it's possible for a transaction to be left open by an operator who has gone off to have dinner! Open transactions can also arise when the transaction's process has become blocked by another process.

To determine whether there are any open transactions in a database, issue the **DBCC OPENTRAN** statement. When you've identified the transaction, either debug your application to determine whether it should be committed or rolled back, or simply kill the process which holds the open transaction. You should then be able to dump/truncate the **Transaction Log**.

Summary

In this chapter, we've looked at general strategies for troubleshooting SQL Server. We started by running through the approach you should take whenever you try to solve problems with SQL Server (or any other software for that matter). In the end it comes down to being methodical and taking your time. The time you can least afford to be hasty is when you're being hassled for a quick remedy.

Next, we looked at more specific ways to isolate the problem. The Error Log and Event Log will probably be sufficient most of the time, but there will be times when both trace flags and other utilities such as ODBC Spy and SQL Trace will prove to be invaluable tools as well.

After discussing how to locate the problem, we looked at where to find the solution. I find that Books Online sorts out about 70% of my problems. 20% of the time I need either the TechNet or the Developer Platform CDs. The other 10% of the time it's down to the Online Knowledge Base for details of bugs (sorry, undocumented behavior!). Finally, we rounded up the chapter with discussions of how to solve problems in two areas that seem to cause the most headaches.

6.5

Replication

Replication is the component of SQL Server that allows logged inserts, updates and deletes occurring on one server, to be distributed to one or more subscribing servers. Additionally, replication allows the synchronization of entire tables across multiple servers. These features provide the ability to keep up-to-date copies of data on multiple servers. Replication can be configured such that all updates occur on one central server and are distributed to the subscribers, or such that each server updates its own unique rows in a table and distributes only those rows to the subscribers. In either case, however, multiple servers should never be allowed to update the same row. In this sense, data is considered to be read-only at the subscriber level.

As a new feature in SQL Server 6.0, replication provided the ability to distribute updates of data between multiple SQL Servers. In version 6.5, Microsoft has extended this capability to include heterogeneous replication to other relational DBMSs, including Access and Oracle. In fact, SQL Server can now replicate to almost any DBMS that supports ODBC. Another enhancement in version 6.5 is the ability to replicate text and image data, which was noticeably lacking in version 6.0.

This chapter begins with the basics, including replication concepts, and how to use Enterprise Manager's GUI to set up and configure replication. Also included are more advanced features of replication, including horizontal and vertical partitioning of data, and a list of replication system stored procedures which may be used to emulate the functionality of the GUI. Finally, sections are provided on what to do when problems occur (and they will occur) and tips to make the life of a SQL Server DBA a little bit easier.

Replication Concepts

In its simplest form, replication can be defined as the duplication of table schemas (definitions) and data from a source database to a target database. There are two models used for replication:

- **Tight consistency** guarantees that all copies will be constantly identical to the original. This model requires a high speed LAN and usually reduces database availability. A tight consistency model is usually implemented with a two-phase commit protocol like that which is used by the Microsoft Distributed Transaction Coordinator.

- **Loose consistency** allows for a time lag between when a change is made to the source data and when the change is reflected in the target copies. This model does *not* guarantee that copies are constantly identical to the original. For example, a server may not receive changes while it is off-line. This does not prevent other servers from receiving the changes. Loose consistency supports replication across LANs, WANs and low-speed communications links as well as intermittently connected databases.

SQL Server's replication uses the loose consistency model.

The Publish/Subscribe Metaphor

SQL Server uses a publish/subscribe metaphor for managing replication. This is a common metaphor for the activities involved in this process. In many ways, replication can be viewed in the same way that you view magazine subscriptions. An organization publishes a magazine. If you subscribe to it, the magazine arrives in your mailbox at a regular interval. The same thing is true of data being replicated by SQL Server. In SQL Server replication, a server can have one or more of three different roles:

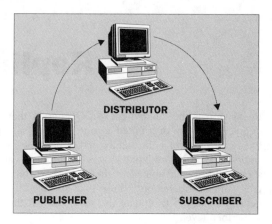

Note that while a single server can play one, two or all three of these roles, the most likely scenario is that one server will be acting as publisher and distributor, with many other servers acting as subscribers. We'll examine the roles of each now.

Publishing

The publisher is the server on which updates to the data originate. Just as a publishing company produces a master copy of a magazine and distributes copies to many subscribers, so also the publishing server produces updates to data which are distributed to subscribing servers. The publisher contains the master copy of the data. All subscribing servers have only copies of the data and should never modify it on their own. All updates should originate from the publisher.

Distributing

The distributor is the server that actually copies the transactions occurring on the publisher to the subscribing servers. Generally, the publishing server can also act as a distributor, but if the load on the publisher is too great, a separate distribution server can be defined. A special database called the distribution database, is automatically created on the distribution server when it is defined. This database contains tables to store transactions to be replicated to all subscribing servers.

Subscribing

The subscriber receives information from the distributor. In SQL Server 6.5, replication has been enhanced to allow other ODBC-based database management systems, such as Oracle or Access, to act as subscribers to SQL Server publications. The specific rules and requirements are spelled out in the *SQL Server Administrator's Companion*, but generally, almost any DBMS that meets Level 1 ODBC standards will be able to receive distributed updates from SQL Server.

The Replication Process

Before we can look at the replication process as a whole we need to define what each of the stages in the process does.

Synchronization

Replication begins with a process called **synchronization,** which makes the table schema, and the table data, at the subscribing location identical to that at the publishing location. This happens only once when a subscriber first subscribes to a publication. All components of a publication are synchronized at once to preserve referential integrity. SQL Server supports automatic synchronization, which is managed by the SQL Server and occurs on a scheduled basis based on the distributor's clock. It also supports manual synchronization where the user takes responsibility for synchronization and notifies SQL Server when it is done.

Log-based Replication

In SQL Server, once the source and target databases are synchronized, replication is primarily done using the transaction log. (There is a provision for full table copy replication–discussed a little later.) With log-based replication, any transaction that affects a published table is marked for replication in the transaction log. There is a process called the **log reader** that continually monitors the log of each publishing database. Any transaction that involves tables which are published will be marked in the transaction log. The log reader picks up these marked transactions and copies them to the distribution database. Only committed transactions are copied. Committed transactions are executed on subscribing servers in the same order that they were done on the source server.

> Note that this process does not purge transactions from the transaction log. In fact, replication changes the definition of an inactive transaction. A transaction which still needs to be replicated will be considered active by the transaction dump process just as an uncommitted transaction will.

It's also worth noting that only inserts, updates and deletes written to the transaction log are replicated. For example, executing the following statement on the publishing server would result in all records in the authors table being deleted, and replicated to all subscribing servers:

```
DELETE authors
```

However, the following statement would not replicate out to any subscribers, since this statement is not logged:

```
TRUNCATE TABLE authors
```

In fact, this statement would not even be allowed on a table that is defined for replication. SQL Server disallows truncate statements on replicated tables. In order to truncate, you would first have to turn off replication to this table.

Partitioning

So we have seen that replication can be set up on individual tables within an SQL Server database, as in the author's example above. However, replication can also be set up to distribute only portions of a table (either restricting columns or rows from being replicated). This process is called **vertical** or **horizontal partitioning**. Before we can consider this process, we need to define a couple of terms.

The basic unit of replication is the **article**. An article consists of a table and any restrictions which may change rows or columns that are to be replicated. Note that an article cannot be composed of a view, or a join of multiple tables.

A **publication** is a collection of articles logically grouped to ease administration. In this sense, a subscriber can subscribe to an entire publication, without having to specify each article. A subscriber can also subscribe to individual articles within a publication. An article must belong to a publication. All the articles in a publication are guaranteed to be initially synchronized (made to match the source database). There are three basic forms used for articles:

Vertical Partitions

A vertical partition is some column subset of the table. The vertical partition must include the primary key. This is a project operation.

PKey	Col1	Col2	Col3	Col4

Vertical Partition

Horizontal Partitions

A horizontal partition is some row subset of the table.

PKey	Col1	Col2	Col3	Col4

Horizontal Partition

Horizontal and Vertical Partitions

A vertical and horizontal partition selects some of the rows and some of the columns. Like a vertical partition, the vertical and horizontal partition must include the primary key.

PKey	Col1	Col2	Col3	Col4

Horizontal and Vertical Partition

SQL Server provides a lot of flexibility in its data distribution scheme. It supports selective subscription to publications in which any given server can subscribe to none, some or all of the publications offered in the enterprise. It also allows selective subscription to articles within a publication. SQL Server publications can also be defined to allow unrestricted access or with access restricted to one or more servers in the enterprise.

Overview of the Replication Process

Replication is actually controlled by three separate NT processes:

- Log reader
- Synchronization
- Distribution

These processes run on the distribution server and are subsystems of the SQL Executive. They can be independently configured and are not started or administered by users. We can now flesh out our initial simplified view of replication into something more specific to our platform:

356

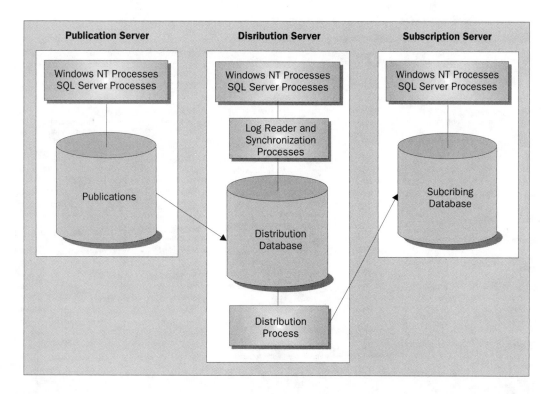

The log reader process is responsible for moving transactions marked for replication from the publisher's transaction log to the distribution database. The synchronization process prepares the initial synchronization files. These include both the schema (the definitions of the tables involved) and the data. This process also stores synchronization files in distribution database and records the completion of synchronization jobs. The distribution process actually moves initial synchronization jobs and subsequent transactions to the subscribing servers.

Distribution Database

There's one part left, central to the whole replication process that we haven't looked at yet, the **distribution database**. This is a store-and-forward database that holds all transactions waiting to be distributed to subscribers as well as any synchronization information. This database does not contain any user tables. The following ER diagram provides a picture of the tables and relationships contained within this database:

SUBSCRIPTION SERVER TABLES   DISTRIBUTION SERVER TABLES

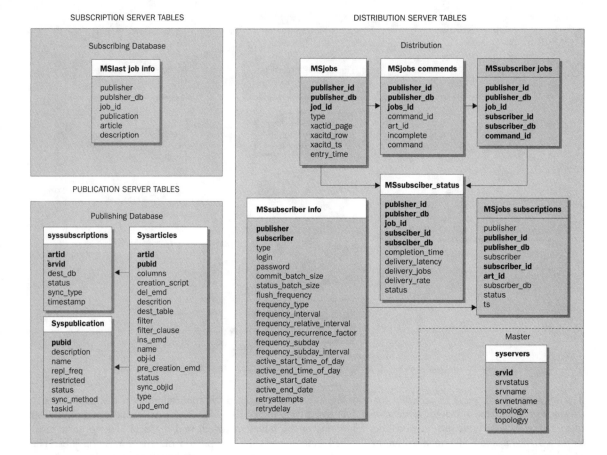

Note that one table (sysservers) is stored in the master database, one table (MSlast_job_info) is stored in the subscribing database of the subscribing server and several tables are stored in the publishing database of the publishing server. Notice also that several of the tables contain fields called job_id and command_id.

To illustrate replication's use of these fields, consider the following SQL statement:

```
UPDATE authors
SET zip = 91111
WHERE city = 'oakland' AND state = 'ca'
```

Now suppose there are five authors in the table from Oakland, CA. Replication will generate one job consisting of five update commands, with each update based on the primary key of the authors table (the au_id column). Each command will be in the form of a T-SQL statement, such as

```
UPDATE authors SET zip = 91111 WHERE au_id = '213-46-8915'
UPDATE authors SET zip = 91111 WHERE au_id = '274-80-9391'
UPDATE authors SET zip = 91111 WHERE au_id = '724-08-9931'
UPDATE authors SET zip = 91111 WHERE au_id = '724-80-9391'
UPDATE authors SET zip = 91111 WHERE au_id = '756-30-7391'
```

So, we see that a job is a grouping of commands. Generally, a transaction that updates multiple records will be scheduled as a job. Each individual record that is updated will be a command within the job.

Also, notice that the updates to the individual records in the authors table were based on the primary key values. For this reason, **all articles defined for replication must be based on tables that have primary keys.**

With this basic information in place, let's look at each individual table in the distribution database:

Table	Contents
MSjobs	Contains one record for each job that is scheduled to be distributed.
MSjob_commands	Contains one record for each command that is scheduled to be distributed. Note the master-detail relationship between this table and the MSjobs table. There may be multiple commands for a given job.
Mssubscriber_jobs	Contains commands to be distributed to one or more subscribing servers. Note that if there are 100 subscribers to an article, each update to a row within that article will generate 100 rows in this table. For this reason, Mssubscriber_jobs can grow very large and result in poor replication performance if not cleaned up periodically. The cleanup tasks are discussed in detail later in this chapter.
Mssubscriber_status	Contains information on jobs that have been successfully distributed to subscribing servers.
Mssubscriber_info	Contains one row for each subscriber of any publication.
MSjob_subscriptions	Contains one row for each article subscribed to by a subscribing server.
Sysservers	Contains one row for each server that is allowed to subscribe to a publication.
Syssubscriptions	Contains a row for each subscriber of each article in the database.
Syspublications	Contains a row for each publication in the database.
Sysarticles	Contains a row for each article in the database.
MSlast_job_info	Contains the last job that has been successfully distributed to a subscriber.

Replication and Triggers

Because replication is log-based, any trigger effects on the source database will be recorded in the log. For example, suppose a publishing database named Fred has two tables, A and B. Table A has an insert trigger that adds a row to table B. Both of these inserts will be recorded in A's transaction log. Now, suppose that a subscribing database wants to subscribe to a publication that contains table A and table B.

If the subscribing database has no trigger on table A, everything will work fine. However, if it has a trigger, that trigger will insert a row into table B. Along will come the replicated table B and a duplicate key situation will arise. You will need to consider this kind of situation when you design replication strategies. It is not uncommon for subscription databases not to have the same triggers as publishing databases, particularly if the only updates are coming through replication.

Implementing Replication

The following sections describe the requirements for a replication server, as well as the steps for setting up replication using SQL Enterprise Manager's graphical user interface.

In most cases, using Enterprise Manager to set up replication is the preferred choice. However, you may also perform almost all of the same tasks using replication stored procedures. The advantage of using stored procedures is that you can save them into a T-SQL script and execute them on many different servers, if needed. Also, using scripts provides a way to automate the re-creation of your replication environment in case of emergency.

Replication Requirements

There are a few special requirements for servers that will be participating in SQL Server replication.

Memory

Any server that acts as a distributor of transactions must have at least 32MB of memory. Furthermore, at least 16MB of this memory must be dedicated to SQL Server. Remember that this is the minimum requirement and performance may be very poor with this amount of memory. It would very prudent to at least double this amount if you are planning to replicate fairly large amounts of data (100MB or bigger) to several servers.

Disk Space

The distribution database will require a minimum of 30MB for the data device and 15MB for the transaction log. Again, this is the minimum value and it is very likely that you will have to expand these devices if you are planning on replicating large amounts of data.

Service Accounts

In order to replicate information using SQL Server, the SQL Executive service must be set up to log on under a user account. When SQL Server 6.5 is installed, you will specify a domain and user name of a Windows NT account, which is assigned to SQL Executive. This account must be given certain privileges within the domain:

- ▲ The account must be a member of the Administrators local group.
- ▲ The account must have the Password Never Expires attribute.

The account must also have been granted the following advanced User Rights:

- ▲ Log on as a service

- ▲ Act as part of the operating system

- ▲ Replace a process level token

- ▲ Increase quotas

Character Set, ODBC Drivers and Networks

In SQL Server 6.0, servers involved in replication must use the same character set. In 6.5, the servers may use different character sets (code pages). For consistent query results across all servers, you will probably want to use the same sort order. However, the sort orders can be different.

Replication (even between SQL Servers) uses ODBC and requires the 32-bit ODBC driver be installed on all *distribution* servers.

Keep in mind that the distribution server connects to subscribing servers with trusted connections, and therefore it must use either the named pipes or multiprotocol netlib. If you want to replicate across domains, you will need to establish the appropriate trust relationships.

Finally, make sure all the tables you plan to replicate have declared primary keys. You must have a primary key constraint on any table (except a subscriber snapshot table) which is to participate in replication.

Setting Up for Replication to ODBC Data Sources

If you are going to replicate SQL Server data to ODBC subscribers, you will need to define appropriate ODBC data source names for them. You do this by using the ODBC administrator tool in Control Panel. You should also note that SQL Server will use quoted identifiers for the tables it creates on the ODBC subscribers. Some third-party query and development tools do not support this feature.

Setting up Replication for Microsoft Access Subscribers

If you want Access databases to subscribe to SQL Server publications, you will need to install the proper ODBC driver. This driver ships with SQL Server 6.5. You install it using the Setup program found in the **\I386\ODBCREPL** subdirectory of the SQL Server 6.5 CD-ROM.

You must also have the MSSQLServer service log on with the same domain user account and privileges as the one assigned to the SQLExecutive. That domain account must also have full access privileges to the Access **.MDB** file.

> **When you register a Microsoft Access DSN on a remote server, be sure to use a Universal Naming Connection (UNC) name, not a redirected drive letter. For example you would use \\SERVER1 instead of mapping a drive to SERVER1.**

Setting up Replication for ORACLE Subscribers

SQL Server 6.5 includes an ODBC driver that allows ORACLE databases to subscribe to SQL Server Publications. This driver was developed by Visigenic™, but is distributed and supported by Microsoft. You need to run the setup program in the **\I386\ODBCREPL** subdirectory to install this driver.

> **The ORACLE ODBC driver is not double-byte (DBCS) character set-enabled.**

When you create a DSN for the ORACLE data source, you will need to supply the ORACLE user name that the distribution process will use to connect to the ORACLE database. The ODBC setup will create a registry key for the ORACLE password in the registry. You can edit this key to supply the desired password. The key is:

```
\HKEY_CURRENT_USER
    \SOFTWARE
        \ODBC
            \ODBC.INI
                \ORACLE\PWD:REG_SZ:password
```

If you provide a password in the registry, the ODBC driver will connect to ORACLE without requesting a password. If you don't provide the password in the registry, you must specify it when you set up subscriptions. If you will have multiple ORACLE subscribers with different user names and/or passwords, you will need to specify them as part of the subscription process.

Other ODBC Subscribers

If you want to have other ODBC data sources subscribe to SQL Server publications, the ODBC driver must:

- ▲ Be ODBC Level 1 compliant
- ▲ Be 32-bit, thread-safe
- ▲ Run on the same processor architecture (Intel, PowerPC, MIPS®, or Alpha AXP™) that the distribution process runs on
- ▲ Be transaction capable
- ▲ Support the Data Definition Language (DDL)

Login IDs Used for Replication

Replication uses remote servers and sets up all the necessary id mappings. When you set up replication, SQL Server creates a repl_publisher login on the subscribing server. This allows the distribution server to log in. It has owner privileges for destination database and should not be modified. Users should not log in as repl_publisher

It also creates a repl_subscriber login on the publishing (or remote distribution) server. This allows the subscribing server to log in. The sa account on subscriber is mapped as a remote login to repl_subscriber account on the publisher. The repl_subscriber login has user privileges in *master*, *distribution*, *msdb* and publishing databases.

Setting Up Replication Using Enterprise Manager

The first step in setting up replication using SQL Enterprise Manager is to install publishing on the server that will act as the 'publisher' of data. If the distribution database is going to be on a remote server, you will have to create it before you install publishing. If it is local, it will be created for you when you install publishing. However, you will need to create devices for the database and its transaction log. You should have a minimum of 30MB of database space and 10MB of log space.

Installing Publishing

To install publishing, first establish a connection to the desired server, then select Replication Configuration from the Server menu and select the Install Publishing option. This will take you to the following dialog:

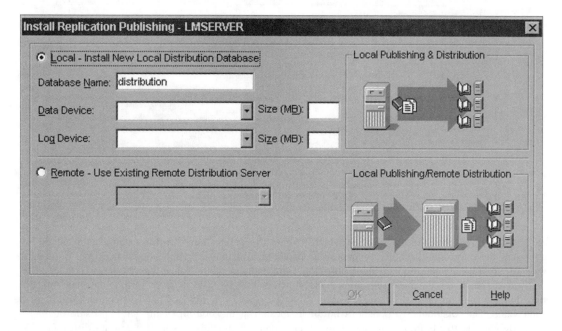

The first half of the screen is used if you are going to use the same server as both publisher and distributor. Note that the option Local is selected by default. If you wish to use a separate server for distribution purposes, select the Remote option on the second half of the screen.

If you are using a local distributor, you must select devices for the creation of the distribution database and its transaction log from the drop-down boxes provided. If you have not created devices for these yet, you will be able to automatically create them from this screen using the New option for device name. If you are using a remote distributor, you must select the name of the distributor from the drop-down box provided. Note that if you are using this option, the publishing server must be defined as a remote server to the distribution server you are connecting to.

Regardless of which option you chose above, you should click on the OK button to define the distribution database. You will then be asked if you are ready to proceed at this point to continue with the next section. If you are not ready, you can always get back to this point at a later time from the Publishing option on the Replication Configuration menu.

Defining a Publication Database

The next step in configuring replication, is to define the database which will be published and a list of servers which may act as subscribers to publications based on this database:

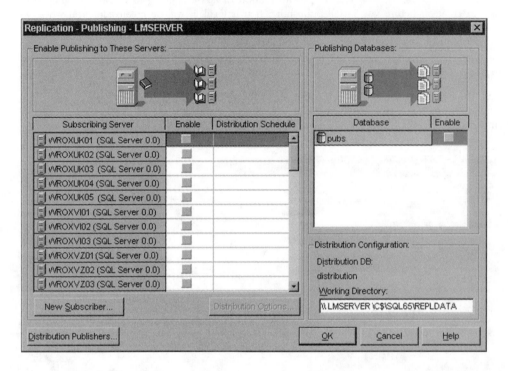

The first task is to select the database on which to base the publication. In this example, the pubs database is the only one available. To make this database available for publication, check the Enable box beside the appropriate selection in the Publishing Databases section. Notice the Working Directory box directly underneath the database selections. This directory will be used to store scripts, data and other replication information created by SQL Server. In most cases, you will not need to change this from the default value. The Distribution Publishers button is located at the bottom of the left-hand side of the screen. By clicking this button, you can allow other servers to use this server as a remote distributor.

Now you are ready to specify which servers are allowed to subscribe to your publication. By checking the Enable box for a server in the Subscribing Server list, you are instructing SQL Server that this particular server *has the ability* to subscribe to your publication. Note that this does *not* mean that the server is actually subscribed. This step is performed later. If you wish to add a server that does not appear in the list, use the New Subscriber button.

Distribution Options

By selecting the Distribution Options button, you will get a dialog with several options that deal with how transactions are to be distributed to the subscriber currently selected in the Enable publishing to list.

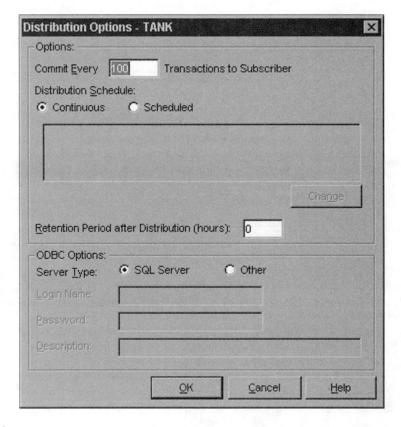

Commit Size

The first choice to make is the commit size for the subscriber. This number specifies how many transactions to apply on the subscriber before issuing a commit statement. Making a wise decision for this parameter can greatly enhance performance of replication. The best value really depends on your specific data and requirements, but in general the default of 100 seems to be quite low. You may want to consider upping this to at least 1000.

Distribution Schedule

Next, you must select a schedule for distribution. By selecting Continuous, transactions are applied to the subscriber as they occur. If you want to schedule transactions to occur on a timed-basis, such as every 5 minutes, or every hour, use the Scheduled selection and press the Change button to define the desired schedule.

Retention Period after Distribution

The Retention Period after Distribution value specifies how long the distributor will maintain transactions that have already been distributed. This parameter works in conjunction with the cleanup tasks which will be discussed later. In most cases, you can leave this at the default value.

ODBC Options

Finally, if you are defining an ODBC subscriber, such as Oracle or Access, you must specify a login and password in order for SQL Server to make the connection when distributing data. If the subscriber is a SQL Server 6.5 database, leave the SQL Server box checked.

Enabling Subscribers

After completing the Install Publishing dialog, the next step to perform is to connect to the subscribing server and allow it to receive information from the distributor. Note that in the previous step, we specified which servers the **distributor could publish to**. In this step, we are specifying which servers the **subscriber can receive information from**.

To perform this step, connect to the subscribing server and select Replication Configuration, Subscribing from the Server menu:

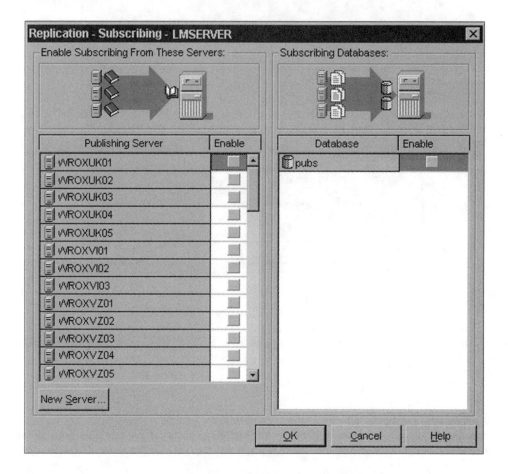

To complete this screen, check the Enable box beside the distribution server that is to replicate to this server. Also, check the databases that are permitted to subscribe to publications.

> Keep in mind that the distribution task is resource intensive and it may not be desirable to have a SQL Server that is heavily used for applications also serving as a distribution server.

Publishing Articles

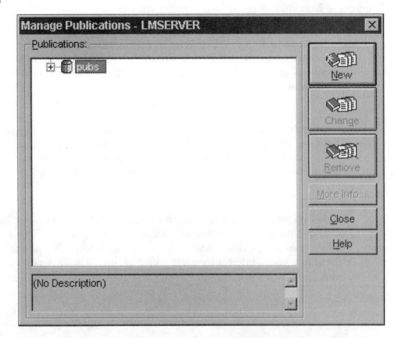

Now that you have defined the
database to be published and the
possible subscribers, you need to
specify the data that is to be
replicated. This is done by
creating *articles* for the
publication. On the publishing
server, select Manage,
Replication, Publications from
the menu. The following screen
will appear:

Notice that pubs is the
only database shown in
the list of publication
databases. This is
because pubs is the
only database that we
defined for replication
in the previous section.
At this point, we need
to create a new
publication on the
pubs database, so click
the New button while
pubs is highlighted to
do this:

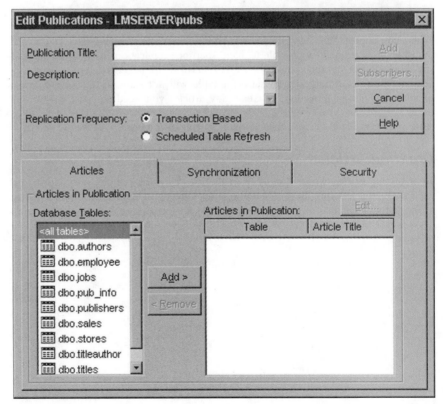

You should first provide a title and description for your publication. The next step is to select a replication frequency. Note that there are two possible choices:

▲ **Transaction Based** publications distribute information to the subscribers, based on updates that are placed in the transaction log of the publishing database. Each time a record is updated, deleted or inserted, these transactions will be read by replication processes and distributed to all subscribers.

▲ **Scheduled Table Refresh** publications are not based on logged transactions. These publications are set up in such a way that a complete copy of the articles in the publication are distributed to all subscribers on a scheduled basis, such as weekly or daily. These types of publication are useful if you do not need immediate updates to the subscribers.

> Actually, when a scheduled table refresh occurs, replication places a request in the distribution database called an 'initial synchronization'. This special command, when read by the distributor, will cause the data on the publisher to be bulk copied (bcp) to a special directory on the distributor. Also, a script containing schema generation for the tables involved is created in this same directory. Replication then uses this script to recreate the table on the subscriber, and bcp the data in. This is how scheduled table refreshes work.

Snapshot Replication

When you choose Scheduled Table Refresh as your replication interval, you create what is called a **snapshot** replication. It is possible to have snapshot replication for a table which does not have a primary key. You will not be able to use the SQL Enterprise Manager to create a snapshot publication if the table does not have a primary key, because the table will not show in the list. You will need to use the sp_addarticle stored procedure to create any articles you need.

After you've selected a replication frequency, you next need to create an article.

Creating Articles

To create an article, choose a table from the list of available tables and add it to the article list. Then click the Edit button to bring up the Manage Article dialog. This is an important dialog, so we will cover each of the parts in detail.

The Article Information Section

There are two check boxes in the Article Information section. These options are new with the 6.5 release; you won't see them if you're running 6.0. Normally, replication assumes that the owner of the source table is *dbo*. If other owners want to publish tables, the replication can be qualified with the owner name. In this case, you must check the Owner-Qualify Table Name option.

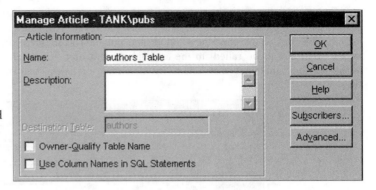

With release 6.5, you are also given the option to have column names included in the insert statements that will be generated. This is how you can make sure that the data populates the correct columns in the target table. In SQL Server 6.0, the column names were not included and this could cause errors when the target table had columns in a different order or a different number of columns from the source table. If you check this option, the insert statements will include column names.

> *Microsoft suggests that you check this box only if you suspect that problems will occur in replication. Their argument against using it is that the insert statements will be longer, resulting in an increase in storage requirements for the distribution database and in higher network traffic. Personally, I'm not sure I agree with them. It is a recommended practice to use the column list on the insert so that the code continues to work even if the table is subsequently altered. I think the same applies to replication. Inserts, as well.*

The Filters Tab

The Filters tab allows you to define the specific contents of the article. This is where you create the vertical and horizontal partitions discussed earlier. You create a vertical partition by using the Replicate column and checking to be included or clearing those that aren't to be replicated. To create a horizontal partition, use the Restriction Clause. This can contain any legitimate **WHERE** clause selection criteria. If you can't express your selection criteria in a **WHERE** clause or if your restrictions are not based on columns of the replicated table, you can click the Advanced button. This will give you an opportunity to use a stored procedure as a filter for the replication.

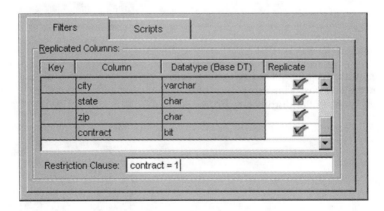

The Scripts Tab

The Scripts tab allows you to define how the article should be replicated. Normally, replication will simply use **INSERT**, **UPDATE** and **DELETE** statements. However, you can specify a stored procedure to be used for any given action by checking Custom and putting **CALL myproc** (where **myproc** is the name of the stored procedure to be called) in the appropriate text box. If you check Custom and put the word NONE in the text box, that particular action (insert, update or delete) will not be replicated.

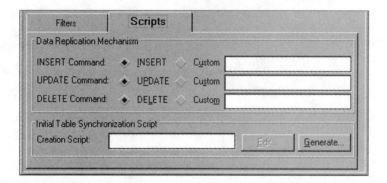

The Initial Table Synchronization Script

The final element of the Scripts dialog is the Initial Table Synchronization Script. This will be blank when you are creating an article. Normally, SQL Server will create this script for you when you save your article. If you subsequently modify it, you will see the full path name of the file that has the schema creation script.

The default options for synchronization are to drop the table if it exists in the subscriber rather than ignoring it, truncating it or deleting data that matches the restriction. Synchronization will also automatically transfer the clustered index but not any non-clustered indices, and will convert user-defined datatypes to base datatypes. Primary and foreign key constraints will not be transferred. If you want to change any of these options, you need to click the Generate button. That will present a dialog box that allows you to specify how you want the synchronization script built. Once the script is defined, you can also edit it by clicking the Edit button. The scripts will be placed in the distribution process' working directory. You can change the working directory in the Publication Options dialog of SQL Enterprise Manager, or by editing the keys under the **Replication** key in the Registry.

You can create your own synchronization script and specify its full path name in the text box. This name must be a UNC name and must point to the distribution process' working directory.

If your synchronization script does not transfer indexes, then the synchronization can use fast bulk copy if the Select Into/Bulk Copy option is turned on in the target database.

Using Stored Procedures to Customize Replication

Stored procedures that are called at **INSERT** time are passed the replicated columns, in order, as parameters. **UPDATE** stored procedures get the replicated columns (whether modified or not), followed by the original values of all columns in the primary key. **DELETE** stored procedures will be passed the values of the primary key. If these stored procedures want to inform the distributor of success or failure, you must include a **RAISERROR** statement in the procedure. If you raise an error with severity 12 or greater, the distribution process to that server will stop. If you are using stored procedures to do insert, update or delete, you must install the stored procedures in the destination database on each subscriber.

If you want to use a stored procedure for a filter, you will need to specify both its name and the synchronization object in the dialog that appears when you click the Advanced button. You must have already defined the stored procedure in the source database.

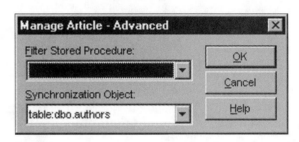

A filter stored procedure must be of the form:

```
IF sql_statement
    RETURN 1
ELSE
    RETURN 0
```

where **sql_statement** is any SQL statement that accomplishes the filtering. Remember that this filter will be processed against every log record for the replicated table and keep it as simple as possible to avoid overhead. The filter will be applied to only one log record at a time. If you are using a filter stored procedure, you may also need to specify a synchronization object. The synchronization object is the source of the data used for initial synchronization of the tables in the publishing and subscribing databases. Normally, the synchronization object is the base table for the article. If the article is a vertical, horizontal or combined partition of the table, SQL Server creates a view that matches the article definition and uses that as the synchronization object. If you have created a filter stored procedure, you may also have to create a view that matches the custom filter.

Publication Synchronization

Open the Synchronization tab to specify how your publication should be synchronized when someone subscribes to it. Note that if you are preparing a publication for replication to ODBC data sources (including Version 6.0 SQL Servers), you must request character mode synchronization.

You determine the frequency of automatic synchronization by specifying the schedule on which you want it to happen. Since this activity can produce a high amount of system overhead, you should schedule it at low-activity periods.

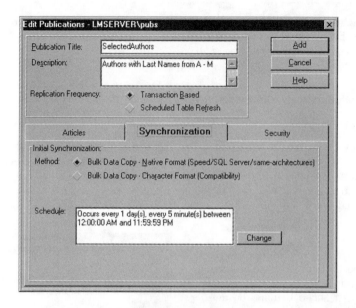

Publication Security

The final thing you need to do is to specify the security of your publication. Use the Security tab to control the visibility of the publication. If you choose Unrestricted, the publication can be seen and subscribed to by any subscribing server. A restricted publication can only be seen and subscribed to by the servers you check off.

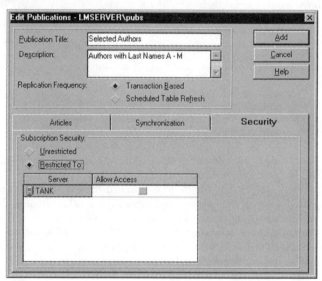

Manual Synchronization

In most cases, you will want automatic synchronization. However, manual synchronization may be appropriate when the publishing and subscribers are connected by a slow network link, or when the table being synchronized is very large.

If you choose to use manual synchronization, you will use the schema and data files which were prepared in the process of setting up the replication. Copy the schema and data files from the distribution server to the target server. You can obtain the name of the schema script by looking at the article. To find the name of the data file, you will need to look at the scheduled synchronization task history. This history will give you the name of the **.TMP** file used to migrate the data. Run the scripts using isql and bcp as appropriate, to manually synchronize the files. Then you must notify the publishing server that the synchronization is complete. You do this with the Manage Subscriptions dialog. Select the publication that is targeted for manual synchronization and click the 'Sync Completed' button. This will present a dialog that will allow you to tell the distribution process that replication should now begin for this subscriber.

It is important that you perform the manual synchronization in a timely manner. Once the scheduled manual synchronization job comes to the top of the task queue, all replication to the target database stops until the synchronization is complete.

Subscribing to Articles

Once you have created a publication, other servers can subscribe to it. SQL Server supports two approaches to subscriptions:

- A **pull** subscription is like the magazine you order. You request it and it arrives. In SQL Server, these subscriptions are created by 'pulling' in a publication or article. The subscriber has a degree of autonomy and does not need to get any unwanted data. Pull subscriptions can be set up from many publishers at once.

- A **push** subscription is like all those magazines and catalogues that arrive that you *didn't* order. Push subscriptions are created by 'pushing' a publication or article to one or more servers. Push subscriptions can simplify and centralize subscription administration. These subscriptions are created simultaneously with the act of publishing, and many subscribers can be set up at once. You must use push subscriptions for ODBC subscribers.

Note that these terms only describe how the subscriptions are set up. Once a subscription is in place, data replication uses the same mechanisms regardless of how it was set up.

Creating Push Subscriptions

Push Subscriptions are aptly named, as they occur on the publisher and are 'pushed' out to the subscriber. They are beneficial for central administration of all subscriptions, and many subscribers can be easily added at once using this method. To add push subscriptions, first select the publication, and click the Change button. The following screen will appear:

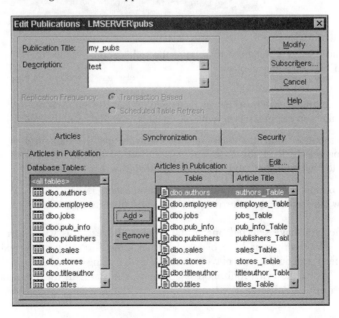

Click the Subscribers button to add subscriptions to the publication. You will then receive the following screen:

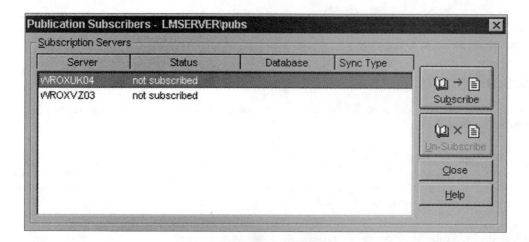

For each server you wish to subscribe to the publication, select the server and click the Subscribe button. If you wish to remove a subscription from a publication, use the Un-Subscribe button. When a subscription is selected, the following screen will appear:

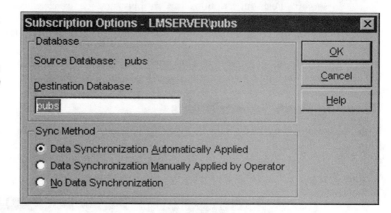

From this screen you must select a database to receive the publication (usually the default), and a method of synchronization from the following choices:

▲ **Automatic:** An initial synchronization is scheduled for the publication and, upon completion, the data on the subscribing server will be equal to the data on the publisher.

▲ **Manual:** This option indicates that you will manually get the data in sync on the subscriber by performing the BCP of the data and creating all tables. When this is accomplished, you must return to the publisher and acknowledge that this has occurred.

▲ **None:** This option indicates that no data synchronization is necessary. This is useful if you already know for certain that the data on the subscriber is up-to-date.

Click the OK button after you have selected one of the choices above. This will return you to the previous screen. When all subscriptions have been added, click the Close button to exit. If initial synchronizations have been scheduled, you may monitor them by using the Manage Scheduled Tasks feature of SQL Server. When the synchronization is complete, the status in the replication window will change from 'not subscribed' to 'subscribed'.

Creating Pull Subscriptions

This same process of subscribing to a publication may also occur on the subscribing server if desired. This method is called a 'Pull Subscription'. Pull subscriptions are beneficial if decentralized administration of subscriptions is desired. As a result, only one subscription at a time can be processed using this method. To add a pull subscription, first connect to the subscribing server. Then select **Manage, Replication, Subscriptions** from the menu. The steps involved are very similar to those described in the previous section, and do not warrant repeating. Regardless of which method you choose, the results should be the same: replication has finally been set up! You should now be able to apply changes to the publisher, and watch them replicate to the subscribers!

Replication Topology

The final feature of Enterprise Manager's GUI for replication is the Replication Topology window. This screen can be accessed by selecting **Server, Replication Configuration, Topology** from the menu. When selected, a graphical representation of your replication hierarchy is presented, starting with the publisher and ending with the subscribers. You may also access many of the other features of the GUI from this screen, such as creating and removing subscriptions.

Stopping Replication

You may want to stop replication either permanently or on a temporary basis. If you want to stop replication from a subscriber, you can cancel a subscription to an article or cancel a subscription to a publication. You can also disable publishing to the subscribing server, but it is best to unsubscribe first.

If you want to stop replication from a publisher, you can remove a publication or an article from it, and disable publishing for a database. If the server is no longer to publish any thing, you can uninstall publishing with SQL Enterprise Manager using the **Server, Replication Configuration, Uninstall Publishing** menu option. This option is only available in SQL Server 6.5

To stop replication from a distributor, you can disable the distribution publisher or stop the log reader, synchronization or distribution process. Both of these are brute force actions. If you no longer want a server to function as a distributor, first redirect any publications to another distributor, and then disable the distribution function.

Replication Stored Procedures

Almost all of the features provided in the Enterprise Manager GUI are also available as stored procedures. The following is a list of a few of the most important replication stored procedures which may be used in lieu of the GUI. For complete syntax, consult your *Transact-SQL Reference Guide* under the 'Stored Procedures - Replication Stored Procedures' heading.

Procedure Name	Functionality
`sp_addpublisher`	Adds a new publication server
`sp_droppublisher`	Removes a publication server
`sp_addsubscriber`	Adds a new subscription server
`sp_dropsubscriber`	Removes a subscription server

Table Continued on Following Page

Procedure Name	Functionality
`sp_addarticle`	Adds a new article to an existing publication
`sp_droparticle`	Removes an article from a publication
`sp_addsubscription`	Adds a subscription to a publication
`sp_dropsubscription`	Drops a subscription from a publication

Managing Tasks

When replication has been successfully set up on a server, several tasks are created which are managed by SQL Executive. These are the sync, log reader, distribution, and cleanup tasks. These tasks may be viewed by selecting Manage Scheduled Tasks from within Enterprise Manager. The following diagram presents a sample task schedule:

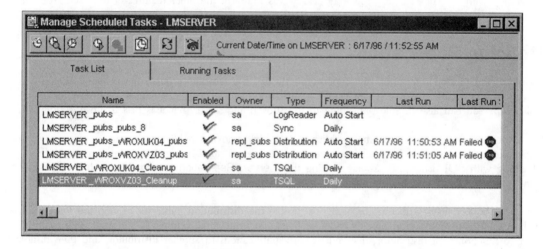

Notice that in this example, there is one task of type 'Sync', one task of type 'LogReader', two tasks of type 'Distribution' and two Cleanup tasks of type 'TSQL'. Now, let's discuss each of these:

Sync

The Sync task is executed whenever an initial synchronization is requested for a publication. It creates a bcp file and schema file for the articles being synched, and places a sync request in the distribution database. The actual synchronization of the data will not take place until the distribution tasks run.

Alternate Delimiters for Synchronization Task

By default, SQL Server uses tab characters to delimit fields and newline characters to delimit rows in the data used for character mode synchronization. If the data used for synchronization contains these characters, the synchronization can fail. SQL Server 6.5 allows you to specify alternate delimiters using switches. Both switches are case-sensitive.

Switch	Function
-r	Row-delimiter
-f	Field-delimiter

The row-delimiter is a sequence of one or more characters used to signal the end of a row of data. The field-delimiter is a sequence of one or more characters used to signal the end of a column of data. These sequences should not appear as data in any table that is being synchronized. Don't leave any spaces between the switch and the delimiter.

To change the delimiters,

- Stop the SQL Executive
- Create your publication
- Set the synchronization method to Bulk Data Copy–Character
- Leave Publication dialog
- Use the Manage Scheduled Tasks dialog to edit the synchronization task
- Add the desired switches in the Command text box
- Modify the task
- Restart the SQL Executive

> **Keep in mind that while the SQL Executive is stopped, none of its activities (other scheduled tasks, other replication, and alerts) can take place. You should make this kind of change when there is little or no activity on the server.**

Log Reader

The Log Reader task is used in transaction-based replication, as opposed to synchronization. The Log Reader continually scans the transaction log of the publication database for any new transactions to be replicated. When one is found, the distribution database is populated with a replication job, and is scheduled to occur on all subscribers.

This task should be monitored often in case of failures. To check the execution history of a task, first select the task in the scheduling window. Then click the Task History button (the white button that resembles a clock directly underneath the word 'Tasks' in the title bar). This will give you a status of the latest runs of the task. If a failure occurs, a descriptive message will be provided.

Replication Log Reader Switches

There are three parameters on the Log Reader that you can modify in order to tune the performance of your system. You want to change these only when you experience delays. They are all switches on the log reader task command line.

Switch	Function
-b	Specifies the transaction batch size
-c	Specifies the commit batch size
-t	Specifies the command threshold

The **transaction batch size** determines the maximum number of transactions to read out of the publishing database's transaction log before the log reader begins the **COMMIT TRANSACTION** process. The default is 100.

The **commit batch size** determines how many transactions are placed in the distribution database before a commit is issued in the distribution database. The default is 100. A large transaction batch size (together with a large commit batch size) will move data out of the transaction log faster but may delay the availability of these data to the subscribers.

The **command threshold** (new with SQL Server 6.5) determines the number of commands within a transaction to accept before issuing a commit transaction in the distribution database. If this is non-zero, the log reader will commit the transaction when it has processed this many commands, whether or not it has reached the commit batch size. This can lessen the impact of large batch sizes by allowing the log reader to commit the transactions as soon as they are completely processed rather than waiting for all pending transactions to be processed. This can improve access for the subscribers.

With SQL Server 6.5, the log reader will commit the current batch to the distribution database when:

▲ The number of jobs exceeds the commit batch size, or

▲ The number of commands in the last job exceeds the command threshold.

To change these parameters you must:

▲ Stop the SQL Executive

▲ Edit the appropriate tasks using the Manage Scheduled tasks window

▲ Modify the text in the command window

▲ Restart SQL Executive

> **Keep in mind that while the SQL Executive is stopped, none of its activities (other scheduled tasks, other replication, and alerts) are taking place. You should make this kind of change when there is little or no activity on the server.**

Distribution

The Distribution Tasks actually read the jobs that have been placed into the distribution database, and apply them on the subscribers. Notice that there is a separate distribution task for each subscriber. Also notice that in the example above, the last execution of the two distribution tasks resulted in a failure! It is important to keep a close watch on these tasks. To find the exact cause of the failure, use the task history button and review the error message that is provided.

Cleanup

The Cleanup Tasks remove replicated jobs from the distribution database. There is a cleanup task provided for each subscriber. These tasks run by default at 1:00 AM each day, although you may modify this schedule by editing the task if you wish. Be sure, however, that they do run often, since performance problems can occur if the distribution database becomes too large. When the publication was first defined, a default retention period for transactions to remain in the distribution database before they are eligible to be removed by the cleanup tasks, was specified. Only jobs that have been successfully distributed to the subscribers and have exceeded the retention period specified, will be removed by the cleanup tasks.

Monitoring Replication

Once the initial setup of replication is complete, the DBA's replication duties become largely that of monitoring and troubleshooting. In fact, depending upon the number of servers involved, the monitoring aspect of replication can quickly become a nightmare. Suppose, for example, that you have a central publisher/distributor with 50 subscribers.

How do you make sure that each of the 50 servers has received and applied the latest batch of replicated transactions? Furthermore, how can you accomplish this without having to manually connect to 50 servers to perform the verification?

Inspecting Task Histories

The first step in ensuring that replication is working correctly is to view the task history for the log reader, sync, distribution, and cleanup tasks. Each one of these tasks will need to be monitored at different times. For example, the sync task only needs to be monitored when an initial synchronization has been scheduled for a subscriber. The log reader and distribution tasks will most likely be running throughout the day, so these will need to be checked more often. The cleanup tasks run by default at 1:00 AM on a daily basis, so only a periodic check of these is necessary.

To view the status of the latest runs of these tasks, select a task and click on its history button. The results will indicate the run dates, run times, status (success or failure), and the duration of the task. Also, a message box is situated at the bottom of the window, and this provides information on the reason for any failures that may have occurred.

To make the verification of these tasks easier, a T-SQL script can be executed which will query the last execution of each task. Save the following as a T-SQL script, and execute from within a query window:

```
SET nocount on
USE msdb
GO
DECLARE @msg varchar(80)
SELECT @msg = "Server:  " + @@servername + '           ' + CONVERT(char(20),getdate())
PRINT " "
PRINT @msg
PRINT " "

SELECT 'Task Name' = substring(name,1,29),
       'Type' =
          CASE
```

```
            WHEN substring(subsystem,1,1) = 'T' THEN 'C'
                ELSE substring(subsystem,1,1)
            END,
        'Run Date' =
        substring(datename(month, CONVERT(smalldatetime,
CONVERT(varchar,lastrundate))) + " " + datename(day,
CONVERT(smalldatetime,convert(varchar,lastrundate))) + + ", " +
datename(year, CONVERT(smalldatetime,
CONVERT(varchar,lastrundate))),1,20),

        'Time' = lastruntime,
        'Status' =
            CASE
                WHEN enabled = 0 THEN 'Disabled'
                WHEN lastruncompletionlevel = 0 THEN 'Failure'
                WHEN lastruncompletionlevel = 1 THEN 'Success'
                ELSE 'Unknown'
            END
FROM systasks
WHERE subsystem in ('distribution', 'sync', 'logreader') or
        name LIKE '%Cleanup%'
ORDER BY subsystem, name

PRINT " "
PRINT " "
GO
```

The results will appear to be similar to the following (note that the Type column indicates D for Distribution, L for LogReader, S for Sync, and C for Cleanup):

Server: SERVER1   Jun 11 1996 10:23AM

Task Name	Type	Run Date	Time	Status
SERVER1_pubs_SERVER2_pubs	D	June 11, 1996	100900	Success
SERVER1_pubs_SERVER3_pubs	D	June 11, 1996	101000	Success
SERVER1_pubs_SERVER4_pubs	D	June 11, 1996	101100	Success
SERVER1_pubs_SERVER5_pubs	D	June 11, 1996	101200	Success
SERVER1_pubs_SERVER6_pubs	D	June 11, 1996	101300	Success
SERVER1_pubs	L	June 11, 1996	100000	Success
SERVER1_pubs_Central	S	June 11, 1996	100000	Success
SERVER1_SERVER2_Cleanup	C	June 11, 1996	010000	Success
SERVER1_SERVER3_Cleanup	C	June 11, 1996	010100	Success
SERVER1_SERVER4_Cleanup	C	June 11, 1996	010200	Success
SERVER1_SERVER5_Cleanup	C	June 11, 1996	010300	Success
SERVER1_SERVER6_Cleanup	C	June 11, 1996	010400	Success

In this example, we see that there is a central server called SERVER1, and five subscribing servers SERVER2, SERVER3, SERVER4, SERVER5, and SERVER6. The database name on which the publication is based is called pubs. Note that the status of all these tasks is 'Success'. This is what you are hoping for! If a failure has occurred, the status would read 'Failure', and further investigation would be necessary.

Verifying Replicated Jobs

On the subscribing database of each subscriber, there exists a special table called MSlast_job_info. This table stores the job_id of the last job that was successfully distributed to the subscriber. For example, the following query executed on SERVER6 can be used to check the last job distributed to the pubs database on this server by SERVER1:

```
/* SUBVER.SQL script */

USE pubs
GO
SELECT job_id FROM mslast_job_info WHERE publisher = 'SERVER1'
GO
```

In order to determine whether SERVER6 has received all replicated transactions from SERVER1, you can compare the results from SUBVER.SQL to the last job_id scheduled for distribution to the subscribers of the publication on SERVER1. If these numbers are equal, SERVER6 is up-to-date with all replicated transactions. We can execute the following query on SERVER1 to obtain this information:

```
/* PUBVER.SQL script */

USE distribution
GO
SELECT max(job_id) FROM msjobs
WHERE publisher_id =
    (SELECT srvid FROM master..sysservers WHERE srvname = 'SERVER1') AND
publisher_db = 'pubs'
GO
```

In order to check whether all servers are up-to-date, you would need to run the first script above for all subscribers, and compare the results to the number obtained from the second script! Naturally, if you have 50 subscribers, this may take some time. Fortunately, this process can be automated by creating a command file consisting of isql commands, with the results written to a file.

First, save the above scripts into files called **SUBVER.SQL** and **PUBVER.SQL**. Then create a command file similar to the following and call it **REPLVER.BAT** (use your server names and database names instead of the ones in the example):

```
/* REPLVER.BAT Command file */

SET SERVER=SERVER1
isql /Usa /n /ddistribution /Pxxx /S%server% /i PUBVER.sql >results.txt
SET SERVER=SERVER2
isql /Usa /n /dpubs /Pxxx /S%server% /i SUBVER.sql >>results.txt
SET SERVER=SERVER3
isql /Usa /n /dpubs /Pxxx /S%server% /i SUBVER.sql >>results.txt
SET SERVER=SERVER4
isql /Usa /n /dpubs /Pxxx /S%server% /i SUBVER.sql >>results.txt
SET SERVER=SERVER5
isql /Usa /n /dpubs /Pxx  /S%server% /i SUBVER.sql >>results.txt
SET SERVER=SERVER6
isql /Usa /n /dpubs /Pxxx /S%server% /i SUBVER.sql >>results.txt
```

Now execute the batch file. This will query the publisher first, and get the last job to be replicated. Then, all of the subscribers are queried, obtaining the last replicated job_id from each. Finally, all the results are written to the **results.txt** file. You can look at this file using file manager, or any editor. If all the numbers match, all servers are up-to-date.

If you want to get really creative, you can even schedule this command file to run as a task within SQL server on a periodic basis. As a result, all you have to do is edit the file several times a day to see how replication is progressing.

Monitoring Replication Performance

Replication performance can be monitored directly by using the SQL Performance Monitor utility. Upon installation of SQL Server, two performance objects are provided for monitoring replication: **SQLServer Replication-PublishedDB** and **SQLServer Replication-Subscriber**. The PublishedDB object allows the DBA to monitor replication's performance as the log reader reads transactions and inserts them into the distribution database. The Subscriber object monitors transactions as they are distributed to the subscribers.

Performance Counters

The following performance counters are contained within these objects, and may be used in a session of SQL Performance Monitor:

SQLServer Replication - PublishedDB Performance Counters	Purpose
Replicated Transactions	Monitors the number of transactions marked for replication in the transaction log that have not yet been read by the log reader.
Replicated Transactions/sec	Monitors the number of transactions per second read by the log reader and placed into the distribution database.
Replication Latency (msec)	Monitors the amount of time a transaction resides in the transaction log before it is read by the log reader and placed into the distribution database.

SQLServer Replication - Subscriber Performance Counters	Purpose
Delivered Transactions	Monitors the number of transactions that have been successfully distributed to the subscriber by the distributor.
Delivered Transactions/sec	Monitors the number of transactions distributed to subscribers per second.
Delivered Latency (sec)	Monitors the number of seconds a transaction remains in the distribution database before it is distributed to the subscriber.
Undelivered Transactions	Monitors the number of transactions in the distribution database that have not been distributed to the subscriber.

Replication between 6.0 and 6.5 SQL Servers

It's possible to have replication between Version 6.0 and Version 6.5 SQL Servers. The publisher and distributor must run on the same version. You will need to administer replication from a SQL Enterprise Manager on a 6.5 server. You must install the **SQLOLE65.SQL** script on the Version 6.0 server.

> **You have probably already done this so that you could use the 6.5 SQL Enterprise Manager to administer your 6.0 servers, but if you didn't, the script is in the platform (e.g.; I386, Alpha, MIPS, etc.) subdirectory on the installation CD.**

When you are replicating from a 6.0 SQL Server to a 6.5 Server, you only get the 6.0 features. This means that you cannot replicate text columns, use owner-qualified table names or different character sets, or have column names in the insert statements.

Replication from SQL Server 6.5 databases to SQL Server 6.0 databases is done as if the 6.0 server were an ODBC data source. This means that you must create a DSN for the 6.0 SQL Server just as you would any ODBC source.

Replication and Your Database Maintenance Plan

When servers are involved in replication schemes, you need to consider a few additional things as you develop your backup and recovery plan. Remember that replication is based on the transaction log. Because database and transaction log dumps affect the contents of the transaction log, you need to take a server's role in replication into consideration when you are backing it up.

Backing Up a Publisher

The transaction log of a database on a publishing server contains all transactions that need to be replicated. Transactions are kept in the log until they are successfully transferred to the distribution database. After that, they are purged with other transactions in the inactive portion of the log. You can dump a published database at any time since that does not truncate the transaction log. However, you will need to coordinate dumps of the transaction log with backups of the distribution database.

If the transaction log should fill up and must be truncated, you should unsubscribe all subscribers. You will then be able to truncate the non-replicated transactions. When you re-subscribe them, there will be a synchronization process to put them back in sync with the publishing database.

Backing Up a Distributor

Remember that the distributor can be on the same server as the publisher, or on a remote server. The considerations in this section apply to the *distribution database,* wherever it resides. All transactions are retained in the distribution database tables until they have been applied to all eligible subscribers. The transaction log of the distribution database does not contain any replication specific information.

The Msjobs table in the distribution database keeps a pointer in the publication database's transaction log so that it knows the last transaction transferred into the distribution database. If you need to recover a distribution server, this pointer must point to a transaction that still exists in the publisher's transaction log.

Since transaction log dumps might truncate these transactions, you need to coordinate the backups of publishing servers and distribution servers. In order to ensure full recovery, you have to back up the distribution server databases and transaction logs after the last transaction log dump of all databases publishing to that distribution server. This means that you need to schedule a full backup on the distribution server after *any* transaction log dump on an associated publishing server.

Backing Up Subscribers

Because replication affects subscribers in exactly the same way as other data applied by client processes, the management of backups for subscribers is relatively straight forward. The administrator can schedule backups in such a fashion that the subscribing database can be recovered to a known point in time. This schedule needs to take into account the retention period after distribution. This interval determines how frequently the replication cleanup process runs. This cleanup process deletes all transactions that have been successfully distributed to subscribers and all synchronization jobs. By coordinating the retention period with the backup of subscribing servers, you can ensure that data can always be recovered at the subscriber.

For example, if a subscribing server is backed up every 24 hours, setting the retention period to 48 hours would guarantee that, even if the subscriber crashed immediately before a backup, the data would still be available in the distribution server's database. It is best to set this interval as a distribution option before setting up any subscriptions. However, you can also set it by editing the appropriate cleanup task. The task uses the **sp_replcleanup** stored procedure which takes 3 parameters:

- ▲ The name of the publishing server,
- ▲ The name of the subscribing server and
- ▲ The retention period.

You can change the retention period and modify the task.

Troubleshooting Replication

It seems sometimes that setting up replication is the easy part. The instructions are fairly straight-forward and the GUI is so easy to use that you could probably set up a simple replication scenario without even reading the manuals. However, things often tend to get more difficult after this initial setup. Remember that replication was new to SQL Server 6.0, and there were many bugs found after the release of the product. The changes in version 6.5 are relatively insignificant compared to the initial release. As a result, replication in version 6.5 should prove to be more stable. However, only time (and DBA experience) will tell.

In most cases, if replicated transactions are not being received by the subscribers, you should start by checking the task histories for the log reader and distribution jobs. If errors have occurred, a message will be given in the task history window.

The following is a just a partial list of problems that can (and most likely will) occur with replication, and what you can do to correct them:

Distribution Database Is Full

If the distribution database fills up, all replication will come to a screeching halt. For this reason, you should keep a close watch on this database to ensure that it is large enough to handle the load of records being inserted into it. Also, frequent dumps of the transaction log will prevent the log from filling up. However, if the distribution database does fill up, the following options are available:

▲   Extend the device the distribution database resides on and the database itself. By giving it more space, replication will be able to continue.

Run the cleanup tasks from the task scheduler. This will remove any transactions that have already been replicated. Note that if the transaction log is full, this will not help, since the records deleted by the cleanup tasks are logged.

Subscribers Aren't Getting Changes

The first thing you need to determine is whether all subscribers are failing to receive changes, or if this is the case with just one. If all subscribers are affected, the problem lies with the log reader or the distribution processes. To find out which has a problem, you need to interrogate the Msjob_commands table in the distribution database. You want to select the Command column. If none of the changes are there, the problem is in the log reader. If they are there, the problem is in the distribution process.

If it's the log reader then use the Task Scheduling dialog in SQL Enterprise Manager to check the status of the log reader task. View its history and see if there are any clues there. Set it to run daily every minute. Stop the SQL Executive, restart it, and then monitor the log reader task. This may give you enough information to solve the problem with.

If it's the distribution task, follow the same process but focus on the task itself. If all subscribers are failing on the same transaction, it is possible to isolate the failing transaction. There are detailed instructions for doing this in the *Administrator's Companion* so we won't repeat them here. If only one subscriber is failing to receive changes, check the following:

▲   Is the subscribing database available and is there space in it?

▲   Is the subscribing server up?

▲   Has someone removed the *repl_publisher* login from the subscribing server?

▲   Is the distribution task waiting on a manual synchronization event?

> You can find the manual synchronization event by interrogating the Mslast_job_info table in the subscription database of the subscription server. If this table contains entries in the publication, article and description columns, the distribution task is paused until the manual synchronization is accomplished. Follow the procedure described above to do the synchronization, and notify the distribution process of the completion of the synchronization.

Publishing Database Transaction Log Problems

If the transaction log is filling up, there is probably a problem with the log reader task. You can troubleshoot it in the same way described for the case where subscribers aren't receiving changes. You can also use two stored procedures to study the contents of the transaction log. The procedure sp_repltrans will show you all the transactions that are awaiting replication. If this command returns results, you can then use the stored procedure sp_replcmds for detailed information about the transactions that are pending. If the transaction log is completely full, and there are unreplicated transactions, you will not be able to truncate the log. There are two ways to deal with this. The first is to increase the transaction log with **ALTER DATABASE**. The second is to clear the non-replicated transactions out of the log. To do this, use the sp_repldone stored procedure with the following parameters

```
sp_repldone 0, 0, NULL, 0, 0, 1
```

This will mark all replicated transactions as having been distributed. Once this is done, you can dump the transaction log with no_log.

> **You should immediately back up the publishing database. You should also unsubscribe all the subscribers and resubscribe them so that they will be resynchronized.**

Initial Synchronization Didn't Happen

Here again, there are two points of failure:

- The sync task
- The distribution task

If the sync task is the problem, the synchronization commands won't appear in the distribution database. Then you can study it using the task history. Here are some things to look at:

- Perhaps it is scheduled far in the future
- Try running it immediately and see if it produces any error messages
- Make sure it has access to the replication working directory

If the problem is in the distribution task, you need to look at whether the task is failing at login. You can turn on the 'audit failed logins' for the subscribing server in SQL Enterprise Manager. If the table has been created but has no data in it, check the bulk copy portion of the task. If this is failing, perhaps you can apply it manually and update the job_id of the corresponding row in the Mslast_job_info table. Perhaps the data contains tabs or linefeeds and you will need to re-run it changing the delimiters.

Monitoring Scheduled Table Refresh

You can monitor the completion of a scheduled table refresh by looking at the MSlast_job_info table in the destination database. If you are synchronizing with deletion or truncation, there will be two jobs. If the job_id in MSlast_job_info increments by 2, the refresh was successful. If you are synchronizing with the existing table being dropped, there are three jobs and an increment of 3 indicates successful completion.

Replication Is Working, but very slowly...

Each distribution task has a default commit size for the number of transactions to apply on the subscriber before issuing a commit. If this number is small, performance of the distribution tasks will suffer. To change this value, perform the following:

Edit the distribution task in the task scheduling window. In the Command box, you will see a line similar to the following:

```
-SSERVER6 -dpubs -pSERVER1 -c100 -npubs -i2000 -t0
```

Notice the -c parameter is set to 100. This means that a commit will be issued on the subscriber after every 100 jobs. Replication may be spending a lot of time issuing commits instead of replicating updates! To make the corrections, edit the line above to read:

```
-SSERVER6 -dpubs -pSERVER1 -c1000 -npubs -i2000 -t0
```

This will change the commit size to 1000. You should experiment with this parameter to find out what works best for you and your particular environment.

Helpful Hints

If you are involved in administering replication in SQL Server, you can expect some problems to occur. There are, however, some preventative maintenance steps that you can take to reduce the number of problems that will occur over time. Listed below are a few hints that can make your life as an SQL Server DBA a little bit easier:

Make Sure the Distribution Cleanup Tasks Run Frequently

This applies especially if you are replicating large amounts of data. In particular, the MSsubscriber_jobs table in the distribution database can become very large if not cleaned up on a daily basis. Naturally, this depends on the number of transactions you are replicating in a day, but replication performance can be adversely affected if the distribution database becomes too large.

In general, we would recommend that the cleanup tasks should be scheduled on a daily basis at a time when no other processing will occur on the system. You can control the scheduling of cleanup tasks by editing them in the Manage Scheduled Tasks window and changing the start time. If possible, you should also disable all other replication tasks (log reader, distribution, and sync) while the cleanups are running. The reason for this is that the cleanup tasks obtain exclusive table locks on several tables in the distribution database. If another replication task starts while the cleanup tasks are running, it will wait until the cleanup finishes. As a result, several tasks could end up waiting for a long period of time.

Also, it is a good idea to avoid running all the cleanup tasks at the same time. For example, if you have 100 subscribing servers, there will be 100 cleanup tasks scheduled to run. Each one of these tasks will establish a connection to the distribution server. Unless your distribution server is a very high-end machine, you probably won't want to add 100 simultaneous connections, each of which is attempting to obtain exclusive table locks on the same tables! For this reason, you should stagger the start times of the cleanup tasks so that each one has time to complete before the next one begins. The time interval will depend on your specific situation, but 5 minutes is probably a good figure to start with. Then monitor them daily and adjust as needed.

Backup the Distribution Database and Transaction Log Frequently

Again, this depends on the volume of replication that you are performing, but generally you should back up the distribution database each time you dump the transaction log of a publishing database.

The records in certain tables in the distribution database (such as MSjobs) contain pointers to records in the transaction log of the publishing database. If the distribution database needs to be recovered, you want to make sure that it is at a point in time after the last transaction log dump of the publishing database. If not, records in the transaction log may be removed when the transaction dump occurs. If these records are referenced by the pointers in the MSjobs table, replication will fail upon recovery. For this reason, you should always coordinate backups of the distribution database with transaction dumps of the publisher.

Schedule Large Replication Jobs for After-hours if Possible

If you are attempting to distribute hundreds of thousands of records during normal business hours, you may affect the performance of your system.

This involves knowing your replication strategy, and what type of updates will occur on your publishing server. For example, in an OLTP environment you will mostly be performing small updates on a frequent basis. This type of replication will be very effective using transaction-based replication. You should probably set the distribution and log reader tasks to run very often during the day, perhaps even on 'Auto Start', where they run continuously.

However, if you regularly perform large batch updates of records (perhaps mainframe downloads or stored procedures that update every record in a table), you should avoid running these during your main business hours. This type of replication is best implemented by using the scheduled table refresh method. In this environment, you should spread out the start times of the log reader, sync, and distribution tasks, perhaps even placing them 'On Demand' where they may be started only as needed.

Stagger the Timing of the Distribution Tasks so that They Don't All Run at the Same Time

If you have many subscribers to the same publication, and they all try to distribute at the same time, you can have some performance problems. As with the cleanup tasks, try staggering the start time of each distribution task by one or two minutes. This will give most of your replication tasks time to finish before the next one starts.

The greater the number of distribution tasks running concurrently, the slower the response time of each will be. Experiment to find out what schedule works best for your particular environment. As stated earlier, an OLTP environment lends itself to frequently scheduled distribution, and batch updates are generally best handled with scheduled table refreshes or infrequently executed distribution tasks.

If You're Updating a Large Percentage of Records in a Table in One Statement, Use a Table Refresh instead of Log-based Replication

First, unsubscribe all servers from the publication. Then make your updates to the data. Finally, re-subscribe all subscribers, causing an initial synchronization to occur. This technique works particularly well with very large tables. As an example, if you are updating every row in a million row table, you will cause 1,000,000 update statements (or perhaps 1,000,000 deletes and 1,000,000 inserts, since SQL Server sometimes logs an update as a delete/insert) to be placed in the distribution database. Each of these million updates will have be scheduled to be distributed to the subscribers. This could take forever to complete, if you don't fill up your distribution database first!

In this situation, it would be much more efficient to remove the article from the publication on the publishing server. Then perform the million row update. No records will be written to the distribution database, because the table is no longer defined for replication. After your update is complete, place the article back into the publication. Just as in a new article, an initial synchronization will occur, and all servers will be updated via replication's use of BCP, which is much faster than using update statements.

Learn Structure of the Distribution Database and the Relationships between the Tables it Contains

A little bit of time spent here (see the ER diagram earlier in this chapter) will pay big dividends when problems with replication occur.

For example, if you are not sure if an update has been scheduled to be replicated to a particular server, you need to know how to query the MSsubscriber_jobs table on the distribution server to find the needed information. In another situation, you may wish to view the actual SQL statement that is being distributed for a particular update. To accomplish this, you would need to query the command field in the MSjob_commands table. In fact, there are many situations where you will need to query the tables in the distribution database. By learning the structure of these tables, you will be able to troubleshoot many of your own problems without having to contact SQL Server support, thus saving you time and money!

Check the Knowledge Base on the Microsoft Web Site for Information on Fixes, Service Packs and Other Helpful Add-ons

The site is **www.microsoft.com/kb**, and allows you to search for a particular product (i.e. SQL Server), and to restrict the search by topic and keyword. This is a great place to start if you are experiencing a problem with SQL Server (not just with replication, but with any aspect of the product), and you want to see if there are any known bugs which may be causing your problem. There are also many useful articles which contain detailed information on how various components (transaction locking, for instance) of SQL Server work. You will find lots of information here that is not present in the SQL Server documentation, and you may solve your own problem without having to contact support. Also, some of the more popular online services, such as CompuServe, have discussion forums dedicated to SQL Server. On CompuServe, the SQL Server forum can be accessed by using **go mssql**. For other services, contact your provider for more information.

Summary

In this chapter, we've presented some of the basic concepts of replication and some of the common replication scenarios. We started by describing the publishing metaphor which replication uses in SQL Server. We then took you through the replication process, discussing concepts such as synchronization and partitioning. We looked at how replication is implemented and how you'd distribute information to many servers. Monitoring was also discussed with details on how to inspect task histories and the process of verifying replicated jobs. Finally we looked at the ways in which replication might go wrong and how you could identify and fix any problems.

6.5

The Web and SQL Server

The Web has become one of the hot buzzwords of the 90s. What's required next is the ability to combine corporate data with the Web. The first and simplest method of doing this is via the CGI interface. Typically, a CGI interface works as follows:

- A request is made from the Web Browser
- The HTTP server receives the request and starts a program
- The program connects to the database
- The program queries the database
- The program returns the result to the HTTP server
- The HTTP server returns the result to the Web Browser

Though this series of sequences may seem simple and straight forward, experience shows that the security of a database on the Web can be problematic. In this chapter we will be talking about web databases that are purely informational.

What is an **informational database**? This is where only the database is read and the pages are prepared based on just this information. It isn't possible for the user to query the database, unless you begin a process of replication and scripting that separates the whole Internet community from the SQL Server.

Typically, a read-only database mimics that of a stack of printouts. The printout is purely informational, and it could be company policies or budget codes. Such printouts are simple and effective and are produced by the millions of pages. These pages are ideally produced with Web Assistant, and you can quickly see the power of running this on your Intranet instead of a heap of Access, SQL Anywhere, VB, Delphi queries that are hitting the SQL Server for basic and regular result sets.

6.5 Web Assistant

Web Assistant is a tool to create read queries in 6.5 only. The unique part of Web Assistant is that it does not require a specific web server to display its pages, because it isn't connected in any form to any one particular web server.

Your users are able to use any Web browser for this, as there are no special Add-Ins or Applets to divulge.

Creating a Query

It's, therefore, very simple and requires the following steps for integration:

Login to the Database

To start the Web Assistant, double click on the SQL Server Web Assistant icon on the Server, or start from client listing. This will cause the following dialog to appear.

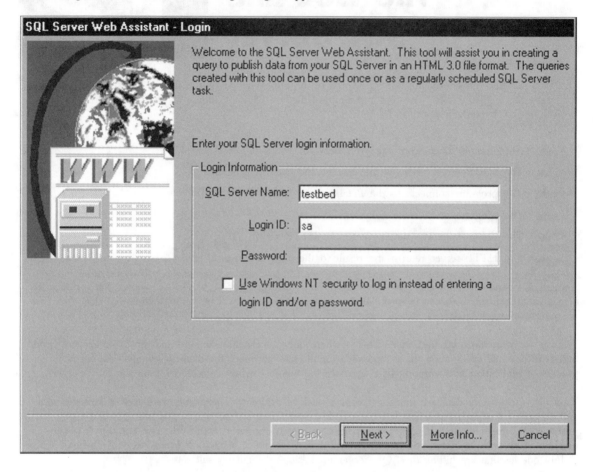

The SQL Server Web Assistant wizard is a program that needs to log onto a database to retrieve information. Enter a valid server name, one that must be registered and be able to appear in the SQL Enterprise list box, and go through to the logon/password. As stated, you can instigate NT secure logon instead if you've set trusted domains from the SQL Server.

Type of Query

There is a basic series of dialogs so that you may:

▲ Build a query from a database hierarchy

▲ Build a query using a stored procedure

▲ Enter a query as free form text

Build a Query from a Database Hierarchy

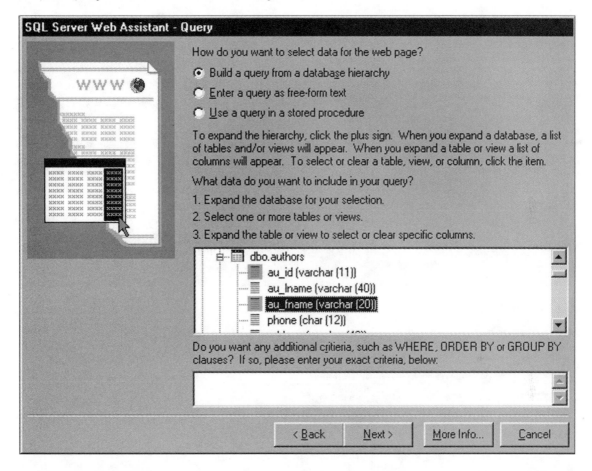

Queries from a hierarchy are based solely on a table or view. It isn't possible to attach several tables together unless the query is a view itself. This is as per the vanilla statement:

```
SELECT * from  (mytable | myview)
```

This offering is simple and straightforward and will default to display all columns in the query. You may set some simple criteria: **WHERE**, **ORDER BY**, etc., to get some selective ordering.

In your list box of database elements you simply select, as normal, tables, etc., to be included in the query. The elements show that they've been selected by turning green. You can dart around the listings grabbing columns and tables ad hoc—but expect some pretty ugly displays as the result set is placed in one big HTML grid table as a default.

Step through the following dialogs, such as setting a timed result set,

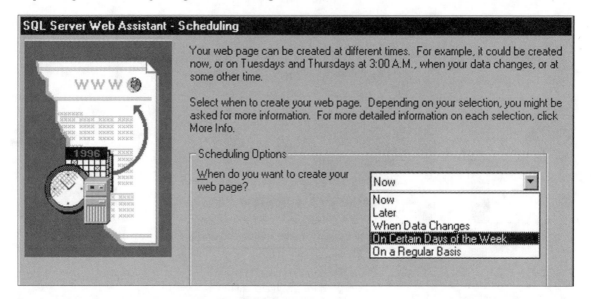

and template / title / font selections:

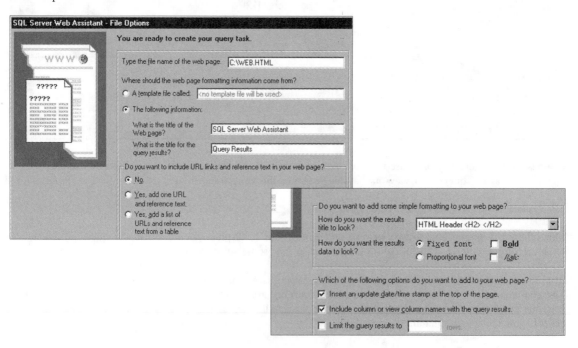

If you want to see a swift result, you can just accept the defaults and get to the finish screen quickly. Then you have to start up a browser and have a look at your work. It's worth a note to say that the HTML file you've created will default to reside on your Server's root–so search out your masterpiece with your browser's Open File... to view your first try. See the following screenshot.

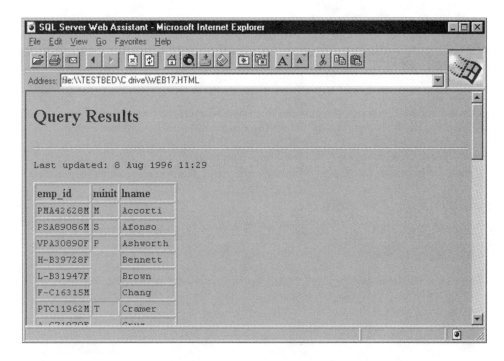

Build a Query Using a Stored Procedure

Select the Use query in a stored procedure option to get the dialog below:

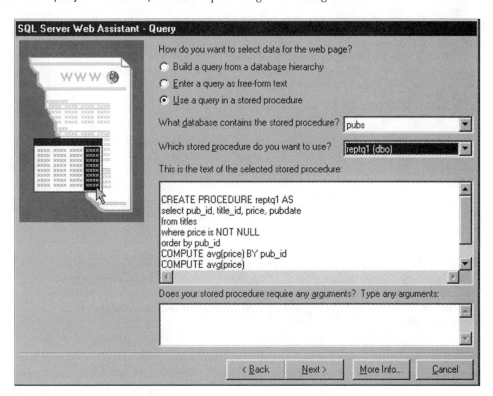

When you have selected a database from the drop-down list, all of the stored procedures that are available to it are viewable in the text area. You must, of course, add your procedure's arguments to this. After that, you simply step through the dialogs, as before, to execute the procedure, set some fonts and schedule the web page and, voilá, another HTML page.

> In the argument dialog box it's possible to enter parameters based on other queries or functions, but be extremely careful on the result set, because more times than not the function will refuse to work. If you desire this type of functionality, it's easier to add a few extra lines into the stored procedure.

Building a Query Using Free Form Text

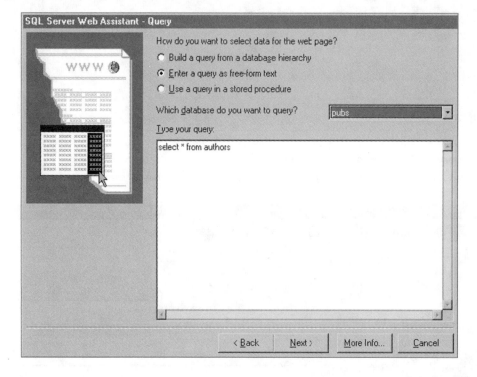

You need to select, as before, which database you would like to use for your query. In the figure above, we've used pubs. In the large text box, you need to type in the query that will return your result. The query must be a valid SQL query string.

> In this free form dialog box, any query that results in a return set is pretty much legal. This includes the calling of stored procedures and any call that is specific to SQL Server. This is where you would process your TSQL script and extended stored procedures.

If there are any incorrect parameters or incorrect statements, the assistant wizard will automatically detect it and prompt you to make the relevant corrections.

Scheduling the Query

The purpose of the Web Assistant is to have SQL Server create a Web page of the output at some point in time. The point in time can be immediate, periodically, or simply when data changes. These features give you the flexibility to rebuild the page with respect to an event that occurs in the database. You can select modes in the dialog:

Now

With now, the web page is created right away and is considered a 'one-off'. The stored procedure that calls this query isn't stored in the database.

Later

This allows you to create your report at a later point in time. However, like the now it's a 'one-off' and can't be reused for another query.

When Data Changes

This allows you to create your report whenever a specific value within a table or column changes. The table that you choose must be in the same database as the one where you are querying. It's possible to set the trigger to cover multiple tables and columns, or any combination of the two. There is a difference though, in that views can't be used to trigger a web page creation.

On Certain Days of the Week

Pretty obvious choices... remember that you're tied to your Server's clock and that there's no facility to track your Web site timers if you're supplying multi or virtual sites with data.

On a Regular Basis

Again obvious choices, although you can't select fractional parts to the given cycles on the wizard.

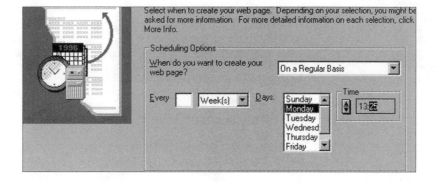

File Options

In this dialog box, you need to specify where the HTML file will be created and how.

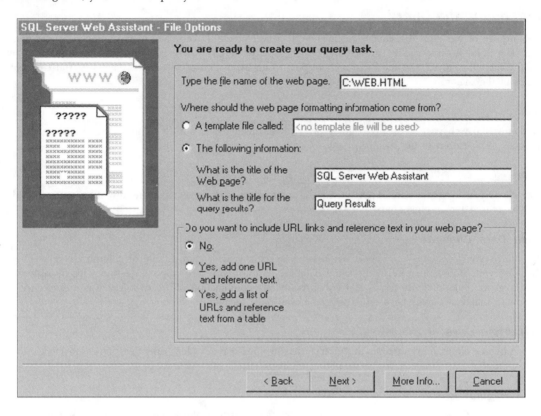

The directory must already exist and the file name must be valid and have the ending **HTM** or **HTML**.

> **This text field does not support UNC naming. For example, you couldn't specify as an output name \\ZEUS\cgross\web.html. It must reference a drive, directory and file name.**

The question 'Where should the web page formatting information come from?' refers to how your output page has to look. By default, the Web Assistant will create a simple table page with a page title and query title as specified (you saw this as our first browser result set shot). However, it's possible to define a custom page using the special tag **<%insert_data_here%>**. The following example HTML page shows how to use this:

```
<HTML>
<HEAD>
<TITLE>My own page</TITLE>
</HEAD>
```

```
<BODY>
<H2>Hey dude this is a query</H2>
<HR>
<%insert_data_here%>
<P>
<P>
<HR>
</BODY>
</HTML>
```

> **Try to reserve time to generate a standard template file. Template files give a more attractive output to the user, thus making any Web based solution more palatable.**

By opting to let Web Assistant create your page, you have the ability to add URLs. The purpose of these would be to create a hyper-link to relevant pages. The 'hot link' to another site/page will be automatically created on your data page.

Formatting Your Output

The dialog below is a result of letting Web Assistant create your page:

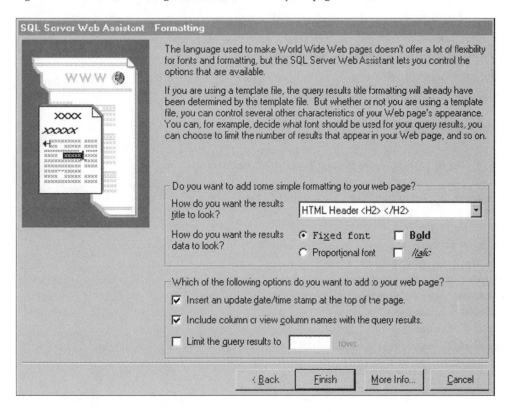

In the combo box 'How do you want the results title to look?', you should specify how the title will appear. Valid options are:

```
HTML Header <H2> </H2> ... HTML Header <H6> </H6>
```

It's possible to set the header types from 2 to 6. The radio button below the title formatting specifies how the data in the results table should appear. There are four possible:

- ▲ **Fixed font:** A fixed font is usually best for financial results because the numbers will cleanly align in a straight column.

- ▲ **Proportional font:** Not recommended for results that require a clean alignment.

- ▲ **Bold (is proportional font based):** Bold fonts are most useful when the font is small and you would like to see a large amount of data. Another very effective use of bold fonts is when you have a textured background on your web page template.

- ▲ **Italic (is proportional font based):** While italic fonts can look cool and nifty on most textured backgrounds, they have a habit of looking very misplaced and should be avoided if at all possible.

You can also add the normal time stamp which defines when the page was created.

Using the Web Specific Stored Procedures

The Web Assistant program is a front end for three specific stored procedures available within SQL Server. Using the three stored procedures, you can create your own HTML enabled programs that are not dependent on a periodic occurrence or data change event.

We're reprinting the procedure here courtesy of the SQLServer Book on-line. We've added our own comments to each parameter to help make it a little easier to read.

sp_makewebtask

This stored procedure creates a task that will produce an HTML document. All of the parameters that are used for this stored procedure are defined in the Web Assistant user interface.

```
sp_makewebtask {@outputfile = 'outputfile', @query = 'query'}
[, [@fixedfont = fixedfont,]
[@bold = bold,]
[@italic = italic,]
[@colheaders = colheaders,]
[@lastupdated = lastupdated,]
[@HTMLHeader = HTMLHeader,]
[@username = username,]
[@dbname = dbname,]
[@templatefile = 'templatefile',]
```

```
[@webpagetitle = 'webpagetitle',]
[@resultstitle = 'resultstitle',]
[[@URL = 'URL', @reftext = 'reftext'] |
[@table_urls = table_urls, @url_query = 'url_query',]]
[@whentype = whentype,] [@targetdate = targetdate,]
[@targettime = targettime,]
[@dayflags = dayflags,]
[@numunits = numunits,]
[@unittype = unittype,]
[@procname = procname, ]
[@maketask = maketask,]
[@rowcnt = rowcnt,]
[@tabborder = tabborder,]
[@singlerow = singlerow,] [@blobfmt = blobfmt]]
```

@outputfile(varchar, length < 255): Defines the location of the generated HTML file. It must be unique for each task created.

@query (text,): This specifies the name of the query to run. If you specify multiple selects within the query, multiple tables will be created.

@fixedfont (default = 0, tinyint,): You can toggle this parameter with the value being either 1 meaning use fixed, and 0 not to. The default is 0. The fixed font specifies the way the resulting query data will appear in the HTML page.

@bold (default = 0, tinyint,): This parameter is a toggle between 0 and 1. The default is 0. A value of 1 specifies that that the output data will appear with a bold font.

@italic (default = 0, tinyint,): This parameter is a toggle between 0 and 1. The default is 0. A value of 1 specifies that the output data will appear with an italic font.

@colheaders (default = 1, tinyint,): Specifies that the query results are displayed by default with column headers. The column header names are the names from the database headers.

@lastupdated (default = 1, tinyint,): Specifies whether the generated query output displays a Last Updated. By default, a timestamp is produced.

@HTMLHeader (tinyint,): Specifies the formatting for **@resultstitle** using the HTML header command. Valid values are given in the table below:

Value	HTML Formatting Code
1	H1
2	H2
3	H3
4	H4
5	H5
6	H6

403

@username (varchar, length <= 30): This specifies the username for running the query. The query runs using this user's security attributes.

@dbname (default to current database, varchar, length <= 30): Specifies the name of the database where the query will be run. If this value isn't given it will use the default value.

@templatefile (default web assistant creates a page based on other parameters, varchar, length <= 255): Specifies the name of a template file that is used for dumping the resulting query into. The HTML page is a normal static web page with the exception that it contains another tag `<%insert_data_here%>`. There are two ways to specify the location of the results of a query in a template file:

- ▲ Simply insert the `<%insert_data_here%>` tag to position the query results within the HTML page.

- ▲ Specify a row format between the tags `<%begindetail%>` and `<%enddetail%>` including `<TR>`, `</TR>`, `<TD>` and `</TD>` HTML tags. Each column is displayed in the column using the tag `<%insert_data_here%>` inside the row format keywords. The `@colheaders` keyword is ignored using this format.

> **If this parameter is used then the following parameters are ignored:**
>
> `@bold @singlerow @fixedfont @tabborder @HTMLHeader @table_urls`
> `@italic @URL @lastupdated @url_query @reftext @webpagetitle`
> `@resultstitle`

@webpagetitle (varchar, length <= 255): Specifies the title of the web page that is created by the HTML query.

@resultstitle (varchar, length <= 255): Specifies the title of the query results. This title is displayed just above the results table.

@URL (varchar, length <= 255): Specifies the addition of hyperlink to a HTML page. The hyperlink is located after the query results. By specifying a URL, you must also specify something for `@reftext`. By specifying a value for `@URL` you can't specify a value for `@table_urls` and `@url_query` or vice-versa. If `@table_urls` is specified, then `@url_query` must be included to specify the query to be executed for retrieving hyperlink information, and `@URL` and `@reftext` can't be specified. Information is specified either in `@URL` and `@reftext`, or in `@url_query` and `@table_urls`.

@reftext (varchar, length <= 255): Describes the hyperlink that is specified from the @URL parameter.

@table_urls (tinyint): Specifies whether the HTML page will contain hyperlinks. By default this value is 0, meaning that no hyperlink queries will be generated. Specifying a value of 1 indicates that the list of hyperlinks will be generated using a query referenced by `@url_query`. The hyperlink list is generated using a **SELECT** statement on a SQL Server. If `@table_urls` is specified, then `@url_query` must be included to specify the query to be executed for retrieving hyperlink information, and `@URL` and `@reftext` can't be specified. Information is specified either in `@URL` and `@reftext`, or in `@url_query` and `@table_urls`.

@url_query (varchar, length < 255): Specifies the **SELECT** statement to create the hyperlink text and its accompanying URL. This parameter allows the creation of multiple hyper-links. The **SELECT** statement must return 2 columns. The first column is the address of the hyperlink or URL and the second column is the description of the URL.

@whentype (default = 1, tinyint): Specifies when the query is to be run. The possible values are:

Value	Description
1	The page is created immediately. The sequence of events for this task are creation, execution and deletion.
2	Create the page some time in the future. The sequence of events for this task are creation and then deletion. Execution is deferred until the specified data and time is reached. The time and data is specified by **@targetdate** and **@targettime**. Note that if **@targettime** isn't specified then the web task will default to be executed at 12:00AM or 0:00.
3	The page is created every n days of the week. The day or days is specified by **@dayflags** and the time specified by **@targettime** (optional), beginning with the date in **@targetdate**. Multiple days can be specific. If a **@targettime** value isn't specified, the default is 12:00 am or 0:00. The **@targetdate** parameter is required when **@whentype** is 3. The web task isn't deleted after it has executed. The task needs to deleted using the stored procedure **sp_dropwebtask**.
4	Creates the web page every n periods. Where the periods span minutes, hours, days or weeks. The first document is created at **@targetdata** and **@targettime**. If a **@targettime** value isn't specified, the default is 12:00AM or 0:00. The period of the task is specified by the **@numunits** and **@unittype** parameters. The task needs to be deleted using the stored procedure sp_dropwebtask.
5	Create page upon request. The procedure is created without automatic scheduling. The user creates a HTML document by running **sp_runwebtask** and deletes it only by using **sp_dropwebtask**.
6	Create page immediately and at some period later in time. The later period in time is according to **@whentype** = 2.
7	Create page now and every *n* day(s) of the week. The HTML document is created immediately and recreated according to **@whentype** = 3, except no **@targetdate** is required.
8	Create page now and periodically from then on. The HTML document is created immediately and recreated according to **@whentype** = 4, except that no **@targetdate** is required.
9	Create page now and upon request. The HTML document is created immediately and recreated according to **@whentype** = 5. The task must be deleted manually.

@targetdate (int): Specifies the date of creation for the HTML page. The format is YYYYMMDD. If **@whentype > 3** is true then the **@targetdate** is important. If that date is specified then the current date is used. For **@whentype** = 2 (later), 3 (dayofweek), 4 (periodic), and 6 (now and later), the **@targetdate** parameter is required.

@targettime (int): Specifies the time of creation for the HTML page. When a starting time is important but not supplied, 12:00AM is the default. The format is HHMMSS. The **targettime** variable is of **int** datatype.

@**dayflags** (**tinyint**): Specifies on what days to create the HTML page. Multiple days are specified by adding the value together. For example, specifying the days Monday and Thursday, the parameter becomes 18. This parameter is required for **@whentype** = 3 (dayofweek), **@whentype** = 7 (now and dayofweek); and in cases in which **@whentype** = 4 (periodic) and **@whentype** = 8 (now and periodic) where the **@unittype** = 3 (weeks). These are the values and their descriptions.

Value	Day of Week
1	Sunday
2	Monday
4	Tuesday
8	Wednesday
16	Thursday
32	Friday
64	Saturday

@**numunits** (**tinyint, 1 <= value <= 255**): Specify how often to create the HTML page. This parameter is used only when **@whentype** = 4 (periodic) or **@whentype** = 8 (now and periodically thereafter). For example, if **@whentype** = 4, **@numunits** = 6, and **@unittype** = 1 (hours), the specified HTML document will be updated every six hours.

@**unittype** (**tinyint**): Specifies the frequency of HTML page create when @numunits = 4 (periodic) or **@whentype** = 8 (now and later). Use 1 (hours), 2 (days), 3 (weeks), or 4 (minutes). The **unittype** variable is of **tinyint** datatype.

@**procname** (**varchar, length <= 28**): Specifies the procedure or task name for the HTML page. If no **@procname** is specified, the procedure name generated by **sp_makewebtask** is in the form of **Web_YYMMDDHHMMSS<spid>**. If it's user-specified, the procedure name must meet the conditions for valid procedure names and the procedure name must be unique.

> **If you use the Web Assistant to create the task, it will use the default name formatting.**

@**maketask** (**tinyint, default is 1**): Specifies whether a task should be created to execute an internal stored procedure that generates an HTML document. A value 1 builds the task, while 0 creates a stored procedure to build the task.

@**rowcnt** (**int, default to display all of the results**): Specifies the maximum number of rows to display in the generated HTML page. The default is to specify that all rows that satisfy the given query will be displayed in the HTML document (0). The **rowcnt** variable is of **int** datatype.

@**tabborder** (**tinyint, default is 1**): Specifies whether a border should be drawn around the results table. The default is to draw a border. 0 specifies that no border should be drawn.

@singlerow (**tinyint, default is** 0): Specifies whether the results are to be displayed as one row per page. By default, all results appear on one page. With a value of 1, **@singlerow** causes a new HTML page to be generated for every qualifying row in the results set. Successive HTML pages are generated with a number appended to the specified **output_filename**. For example, if **web.html** is specified as the output filename, by using **@singlerow** = 1, pages are called **web1.html**, **web2.html**, and so on. The **singlerow** variable is of **tinyint** datatype.

@blobfmt (**image or text, default is NULL**): Specifies whether all columns of **text** or **image** datatypes should be embedded in the same results page, by default, or whether these fields should be saved in another page and linked to the main HTML document by an URL. To place the *text* or *image* data in a separate HTML page, use the following format:

```
"%n%    FILE=output_filename    TPLT=template_filename
            URL=url_link_name..."
```

where:

> **n** is the column number in the results list corresponding to a text field, and **n+1** is the URL hyperlink text to the separate text or image HTML file. If a **template_filename** is provided, the **<%insert_data_here%>** marker should be used to indicate the data insertion point.

Output filenames end with a number indicating successive rows similar to **@singlerow**. The **output_filename** parameter is required, but the **template_filename** and **url_link_name** parameters are optional. The **FILE output_filename** is the full path to the **output_file** location. If provided, the **url_link_name** is the http:// link to the file that is accessible through the World Wide Web. If the **url_link_name** parameter isn't provided, then the full physical filename preceded with the "file:///" tag will be used as the **url_link_name**. The same syntax in **@blobfmt ("%n% FILE=...")** can be repeated for multiple **text** or **image** columns.

> **Do not add spaces before or after the equal sign (=) and don't put filenames in quotation marks (').**

This stored procedure reports all of its errors in the Windows NT event log under the application event list. The source of the events are entitled **xpsqlweb**.

sp_dropwebtask

Used to delete an already defined web task. The task can be referenced by the output filename, procedure name, or by using a combination of both parameters. To delete the web task, the task must reside in the same database from where the stored procedure is called.

sp_dropwebtask {@procname = *procname* | **@outputfile** = *outputfile* | **@procname** = *procname*, **@outputfile** = *outputfile*}

where:

> **@outputfile** (**varchar, length** <= 255): Specifies the name of the web task to be deleted.

> **@procname** (**varchar, length** <= 255): Specifies the name of the web task procedure to delete. The named procedure describes the query for the web task.

sp_runwebtask

Executes a previously defined web task and creates the HTML page. The task to be run can be identified by the output filename, procedure name, or by a combination of the two parameters. The web task to be run must exist in the same database as specified by the **@dbname** parameter of **sp_makewebtask**.

```
sp_runwebtask {@procname = procname | @outputfile = outputfile |
@procname = procname, @outputfile = outputfile}
```

where:

> **@outputfile (varchar, length <= 255)**: Specifies the name of the web task to run.

> **@procname (varchar, length <= 28)**: Specifies the name of the web task procedure to run. The named procedure defines the query for the web task.

These are your raw tools for setting some basic page creation schemes going. For really fancy HTML tricks, you have to read a book on the present standard (2.0 or 3.2?) and also have something like 'Front Page' ready while reading it.

Meanwhile, we are going to try and stretch the envelope of Web Assistant and push it to do a simple version of a larger concern. This is a perfect use for an hermetic information 'pull' machine such as SQL Server.

Example: Preparing a Mini-data Warehouse

A data warehouse isn't an operational database (OLTP). It's the following things:

▲ **Subject oriented**: The data is organized specifically according to the requirements of the end users. That means that the data is typically de-normalized.

▲ **Very big**: The data warehouse is used for statistical purposes and ancient data history.

▲ **Not necessarily the same format**: Because of the ages the data warehouse spans, it does not necessarily mean that all of the data uses the same criteria.

▲ **Not necessarily the same schema**: The original transactional database evolves and the original schema evolves, and the data warehouse must adapt.

▲ **A synopsis**: A good data warehouse is a little like the cheat book of 'War & Peace'. Typically, data is too vast for anyone to look at it and see any trends, so instead the data must be compressed and summarized.

▲ **And it integrates data from many sources**.

Looking back to the opening paragraph to this chapter we see that, in fact, a data warehouse is an informational database and, as such, using Web Assistant is a perfect mini-data warehouse builder. Why mini-data warehouse? Web Assistant is only good for SQL Server and is on a per database dependency.

Users

The DBA knows which database generates the most traffic and which causes the most headache. The users of the databases are simply in tune with the data–let them take charge of their own databases.

Splitting the Database

The data warehouse should under no circumstance reside on the same database as the production machine.

Because we are building a mini-data warehouse, we use the SQL Server replication method. The advantage of using an automatic replication is that combining this with an HTML update, it becomes a complete self contained system. We will be using a distribution replication mechanism for our data warehouse. This method is outlined in the following diagram.

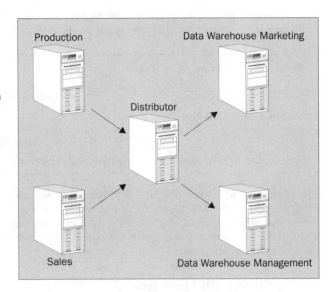

Looking at the above diagram we see that sales and production are the productive OLTP databases, and that both databases will publish to the Distributor which allows subscribers. We're basically in sound form to continue as we have:

▲   Database independence

▲   Replication resources are minimized

▲   Central knowledge of what data does exist within the corporation

So, split the database as normal (see Chapter 11 for much more):

1   Open the SQL Enterprise manager and logon as sa.

2   Check to make sure all databases (local and remote) are registered with the local SQL Enterprise manager. If not then all the databases need to be added. If some databases can't be added because they do not exist then create them.

3   Publishing needs to be installed. Check the Server->Replication tool.   A dialog box will appear with all currently registered servers.

4   Select the production databases and enable them to be subscribing servers.

5   Set the replication not to be continuous, and set it to a time when resources are not required.

6   Set the Distribution database to be subscribed to all.

7   Set the Distribution database to be a Replication Distribution database.

Finally, subscribe the data warehouses to the Distribution database.

And there you have it, a replication scheme for your data warehouse. Create the individual databases for a small example. As with the pubs, we could implement it as follows:

Type	Name	Tables
Production	Publisher	employee, jobs, pub_info, publishers
Distribution	Distributor	titleview
Production	Stores	sales(title id is replaced with reference to titleview.title), stores, discount
Production	Authors	authors, titles, titleauthor, roysched

The pubs database, which was one only, has now been split into three production databases with one table being created on the Distribution. The purpose of creating this table is that it is in fact a pseudo 'data warehouse'. The two tables that reference this table are sales and titleview. These two tables are history tables. That means that it does not matter whether the reference to the title exists or does not exist, because it did at some time.

Performance and Net traffic

Net performance, i.e. Network, Intranet or Internet, is an important item to consider when building any data warehouse example. Some easy tips are:

▲   Send SQL commands and not data.

▲   Use a time based replication–continuous update will follow peak traffic and give you a double headache.

▲   Have the replicated data & HTTP servers on a different network loop to your Intranet users so it'll be easier to make sure that they get to talk to each other at high speed.

Performance Monitor

Performance monitor is a regular haunt for DBAs analysing the NT and/or the SQL Server statistics. The good news is that there's a set of performance counters for Microsoft's Internet Information Server (IIS) as well. As you get IIS with NT4, and Web Assistant is only valid (at present) on the Intel Server platforms, then this Web Server is a natural choice to run your initial experiments in publishing on a 'net. Between your various performance counters you can plan for reasonable hardware upgrades and data replication times for your data site.

Creating the Data Warehouse

Now we have come to the stage of setting up our data warehouse. The data warehouse computer should contain both the database and the HTTP server. This suggestion may run contrary to security requirements, but the point with creating a distributed data warehouse is that only the data to be published is stored. Therefore, if anyone does happen to break into the server, only data that is already published will be available.

Select a Web Server

The web server that you use is irrelevant to Web Assistant. Web Assistant generates HTML pages and therefore does not need to know what the web server is. It's even possible, using technology like NFS or SAMBA, to write files that will be used by a UNIX-based HTML server.

What Things Do We Want to See?

Looking at our Pubs example for the database, we would like to see answers to the following questions:

- Which store orders the most?
- Which publisher brings in the largest revenue?
- Which publisher has the best revenue to profitability ratio (a volume author may bring revenue, but not a large amount of profitability)?
- Which store brings in the most profitability in terms of books ordered and the cost of those books?

All of these are queries that can be repeated time after time. Comparing these queries on a period basis allows us to monitor our progress or loss.

Using the Web Assistant to Build a Revenue Query

Let's use web assistant to build a query that will show what our revenue has been for the past 2 years. We will start with a very simple query and then show more complex examples of the same query.

A Simple Query

What is the revenue made for the past 2 years? The query is as follows:

```
SELECT sales.stor_id, sales.ord_num, sales.ord_date, sales.qty,
sales.title_id, titles.price, (qty * price)
FROM titles INNER JOIN sales ON titles.title_id = sales.title_id
WHERE DATEDIFF(year, ord_date, getdate()) < 3
ORDER BY stor_id, sales.ord_date
```

We use the **DATADIFF** function that compares the date of sales function with the current date. If this difference is less than 3 years then we have found a record. The query is created using the web assistant and cutting and pasting this **SELECT** into the free form text query.

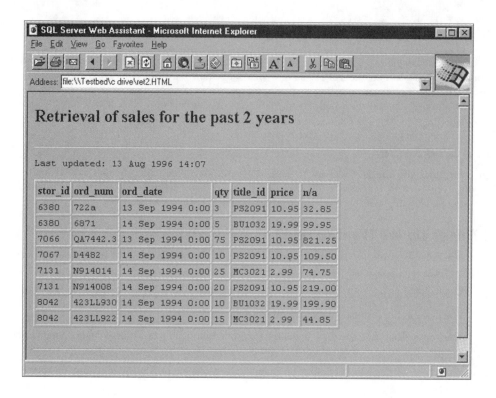

Creating a Stored Procedure

Now, instead of using Web Assistant to create that query, let's create the same query, except using the stored procedure **sp_webmaketask**. Try inserting this query as arguments in your "Use query in stored procedure" selection. Remember the procedure is in the Master database, and to copy the template file **simple.tpl** to a suitable directory (e.g. c:\web\simple.tpl).

```
@outputfile = 'C:\WEB\SIMPLE.HTM',
@query = 'SELECT sales.stor_id, sales.ord_num, sales.ord_date, sales.qty,
sales.title_id, titles.price, (qty * price)
FROM titles INNER JOIN sales ON titles.title_id = sales.title_id
WHERE DATEDIFF(year, ord_date, getdate()) < 3
ORDER BY stor_id, sales.ord_date',
@templatefile = 'C:\WEB\SIMPLE.TPL',
@dbname = 'PUBS',
@whentype = 9
```

This stored procedure can be called at the ISQL level and will generate the same results as the web page before. The only difference is that a specific web page has been specified. Our web page template file looks like the following:

```
<HTML>
  <HEAD>
  <TITLE>SQL Server Queries</TITLE>
```

```
  <BODY>
  <H1>Hey yet another query </H1>
<HR>
<P>
<%insert_data_here%>
</BODY>
</HTML>
```

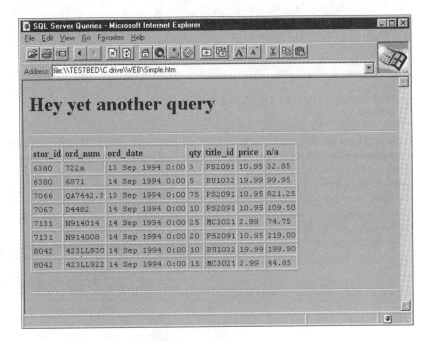

This is an example of the simplest possible template file. The query results are inserted in the section where it says **<%insert_data_here%>**. The output looks as follows on any browser:

Using a Stored Procedure with Specific Formatting

Let's add proper formatting for each element of the query result. In the previous example, our template dumped all of the data in one location. The output is ready for a customized template file. Ensure you replace **simple.tpl** with the new script below before running **sp_webmaketask** again.

```
<HTML>
<HEAD>
<TITLE>SQL Server Queries</TITLE>
<BODY>
<H1>Same ol' query</H1>
<HR>
<P>
<TABLE BORDER>
<TR>
<TH><I>Store Id</I></TH>
<TH><B>Order Number</B></TH>
<TH><B>Order Date</B></TH>
<TH><B>Quantity</B></TH>
<TH><B>Title Id</B></TH>
<TH><B>Price/Book</B></TH>
```

413

```
<TH><B>Total Price</B></TH>
</TR>
<%begindetail%>
<TR>
<TD><I><%insert_data_here%></I> </TD>
<TD><%insert_data_here%></TD>
<TD><%insert_data_here%></TD>
<TD><B><%insert_data_here%></B></TD>
<TD><%insert_data_here%></TD>
<TD>$<%insert_data_here%></TD>
<TD><B>$<%insert_data_here%></B></TD>
</TR>
<%enddetail%>
</TABLE>
<P>
</BODY>
</HTML>
```

Looking closer at this improved template, we have two new keywords: **<%begindetail%>** and
<%enddetail%>. These keywords define the beginning and end boundary for the results query.

Looking back to the original query, we see that it generates seven columns of output. Therefore, in our
template we must add the keyword **<%insert_data_here%>** seven times. Each keyword instance
represents a column. The tag **<TR>** refers to a row which is used by the web assistant when generating the
table.

Our example output
therefore looks like that
opposite, in any browser.

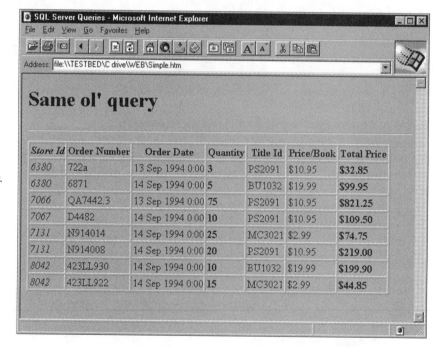

Creating a Page with Multiple Queries

We have created a page that uses one query, now we would like to create a web page display using multiple queries. Currently, our revenue stream is only defined for a year. Instead, we will create a query that displays year 2 and year 3. To do this, we must again modify the stored procedure and the template file:

```
@outputfile = 'C:\WEB\SIMPLE.HTM',
@query = 'SELECT sales.stor_id, sales.ord_num, sales.ord_date, sales.qty,
sales.title_id, titles.price, (qty * price)
FROM titles INNER JOIN sales ON titles.title_id = sales.title_id
WHERE DATEDIFF(year, ord_date, getdate()) = 2
ORDER BY stor_id, sales.ord_date
SELECT sales.stor_id, sales.ord_num, sales.ord_date, sales.qty, sales.title_id,
titles.price, (qty * price)
FROM titles INNER JOIN sales ON titles.title_id = sales.title_id
WHERE DATEDIFF(year, ord_date, getdate()) = 3
ORDER BY stor_id, sales.ord_date',
@templatefile = 'C:\WEB\SIMPLE.TPL',
@dbname = 'PUBS',
@whentype = 9
```

Adding multiple queries is very simple with the parameter **@query**. The **@query** parameter has multiple **SELECT** statements contained within it. Each select statement refers to one result set. The template file should look as follows:

```
<HTML>
<HEAD>
<TITLE>SQL Server Multiple Queries</TITLE>
<BODY>
<H1>Same ol' query</H1>
<HR>
<H2>Year 1</H2>
<P>
<TABLE BORDER>
<TR>
<TH><I>Store Id</I></TH>
<TH><B>Order Number</B></TH>
<TH><B>Order Date</B></TH>
<TH><B>Quantity</B></TH>
<TH><B>Title Id</B></TH>
<TH><B>Price/Book</B></TH>
<TH><B>Total Price</B></TH>
</TR>
<%begindetail%>
<TR>
<TD><I><%insert_data_here%></I> </TD>
<TD><%insert_data_here%></TD>
<TD><%insert_data_here%></TD>
<TD><B><%insert_data_here%></B></TD>
<TD><%insert_data_here%></TD>
<TD>$<%insert_data_here%></TD>
```

```
<TD><B>$<%insert_data_here%></B></TD>
</TR>
<%enddetail%>
</TABLE>
<P>
<H2>Year 2</H2>
<TABLE BORDER>
<TR>
<TH><I>Store Id</I></TH>
<TH><B>Order Number</B></TH>
<TH><B>Order Date</B></TH>
<TH><B>Quantity</B></TH>
<TH><B>Title Id</B></TH>
<TH><B>Price/Book</B></TH>
<TH><B>Total Price</B></TH>
</TR>
<%begindetail%>
<TR>
<TD><I><%insert_data_here%></I> </TD>
<TD><%insert_data_here%></TD>
<TD><%insert_data_here%></TD>
<TD><B><%insert_data_here%></B></TD>
<TD><%insert_data_here%></TD>
<TD>$<%insert_data_here%></TD>
<TD><B>$<%insert_data_here%></B></TD>
</TR>
<%enddetail%>
</TABLE>
<P>
</BODY>
</HTML>
```

The template contains 2 instances of **<%begindetail%>** and **<%enddetail%>**.

Each tag defines a boundary. Using the multiple queries you must be aware that each result set is bounded with **<%begindetail%>** and **<%enddetail%>** or a single **<%insert_data_here%>**.

The resulting output set looks as follows:

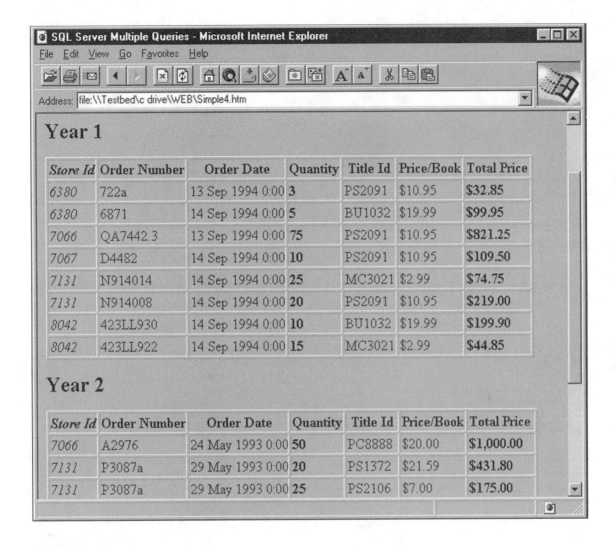

Summary

With this final chapter, we have learned to build read only queries and have retrieved data using Web Assistant from SQL Server. With NT4 comes the really powerful 'Front Page' HTML editing suite and the prospect of hundreds of DBAs using thousands of hours to build useful and slick-looking Web Data pages. Well, as long as the databases run themselves and nobody wants a new report for the next 6 months, that'll be fine. In reality, this is a great tool to use to get Intranet pages published quickly, while you're fixing yet another bottleneck on those order transactions... and maybe, just maybe, the way to encourage M.I.S. departments to stop using so many trees. As far as the Internet's concerned, well, you've got to get your Merchant service up and running by next week!

6.5

Transact-SQL Tutorial

SQL (Structured Query Language) is a standard language used to access and manipulate relational databases. SQL can be used to query a database, manipulate information in database tables and create and change the database structure, among other things. Although SQL is standardized, many versions of SQL contain vendor-supplied extensions and alterations. Transact-SQL is the SQL language variety that is used to communicate with SQL Server.

This section isn't intended to be a comprehensive treatment of Transact-SQL. In fact, only a limited subset of Transact-SQL statements are presented here. Those missing statements are covered elsewhere in this text and in the Microsoft documentation. This section will demonstrate the use of Transact-SQL and its programming constructs and will aid you in using the system documentation and other resources. Before you start, there are three items that you should have:

- You should have a basic knowledge of Structured Query Language. This tutorial will provide some introductory material, but if you require a more detailed introduction to SQL then *Instant SQL Programming*, written by Joe Celko and published by Wrox Press, should meet your needs.

- You should have access to the Microsoft Transact-SQL documentation. Either the printed manual or SQL Server Books Online is sufficient.

- You should have installed the **pubs** database and Interactive SQL for Windows (ISQL/w) or Enterprise Manager. If you haven't loaded the **pubs** database and the SQL Server Client Tools, you should do so before continuing.

Programming with Transact-SQL

If you have limited past SQL experience, you might view SQL as simply **SELECT**, **INSERT**, **UPDATE** and **DELETE** statements used to query and manipulate data. If you have additional experience, you may have the view that SQL is a restrictive database creation and data query tool and not what you consider a programming language in the full sense of the phrase. However, with Microsoft SQL Server Transact-SQL whatever your view, you might just be in for a pleasant surprise.

Microsoft SQL Server Transact-SQL has a comprehensive set of SQL statements, an extensive list of functions and system stored procedures and a fairly rich set of programming extensions that make it a considerable programming language.

SQL itself can actually be broken up into three sublanguages: the Data Manipulation Language(DML), the Data Definition Language(DDL) and the Data Control Language(DCL), each of which fulfills a different function.

▲ DML is used to query and manipulate the data in a database but it can't be used to change the structure of the database.

▲ DDL allows you to create, change and delete database structures.

▲ DCL enables you to control security permissions on statements and tables and views.

We'll explore each subsection of the SQL language separately in this appendix. In between, we'll look at language extensions and treatments of some of the more complex aspects of the language.

Statement Syntax

The conventions used for syntax in this appendix and in the book as a whole follow those used in the SQL Server documentation and SQL Server Books Online. Most of them should be self-evident, but here are a couple of reminders:

▲ Braces **{parameter}**, are used to indicate required parameters.

▲ Brackets **[parameter]**, are used to indicate optional parameters.

▲ The pipe, **|**, is used to indicate a choice must be made between competing parameters, e.g. **[parameter_choice1]| [parameter_choice2]**.

Capitalization

The SQL examples shown here have the Transact-SQL keywords capitalized for demonstration purposes and to be consistent with the Microsoft documentation. You don't need to capitalize the keywords. To SQL Server **select** is the same as **SELECT**.

Capitalization is also used to indicate a required part of a keyword. For example, the keyword **EXECute** indicates that only **EXEC** is required and the rest of the keyword is optional.

Lists

It's often the case that either a name or a list of names can be used in Transact-SQL statements. Such an option is shown in the syntax example as,

VERB OBJECT_TYPE {*object_name* | *object_list*}

where *object_list* would be a comma-delimited list of object names.

For example, the **DROP DATABASE** statement's syntax is:

DROP DATABASE {*database_name* | *database_list*}

The syntax example clearly indicates that you can specify a single database or a list of databases in this statement.

To **DROP** a single database, you would write the statement as:

```
DROP DATABASE myFirstDB
```

A similar example that uses a list in order to **DROP** multiple databases would be written as:

```
DROP DATABASE myFirstDB, mySecondDB, myThirdDB
```

Example Databases

The SQL examples shown here use the **pubs** database and a **test_pubs** database. The **pubs** database is provided with SQL Server to provide a sample database. Most books use **pubs** for demonstration purposes. As some of the examples provided are intended to modify the contents of the database we will use another database, the **test_pubs** database. This is created during the course of the tutorial and is utilized whenever structural modifications to the database or content modification to the tables need to be demonstrated.

ISQL/w

Although SQL statements can be submitted to SQL Server from a variety of programming languages and sources, for the purpose of this tutorial, you should use the Interactive SQL for Windows (ISQL/w). The ISQL/w tool can be used to establish connections to SQL Server and run SQL statements, groups of statements called scripts and stored procedures. This is an alternative to the SQL Query Tool in the Enterprise Manager.

You can invoke ISQL/w from the Client Tools program group on a client or from the SQL Tools program group on the server.

If you open an ISQL/w window, you'll be presented with this screen:

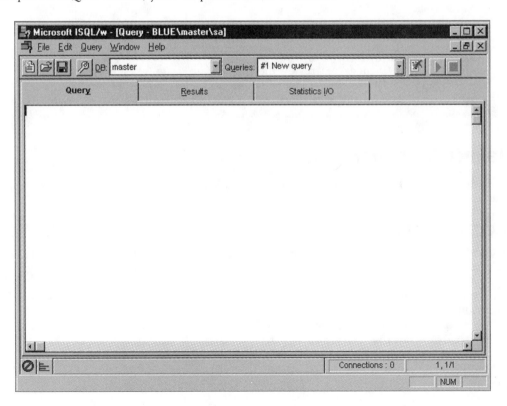

The central window of ISQL/w is a tabbed dialogue box with three tabs. The Query tab is the window you use to prepare your Transact-SQL query. The Results tab is a window that contains the results of executing your query. The central tab window is surrounded by the tool bar and status bar. The tool bar, at the top of the screen, displays various tool icons and two drop-down list boxes. The DB drop-down box in the ISQL/w window contains master and the Queries box contains #1 New query.

On the right side of the toolbar there is a green arrow that points to the right. This is the Execute Query button.

The status bar at the bottom shows the number of open connections. In this example, there are no connections currently open. You can have multiple queries and multiple connections open.

> It's important to note that each ISQL/w connection counts as a connection to SQL Server. It's possible, depending on your server configuration, that you won't be able to open another connection. Be aware of the number of connections you have.

Data Definition Language (DDL)

The primary DDL statements are **CREATE**, **ALTER** and **DROP** statements but there are different DDL statements for each object type. For example, there are **CREATE TABLE** and **CREATE RULE** statements. Although they are both **CREATE** statements and they act on two very different database objects, they don't share a common syntax.

> It's important that you have an understanding of SQL Server data types. Before you undertake any DDL endeavors, review the appropriate sections in this book and the SQL Server documentation. Demonstrations in this tutorial will be limited to a small subset of the available data types.

Database Statements

The first segment of the DDL that we'll consider are the database creation, alteration and destruction statements.

CREATE DATABASE

The **CREATE DATABASE** statement creates a new database. You must be in the master database to create a new database.

```
CREATE DATABASE  database_name
[ON {DEFAULT | database_device} [= size]
     [, database_device [= size]]...]
[LOG ON database_device [= size]
     [, database_device [= size]]...]
[FOR LOAD]
```

To create a new database for the tutorial examples, you can use the DDL statement **CREATE DATABASE**. Change the ISQL/w DB drop-down box to master and enter SQL statements in the Query window as shown below.

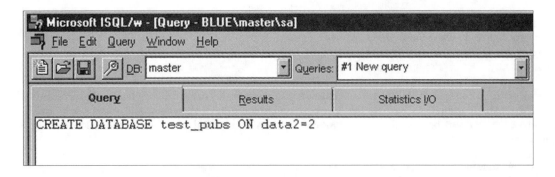

> You should specify any device on your system that has 2MB of space available. If no device has 2MB available, you will have to create a new device before proceeding. Because the following example requires an additional 1MB, you can save time by allocating the 2MB on a device that has at least 3MB available.

When this statement is executed, SQL Server creates a 2MB database named **test_pubs** on the device **data2**. When you click on the Execute Query button in the tool bar (or *Alt-x*) the Results tab in ISQL/w displays the results of the query as shown:

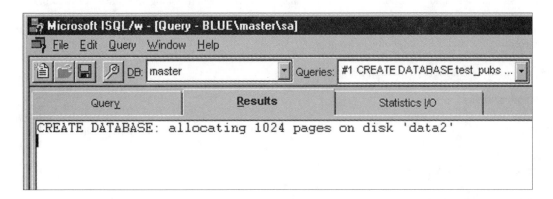

The message displayed in the Results tab refers to 1024 2K pages required for the 2MB allocation.

ALTER DATABASE

The **ALTER DATABASE** statement is used to increase the amount of device space that a database occupies. The statement syntax is:

```
ALTER DATABASE  database_name
[ON {DEFAULT |  database_device} [= size]
[,  database_device [= size]]...]
[FOR LOAD]
```

The size that you specify in the **ALTER DATABASE** statement is the size of the increase, not the size of the entire database allocation. To increase the **test_pubs** database to 3MB, you would specify only 1MB in the **ALTER DATABASE** because the initial **CREATE DATABASE** allocated 2MB. Enter the following SQL statement:

```
ALTER DATABASE test_pubs on data2=1
```

After the **ALTER** statement is executed, the message Extending database by 512 pages on disk data2 is returned informing you of the amount, in 2K pages, that the database was extended on the device:

DROP DATABASE

The **DROP DATABASE** statement is used to delete a database from SQL Server. The syntax for this statement is:

```
DROP DATABASE {database_name |  database_list}
```

Only the database owner (dbo), the person who created the database, is allowed to issue the **DROP DATABASE** statement and the dbo must be in the master database when issuing the **DROP DATABASE**.

Once you've dropped a database, you can only recover it by recreating it from backups. The database, its associated objects and its storage areas are gone.

This statement is effective for dropping a single database:

```
DROP DATABASE x
```

To drop several databases, you would use the next statement. It also demonstrates the list option in the syntax:

```
DROP DATABASE x, y, z
```

Now run the following drop operation for the **test_pubs** database:

```
DROP DATABASE test_pubs
```

The statement results in a message stating This command did not return data, and it did not return any rows. No rows of data were returned in a result set because the **DROP DATABASE** statement doesn't return data. No error messages were returned either. This message usually means that what you wanted to execute did so without generating any error messages.

There is one instance where you may misinterpret this message. Examine the ISQL/w window shown:

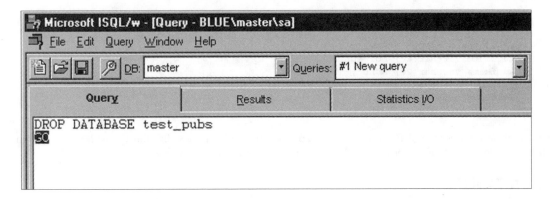

Note that GO is highlighted. (**GO** is a simple directive to SQL Server to execute the statements that preceded the **GO**.) If this query is executed, only the highlighted statements are sent to SQL Server for execution. Only the GO is executed in this case and the resulting message, This command did not return data, and it did not return any rows, gives no indication that only some of the statements in the window were executed. The database is not dropped. Be careful to avoid inadvertent selections.

Before continuing, recreate the **test_pubs** database with the following statement:

```
CREATE DATABASE test_pubs ON data2=3
```

Table Statements

Tables are the basic entity for data storage within a database. They are composed of columns and rows. The Transact-SQL DDL contains various statements for creating and manipulating tables.

CREATE TABLE

The **CREATE TABLE** statement is used to direct SQL Server to create a table in a particular database. The table is described by its columns and the data type associated with that column.

The syntax of the **CREATE TABLE** statement is:

```
CREATE TABLE [database.[owner].]table_name
(
    {col_name column_properties [constraint [constraint [...constraint]]]
    | [[,] constraint]}
        [[,] {next_col_name | next_constraint}...]
)
```

Assume there's a need for a separate table to record the last date an author was contacted by an editor. You need to create a table, called Author_contact, containing five columns: ac_id, au_lname, au_fname, contact_date and editor.

```
USE test_pubs
GO

CREATE TABLE author_contact
(
    ac_id int NOT NULL IDENTITY ,
    au_lname varchar(40) NOT NULL ,
    au_fname varchar(20) NULL ,
    contact_date smalldatetime NULL ,
    editor varchar(40) NULL
)
```

The **IDENTITY** property is defined for the **ac_id** column. This indicates that the values for this column will be maintained by the system to produce a unique identifier for every row.

ALTER TABLE

To change an existing table without deleting columns, you use the **ALTER TABLE** statement. This is the syntax:

```
ALTER TABLE [database.[owner].]table_name
[WITH NOCHECK]
[ADD
    {col_name column_properties [column_constraints]
    | [[,] table_constraint]}
        [, {next_col_name | next_table_constraint}]...]
|
[DROP [CONSTRAINT]
    constraint_name [, constraint_name2]...]
```

If you needed to add a 'response' column to the Author_contact table, you could do so with this example:

```
USE test_pubs
GO

ALTER TABLE author_contact
ADD
response varchar(40) NULL
```

DROP TABLE

The **DROP TABLE** statement deletes a table and its data from the database. It also drops associated indexes, constraints and triggers. Rules are unbound from the table but are not dropped.

```
DROP TABLE [[database.]owner.]table_name
[, [[database.]owner.]table_name...]
```

To drop a table:

```
DROP TABLE newauthors
```

To drop a table when you're in a different database:

```
DROP TABLE pubs.dbo.newauthors
```

Default Statements

A default specifies the value that will be inserted into a column if no other value is supplied. It's an object that's associated (bound) to either a user-defined datatype or a column.

> See **DEFAULT** elsewhere in this text or in the SQL Server documentation for further information.

CREATE DEFAULT

The syntax of the **CREATE DEFAULT** statement is:

```
CREATE DEFAULT [owner.]default_name
AS constant_expression
```

You place the default on the response column in two steps:

- ▲ Create the default.
- ▲ Bind the default, or associate it, to a particular column.

The default is an object that exists in the database independent of any table columns. This allows you to create a single object and bind it to multiple columns in multiple tables.

If there was a typical response from an author, you might want to place a default on the response column in the Author_contact table to add that response, if no response was given. It would be more efficient in place of the NULLS you would otherwise get. You could do this with:

```
CREATE DEFAULT respdflt as 'Offered endless lame excuses'
GO
sp_bindefault respdflt, 'author_contact.response'
GO
```

If the statement is successful, the message Default Bound to Column will be displayed in the results window.

> You probably noticed that the CREATE DEFAULT statement is followed by a GO statement and then **sp_bindefault**. The GO statement forces the execution of the CREATE DEFAULT statement before the system stored procedure, **sp_bindefault**, is executed. The GO statement is discussed later in the SQL Batching section and system stored procedures are also treated later.

DROP DEFAULT

The **DROP DEFAULT** statement deletes a user-defined default from a database.

```
DROP DEFAULT [owner.]default_name [, [owner.]default_name...]
```

> Before issuing the DROP DEFAULT statement, you must first unbind it with the
> sp_unbindefault system stored procedure.

To unbind and drop the default **respdflt**:

```
sp_unbindefault 'author_contact.response'
go
DROP DEFAULT respdflt
```

The **DROP DEFAULT** statement is relatively simple. As such, it doesn't really warrant treatment beyond
what is supplied in the system documentation. However, we can use it to further illustrate the need to
think about what you're doing at all times. Not thinking about the potential effects of what you're doing is
the cause of most SQL programming errors. The **DROP DEFAULT** command is a perfect example. If you
don't use it sensibly, it will result in an error being returned from a subsequent **INSERT** action.

The problem stems from the fact that columns can be declared so that they accept or reject NULL values.
If you dropped the default on a column that accepted NULL value then NULL values would become the
default for that column. If the column value is not specified on a subsequent **INSERT**, the column would
get NULL values inserted. Everything would work.

If, however, you dropped the default on a column that can't accept NULL then SQL Server has no
alternative but to issue an error message. What value should be entered in that column if the value is not
explicitly stated? If it can't be NULL, how can SQL Server possibly choose a value?

You should always consider all of the potential side-effects of dropping any part of the database, not just
the tables.

Data Manipulation Language (DML)

While the DML can't be used to change the actual structure of the database, it can be used to do
practically everything else, from inserting new data and keeping the database up to date, to running any
kind of query against the database. Despite the wide-ranging nature of these tasks, data manipulation in
SQL Server is accomplished by only four statements: **SELECT**, **INSERT**, **UPDATE** and **DELETE**.

SELECT

The **SELECT** statement is the fundamental SQL statement. If any single statement can be said to embody
the spirit of SQL it must be the **SELECT** statement. It's through the **SELECT** statement that data is
returned. You should commit the format of the **SELECT** statement to memory (especially if you're
intending to take the Microsoft certification exams.)

The format of the **SELECT** statement is:

```
SELECT [ALL | DISTINCT] select_list
     [INTO [new_table_name]]
[FROM {table_name_1 | view_name_1}[(optimizer_hints)]
     [[, {table_name_2 | view_name_2}[(optimizer_hints)]
     [..., {table_name_16 | view_name_16}[(optimizer_hints)]]]
[WHERE clause]
[GROUP BY clause]
[HAVING clause]
[ORDER BY clause]
[COMPUTE clause]
[FOR BROWSE]
```

The format looks complex at first glance but, as with most languages, what you can do is not necessarily what you will do. For example, you can see from the format that you can specify up to 16 tables or views in a single **SELECT** statement. Ordinarily, you won't access that many tables.

The majority of data retrieval statements that you'll use will probably be relatively simple. You might return all rows and columns or a subset of rows and columns from a table and you might want to sort the result of your query. In that case, *select_list* specifies which columns are to be returned and the **WHERE** clause determines the rows. The **ORDER BY** clause determines the sort order of the results.

Here are several examples of simple **SELECT**s that use the pubs database.

To return all the rows and columns of the authors table:

```
SELECT * FROM authors
```

> The asterisk is a wildcard character that is used instead of specifying each column name separately. Here, it means all columns in the table specified in the FROM clause.

To return just the first and last name from the authors table:

```
SELECT au_fname, au_lname FROM authors
```

To return just the first and last name from the authors table for authors who live in California:

```
SELECT au_fname, au_lname FROM authors WHERE state = 'CA'
```

To return just the first and last name from the Authors table for authors who live in California and sort by name (ascending):

```
SELECT au_fname, au_lname FROM authors WHERE state = 'CA' ORDER BY au_lname, au_fname
```

To create a new table, **author_name**, containing just the first and last name from the Authors table:

```
SELECT au_fname, au_lname INTO author_name FROM authors
```

> The previous statement can't be executed without SELECT...INTO authority. See
> sp_dboption later in this appendix.

JOINS

The **SELECT** examples up to this point all accessed a single table to retrieve the requested rows. It's more often the case that the data you want to retrieve exists in several tables. The **JOIN** statement allows you to **SELECT** from multiple tables to produce a single result set of rows. The **JOIN** syntax (in the context of the **SELECT** syntax) is:

```
SELECT ...
    [FROM {table_name | view_name}
    [CROSS | INNER | LEFT [OUTER] | RIGHT [OUTER] | FULL [OUTER]]
    JOIN {table_name | view_name}
    [ON search_condition]
```

There are several types of **JOINS**.

Cross Joins

A **CROSS JOIN** is the product of two tables. Each row of the first table is joined with every row of the second table. There is no **WHERE** clause to restrict the number of rows involved. This produces a Cartesian product that is, in most circumstances, useless. To create a cross product of publishers and stores:

```
SELECT pub_name, stor_name FROM publishers CROSS JOIN stores
```

Inner Joins

An **INNER JOIN** returns only the rows of the first table and those rows of the second table that match. To create a list of stores that had sales:

```
SELECT stor_name FROM stores INNER JOIN sales ON stores.stor_id = sales.stor_id
```

To create list of authors and the books they wrote:

```
SELECT a.au_lname, a.au_fname, t.title
FROM authors a
INNER JOIN titleauthor ta ON a.au_id = ta.au_id
INNER JOIN titles t ON ta.title_id = t.title_id
ORDER BY a.au_lname, a.au_fname, t.title
```

This example required three tables to obtain the requested information. The intermediate table, **titleauthor**, was required to link the authors with the titles they wrote.

This example also demonstrates the use of table aliases. Table aliases are used to simplify the SQL so that it's easier to write, maintain and debug. Instead of qualifying the **au_id** column of the authors table with the full table name, **authors.au_id**, you can specify an alias and use that instead as in **a.au_id**. The other tables in the example are also aliased.

There's only one thing to remember about table aliases. If you use a table alias, you must continue to use it in all subsequent references to the table in that statement. For example, you could not write **FROM authors a** then write **ORDER BY authors.au_lname**. The **ORDER BY** clause must specify the alias when qualifying the column.

Left Outer Joins

A **LEFT OUTER JOIN** returns all the rows of the first table and only those rows of the second table that match the first. All the rows of the first table are returned regardless of any match. Corresponding unmatched columns are set to **NULL**.

To create a list of all publishers and their book titles, if any:

```
SELECT p.pub_name, t.title
FROM publishers p
LEFT JOIN titles t ON p.pub_id = t.pub_id
ORDER BY p.pub_name, t.title
```

To create a list of all authors and any book titles:

```
SELECT a.au_lname, a.au_fname, t.title
FROM authors a
LEFT JOIN titleauthor ta ON a.au_id = ta.au_id
LEFT JOIN titles t ON ta.title_id = t.title_id
ORDER BY a.au_lname, a.au_fname, t.title
```

Right Outer Joins

A **RIGHT OUTER JOIN** returns all the rows of the second table and only those rows of the first table that match the second. Corresponding unmatched columns are set to **NULL**.

To create a list of all titles and any associated publishers:

```
SELECT t.title, p.pub_name
FROM publishers p
RIGHT JOIN titles t ON p.pub_id = t.pub_id
ORDER BY t.title, p.pub_name
```

Full Outer Joins

This is a combination of the **LEFT OUTER JOIN** and **RIGHT OUTER JOIN.** It returns all the rows of the both tables and sets the result set columns for any corresponding unmatched table to **NULL**.

To create a list of all publisher names and all book titles:

```
SELECT p.pub_name, t.title
FROM publishers p
FULL OUTER JOIN titles t ON p.pub_id = t.pub_id
ORDER BY p.pub_name, t.title
```

To create a list of all publishers without book titles and all book titles without publishers:

```
SELECT p.pub_name, t.title
FROM publishers p
FULL OUTER JOIN titles t ON p.pub_id = t.pub_id
WHERE p.pub_id IS NULL OR t.pub_id IS NULL
ORDER BY p.pub_name, t.title
```

Join Operators

Prior to release 6.5, SQL Server didn't support the ANSI join syntax described above. It required that you use join operators instead. These were ***=** and **=*** for left outer join and right outer join respectively. Releases of SQL Server beyond 6.5 will probably not support these join operators. You should only use the ANSI join syntax with SQL Server 6.5 and later.

Compatibility with Access

The ANSI join syntax allows you to write SQL that is compatible across many database management systems. If you don't use the optional **OUTER** keyword and you do use the optional **INNER** keyword, you can construct joins that you can transport to Microsoft ACCESS.

INSERT

The **INSERT** statement is used to add rows to a table.

```
INSERT [INTO] {table_name | view_name} [(column_list)]
       {DEFAULT VALUES | values_list | select_statement}
```

If we go back to the example database, **test_pubs**, that we created earlier, we can use the following statement adds one row in the Author_contact table for each author in the authors table in the **pubs** database.

```
INSERT author_contact (au_lname, au_fname)
SELECT au_lname, au_fname FROM pubs.dbo.authors
```

UPDATE

We use **UPDATE** to change the data in a table or view. The **SET** keyword is used in conjunction with the **UPDATE** to accomplish this. The general syntax of the **UPDATE** statement is:

```
UPDATE {table_name | view_name}
SET [{table_name | view_name}]
    {column_list_1
    | variable_list_1
    | variable_and_column_list_1}
        [, {column_list2
            | variable_list2
            | variable_and_column_list2}
        ... [, {column_listN
                | variable_listN
                | variable_and_column_listN}]]
[WHERE clause]
```

Like the **SELECT** statement, the **UPDATE** statement format seems very complex but is quite simple when you come to use it. The next example uses **test_pubs** again and demonstrates how to update the author_contact table by changing the contents of the **response** column for authors with a particular last name.

```
UPDATE author_contact
SET response =  '15 Jun 96' WHERE au_lname = 'Ringer'
```

The table, author_contact is identified after the keyword **UPDATE**. The column, **response**, is identified after the keyword **SET** and the value is provided after the equal sign. The **WHERE** clause determines which rows will be selected for the update operation.

DELETE

We use the **DELETE** statement to delete rows from a table or view. The syntax is:

```
DELETE [FROM] {table_name | view_name}
    [FROM {table_name_1 | view_name_1}
        [, {table_name_2 | view_name_2}]...]
            [..., {table_name_16 | view_name_16}]]
[WHERE clause]
```

Transact-SQL allows you to specify up to 16 tables or views to be used in the subsequent **WHERE** clause to determine which rows (in the table or view specified immediately after the word **DELETE**) are to be deleted.

The **DELETE** statement with no **WHERE** clause will delete all rows from the table, much like the **TRUNCATE TABLE** statement described below. Remember, the difference is that the **DELETE** operation logs the deletions and doesn't reset any **IDENTITY** column while the **TRUNCATE TABLE** operation doesn't log the row deletions and resets the **IDENTITY**. To delete all authors from New Jersey:

```
DELETE FROM authors WHERE state = 'NJ'
```

To delete all authors (without the optional **FROM**):

```
DELETE authors
```

TRUNCATE TABLE

The **TRUNCATE TABLE** statement deletes all rows from a table but leaves the table structure and indexes intact. The syntax is:

```
TRUNCATE TABLE [[database.]owner.]table_name
```

The **TRUNCATE TABLE** operation is not logged. There is no record of the deleted rows and any **IDENTITY** column will be reset. This is the fastest way to empty a table of its data while retaining its structure.

The **DELETE** statement is explained in the DML section later. It's important to note that the **DELETE** statement with no **WHERE** clause will also empty the data from the table. The difference is that the **DELETE** logs the deletions and does not reset any **IDENTITY** column.

To empty the Newauthors table:

```
TRUNCATE TABLE newauthors
```

Data Control Language (DCL)

The DCL is used to control security and administer permissions in SQL. The primary DCL statements are **GRANT** and **REVOKE**.

GRANT

There are two distinct forms of the **GRANT** statement. The first is used to grant data manipulation and access permissions to users. This is the most common use of the **GRANT** statement and its syntax is as follows:

```
GRANT {ALL  |  permission_list}
ON {table_name [(column_list)]  |  view_name [(column_list)]  |
stored_procedure_name  |  extended_stored_procedure_name}
TO {PUBLIC  |  user/group_list}
```

You can grant **INSERT**, **UPDATE**, **DELETE** and **SELECT** permissions to users for tables or views. You can specify individual users or user groups. A separate **REFERENCES** permission is available for users who need to create **FOREIGN KEY** constraints that reference a table where they have no **SELECT** permission. You can also use this form of the **GRANT** statement to allow the execution of stored procedures.

```
GRANT {ALL  |  statement_list}
TO {PUBLIC  |  user/group _list}:
```

The second form of the **GRANT** statement is used to control access to certain **CREATE** and **DUMP** Transact-SQL statements (e.g. **CREATE DATABASE**, **CREATE DEFAULT**, **CREATE PROCEDURE**, **CREATE RULE**, **CREATE TABLE**, **CREATE VIEW**, **DUMP DATABASE**, and **DUMP TRANSACTION**.)

Here are several examples of both applications of the **GRANT** statement.

To allow all users **SELECT** permission on the authors table in the **pubs** database:

```
GRANT SELECT ON authors TO PUBLIC
```

To allow all members of the group **DEV_GROUP** to issue **SELECT**, **INSERT**, **UPDATE** and **DELETE** statements on the authors:

```
GRANT ALL ON authors to DEV_GROUP
```

To allow the users **johnf**, **tomw**, and **jans** to issue **SELECT** and **INSERT** statements against the **publishers** table:

```
GRANT SELECT, INSERT ON publishers TO johnf, tomw, jans
```

To allow **tomw** to **EXECUTE** the stored procedure **sp_helpserver**:

```
GRANT EXECUTE ON sp_helpserver TO tomw
```

REVOKE

The **REVOKE** statement is the opposite of **GRANT**. It removes the permissions granted in the previous statement.

```
REVOKE {ALL  |  statement_list}
FROM {PUBLIC  |  name_list}

REVOKE {ALL  |  permission_list}
ON {table_name [(column_list)]  |  view_name [(column_list)]  |
stored_procedure_name  |  extended_stored_procedure_name}
FROM {PUBLIC  |  name_list}
```

Batching SQL Statements

Transact-SQL statements can be grouped together and run in a batch. This feature allows you to control the execution of groups of SQL statements.

To copy tables from the **pubs** database to the new **test_pubs** database, you should use the **SELECT...INTO** statement. Before you can do this, though, you must set the **select into/bulkcopy** database option in the **test_pubs** database. As we have just created **test_pubs**, no database options are currently set. To change the database options, you should use the system stored procedure, **sp_dboption**.

> System stored procedures are, like stored procedures in general, precompiled SQL statements, but they operate on system tables rather than user tables. This particular system stored procedure changes the database options.

If you look up **sp_dboption** in the reference material, you'll see that it takes three parameters: the database name, the database option name and a true or false indicator. Open an ISQL/w window, select the **master** database and enter the following statements:

```
sp_dboption test_pubs, 'select into/bulkcopy', true
go
sp_dboption test_pubs
```

You'll get this result:

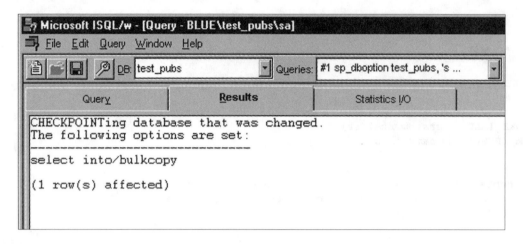

The first line in the Results window, CHECKPOINTing database that was changed is the result of the first **sp_dboption**. The first occurrence of **sp_dboption** turns on the **select into/bulkcopy** option for the table **test_pubs**. The succeeding **GO** statement forces the execution of the first **sp_dboption** before the second **sp_dboption** can be executed. The **sp_dboption** with only the database name displays all the options set for that database, so this second **sp_dboption** will show the effect of the first **sp_dboption**.

Therefore, it's the **GO** statement that actually defines a group of statements known as a **batch**. The first batch is processed as a group, then the next batch is processed. (In this case the second batch is the last **sp_dboption** statement.) Batching is important when you need some SQL statements to be run before others, usually because you need the latter statements to have access to what was affected by the former.

The next example further demonstrates the concept of a SQL batch with SQL statements that copy tables from the **pubs** database to the **test_pubs** database. Before you type the following statements, you should select the New Query button in the toolbar. When you do this, notice that the Queries drop-down box now displays #2 New query.

```
USE test_pubs
GO

SELECT *
INTO authors
FROM pubs.dbo.authors

SELECT *
INTO publishers
FROM pubs.dbo.publishers

SELECT *
INTO pub_info
FROM pubs.dbo.pub_info

SELECT *
INTO titleauthor
```

```
FROM pubs.dbo.titleauthor

SELECT *
INTO titles
FROM pubs.dbo.titles
```

These statements copy the data from five tables in the **pubs** database into five corresponding tables in the **test_pubs** database.

The first statement, **USE test_pubs**, is the same as selecting **test_pubs** in the ISQL/w drop-down list box. This ensures that all subsequent processing will be confined to the **test_pubs** database unless specifically noted otherwise as in the **FROM** lines in the **SELECT** statements.

Comments

Since this query is longer than a line or two and you may want to run it again, you should consider saving it. If you save queries for future use, you should consider adding comments to them. It's always advisable to add comments to your SQL code in order to provide sufficient information to run the code or change it. Always remember that it may be another person who needs to make alterations to the SQL statements, or worse, you might need to do it yourself a long time after you wrote them.

There are two types of comments in Transact-SQL.

The C-type of comment can be placed anywhere. It begins with **/*** and terminates with ***/**. It can be on one line or span many lines.

```
/* the following statements
display the last names and states
in the authors table */
SELECT au_lname, state FROM authors
```

The line comment comments an entire line beginning with double dashes **--**. The comments continue to the end of the line only. The next example uses both types of comments:

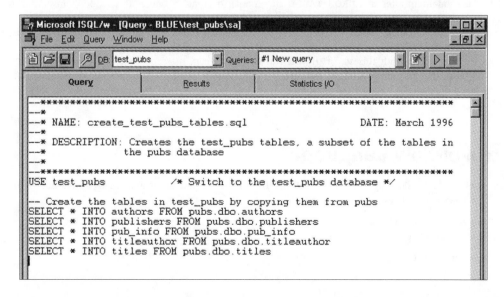

Scripts

You can save your query as a script that you can re-open in ISQL/w and run again. The **SAVE AS** command (or tool bar button) will prompt you for a file name with a **.sql** extension.

The only problem with saving the current group of SQL statements is that it can't be re-run without first dropping the tables. If, however, you add the **DROP TABLE** statements, as shown, you can save this group of SQL statements as a script (**create_test_pubs_tables.sql**, in this example) and run it at any time:

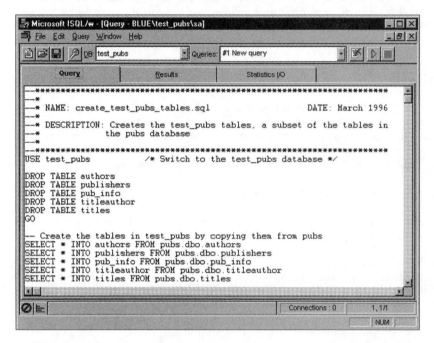

We need the **GO** statement after the **DROP TABLE** statements to create a batch. If you don't insert the **GO** statement, the subsequent **SELECT** statements won't run because the table objects haven't yet been dropped from the **test_pubs** database. You won't be allowed to create the tables if they already exist.

There's one other problem with this script. If you run it, you'll get a message returned from the **DROP** statements because, the first time through, the tables are not there to drop. You can avoid this Cannot drop the table... message by using two additional Transact-SQL constructs subqueries and control-of-flow language.

Control-of-flow Language

There are control-of-flow language enhancements in Transact-SQL that allow you to treat Transact-SQL as a programming language. These statements are:

- **CASE** expression

- **BEGIN...END**

▲   GOTO

▲   IF...ELSE

▲   PRINT

▲   RAISERROR

▲   WAITFOR TIME

▲   WAITFOR DELAY

▲   WHILE

▲   WHILE...BREAK

▲   WHILE...CONTINUE

IF Statement

You can use an **IF** statement to control whether or not the **DROP** is executed:

```
--**********************************************************************
USE test_pubs        /* Switch to the test_pubs database */
GO

-- Drop the tables before re-creating them with a SELECT INTO
IF EXISTS (SELECT * from sysobjects where id=object_id('dbo.authors'))
      DROP TABLE authors
IF EXISTS (SELECT * from sysobjects where id=object_id('dbo.publishers'))
      DROP TABLE publishers
IF EXISTS (SELECT * from sysobjects where id=object_id('dbo.pub_info'))
      DROP TABLE pub_info
IF EXISTS (SELECT * from sysobjects where id=object_id('dbo.titleauthor'))
      DROP TABLE titleauthor
IF EXISTS (SELECT * from sysobjects where id = object_id('dbo.titles'))
      DROP TABLE titles
GO

-- Create the tables in test_pubs by copying them from pubs
SELECT * INTO authors FROM pubs.dbo.authors
SELECT * INTO publishers FROM pubs.dbo.publishers
SELECT * INTO pub_info FROM pubs.dbo.pub_info
SELECT * INTO titleauthor FROM pubs.dbo.titleauthor
SELECT * INTO titles FROM pubs.dbo.titles
```

In this example, **IF** statements and a subquery are used to determine whether a table exists before dropping it.

Statement Blocking with BEGIN...END

The **IF** statement normally allows a single statement to be executed only if the condition is true. If you want to execute more than one statement, you need to write a statement block with the **BEGIN** and **END** keywords surrounding the multiple SQL lines:

```
IF EXISTS (SELECT * from sysobjects where id = object_id('dbo.authors'))
    BEGIN
```

```
        DROP TABLE authors
        PRINT "author table dropped"
  END
```

In this case, there's no need for more than a single line of code.

CASE Statement

The **IF** statement is be used to direct code execution based on one condition. In the previous example, only the existence of a certain **object_id** was necessary to direct the code. The table existed or didn't and code appropriate to that situation was executed. The **CASE** statement is better suited to circumstances where there are multiple conditions possible.

For example, if there's a month column in a table, **year**, you could direct code execution based upon the value of the month column.

```
SELECT month, "How many days"
    CASE month
            WHEN 'January' THEN '31'
            WHEN 'February' THEN '28????'
            WHEN 'March' THEN '31'
            WHEN 'April' THEN '30'
            WHEN 'May' THEN '31'
            WHEN 'June' THEN '30'
            WHEN 'July' THEN '31'
            WHEN 'August' THEN '31'
            WHEN 'September' THEN '30'
            WHEN 'October' THEN '31'
            WHEN 'November' THEN '30'
            WHEN 'December' THEN '31'
            ELSE 'very bad month'
    END
FROM year_table
```

Subqueries

A subquery is a **SELECT** statement embedded within another query. In the previous example, it follows the word **EXISTS**.

Transact-SQL allows you to write a **SELECT** statement in place of an expression as long as the expression that contains the subquery returns a TRUE or FALSE. You can also embed a **SELECT** in a **SELECT**, **INSERT**, **UPDATE** or **DELETE** statement. The **SELECT** statement used in a subquery is slightly different from a normal **SELECT**. The syntax is:

```
SELECT [ALL | DISTINCT] subquery_select_list
  [FROM {table_name_1 | view_name_1}[(optimizer_hints)]
     [[, {table_name_2 | view_name_2}[(optimizer_hints)]
     [..., {table_name_16 | view_name_16}[(optimizer_hints)]]]]
[WHERE clause]
[GROUP BY clause]
[HAVING clause]
```

The subquery in the example returns all the columns in the **sysobjects** table in the **test_pubs** database where the ID column value is equal to the object id of the table in question. The **object_id()** function is used to return the ID value when supplied with a table name.

Functions

In the last subquery example, we used an **object_id()** function. Transact-SQL has various types of functions. Mathematical, date, aggregate, niladic, string, system, text/image and type conversion functions are available.

COUNT(*)

The **COUNT(*)** function returns a summary value of all selected rows:

```
USE pubs
GO

SELECT COUNT(*) FROM author_contact
```

This returns the count of all rows in the authors table, while:

```
USE pubs
GO

SELECT COUNT(*) FROM authors WHERE state = 'CA'
```

returns the count of all rows in the authors table that have California specified in the state column.

COUNT

The **COUNT** function has the format of **COUNT(expression)**. It returns a summary value of all non-null items in the expression. For example:

```
USE test_pubs
GO

SELECT COUNT(response) FROM author_contact
```

This statement will return a count of the rows where the response column is not NULL.

Finding Duplicate Values

We can use the **COUNT** functions to locate duplicate values. For example, if you need to find out whether there are any duplicated last names in the authors table, you could create a query similar to this:

```
USE test_pubs
GO

SELECT au_lname FROM author_contact
```

```
GROUP BY au_lname
HAVING COUNT(*) > 1
```

The **SELECT** statement used here is different from previous examples as it's used in conjunction with the **GROUP BY** and **HAVING** clauses, as well as the **COUNT(*)** function. The **GROUP BY** clause divides the table up by the specified group, in this case **au_lname**. The **COUNT(*)** within the **HAVING** clause counts the number of rows in each of the groups. The remainder of the **HAVING** clause causes only those groups with more than one row to be selected. In this case, only the groups with more than one of the same last names are selected.

The **SELECT** specifies that the **au_lname** column be returned. The **SELECT** statement requires that only columns specified in the **GROUP BY** clause or in an aggregate function (such as **COUNT**) can be specified. The results show all of the duplicate names in the database.

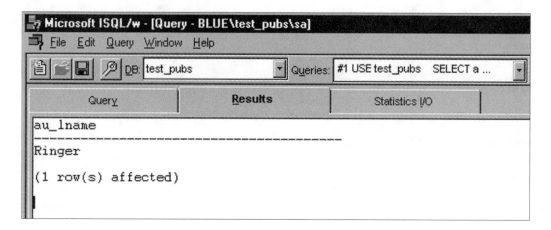

Variables

One important adjunct to the use of functions is the use of variables. Variables are defined with a **DECLARE** statement. Variables are assigned initial values with a **SELECT** statement. SQL Server supports local variables and global variables.

Local variables are prefixed with a **@** and are available only to the SQL batch in which they were created. Global variables are prefixed with **@@**. There are predefined global variables for system use that don't need to be declared. **@@ROWCOUNT**, for example, is a system global variable that contains the number of rows affected by the last statement executed.

The Use of Variables and Functions

To demonstrate the integration of variables and functions, we'll consider the following example. In this example, we'll create a table, named **process_date**, that has one row with one column, **process_yyyymm**. That column is a six character field containing the processing year (four characters) and month (two characters). There's a further restriction that the **process_yyyymm** column must contain a value based upon the date when the SQL is executed. If the SQL is executed in the first half of the month the value in **process_yyyymm** must reflect the previous month. If the SQL is executed past the 15th of the month then the current month must be inserted. The code is as follows:

```
USE test_pubs
GO

DECLARE @dt DATETIME
DECLARE @d CHAR(6)

-- If the current date is past the mid-point of the month use the
-- current month to seed the processing month
-- If the current date is before the mid-point use the previous
-- month to seed the process month

IF DATEPART(dd, GETDATE()) > 15
    SELECT @d = CONVERT (CHAR(6), GETDATE(), 112)
ELSE
    BEGIN
        SELECT @dt = DATEADD(mm, -1, getdate())
        SELECT @d = CONVERT (char(6), @dt, 112)
    END

CREATE TABLE process_date
(
    process_yyyymm CHAR (6) NOT NULL
)

INSERT INTO process_date (process_yyyymm)
    VALUES(@d)

SELECT * FROM process_date
```

The first two **DECLARE** statements declare two local variables. One variable is a **DATETIME** datatype and the other is a character datatype with a length of 6.

The **IF** statement determines whether the current month or the previous month is used to populate the column. This line of SQL code first uses the **GETDATE** function to get the current date and time. It then uses the **DATEPART** function to extract the day value from the result of **GETDATE**. The **DATEPART** function uses various abbreviations to identify the part of the date to be returned. In this case, **dd** is the abbreviation for day.

In the event that the current day is larger than 15, the current date is used. This is achieved by the **SELECT** statement. The **SELECT** sets the value of the **@d** local variable to the result of the **CONVERT** function. The **CONVERT** function can be used to format dates and the **112** parameter is the designation for the ISO date format (**yyyymmdd**) and converted to six characters.

If the day is less than 15, the **BEGIN...END** statement block will be executed. The first **SELECT** sets the value of the local variable, @d, to the result of the **DATEADD** function. The **DATEADD** function has the syntax:

```
(datepart, number, date)
```

and adds the number of dateparts to the date. In this case, it take the current date (**GETDATE**) and add a negative 1 month (**mm**) to it. **The SELECT...CONVERT** is the same as the previous condition.

The next two statements create the table and insert the value from the local variable into the column.

Controlling the Output

The output from queries is not always detailed. Consider the following example:

```
--***************************************************************************
USE test_pubs        /* Switch to the test_pubs database */
GO

-- Drop the tables before re-creating them with a SELECT INTO
IF EXISTS (SELECT * from sysobjects where id=object_id('dbo.authors'))
     DROP TABLE authors
IF EXISTS (SELECT * from sysobjects where id=object_id('dbo.publishers'))
     DROP TABLE publishers
IF EXISTS (SELECT * from sysobjects where id=object_id('dbo.pub_info'))
     DROP TABLE pub_info
IF EXISTS (SELECT * from sysobjects where id=object_id('dbo.titleauthor'))
     DROP TABLE titleauthor
IF EXISTS (SELECT * from sysobjects where id = object_id('dbo.titles'))
     DROP TABLE titles
GO

-- Create the tables in test_pubs by copying them from pubs
SELECT * INTO authors FROM pubs.dbo.authors
SELECT * INTO publishers FROM pubs.dbo.publishers
SELECT * INTO pub_info FROM pubs.dbo.pub_info
SELECT * INTO titleauthor FROM pubs.dbo.titleauthor
SELECT * INTO titles FROM pubs.dbo.titles
```

The messages returned only indicate the number of rows affected. To associate a message with a particular SQL statement, you must return to the original query and match them in sequence.

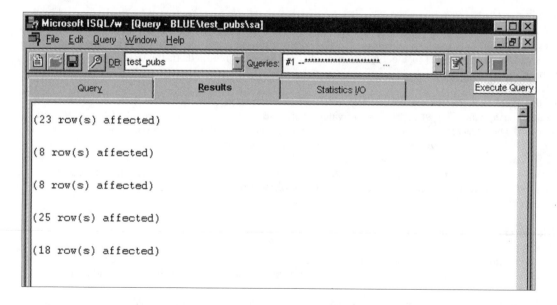

We can make several improvements to the original query so more meaningful messages will be returned.

The **GETDATE()** function can be used in a simple **SELECT** statement to force a time stamp to be printed in the results window. This is particularly useful for queries that need to have their process times recorded.

```
--*******************************************************************
--*
--* NAME: create_test_pubs_tables.sql          DATE: March 1996
--*
--* DESCRIPTION: Creates the test_pubs tables, a subset of the tables in
--*      the pubs database
--*
--*******************************************************************
USE test_pubs         /* Switch to the test_pubs database */
GO

SELECT GETDATE() /*Added to record the process duration of this script*/

-- Drop the tables before re-creating them with a SELECT INTO
IF EXISTS (SELECT * from sysobjects where id = object_id('dbo.authors'))
    DROP TABLE authors
IF EXISTS (SELECT * from sysobjects where id = object_id('dbo.publishers'))
    DROP TABLE publishers
IF EXISTS (SELECT * from sysobjects where id = object_id('dbo.pub_info'))
    DROP TABLE pub_info
IF EXISTS (SELECT * from sysobjects where id = object_id('dbo.titleauthor'))
    DROP TABLE titleauthor
IF EXISTS (SELECT * from sysobjects where id = object_id('dbo.titles'))
    DROP TABLE titles
GO


-- Create the tables in test_pubs by copying them from pubs
SELECT * INTO authors FROM pubs.dbo.authors
SELECT * INTO publishers FROM pubs.dbo.publishers
SELECT * INTO pub_info FROM pubs.dbo.pub_info
SELECT * INTO titleauthor FROM pubs.dbo.titleauthor
SELECT * INTO titles FROM pubs.dbo.titles

SELECT GETDATE() /*Added to record the process duration of this script*/
```

The output is then broken up at two points with the time stamp:

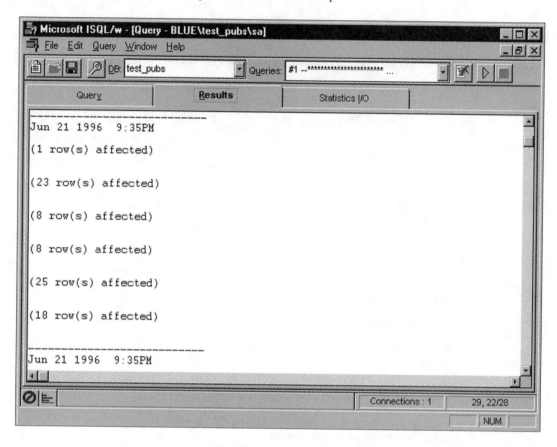

This addition is useful, but there is still no association of the result message to query statement other than the order of execution. To provide meaningful result messages, you must control the printing of the messages in the Results window from with the SQL query. This example relies on local variables, a global variable called **@@ROWCOUNT**, some functions and a **PRINT** statement. It also performs string concatenation with the **+** operator.

```
SET NOCOUNT ON

DECLARE @mymsg varchar(255)            /* Establish a message variable */
SELECT @mymsg = '*** script started at ' + convert(char(19),getdate())
PRINT @mymsg
PRINT ''

-- Drop the tables before re-creating them with a SELECT INTO
IF EXISTS (SELECT * from sysobjects where id = object_id('dbo.authors'))
   DROP TABLE authors
IF EXISTS (SELECT * from sysobjects where id = object_id('dbo.publishers'))
   DROP TABLE publishers
IF EXISTS (SELECT * from sysobjects where id = object_id('dbo.pub_info'))
   DROP TABLE pub_info
```

```
IF EXISTS (SELECT * from sysobjects where id = object_id('dbo.titleauthor'))
    DROP TABLE titleauthor
IF EXISTS (SELECT * from sysobjects where id = object_id('dbo.titles'))
    DROP TABLE titles
GO


-- Create the tables in test_pubs by copying them from pubs

DECLARE @mymsg varchar(255)              /* Establish a message variable */

SELECT * INTO authors FROM pubs.dbo.authors
SELECT @mymsg = 'authors processing ended at ' + convert(char(19),getdate()) + ' -
Rows affected: ' + convert(char(12),@@ROWCOUNT)
PRINT @mymsg
PRINT ''

SELECT * INTO publishers FROM pubs.dbo.publishers
SELECT @mymsg = 'publishers processing ended at ' + convert(char(19),getdate()) + ' -
Rows affected: ' + convert(char(12),@@ROWCOUNT)
PRINT @mymsg
PRINT ''

SELECT * INTO pub_info FROM pubs.dbo.pub_info
SELECT @mymsg = 'pub_info processing ended at ' + convert(char(19),getdate()) + ' -
Rows affected: ' + convert(char(12),@@ROWCOUNT)
PRINT @mymsg
PRINT ''

SELECT * INTO titleauthor FROM pubs.dbo.titleauthor
SELECT @mymsg = 'titleauthor processing ended at ' + convert(char(19),getdate()) + ' -
Rows affected: ' + convert(char(12),@@ROWCOUNT)
PRINT @mymsg
PRINT ''

SELECT * INTO titles FROM pubs.dbo.titles
SELECT @mymsg = 'titles processing ended at ' + convert(char(19),getdate()) + ' - Rows
affected: ' + convert(char(12),@@ROWCOUNT)
PRINT @mymsg
PRINT ''
SELECT @mymsg = '*** script ended at ' + convert(char(19),getdate())
PRINT @mymsg
```

The **SET NOCOUNT ON** directive on the first line stops the row count messages from being displayed in the results window. A local variable, **@mymsg**, is declared to hold the message string and it's populated with a **SELECT** statement that concatenates a constant with the output of the **CONVERT()** function. The **CONVERT()** function simply ensures that the date supplied by the **GETDATE()** function includes the seconds and is not truncated. **GETDATE()** also turns the internal date format into a string so that any subsequent concatenation operator will work.

Most of the rest of the example is unchanged from the previous, except for concatenating the **@@ROWCOUNT** global variable to the string constant and date for the messages displayed after the **SELECT...INTO** statements. This is simply to provide a record of the rows affected by the **SELECT...INTO**.

The **PRINT** statement is used to display the message in the Results tab window of ISQL/w:

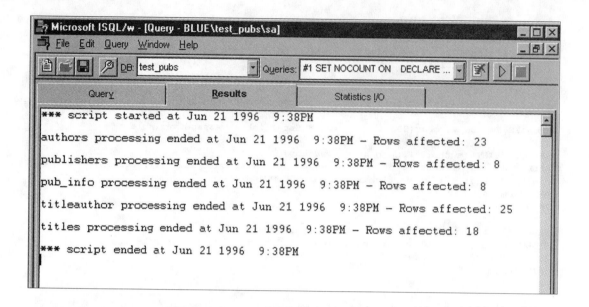

> You should be careful when you use PRINT outside the ISQL/w environment. For example, you should never use it in stored procedures, since it will return the message to the clients message handler, not as the regular rows returned by the select

Temporary Tables

You can use temporary tables to store intermediate results for subsequent processing. These tables exist only for the duration of the session in which they were created. They are stored in the **tempdb** database.

To create a temporary table in **tempdb** open an ISQL/w session and execute the following:

```
SELECT * INTO #mytemp FROM pubs.dbo.authors
```

To display the rows of the temporary table you just created enter the following in the same ISQL/w window:

```
SELECT * FROM #mytemp
```

Open a second ISQL/w sessions by selecting the New Query option from the File menu or by using the New Query button on the tool bar. Switch to the **tempdb** database and execute the following:

```
SELECT * FROM #mytemp
```

Notice that an error message Invalid object name '#mytemp' is returned. If you return to the first ISQL/w session and execute the same **SELECT** it will return the rows in the table. This is because the temporary table isn't available to any session except the creating session.

To allow another session access to that temporary table, you must make it global. Global temporary tables are identified by having the prefix of **##** instead of the single **#**. Global temporary tables are available to other sessions, but cease to exist when the creating session is terminated.

```
SELECT * INTO ##mytemp FROM pubs.dbo.authors
```

You can also create a temporary table if you simply create a table in **tempdb**.

```
SELECT * INTO tempdb..myauthors FROM pubs.dbo.authors
```

When SQL Server is restarted, the table will be gone but it will exist until explicitly dropped or SQL Server is restarted.

Views

A view is a construct for presenting data from one or more tables and making it look like it was a single table. The data resides in the table or tables of origin and not in the view. A view is considered a 'virtual table', another way of looking at data in a table or tables. It's often the case that you want to restrict the user to selected columns or rows within a specific table. Some columns in a table may contain sensitive information that you want to secure from a user. Sometimes, the user should only have access to certain rows within a table. Another use of views is to simplify the access to the underlying tables without duplicating data. In this case, you can create a view that contains columns from several base tables.

CREATE VIEW

The **CREATE VIEW** statement has this syntax:

```
CREATE VIEW [owner.]view_name
[(column_name [, column_name]...)]
[WITH ENCRYPTION]
AS select_statement [WITH CHECK OPTION]
```

Please note that the nested **SELECT** can't contain an **ORDER BY**, **COMPUTE** or **COMPUTE BY** clause, the **INTO** or **UNION** keywords or reference a temporary table.

To create the view **v_calauthors**   restricting the user to those rows that match the stated criteria:

```
USE pubs
GO

CREATE VIEW v_calauthors AS
    SELECT au_lname, au_fname FROM authors WHERE state = 'CA'
```

To create the view **v_author_title**:

```
USE pubs
GO

CREATE VIEW v_author_title AS
    SELECT a.au_lname, a.au_fname, t.title
```

```
FROM authors a
LEFT JOIN titleauthor ta ON a.au_id = ta.au_id
LEFT JOIN titles t ON ta.title_id = t.title_id
```

Note that this latter view simplifies subsequent access, i.e. you no longer have to use a **join** to obtain author names and associated titles, and it also restricts the users of this view to only the three columns specified.

DROP VIEW

DROP VIEW deletes a view from the database.

DROP VIEW {[*owner.*]*view_name* | *view_list*}

To delete the view **v_calauthors**:

```
DROP VIEW v_calauthors
```

Summary

This appendix has presented an overview of Transact-SQL. We've introduced the major language sections, DDL, DML & DCL, and demonstrated language extensions and other features, such as control-of-flow language, temporary tables, views and subqueries. We've also presented programming techniques to control script output.

As we stated earlier, we never intended this appendix to be a comprehensive treatment of the SQL language. It should have given you enough information to be a productive Transact-SQL programmer while you investigate the language further by studying this text and the Transact-SQL documentation.

6.5

The Microsoft Distributed Transaction Coordinator

New with the 6.5 release of Microsoft SQL Server is the Distributed Transaction Coordinator (MS DTC). This service makes it possible to define transactions that span multiple SQL Servers. In previous versions of SQL Server, this could be done only when applications themselves implemented what's called a 'two-phase' commit protocol. The MS DTC is a distributed transaction manager that allows SQL Server to participate in transactions controlled by transaction processing (TP) monitors such as Transarc's Encina®, Tuxedo® and AT&T Global Information Solutions Companies Top End®, as well as any other distributed transaction processing monitors that are compliant with the XA specification. This new product will present a lot of additional capability for application developers as well as a new set of challenges for the SQL Server administrator.

In this appendix, we'll provide some background material about distributed transactions and the two-phase commit protocol. Then we'll explain how the MS DTC interacts with the SQL Servers to manage the distributed transactions. After that, we'll discuss the set up and configuration of the MS DTC as well as the front end that SQL Enterprise Manager provides for administering the DTC. Finally, we'll present a few troubleshooting tips for this new product.

Distributed Transactions

In Chapter 8, transactions were described as a **logical unit of work**: something in which either all database updates must complete or must be rolled back. We also presented the ACID properties of a transaction:

- Atomicity
- Consistency
- Isolation
- Durability

We discussed transactions that operate locally; that is, within the context of a single server. SQL Server provides commands for defining transaction boundaries:

- **BEGIN TRANSACTION**
- **COMMIT TRANSACTION**
- **ROLLBACK TRANSACTION**

These allow the SQL Server to insure that the ACID properties are observed. In a SQL Server, transaction management is handled by a process called the **resource manager**.

It's been possible to perform database updates on several servers for several releases now. In Transact-SQL, you can execute remote procedure calls. With DBLibrary, it's possible to do any legitimate database modifications when connected to several different SQL Servers. Both of these are **distributed transactions**. However, SQL Server hasn't previously provided any way to make these distributed transactions observe the ACID requirements. Application developers were forced to do that themselves. Enforcing the ACID properties with distributed transactions requires the **two-phase commit protocol**.

Two-phase Commit Protocol

In a simple local transaction, there's only one resource manager. That process can determine whether the transaction will succeed by looking at the resources under its control. If it can acquire the necessary resources and make the update in such a fashion that the database will be consistent, it allows the transaction to commit. If it can't acquire the resources (for example, in a deadlock situation) or the transaction will make the database inconsistent (for example, the update will violate a referential integrity rule), the resource manager rolls the transaction back. If the system crashes, the resource manager decides what to do with the interrupted transaction when the system comes back up. If it has sufficient information to complete the transaction, it completes it and commits it otherwise it rolls it back.

When a transaction is distributed, one resource manager can't determine whether a transaction will succeed or fail. Instead, there must be some central governing process that coordinates the efforts of the individual resource manager. This process is called a **transaction manager**. When a resource manager knows that it is to participate in a distributed transaction, it 'signs up' with the transaction manager. When it's time to commit the transaction, it's the transaction manager's job to manage the two phases of the protocol:

 Prepare

 Commit

In the **prepare** phase, the transaction manager asks each resource manager that has signed up if it will be able to commit. If all of the resource managers say 'yes', the transaction manager tells them to go ahead with the second, **commit**, phase. If any one says 'no', all resource managers are notified that they must roll back. If the decision was to commit, each resource manager notifies the transaction manager when its commit is complete. When all have completed, the transaction is durable and the transaction is no longer active.

The Microsoft Distributed Transaction Coordinator is a transaction manager. Currently it interacts with only one resource manager, SQL Server. The following figures illustrate how this process works. In the first diagram, the application has completed the database updates and tells the MS DTC that it wants to commit the distributed transaction. MS DTC tells each SQL Server's resource manager that the commit is about to happen, and that they better get ready.

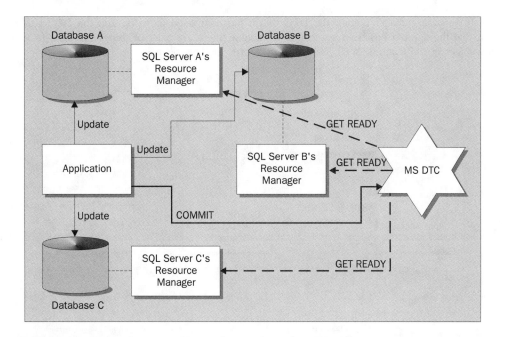

Next, the resource managers tell the DTC that they're ready, and the DTC sends back the instructions for them to commit.

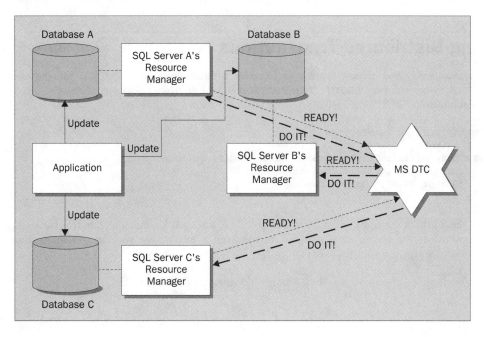

Finally, each resource manager notifies the DTC that it has completed its work, and the DTC tells the application that the commit has been successful. Of course, there are a lot of things that can go wrong during the stages of the commit. We'll look at those more closely a bit later.

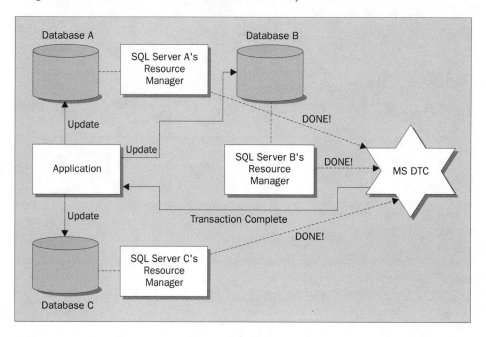

Defining Distributed Transactions

From the application's point of view, it's simple to create a distributed transaction. Just add the word **DISTRIBUTED** to the familiar **BEGIN TRANSACTION** statement. Here's a sample Transact-SQL distributed transaction.

```
BEGIN DISTRIBUTED TRANSACTION
UPDATE authors
    SET city = 'Philadelphia' WHERE au_id = '409-56-7008'
    EXECUTE remote.pubs.dbo.changeauth_city
        '409-56-7008','Philadelphia'
COMMIT TRAN
```

Notice that the **COMMIT** statement remains unchanged. The **ROLLBACK** statement doesn't change, either. If all the transactions in the session are distributed, there's even a **SET** option you can use so the transactions are automatically assumed to be distributed.

There are also facilities to support distributed transactions in the DBLibrary API.

Installing the Distributed Transaction Coordinator

There are two forms of the Distributed Transaction Coordinator: a complete DTC and a DTC client utility. The client utility should be installed on any computer that will initiate a distributed transaction using the C or C++ **BEGIN TRANSACTION** statement. You don't need to install this utility if the client applications uses the Transact-SQL **BEGIN DISTRIBUTED TRANSACTION** statement since that statement will execute on the server. The DTC client utility requires Windows NT Server version 3.51 or later, Windows NT Workstation version 3.51 or later, or Windows 95. The complete DTC should be installed on any SQL Server that will participate in distributed transactions.

Installing the Complete DTC

When you run Setup to install the SQL Server, the DTC is automatically installed for you along with the extensions to SQL Enterprise Manager to allow you to manage it and the interfaces necessary for applications to begin distributed transactions. The DTC is installed as an NT service. The client utility is also automatically installed together with an icon in the control panel that allows you to name the transaction coordinator and the underlying network protocol.

You can start the MS DTC with SQL Enterprise Manager, with the SQL Service Manager, from the Services application in Control Panel or from the command prompt.

Installing the DTC Client Utility

To install the DTC client utility, run the SQL Server Setup program on the client computer. This will install the features you need for the utility. This installation will put an icon for MS DTC in the control panel. You must configure the client utility using this icon before you can work with it.

> If you're installing the client utility on a Windows 95 machine, you must also install the Microsoft Remote Registry Service before you can configure the utility. The Windows 95 machine will need access to the SQL Server setup CD. Here's what you need to do to install the service.
>
> Open the **Network** applet in **Control Panel** and click **Add**. Then click **Add** again on the **Services** dialog.
>
> In the **Select Network Service** dialog, click 'Have Disk'. When you see the prompt for the directory, either type x:\i386\remotereg where x is the drive letter of the CD drive that contains the SQL Server CD or browse until you find the appropriate directory.
>
> **OK** your way back out and the service will be installed.

Once you've installed the client utility, you must tell it which computer houses its distributed transaction coordinator and the network protocol to use. You do this by double-clicking the MS DTC icon in the control panel and filling in the following dialog:

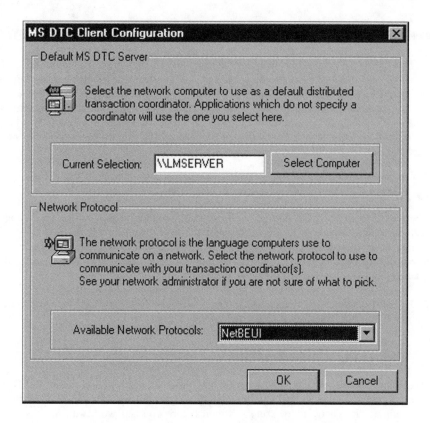

Monitoring and Troubleshooting Distributed Transactions

SQL Enterprise Manager allows you to manage and configure the Distributed Transaction Coordinator. There are four basic functions it supports:

- ▲ Starting and stopping the DTC
- ▲ Dealing with in-doubt transactions
- ▲ Monitoring transactions, statistics and traces
- ▲ Setting global options

The DTC is shown in the Server Manager Display after you register the server.

As usual, the green light shows that it's running.

If you want to administer the DTC remotely, you'll need to make some changes to the registry. See the *Guide to Microsoft Distributed Transaction Coordinator* in SQL Books Online for instructions.

Configuring the MS DTC

To configure the MS DTC and the Enterprise Manager displays of its information, right click on its icon in the Server Manager window and choose Configure.

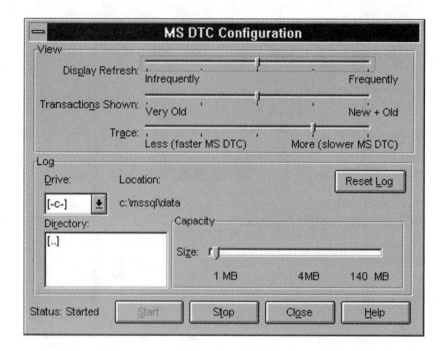

The first slider controls the refresh rate of the displays. An 'infrequent' display refresh means every 20 seconds, a 'frequent' one means every second. You choose how long a transaction must be active before it's displayed with the second slider. A 'very old' transaction has been active for 5 minutes. A New+Old transaction (why didn't they call it very young?) has been active for only 1 second. For traces, you can select:

▲ None

▲ Error traces

▲ Error and warning traces

▲ Error, warning and informational traces

▲ All traces

> **Note that you slow down MS DTC if you request more detail in the trace.**

Finally, this dialog allows you to change the size of the MS DTC log. The size of the log file determines the number of concurrent transactions this MS DTC can handle. Once a transaction has committed or aborted, it's removed from the log file. If the log file is full, MS DTC can't accept new transactions until space is available again.

> **Be very careful not to mess with the log file while there are any unresolved transactions.**

You should stop the MS DTC before changing the directory or the size of the log.

Monitoring and Resolving Transactions

When you choose Transactions from the MS DTC drop-down menu, you'll see a display that includes only:

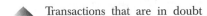 Transactions that are in doubt

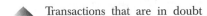 Transactions that have been in the same state for the time you specified in the configuration dialog

Each transaction will have an associated icon that indicates its state. Because locks are held while a transaction is in doubt, there may be occasions when you need to manually resolve these transactions. The transactions you may need to resolve are in-doubt transactions, which are usually the result of a failed connection between two servers, and transactions that have been committed but not acknowledged by a SQL Server. This usually happens because the Server went down before sending its 'done' message or because it lost its log.

When either of these situations exists, you may resolve them manually by telling the DTC to commit, abort or forget a transaction on a particular node.

Here's an example in which it's appropriate to manually commit a transaction. SQL Server A is the commit coordinator for the transaction. The flow of communication for the two phase commit is from A to B to C to D. This is the state during the second phase.

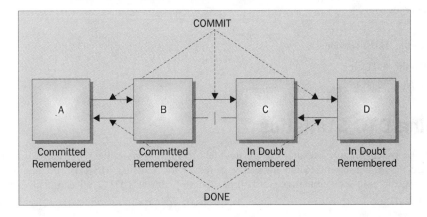

At the point illustrated, all the servers have received the message to commit. There's a break in communication between C and B so the DONE message didn't get to B. We don't know whether C actually committed. A and B can't forget the transaction and release locks because B hasn't heard from C. The database administrator must force a commit on C, which will allow a commit on D. C and D will now forget the transaction. However, C still can't communicate with B, so the administrator must force B to forget the transaction, which lets A forget it too. At this point all locks are freed and the system is back in business. (Of course, somebody still has to deal with the communication failure between B and C, but hopefully that's someone other than you!)

You should always resolve the transactions on the nodes closest to the break. The Transactions display will show you in-doubt transactions and the parents. It's much easier to resolve these because there's enough information to determine where the problem lies. It's much harder to resolve the failed-to-respond situation. You'll need to look at each system involved in the transactions and match global identifiers to find parents and children so that you can commit (or abort) and forget as appropriate.

Mechanics

You manually resolve a transaction by right-clicking on its icon in the MS DTC transactions display. The drop-down menu allows you to view or resolve the transaction. If you choose resolve, a further drop-down menu will allow you to commit, abort or forget the transaction.

Tracing Distributed Transactions

The MS DTC trace window shows you messages that have been issued by the Distributed Transaction Coordinator. There are four severity levels:

▲ Error-something bad has happened and you must restart the MS DTC.

▲ Warning-something bad may be going to happen very soon.

▲ Information-an infrequent event, such as startup or shut down, has happened.

▲ Trace-debugging information.

Even if you're not running the trace, *all* error, warning and informational messages are sent to the Windows NT application event log. Both the event log and the trace window will show you the source of the message. Sources are:

▲ SVC–the DTC service

▲ LOG–the DTC log

▲ CM–the network connection manager

Monitoring DTC Statistics

Each MS DTC keeps cumulative statistics during its 'life'. You can review these statistics to monitor system performance and make adjustments when necessary. Some of the statistics MS DTC maintains are about current operations, the rest are cumulative. Each time you stop the MS DTC, all cumulative statistics will be reset to zero.

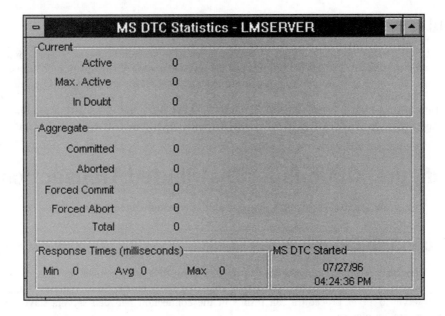

There are three types of DTC statistics: Current, Aggregate and Response Times. In the Current group, you see the information for this monitoring session. An Active transaction is one which hasn't completed the two-phase commit protocol. The Max Active is the highest number of active transactions since you started watching it this time. You also see the current number of in-doubt transactions.

The Aggregate part of the display shows you cumulative values since the DTC was last started. You should note that the committed and aborted figures don't include the Forced Commit or Forced Abort values.

Response Times tells you the duration of transactions from their start point to commit time. This doesn't include time for aborted transactions or transactions whose outcome was forced.

Deadlock and Distributed Transactions

When there's only one resource manager involved, it can detect and resolve deadlock. This is the normal behavior for a SQL Server. However, when a transaction is distributed across multiple servers, deadlock isn't automatically detected. Application developers need to plan for deadlock avoidance. There are two basic choices:

- Serialize access to common tables
- Implement time-outs in the application or with server-wide trace flags

Serializing Access

This is the same technique as is recommended for deadlock avoidance on a single server. It works like this: if you plan to have a distributed transaction affecting Table1 on Server A, Table2 on Server B and Table3 on Server C, always issue the updates in the same order. For example, updates to Table2, then Table1, then Table3 will only work if you have tight control over the design of the distributed transactions. If you don't have control, you need to consider time-out strategies.

Time-out Strategies

Remember that SQL Server normally allows a process to wait forever for a resource. This continues to be the way it behaves even with distributed transactions. If you anticipate a lot of distributed transactions that you don't control, you may want to establish a time-out value. In DBLibrary and ODBC applications, this can be done in the calling program. For ad hoc Transact-SQL usage, you can start the server with trace flag T8503. This will establish a server-wide DTC time-out value that's the same as the remote conn timeout specified with **sp_configure** (see below). A remote conn timeout value of 0 is an infinite wait.

sp_configure: Options for Distributed Transactions

There are two **sp_configure** options that interact with distributed transactions.

remote conn timeout

remote conn timeout specifies a time limit to break a server-to-server connection. The connection will be broken only when the connection has been inactive for the user-defined time. Without this time-out mechanism any server-to-server procedure call results in the connection between servers staying alive until the originating session terminates.

> If a connection is involved in an MS DTC-coordinated distributed transaction, the connection will not be timed out even if its inactivity period has expired unless you have enabled trace flag 8503.

remote proc trans

remote proc trans allows users to protect the actions of a server-to-server procedure through an MS DTC-coordinated distributed transaction. When set to true, it provides an MS DTC-coordinated distributed transaction that protects the ACID properties of transactions whether or not the user says **BEGIN DISTRIBUTED TRANSACTION**. Sessions begun after this option is set will inherit the configuration setting as their default.

6.5

INDEX

Q

U

V

6.5